Raspberry Pi Compute Module 5
IoT In C
Using Linux Drivers and Gpio5

Harry Fairhead

I/O Press
I Programmer Library

Harry Fairhead,
Raspberry Pi Compute Module 5 IoT In C
ISBN: 9781871962956 (Paperback)
ISBN: 9781871962338   (Hardback)

First Printing, April 2025
Revision 0

Published by IO Press   www.iopress.info
in association with I Programmer   www.i-programmer.info
and with I o T Programmer   www.iot-programmer.com

For updates, errata, links to resources and the source code for the programs in this book visit its dedicated page on the IO Press website: www.iopress.info.

Preface

The Raspberry Pi Compute Module 5, CM5 is designed specifically to be used in IoT and embedded applications, but differs considerably from other IoT devices you might be familiar with. The key difference is that it has enough power to run an operating system, usually Linux. While this has obvious advantages in terms of what the CM5 can do, it also complicates things. Linux is a multitasking operating system and your code now has to take account of the possibility that another piece of code might be using the hardware that previously you regarded as completely under your control.

With Linux, the accepted way to access the outside world and other devices avoiding any conflicts that might arise is via a driver. If you are lucky you will find that suitable drivers already exist for your purpose but even so there can be problems with installing and configuring them, particularly as they are often not well documented. Then there is the problem of bit rot. Drivers are often so poorly supported that they stop working following a Linux upgrade. Even so, especially if you are working with popular devices, drivers work very well and can save you a lot of time.

The alternative approach is direct interfacing, bypassing any Linux drivers. This has some advantages – it can access obscure hardware and modes of operation, it can minimize bit rot, hardware doesn't change that fast, and, perhaps most importantly, provide faster operation. If you take the trouble to understand the deeper basic workings of a device, you will be in a good position to take advantage of any advanced modes.

Direct access to the hardware was and is a very attractive proposition on Raspberry Pi devices before the CM5 as their documentation is good. This resulted in a number of standard libraries, Wiring Pi, bcm2835, pigpio, etc, that facilitated interacting with the hardware. Like the Pi 5, the CM5 breaks compatibility with previous versions because it uses Raspberry Pi's newly developed and currently under-documented RP1 chip to interface to the outside world and the standard libraries simply do not work.

While this breaking change makes direct access to the hardware more difficult than it should be, with some reverse engineering, it is possible to write functions that allow direct access to the GPIO, PWM, SPI, I2C and PIO features of the RP1. That is exactly what I have done for the purpose of making the CM5 ideal for working with external devices. They are collected together in an open source library called Gpio5. The inner workings of Gpio5 are presented in this book and you can find its full listing on the book's web page at www.iopress.info and download it from Github: https://github.com/IOPress/Gpio5.
Gpio5 is fully open source, under the MIT License. It is easy to use and can be forked.

This book opens with a brief look at how the Raspberry Pi has disrupted embedded computing. Moving on to the Compute Module, we look specifically at the way the CM5 is supported by the CM5IO board and how to install Pi OS and use other storage devices. Next we move on to Visual Studio Code and how it can be used to develop remotely. The first IoT program anyone writes is "Blinky" to flash an LED and this book is no exception, but it might not be quite what you expect. Instead of using a GPIO (General Purpose Input Output) line we use the Linux LED driver to flash an LED on the board – no hardware and no fuss. The GPIO isn't left out, however, as the next three chapters focus on its use via the GPIO character driver. In a later chapter we discover how to do the same job directly using Gpio5 with direct access to the GPIO lines.

A key component in any look at Linux and its relationship to hardware is the relatively new Device Tree, DT. Most accounts of the device tree are aimed at device driver writers. My account is aimed at device driver users and to this end we look at the DHT22 temperature and humidity driver. Next we look at Pulse Width Modulation via a driver and then directly using Gpio5. From here we tackle the two standard buses, I2C and SPI, and also the 1-Wire bus In each case Gpio5 is used to implement the same devices without the help of drivers.

We next come to the PIO, the Programmable Input Output, first introduced by the Raspberry Pi Pico, a unique way to interface the CM5 to the outside world without the need to use the CPU. After covering the basics, we look at three examples of the most sophisticated PIO programs you are likely to encounter.

The penultimate chapter takes drivers to the next level, showing you how to create your own custom overlays by writing fragments of the device tree and the final chapter is about advanced scheduling and dealing with problems encountered in running a real-time system.

Thanks as ever to my painstaking editors, Sue Gee and Kay Ewbank, for dealing with the many errors of my initial draft, hopefully few remain.

Harry Fairhead
April 2025

Table of Contents

Chapter 4

Drivers: A First Program   **49**

Chapter 5

The GPIO Character Driver   **57**

Chapter 6

GPIO Using I/O Control   **77**

Chapter 7

GPIO Events   **87**

Chapter 11

Pulse Width Modulation 171

Chapter 12

SPI Devices 209

Chapter 13
I2C Driver and Gpio5   **239**

Chapter 14
Sensor Drivers – Linux IIO & hwmon   **279**

Chapter 15
1-Wire Bus   **293**

Chapter 16
The PIO   **321**

Chapter 1
The CM5 For The IoT

The Raspberry Pi family of small computing devices has changed the nature of embedded or physical computing generally known as the Internet of Things (IoT) and Industrial Internet of Things (IIoT). The reason is very simple – they provide a full Linux system at a price that makes it possible to use what most would consider a "full" computer for tasks that previously demanded a cut-down device that was only capable of running custom written code. This makes it possible for programmers more familiar with desktop development to consider using their skills to implement novel applications that look nothing like desktop applications.

It also allows physical computing tasks to be implemented at a level much richer and more complex than a microprocessor allows. For example, if you use a small device to implement some sort of sensor-based monitoring system then it is up to you to code an interaction with the external world such as serving a web page. This isn't impossible, but it is difficult enough to mean that limiting the sophistication of the interface is a wise move. Compare this to using a Linux-based processor. In this case you can install one of the standard web servers, Apache or NGINX say, and with this onboard you can implement as rich a web experience as you desire with little effort.

Perhaps more importantly, Linux will also take care of your security. It has facilities for managing users, making secure connections using SSH and HTTPS and it will connect with secure WiFi.

In short, using a Linux system for IoT devices allows the use of a huge range of off-the-shelf software aimed at desktop and server hardware.

Of course, for lower-level tasks, such as responding to the outside world, the use of a general multitasking operating system brings with it new problems. No longer can you write a program that interacts with sensors and transducers in a way that can ignore what the rest of the system is doing. Your code has to work nicely with the other applications that are running on the same system. In particular, you cannot assume that your program is running at all times and is capable of near instant real-time responses.

What is new here is the need to integrate well-known systems such as web servers with low-level code that interacts with the hardware and this is a relatively new requirement. You need to know about Linux and you need to know how the hardware works and this is what this book is all about.

Raspberry Pi Compute Modules

The Raspberry Pi Compute Module was introduced to provide the core Raspberry Pi functionality in a more flexible, industrial-friendly form factor. Essentially each generation of the Raspberry Pi had its associated Compute Module which was the same hardware – CPU, GPU, memory and peripherals - but with no onboard connectors. Instead the Compute Module was connected to a development board which did have all of the connectors. The idea was that you used this to develop the software and hardware you needed and then you designed your own main board complete with just the connectors and additional hardware required. This may have been the intention, but many a prototype based on the development board made it into limited production devices.

The early versions of the Compute Module based on the original Pi (CM1) and on the Pi 3 (CM3/CM3+) used a DDR2 SO-DIMM form factor.

While these are still available, in the more recent versions a higher density connector is incorporated into a credit-card sized board.

The CM4 and CM5, based on the Pi 4 and Pi 5, respectively are much more powerful than their predecessors. While there is some hardware compatibility between them in that you can plug a CM5 into a board designed for the CM4 and it will usually work, there is a major incompatibility in the software if you use any direct access to the hardware as discussed below.

Compute Module 5

The Compute Module 5, CM5, is a cut-down Pi 5. All of the external connectors have been removed and signals are only available on the two high density connectors on the bottom of the board. It is at the same time a full Pi 5 and the software you write for a main Pi model needs little, if any, change to run on it, but you will need to design a PCB motherboard for it to connect to the outside world or use the CM5IO development board.

It is important to bear in mind that the CM5 is different from the CM4 and all similar Pis in that it uses the RP1 to connect to the outside world. This makes it incompatible in terms of memory map, registers and peripheral hardware with its predecessor the CM4 and other members of the Pi family apart from the Pi 5.

The CM5

When it comes to buying a CM5 there are many models to choose between. You can select from a range of RAM capacities, a range of Flash eMMC capacities for storage and radio or no radio. At the time of writing the available configurations are:

RAM (GB)	2	4	8	16
Storage (GB)	0	16	32	64

and wireless or no wireless.

To get started, a 4GB RAM, 32GB storage with WiFi is a good choice and it is the model included in the official getting started kit.

It is worth mentioning that the CM5 with no storage is referred to as "CM5 Lite" and it needs an SD card to boot. The CM5IO development board has an SD card reader, but this only works with the CM5 Lite. If a CM5 has eMMC flash memory installed then it has to be used to boot the system and the SD card reader on the CM5IO board is non-functioning.

Although the CM5 has its own CM5IO board it will work in the CM4IO board. That is, the CM5 can be used as a drop-in upgrade to an existing CM4 system, although usually with some loss of functionality. For example, there are no USB 3 ports and no M.2.M port on the CM4IO.

Just plugging in a CM5 is an easy way to make a CM4 based system work faster without having to design them. Of course, as the CM5 uses the RP1 and hence the standard GPIO libraries no longer work you may have to modify the software.

The CM5IO Board

The CM5IO board is the most obvious way to get started with a new CM5 project. Its advantage is that it can be used to add mouse, keyboard and monitor to turn the CM5 into a workable desktop computer. However, it also has another important role to play. It can be used as a template for your own custom expansion cards. A full schematic diagram is available and this reveals how little is actually done to present the control and data lines from the CM5 to the outside world. The CM5IO is mainly a collection of connectors and PCB traces but it provides a starting point for your own designs.

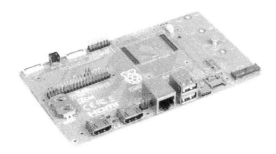

There is also a starter kit that contains a CM5, CM5IO, case, cooler, antenna and power supply.

In most cases, the custom PCB that you need to implement starts life as a clone of the CM5IO board. As well as the schematic, there are also layout files for use with KiCad, an open source PCB design program:

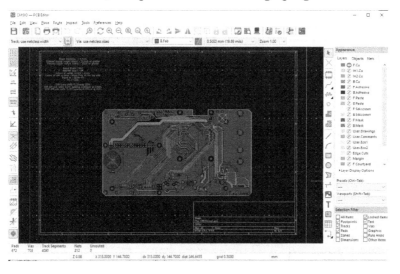

Starting from the CM5IO design you can remove components that you don't need and add components and wire them to the CM5. Of course, KiCad is a complicated application and it takes a lot of time to learn it and the art of layout. This is a task best left to an electronics engineer. Once you have your design you can send it to a PCB prototyping company and have the finished product back quite quickly. There are also companies that will add the components to the finished board.

Pi 5 or CM5?

Given that the CM5 is just a Pi 5 without all of the connectors this raises the valid question of why not just use a Pi 5? You can use either the Pi 5 or the CM5 for IoT application development, but in many cases the CM5 is a better choice.

The software you write for a main Pi model needs little, if any, change to run on the CM5. For example, all of the programs in this book work perfectly on a Pi 5 without modification.

You could use a Pi 5 as your prototyping system but the CM5 plus CM5IO has a number of advantages. The most obvious is that there is more room to work in! It has the same GPIO connector and can accept standard HATs, the Raspberry Pi expansion boards. You also have the option of using eMMC flash memory integrated into the CM5's board. This replaces the usual plugin SD card flash memory and is much faster and more reliable. You can still opt to use an SD card, but only if you select the CM5 Lite option which doesn't have eMMC memory.

Using the CM5IO board also has the advantage of offering full size HDMI connectors, an RTC battery connector and a M2M PCIe socket. You can add a M2M socket to the standard Pi 5 but you need an expansion HAT to make use of it. The M2M socket can be used to add solid state drives which offer high performance and large amounts of storage you can also arrange to boot the system from the M2M drive. In principle, is it possible to use other PCIe expansion cards with the CM5, but in practice this is best avoided as support is inadequate. Another advantage of the CM5 is that it is easy to attach an external WiFi antenna.

Pi Family Compatibility - The RP1 Problem

As already mentioned, the Pi5 and CM5 use the RP1 microprocessor making them incompatible with all earlier models of the Pi family when it comes to interacting with the external world.

All of the models from the original Pi 1 through to the Pi 4 and the Pi Zero are very compatible with one another from an IoT point of view. The reason is that all of their external connections are made via the Broadcom family of chips. The BCM2835 was used in the first version of the Pi, in CM1 and in the Pi Zero, the BCM2837 in the Pi 2, 3 and CM3 and the BCM2711 in the Pi 4 and CM4. They are all so similar that it is possible to write I/O libraries that work with all of them with minimal modification.

For the Pi 5 and the CM5, currently the top of the range of the Raspberry Pi family, the decision was taken to use the RP1, a custom interface chip based on the 2024 processor that powers the Raspberry Pi Pico, making them incompatible with all previous Pis from the point of view of peripherals, including the GPIO lines. The memory map and the registers that control the standard peripherals are different. This means that none of the familiar GPIO libraries, Wiring Pi, bcm2835, pigpio and so on, do not work on the CM5.

The recommended way to work with the IoT via the CM5 is to use Linux drivers and this has lots of advantages when it is suitable. Linux drivers however are very variable in how well they are supported. Most lack adequate documentation and many are poorly supported with bug fixes and updates. In addition most Linux drivers only deliver a subset of what the device is generally capable of.

This book offers an alternative approach to using drivers – that of direct access to the hardware via the Gpio5 library which is developed in subsequent chapters and is a pure C-based open source library which runs exclusively on the CM5, Pi 5 and Pi500 and as far as possible is based on the Pico's SDK.

The fact that the RP1 is based on the processor used in the Pico means that from an IoT point of view the CM5 has more in common with the Pico than with past versions of the Pi.

The Raspberry Pi Pico

The Pico is a small IoT system launched by Raspberry Pi in 2021 using the 2040 processor which was custom designed by Raspberry Pi. It isn't powerful enough to run Linux and so has little in common with the other members of the Pi family.

The importance of the Pico to the CM5 is that Pico was the first device to use the 2040 chip which the Pi 5's RP1 chip is based on. and. This means the I/O devices, GPIO, SPI, I2C and so on have more in common with the Pico than they do with the CM4 or the Pi 4 and it is the Pico's SDK that is the basis on which Gpio5 has been built

The Pico W

What To Expect

There are no complete projects in this book – although some examples come very close and it is clear that some of them could be used together to create finished projects. The focus here is on learning how things work so that you can move on and do things that are non-standard. What matters is that you can reason about what the processor is doing and how it interacts with the real world in real time.

This is the key difference between desktop and embedded programming: timing matters in embedded programming, but not so much in desktop programming.

This is a book about understanding the general principle and making things work. If you read to the end of this book you will have a good understanding of what is going on when you make use of a range of different types of interfacing that typically go together to make a complete system.

There are two distinct approaches to implementing IoT programs on a Linux machine. You can make use of the standard Linux drivers or you can program directly to the hardware. The advantage of Linux drivers is that they work irrespective of the hardware you are using. This means they iron out the differences between the CM4 and CM5. There are disadvantages of using drivers – they can be slow, poorly documented and tend not to support all of the features of the hardware. The alternative is to program directly to the hardware and this is what the GPIO5 library allows you to do without having to master the details of the hardware. In the following chapters both approaches are used.

What Do You Need?

To follow the examples in this book you will need a CM5 and a CM5IO board. It is also worth knowing that while the CM5 is capable of running a development environment and running IoT programs at the same time there are many advantages to using another machine as the development machine and running programs on the Pi using a remote connection.

Either the CM5 or the remote development machine needs to be set up with Pi OS and you need to know how to connect to it and use it via a serial console. You also need to be comfortable with Linux in the sense that while you might not know how to do something, you know how to look it up and follow the instructions. It is also assumed that you are able to program in C. There isn't enough space to teach the elements of the C programming language in this book. If you need to learn C first or brush up on some of the finer points of C and Linux then see *Fundamental C*, ISBN: 9781871962604 and *Applying C for the IoT with Linux*, ISBN: 9781871962611.

It is assumed that you have some experience with creating prototype electronics using a prototype board and hookup wires. If you need help with this side of development then you can consult the book's resources page on the I/O Press website.

One item of test equipment that is more or less essential is a logic analyzer. You may have an oscilloscope and may think that this is enough to examine and analyze the sort of signal an IoT device produces, but unless you have a scope with logic analyzer features it is harder to use than a lower cost logic analyzer.

It is worth noting that the CM5 can generate signals that are too fast to be reliably detected by low-cost oscilloscopes and logic analyzers which work at between 1MHz and 25MHz. This can mean that working with pulses much faster than 1 microsecond can be difficult as you cannot rely on your instruments.

An Information Gap

One of the problems in using Linux device drivers is finding information about them. A search of the web reveals lots of sources, but many are old and there is a great deal of duplication. Here are useful links on specific topics:

Configuration:

https://www.raspberrypi.org/documentation/configuration/config-txt/README.md

Overlay Source:

https://github.com/raspberrypi/firmware/tree/master/boot

Overlay Documentation:

https://github.com/raspberrypi/firmware/blob/master/boot/overlays/README

GitHub Pi OS Repository:

https://github.com/raspberrypi/linux

Hardware details:

https://www.raspberrypi.org/documentation/hardware/raspberrypi/datasheets.md

You can find these links on this book's webpage at www.iopress.info.

Summary

- The Compute Module 5 (CM5) is a Pi 5 packaged as a credit card sized industrial device. It needs a custom I/O board or a development board to make use of it.

- There is a range of options for RAM and eMMC Flash storage. The Lite range of CM5s doesn't have any eMMC and it can be used with a standard SD card. Useful links to actual products used in this book are on its web page at www.iopress.info.

- To make use of the CM5 for development of a custom system you generally use a CM5IO board which provides connections to the usual peripherals – video, USB, GPIO and an M2M disk connector.

- Due to the use of the RP1 to interface to the outside world none of the previous Pi GPIO libraries work with the CM5.

- The Gpio5 library developed for and presented in this book works with GPIO, PWM, I2C and SPI specifically on the Pi 5, P500 and CM5. It is an open source project hosted on GitHub https://github.com/IOPress/Gpio5

- Finding accurate and up-to-date information about the availability of Linux drivers on the Internet is difficult. The useful links in this chapter are kept updated on the book's page on www.iopress.info.

Chapter 2
Setting Up the CM5

The CM5 is a little different to the other members of the Pi family and setting it up before you get started on software development is a little more complicated. In particular, you need to put a CM5 and a CM5IO together. If you haven't bought a CM5 Lite then you have to find a way of installing the OS into the eMMC and there is the problem of how to deal with the boot loader stored in EPROM.

The CM5IO

Although you can use a CM4IO board with the CM5, new projects should always select the CM5IO board. It's specification is given as:

- HAT footprint with 40-pin GPIO connector
- PoE header
- 2× HDMI ports
- 2× USB 3.0 ports
- Gigabit Ethernet RJ45 with PoE support
- M.2 M key PCIe socket compatible with the 2230, 2242, 2260, and 2280 form factors
- MicroSD card slot (only for use with Lite variants with no eMMC; other variants ignore the slot)
- 2× MIPI DSI/CSI-2 combined display/camera FPC connectors (22-pin 0.5 mm pitch cable)
- Real-time clock with battery socket
- 4-pin JST-SH PWM fan connector
- USB-C power using the same standard as Raspberry Pi 5 (5V, 5A (25W) or 5V, 3A (15W) with a 600mA peripheral limit)
- Jumpers to disable features such as eMMC boot, EEPROM write, and the USB OTG connection

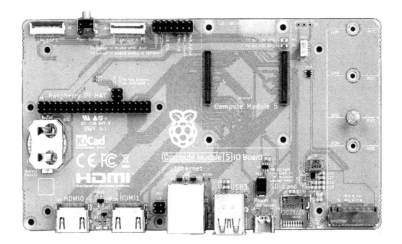

You can see the connectors and jumpers in the image above. They are mostly self explanatory, but there are a few things to note:

- CAM/DISP 0 at the left is always ready to be used but CAM/DISP 1 needs two jumpers to be fitted to J6.

- The GPIO connector, labeled Raspberry PI HAT on the board, can be used to fit a standard Pi 40-way HAT and there are four mounting holes to let you position the expansion cards.

- You can select 1.8V or the standard 3.3V GPIO lines by moving the resistor at R5 to R4 – as this is a surface mount resistor it requires a soldering iron and skill.

- The RTC battery holder takes a CR2032 battery and if fitted it supplies power to the onboard RTC.

- The PoE Power over Ethernet connector J9 supplies the raw PoE signals and needs to be connected to a PoE hat to make use of it.

- If the board has eMMC Flash installed then the SD card reader is ignored.

- J2 at the top left of the board sets a number of useful defaults using jumpers:

Pin	Function	
1-2	nRPIBOOT	If fitted, disables eMMC Boot
3-4	EEPROM_nWP	If fitted, write-protects the EEPROM
5-6	USB_OTG	If fitted, enables OTG mode
8	SYNC_OUT	IEEE1588 timing pin - can be configured as input
12	PMIC_ENABLE	Enable power control
13-14	Wake up	Connects a push button to wake up or shut down CM5

Installing Pi OS

The latest Pi OS is based on Debian Bookworm and is available in 32- and 64-bit versions. This is a very standard implementation of Linux. There are some minor irritations in that some drivers have been renamed, but this is relatively easy to cope with. A bigger difference affects any program planning to make use of graphics. Bookworm has taken the big step of using Wayland in place of the X graphics system that previous versions used. In most cases you can isolate your programs from this change by using a suitable graphics library, but if you plan to interact at a low level with graphics you need to find out more about Wayland.

If you are using a Lite version of the CM5 then you simply use the Raspberry Pi Imager to write an OS to an SD card. Then simply insert the SD card into the card reader on the CM5IO and reboot.

Versions of the CM5 that have eMMC flash memory have to be setup so that the flash memory presents itself to a host machine as removable storage. For this to happen you have to disable booting from the eMMC and install a driver into the host operating system. Once the eMMC is mounted as a disk drive, the Raspberry Pi Imager can be used to install the operating system.

The step-by-step instructions are:

1) Place a jumper to short the pins of J2 on the IO board labeled Fit jumper to disable eMMC Boot:

2) Connect the IO board to the host system using the USB C port J11.

3) Install `rpiboot`:

> Linux: `sudo app install rpiboot`
> Windows: Download the Windows installer from
> `https://github.com/raspberrypi/usbboot/raw/master/`
> `win32/rpiboot_setup.exe`
> Run the installer and reboot the Windows machine.

4) Run `rpiboot`, select the CM5 version under Windows and wait until the storage device appears.

5) Run the Raspberry Pi Imager and install the OS.

6) Remove the jumper on J2 and reboot the CM5.

If you don't want to use the Raspberry Pi Imager you can also arrange to copy the raw OS image using the usual file copy commands.

Using NVMe

If you need to expand the storage capacity of the CM5 then the simplest and best way is to add a Non-Volatile Memory Express, NVMe, disk to the CM5IO board. To do this all you have to do is plug an NVMe module into place on the CM5IO board:

 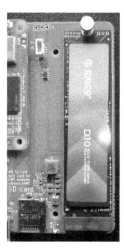

When you reboot the CM5 the NVMe disk will be recognized but it will need to be partitioned, formatted and mounted unless these things have already been done.

To check that the dive has been installed use `lsblk` to list all of the block storage devices:

```
NAME          MAJ:MIN RM    SIZE RO TYPE MOUNTPOINTS
mmcblk0       179:0    0   29.1G  0 disk
├─mmcblk0p1   179:1    0    512M  0 part /boot/firmware
└─mmcblk0p2   179:2    0   28.6G  0 part /
mmcblk0boot0  179:32   0      4M  1 disk
mmcblk0boot1  179:64   0      4M  1 disk
nvme0n1       259:0    0  119.2G  0 disk
```

If you can see `nvme0n1` then the drive is installed correctly.

Next task is to create a partition table:

`sudo parted -a optimal /dev/nvme0n1 mklabel gpt`

then create an ext4 partition using the whole disk:

`sudo parted -a optimal /dev/nvme0n1 mkpart primary ext4 0% 100%`

You can change the amount of the disk used if you want to create multiple partitions. The new partition is named `nvme0n1p1` and this needs to be formatted before it can be used:

```
sudo mkfs.ext4 /dev/nvme0n1p1
```

Creating a formatted partition is something you only have to do once, but to make use of it you have to mount the drive each time the machine boots. To mount the drive manually you can use:

```
sudo mkdir /mnt/data
```

to create the mount point and:

```
sudo mount /dev/nvme0n1p1 /mnt/data -t ext4
```

to mount it. After this you can access the extra storage via the `/mnt/data` directory.

To make the mount permanent you need to edit the fstab table. To do this you need the UUID of the new drive using the `sudo blkid` command which produces something like:

```
/dev/mmcblk0p1: LABEL_FATBOOT="bootfs" LABEL="bootfs" UUID="5DC7-
F115" BLOCK_SIZE="512" TYPE="vfat" PARTUUID="1bf18e19-01"

/dev/mmcblk0p2: LABEL="rootfs"
UUID="a36be96c-66be-4487-a7a6-0481bca99d89" BLOCK_SIZE="4096"
TYPE="ext4" PARTUUID="1bf18e19-02"

/dev/nvme0n1p1: UUID="f003b110-baa9-4270-83f7-a87adddd8c7f"
BLOCK_SIZE="4096" TYPE="ext4" PARTLABEL="primary"
PARTUUID="21361da3-df96-42c6-8fba-3225b18737f3"
```

The important part of the listing is `UUID="f003b110-baa9-4270-83f7-a87adddd8c7f"` which identifies the new partition. Once you have the UUID for the new partition you can edit the `/etc/fstab` table and add to the end the line :

```
UUID=f003b110-baa9-4270-83f7-a87adddd8c7f
                    /mnt/data ext4    defaults    0   0
```

Where the `UUID` is changed to the one reported by `blkid`.

After this the NVMe drive will be accessible for general storage after every boot.

Boot EPROM

The CM5 uses a separate EPROM to hold the boot code. Previous versions of the Pi stored the boot code in the file `bootcode.bin` in the boot partition of the device being used to boot the system. The CM5 doesn't automatically update the boot loader and it is up to you to ensure that you are working with the latest version. First update Linux and dependencies on the CM5:

```
sudo apt update
sudo apt upgrade
```

and to sure you have the latest EEPROM

```
sudo rpi-eeprom-update -a
```

You have to reboot to make any changes and you can check what version you have using:

```
sudo rpi-eeprom-update
```

You can disable any changes to the boot loader by placing a jumper on the correct pins of J2:

The boot loader can be configured using the `rpi-eeprom-config` command which, with no parameters will display the current configuration:

```
@cm5dev:~ $ rpi-eeprom-config
[all]
BOOT_UART=1
BOOT_ORDER=0xf461
NET_INSTALL_AT_POWER_ON=1
```

To change the configuration you can use the command:

```
 sudo -E rpi-eeprom-config --edit
```

This loads the current configuration into the nano editor and saves it using:

```
sudo rpi-eeprom-update
```

Probably the most used boot configuration parameter is `BOOT_ORDER` which you can use to set the CM5 to boot from NVMe. USB etc.

The documentation lists the possible values and refers to other parts of the documentation for more information:

Value	Mode	Description
0x0	SD CARD DETECT	Tries SD then waits for card-detect to indicate that the card has changed. Deprecated now that `0xf` (`RESTART`) is available.
0x1	SD CARD	SD card (or eMMC on Compute Module 4/5).
0x2	NETWORK	Network boot - Refer to Network boot server tutorial.
0x3	RPIBOOT	RPIBOOT - See usbboot.
0x4	USB-MSD	USB mass storage boot - See USB mass storage boot.
0x6	NVME	Boots from an NVMe SSD connected to the PCIe interface. See NVMe boot for more details.
0x7	HTTP	HTTP boot over ethernet. See HTTP boot for more details.
0xe	STOP	Stop and display error pattern. A power cycle is required to exit this state.
0xf	RESTART	Restarts from the first boot-mode in the `BOOT_ORDER` field i.e. loop.

To specify a boot order you put the hex codes together with the right-most code tried first and so on. For example, to boot from NVMe and then try eMMC if that fails you would use:

```
BOOT_ORDER=0xf16
```

Notice that the initial f means that the boot sequence will be cycled through until the number of attempts exceeds MAX_RESTARTS.

There are lots of additional boot configuration parameters and you can look them up at:

```
https://www.raspberrypi.com/documentation/computers/
    raspberry-pi.html#raspberry-pi-bootloader-configuration
```

If you are concerned about security then make sure that you only boot from the internal eMMC.

Booting From NVMe

As an example of how to modify where the CM5 boots from, let's use the NVMe drive installed as a data drive earlier. The first problem we have to solve is getting the OS onto the new boot device. The best way of doing this is to use the Raspberry Pi Imager. You can do this by connecting the NVMe drive to a host machine via an adapter or you can run the Imager on the CM5 itself. You can install the Imager using:

```
sudo apt install rpi-imager
```

After you have installed the Imager you can use it to install the OS of your choice onto the NVMe drive. Note: if you have setup the NVMe drive to be a data storage device and added it to fstab then you need to remove it before proceeding as the Imager will repartition the drive.

After the Imager has finished you can use:

```
sudo blkid
```

to see the details of all of the block devices.

```
NAME            MAJ:MIN RM    SIZE RO TYPE MOUNTPOINTS
mmcblk0          179:0    0   29.1G  0 disk
├─mmcblk0p1      179:1    0    512M  0 part /boot/firmware
└─mmcblk0p2      179:2    0   28.6G  0 part /
mmcblk0boot0    179:32    0      4M  1 disk
mmcblk0boot1    179:64    0      4M  1 disk
nvme0n1          259:0    0  119.2G  0 disk
├─nvme0n1p1      259:1    0    512M  0 part
└─nvme0n1p2      259:2    0    5.1G  0 part
```

You can see that now the NVMe drive has been divided into two partitions, where p1 is the boot partition and p2 is the working partition.

To boot from the new device you have to configure the bootloader. Use:

```
sudo -E rpi-eeprom-config --edit
```

and change the line with BOOT_ORDER on it to read:

```
BOOT_ORDER=0xf16
```

which sets it to boot first from NVMe and if that doesn't work try to boot from eMMC and keep trying in that order.

With this change you should discover that the system reboots using the NVMe drive and it takes longer. If you want to use the eMMC drive as a data store then you will need to mount it and this is done in the same way as for mounting the NVMe drive.

Security

Security is more difficult to enforce for an IoT device than for a server. The difference is that you cannot rule out the situation that the attacker has physical possession of the device. You can keep a server physically secure by locking it in a server room, but in general IoT devices are out in the real world.

One simple way of ensuring security is to lock the boot EPROM so that it cannot be written to. This is just a matter of setting an input line high, which you can do on the CM5IO board with a jumper on J2 and more securely with a hard connection on a custom board. Of course, it doesn't take much skill to remove the connection.

A more secure system is to use secure boot. If you select this option the operating system installed has to be signed with a private key. The bootloader has a copy of the public key which it uses to validate that the OS has been signed by you. The public key is written into One Time Programmable (OTP) memory, which means it cannot be changed and the device is forever locked to only running code signed by the private key.

Exactly how all of this is achieved is fairly involved and beyond the scope of this book but if you want to know more see:

https://github.com/raspberrypi/usbboot/blob/master/
secure-boot-example/README.md

and

https://github.com/raspberrypi/rpi-sb-provisioner

Summary

- The CM5 generally has to be used with the CM5IO board to get started on developing software.

- There are a range of jumpers and connectors on the CM5IO board that allow you to configure some aspects of the CM5.

- Installing an operating system on a CM5 that has eMMC Flash is different from how it works with other models of the Pi.

- You can also install NVMe using the M2M slot on the CM5IO card and this can be used for data storage or for booting the system.

- The boot loader in the CM5 is stored in a separate EPROM and there are commands to examine and configure it.

- You can stop the boot loader being updated using a jumper on the CM5IO.

- Creating a secure IoT system is difficult because you have to assume that the attacker has access to the physical hardware.

Chapter 3
C and Visual Studio Code

C is a good language to use for low-level apps. It is the language that Linux is written in, as are all of the Linux drivers that we are going to use in the rest of the book. It is fast and efficient and you can tailor your code to make the best of the hardware you have. You can describe C as a machine-independent assembly language and hence when you learn it you get deeper into the system than with other languages and discover what is really going on. This makes it a good way to improve your understanding of computers and computing in general. If you need to learn C as it is used in IoT programming then see *Fundamental C: Getting Closer To The Machine*, ISBN: 9781871962604.

Sometimes you don't need speed, even in an IoT application. For example, if you just want to flash a few LEDs or read a temperature sensor in a human timescale, then you can program in almost any language. Even so, it is good to have plenty of headroom when it comes to speed and memory demands and C excels in these respects. Only when it comes to complex high-level data processing and implementing a sophisticated UI do other languages offer a more compact solution than C. In such cases, a mixed language approach often works. However, for the remainder of this book programming in C is our focus.

Getting Started In C

You can program in C in many different ways. All of the software you need to run a C program is already installed on a standard Pi running Pi OS, formerly known as Raspbian. You can use an editor on the Pi to create your program and then compile and run it using the command line. However, there are easy-to-use IDEs that make programming in C fast and painless, and they provide debugging facilities that make finding errors much quicker.

You could use Genny, Eclipse, Code::Blocks or NetBeans, all of which are open source. Genny has the advantage of being installed by default on the Pi, but the others are easy enough to install.

Because of its popularity and ubiquity, Visual Studio Code, VS Code, is the code editor used in the rest of this book. This is a free, open-source, multi-language, multi-platform code editor that is worth the time to get to know. It also supports remote development which is a huge plus point.

Local or Remote

There are two distinct ways you can work with any development environment:

- ◆ Install VS Code on a CM5 and work with it via the GUI desktop, i.e. directly on the CM5. In this case you are using the CM5 as if it was a full desktop computer and it is your development and test machine.

- ◆ Connect the CM5 to a desktop machine and make use of it to write your program and then download and run it on the CM5. In this case the desktop machine is your development machine and the CM5 is your test machine.

Remote development can be implemented in a number of ways. For example a cross compiler could be used on the desktop machine and the compiled program could be downloaded to the Pi to be tested. This is not a common approach to Pi remote development as the Pi is powerful enough to do its own compiling. In general, what happens is that the source code is downloaded to the Pi which then compiles and runs it.

In practice, the remote development approach tends to work better because the desktop machine has the power to run the editor reasonably fast. Another advantage of remote development is that you can easily change the Pi that you are testing the code on, preserving all of the code stored on the desktop machine. This is very useful when working on multiple projects because you can try out your program on multiple Raspberry Pis and swap machines simply by changing the build host used for the project.

Put simply, local development is easier, but remote development is more flexible.

Local VS Code

VS Code can be installed on a CM5 and used to develop programs that run on the same machine, i.e. as local development. This isn't the best way to work, but it is the simplest.

The recommended way to install VS Code is to use the Recommended Software utility from the desktop.

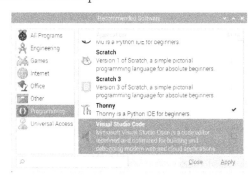

You can also install it using the package manager:

```
sudo apt install code
```

or from the VS Code web site using the Debian release.

After installing VS Code, either on your desktop machine or a Pi, your next step has to be to install the Microsoft C/C++ code extension:

Once you have VS Code installed, you can try a simple hello world program running on the local machine. First select File and click the Open Folder menu option, navigate to a suitable location, Documents in your home folder is a good choice, create a folder called CPROJECTS, open it and create another folder called HelloWorld:

Finally create a file called hello.c in the HelloWorld folder and enter:

```c
#include <stdio.h>
#include <stdlib.h>
int main(int argc, char **argv)
{
        printf("Hello C World");
        int test = 42;
        printf("%d\n", test);
        return (EXIT_SUCCESS);
}
```

You don't have to organize your projects in this way, but it is easier if each C program has its own folder within a top-level workspace folder.

When you come to run the program for the first time you will have to select a compiler. As you are running on a CM5, you can use the latest GCC compiler which is already installed.

This creates a `tasks.json` and a `launch.json` file in the `.vscode` directory which you can edit to customize the way the compiler and linker run, although in most cases this isn't necessary.

If you need to manually create or regenerate these files the simplest way is to click on the gear icon at the far right of the top bar:

This only appears when you have a C file open in the editor. If you select the Add Debug Configuration you will be presented with a selection of possible configurations. It is worth knowing what the two configuration files do.

The `launch.json` file defines how the debugger will be run and it usually doesn't need to be changed. At the end of the `launch.json` file is the command:

```
"preLaunchTask": "C/C++: gcc-12 build active file",
```

This invokes the named task in the `tasks.json` file used to compile the active file before the debugger runs it. The `tasks.json` file is the one you need to change to configure how the compiler works and you do need to do this to include additional libraries etc.

Notice that this is a very simple run and debug implementation and it is really only suited to simple projects with few files and few dependencies. If you want to build projects with many different files then you need to move to a build system such as CMake which is supported in VS Code. However, for simple projects of the sort listed in this book the simple build and run system works well.

Once you have the debug configured you can run the active file, i.e. the one open in the editor using the Run and Debug icon in the left hand bar:

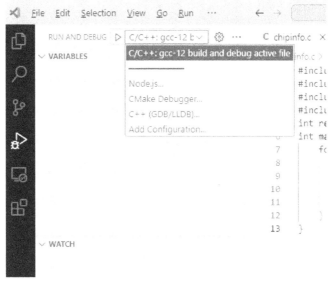

If you select this option the file is built, the debugger started and the program run. You can use the usual debugger facilities – single step, breakpoints and so on and inspect and change the values in variables.

To try this out, place some breakpoints in the program:

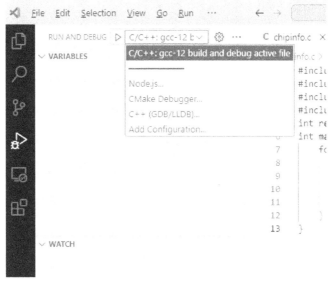

You can make use of the floating menu to control what happens to the program:

Run Without Debug

At the time of writing there is no standard way to run a C program using VS Code without loading the debugger first. This is usually not a problem, but occasionally you do need to run a program at its maximum speed and this means not using a debugger. You can always run the program from the command line, but it is also easy to add a task to the `tasks.json` file that will simply run the existing compiled program in the directory of the currently active file. Open `tasks.json` and add:

```
{
    "label": "run C",
    "type": "shell",
    "command": "${fileDirname}/${fileBasenameNoExtension} ",
    "presentation": {
        "reveal": "always",
        "panel": "shared"
    },
    "group": {
        "kind": "build",
        "isDefault": true
    }
}
```

to the end of the array of tasks. Now you can use the command `Terminal, Run Task` and select run C from the dropdown list of tasks. This will run the executable with the same name as the currently active file in the editor. Notice that it is up to you to ensure that this exists by building or debugging the program first.

Remote Development

If you can use VS Code on a CM5 to develop and run code on it then this is as simple as it gets. A possibly better approach is that of full remote C development. That is, you write your program on a more powerful desktop machine, and run it on a CM5 connected over SSH.

The only other problem with this is that VS Code has more facilities than you need just to run C and this can make it confusing. However, after you have run your first program, it all becomes so much easier. If you are going to be doing much programming on Pis, it is worth the effort in setting up and mastering remote development.

The good news is that once you have set up remote development VS Code works in more or less the same way as in local development mode. That is you can run and debug the program as if it was local.

Before we can get started with VS Code remote development we need to setup SSH.

SSH Without a Password

Before trying to make any of the following work, you need to have set up SSH access using a Key file. Some of the commands work if you simply supply a password, but the debugging commands don't.

Using a password to connect over SSH is fine when you are just testing the installation, but the number of times you are asked to provide it quickly becomes irritating. The solution is to create a key pair to use. If you look up the instructions for doing this, you might conclude that it is very difficult. This is because every effort is make to ensure security is enforced. If you simply want to use a key as a way of avoiding having to supply a password then you can take shortcuts. As long as you keep your private key safe, the setup is secure.

The first step is generating a key pair on the local machine. As long as you have OpenSSH installed, this is easy. The steps described here will work on Windows, Mac and Linux. If you are using Windows, start a PowerShell session:

```
cd ~\.ssh
ssh-keygen -t rsa
```

This generates a default RSA key in the .ssh directory within the current user's home directory. You can provide a name for the key files and in this example the name pi is used, although this doesn't affect what device you can use them for. There are advantages in using the default name.

You will see output something like:

```
Generating public/private rsa key pair.
Enter file in which to save the key (C:\Users\
userhome/.ssh/id_rsa): pi
Enter passphrase (empty for no passphrase):
Enter same passphrase again:
Your identification has been saved in pi.
Your public key has been saved in pi.pub.
The key fingerprint is:
SHA256:UtiQ3RMYpluJb+nx8n5pqsbLXHgiYv2hKs1EVoF7vqQ user@Rockrose
```

```
The key's randomart image is:
+---[RSA 2048]----+
|      .o+o+..    |
|     . oBo.o     |
|       o+ =  .   |
|      + .= .     |
|     o oo S      |
|      ..o+ +     |
|     +oooo* +  . |
|     ..E..*oB  + |
|     .....*+++   |
+----[SHA256]-----+
```

If you really are using the keys for security purposes you should supply a passphrase, which is requested when the key pair is used. If you are simply using the keys to avoid entering a password then leave the passphrase blank for simplicity.

The key generation will leave two files in the `.ssh` directory – in this case `pi` and `pi.pub`. The first is the private key and this you keep to yourself as it is what proves that the machine is the one that the public key belongs to. The `pi.pub` file contains the public key and this is the one that has to be copied to the remote machine. The remote machine uses the public key to challenge the local machine to decode something which can only be done with the private key, so proving that the machine is legitimate, or rather that it has the private key.

Notice that the name of the keys is not the user name that you will use them with, but simply the name of the keys to be used. That is, the fact that we have called the keys `pi` does not mean that they can only be used with user `pi`. Any user who has access to the private key can use the public key to set up a secure SSH connection.

You can use the public key with as many remote machines as you need to. The key identifies you as being allowed to connect to a machine that has it using SSH. To make this happen, you have to enter the details of the file into `.ssh/authorized_keys`. You can do this any way you know how to, but the public key file has to be copied to `~/.ssh/` on the remote machine and renamed `authorized_keys`. As you have SSH working, the simplest thing to do is:

```
scp pi.pub pi@192.168.11.151:~/.ssh/authorized_keys
```

You might have to make the `.ssh` folder on the remote machine first. You will have to provide the user's, pi in this case, password. If this works you will find `authorized_keys` in the `.ssh` directory. If you want to store more public keys in `authorized_keys` so that more than one user can log on, you have to append additional public key files to `authorized_keys`.

SSH will not use the key file if `~/.ssh` or `~` are writable by Group or Others. One way of ensuring this is not the case:

```
chmod 700 ~/.ssh
chmod 600 ~/.ssh/authorized_keys
```

As long as the permissions are set correctly, you should be able to connect without a password using:

```
ssh -i ~/.ssh/pi pi@192.168.11.151
```

If you don't use `-i ~/.ssh/pi` to specify the private key file, you might be asked for a password as well as the key file. You also have to specify the correct user name. As already noted the name of the key file does not have to be the same as the user name.

If you want to log on and not specify the key file, i.e. just using:

```
pi@192.168.11.151
```

then you need to make sure your key files have the correct default names. For protocol 2 the keys have to be called `id_rsa` and `id_rsa.pub`. If you use these default names for RSA keys then the SSH agent will use them automatically. If you use any other names, like `pi` and `pi.pub`, you will need an Identity file specified in `.ssh config`.

Open the file `config` in the `C:\Users\user\.ssh directory` on the local machine (`~/.ssh` under Linux) and enter:

```
Host 192.168.11.151
    HostName 192.168.11.151
    User pi
    PubKeyAuthentication yes
    IdentityFile ~/.ssh/pi
```

Of course, you have to change the IP address, user name and the location of the key file to be correct for the machine you are trying to connect to. You can enter additional Host specifications for each machine you want to connect to.

After this you should be able to connect and work with the remote Pi without providing a password when using VS Code. You can also just use:

```
ssh pi@192.168.11.151
```

at the command line.

Notice that this is low security as we didn't specify a passphrase to use with the private key. If you need security from the outside world, you need to create a key with a passphrase and then you need to use the SSH agent to supply it automatically.

Remote SSH

To run the remote development extension you need to have an OpenSSH client running on the development machine. Windows 10 has its own version of OpenSSH client. You next need to install the remote development pack. You only need to install Remote SSH.

After you have installed Remote SSH you can add the details of the Pi you want to use to develop programs on. To do this click on the `Remote Explorer` icon in the left panel and you will see that there are no SSH clients installed.

Next click on the + that appears when you hover over SSH Targets and enter the details for the Pi you want to connect to:

You specify the host using the format:

```
ssh user@ipaddress
```

When you press `Enter`, select a configuration file to use and you are ready to connect to the new host. Right-click on the new host and select "Connect in this window". Next, you will be asked for your password. You will be asked for the password each time you connect unless you create a private key and use it for authentication as detailed earlier.

When you open the file explorer and select `Open Folder` you will see a list of folders stored in your home folder on the host machine. Create a new folder suitable for storing your C programs and create a file called `hello.c` in it. You will be prompted to install the C extensions on the remote machine. If not you need to install them manually. After this you will be able to run the program on the remote machine. Notice that the program files are stored and compiled on the remote machine. A code server is installed on the remote machine the first time you connect to it.

From here on you can learn about VS Code and slowly customize it to make your work easier.

Local Remote Synchronization

It is important to realize that the C programs you create are stored on the remote host. This means that, if you do nothing about it, your entire program could be stored solely on a Pi, waiting for something bad to happen to it. Even if you consider this a safe option, you have the problem of transferring the program to another Pi if you want to run it there. The best solution is to keep a copy of your programs on a machine that you consider safe, and share them with any Pi you might want to run them on.

The most attractive option is to use source code management. Visual Studio Code supports Git without you having to install any extensions, although you do need to install git on the local machine. Once you have it all set up this works well, but setting it up is a time-consuming process and it requires that you understand how Git, and usually GitHub, works. For small and simple projects this is generally more than you need and you could spend a lot of valuable programming time learning to use a tool that you barely make use of. This said, if you are planning a large project, or a collaborative project, then source code management is your best option, even if it does involve additional initial work.

In most cases we can achieve what we need using simpler tools. You can copy a single file or folder from a remote machine by drag-and-dropping it from the VS Code Explorer to a folder in the local machine. Unfortunately, this doesn't work for remote Linux machines, and this includes Pi OS, so it isn't a method that works for us. However, you can drag-and-drop files and folders from the local machine to the Explorer window on the remote machine.

Now we only have the problem of copying files from the remote machine to the local machine. This can be done by selecting a file or folder in the Explorer and right-clicking to display the context menu. You will see Download in the same section as Copy. Selecting this downloads the entire folder and its contents or the single file. You can pick where you want the file or folder to be copied to and so manually maintain a central copy of anything you are working on.

An alternative way of saving a remote file on the local machine is to use the File, Save As menu option and select the Show Local button.

This allows you to save the file on the local machine under whatever name you want to use.

There are ways of automating the copying of files, but manual copying works well and most of the automatic synchronizing methods have their own drawbacks.

Running and Debugging Remotely

With a remote connection setup as described above you can build, debug and run a program as if you were working locally. The only difference might be a slight pause as things are uploaded. The program is stored, built and debugged on the remote machine. Select the Run and Debug option as before and the debug configuration that you have set up. If you need to run a file without building or debugging then you can use the run task listed earlier.

Customizing Compile - Using Libraries

Sometimes you need to specify a library file for the program to use. You have to include the appropriate header file and you also have to specify the name of the library, gpiod say, that you want the linker to add to your program.

To add a library to the build we need to edit the tasks.json file. If you examine it you will find the args parameter which specifies the option passed to the compiler. To load a library you simply add -lname to the list of parameters.

For example to use `pthread` you would change the `args` to read:

```
"args": [
    "-fdiagnostics-color=always",
    "-g",
    "${file}",
    "-o",
    "${fileDirname}/${fileBasenameNoExtension}",
     "-lpthread"
],
```

which adds `-lpthread` to the end.

If you run into trouble it is worth knowing that the library file specified *lname* corresponds to a file name of `lib`*name*`.a`. For example, `-lpthread` loads and uses the library file named `libpthread`.

You can also add folders to search for include files using `-Ifolderpath`.

Another useful customization is to create a "release" build, i.e. an optimized program with no debug information. To do this replace the "`-g`" option with "`-03`".

Running as Root

There are many hardware facilities that a C program cannot access unless it is running with root privileges. Security is a big problem for Linux programmers, and IoT programmers in particular, because it tends to get in the way of what we are trying to do. For example, running a program as `root` is considered to be very bad practice, but if that program wants to access hardware directly it has no choice but to require root privileges and you have no choice but to supply them, no matter what less well-informed programmers have to say about security risks.

The usual way of running a program with root privileges is to use `sudo`. If the program is called `HelloWorld` then all you have to do to run it as root is:

`sudo ./HelloWorld`

You might well be asked to supply your password and your account needs to be a member of the root group.

At the time of writing, using `sudo` to run VS Code as `root` doesn't work. It might in a future version and it is worth checking, but for the moment the only workable solution is to log on as `root`. Exactly how this works depends on whether you are working with VS Code locally or remotely. In either case, you first need to allow root to log on with a password.

To set a password for root:

```
sudo passwd root
```

and enter the new password.

With this change you can now log on as `root`. However, when the desktop starts up, you will notice that there is no taskbar. This is another security mechanism, but why it is necessary isn't clear.

You can start VS Code using Ctrl-Alt-T to open a terminal and then use the command:

```
code --no-sandbox —user-data-dir=/root/.data
```

This is necessary because VS Code applies more security when running as root. The `user-data-dir` you specify is created and used to store session data for VS Code and you can mostly ignore it. Once you have VS Code loaded you can use it as normal and your programs will be run with root permissions.

You can also start a file manager using:

```
pcmanfm
```

at the command prompt.

If you want to work remotely then you also need to allow root login via SSH. To do this use:

```
sudo nano /etc/ssh/sshd_config
```

and add the line:

```
PermitRootLogin yes
```

After a reboot you can log in with the name "`root`" with the password you set.

Logging in as root using a password is considered insecure and inconvenient. The best advice is to copy the public key, see earlier, using the usual `scp` command at the SSH prompt:

```
scp pi.pub root@192.168.11.151:~/.ssh/authorized_keys
```

You will have to provide the root password and, of course, modify the IP address and the path to the public key. You also need to modify the `.ssh/config` file on the local machine to associate the key to the remote machine.

After you have done this, you can remove the permission to log in using a password by using:

```
sudo nano /etc/ssh/sshd_config
```

and changing the line to read:

```
PermitRootLogin without-password
```

Make sure you can log in using the public key first.

At this point you can start VS Code and set up a remote connection using the root user. This works in exactly the same way as described earlier for a general user and will allow you to run and debug programs with root privileges.

If you want to use the VS Code tasks for remote development then simply change the user to `root` in `settings.json`. You will also have to create the `Documents` directory in `/root` if you want to make use of it.

Summary

- C is a good choice of language for IoT applications – it is the language of Linux and it is efficient and easy to use.

- You can use either local or remote development environments. Local is where you use the same machine to create and run a program. Remote is where the development and machine used to run the program are different.

- For IoT work, remote development has big advantages.

- If you want to use local development you can install and use any of Genny, Eclipse, Code::Blocks, NetBeans or VS Code, which is the IDE used in this book as it has many advantages when it comes to remote development.

- VS Code can be installed on Windows, Linux or OSX.

- To access hardware, programs often need to run with root permissions and the simplest way to do this is to log in as root. However, this can be tricky as the system doesn't always interact well with the root user.

Chapter 4

Drivers: A First Program

The easiest approach to using the hardware of the CM5 is to work with the Linux device drivers that allow user space programs to communicate with hardware via kernel space. This approach has the advantage that you don't have to worry about implementing the low-level protocol that is used to "talk" to the device. You might, however, have to implement the commands that make the device work and to read and write data to configure it. Not all of the work is necessarily done for you. Another big advantage is that the driver runs in kernel mode and this means that it can run without interruption by the operating system. The downside is that most Linux device drivers are poorly documented, usually from the point of view of driver writers rather than users, and suffer from either a lack of support or updates that break your existing programs. With care, however, both situations can be managed.

The most common problem with using drivers is they aren't as fast as direct access to the hardware and this is something we look at in later chapters. Working directly with the hardware is much more complicated but sometimes it cannot be avoided.

Linux drivers work with almost any programming language as they usually only require file I/O and some limited system calls. This means that to make use of them all you need to know is how to open, close, read and write a file, making use of Linux/POSIX file descriptors rather than C file streams. POSIX file descriptors are covered in *Applying C for the IoT with Linux*, ISBN: 9781871962611.

This makes using drivers sound easy, but there are a lot of fine details. How do you get a custom driver loaded and configured for the particular hardware you are using? How can you do this from within your program rather than having to ask the user to perform the configuration? What files do you read or write to achieve any desired result? Answering these questions is what this book is all about.

Using a Driver

A key principle of Unix and Linux is that, as much as possible, every interaction with the outside world is represented as a file. This isn't as crazy as it sounds as reading and writing to a file can be thought of as sending data to and from a device. When you use a standard file you are sending data to and from a disk drive or a storage device. When you send data to a "pseudo" file you are sending the data to and from some more general device, or even an internal part of the operating system.

External devices, such as disk drives, keyboards and so on, are represented as files in the /dev folder. Internal devices such as GPIO lines, timers and so on are represented as files in the /sys folder. This said, there is a great deal of inherited illogicality in the organization.

Most of the devices that we consider in this book have drivers that represent them as folders and files in the /sys folder. The files can be used as if they were perfectly standard files and read and written using the file handling commands available in whatever language you are using. In C it is usually more appropriate to use Linux file descriptors as the buffering isn't appropriate for most devices, as explained in *Applying C for the IoT with Linux*.

When using a driver, the problems are generally just finding out which folders do what and what the allowable values are. The obvious solution to this problem is to find the documentation for the driver, but often this doesn't supply the information you need, in which you need to engage in interactive reverse engineering.

LEDs

It is usual to first write the IoT equivalent of a Hello World program, i.e. Blinky. This is a program that simply flashes an LED. Usually you have to go over the details of connecting an LED to a GPIO line and then how to use software to make it flash at a set rate. Here, however, we want to use a driver to show how this approach to the IoT works and the good news is that there is an LED driver.

If you are familiar with IoT programming you might find this news slightly disturbing. Flashing an LED is the simplest of programs and using a Linux driver by comparison is grossly inefficient, involving layers of intermediate code. This is true, but using a Linux driver has the advantage of being easier to move to another Linux system and is more sophisticated. If you compare what is easy to implement using the LED driver with its equivalent direct implementation, you will see that the inefficient layers are actually doing something useful.

The Linux LED driver, gpio-leds is installed by default and it automatically creates a /sys/class/leds folder which contains a folder for each LED device the system uses and some that it might not.

The two of interest for the CM5 are called ACT and PWR. They were called led0 and led1 under earlier operating systems. The ACT folder corresponds to the green activity LED on all Pis and the PWR folder corresponds to the red power LED on all Pis apart from the Pi Zero.

If you open the ACT folder you will see a number of folders and files:

device   power   subsystem   brightness   max_bright-   trigger   uevent
                                               ness

The ones that are important to us at the moment start with brightness, which gets/sets the brightness of the LED. This is a value between 0 and 1, but most LEDs are either on or off and writing anything greater than 0 generally turns the LED full on. The trigger folder sets an association between the LED and various signal sources. By default trigger is set to mmc0 which flashes the LED according to how much memory I/O there is and hence provides an indication of processor activity. It is the ability to connect the LED to a signal source that makes the LED driver more sophisticated than simply connecting an LED to a GPIO line.

Blinky

Time to write a Blinky program for ACT. All we have to do is write none to trigger and then write a 0 or a 1 to the brightness file:

```
#include <stdio.h>
#include <unistd.h>
#include <fcntl.h>
int main(int argc, char **argv)
{
    int fd = open("/sys/class/leds/ACT/trigger", O_WRONLY);
    write(fd, "none",4);
    close(fd);
    fd = open("/sys/class/leds/ACT/brightness", O_WRONLY);
    while (1)
    {
        write(fd, "0",1);
        sleep(1);
        write(fd, "1",1);
        sleep(1);
    }
}
```

You can see the basic idea – we first open the trigger file and write none to it to disassociate the ACT LED from its standard trigger. Next we open the brightness file and write 0 and 1 to it to set the LED off and on.

Unless you have logged in as root, either locally or via remote, see the previous chapter, then this program will not work. To access the LEDs you need root privileges. If you are not logged in as root then simplest way to run your program with root permissions is to use:

```
sudo ./blinky
```

in the terminal after you have compiled it.

You can also try changing the permissions on the driver:

```
sudo chmod -R  a+rwx /sys/class/leds/ACT
```

Following this the program should work in VS Code, but notice that as sys files are not real files they are constructed when the system boots and this is not a permanent change to the permissions.

For all of the programs in the remainder of this book it is assumed that you have root privileges.

A Blinky implementation more in keeping with the LED driver is to use a trigger rather than a loop to flash the on-board LED together with a sleep. When you set trigger to timer the driver automatically creates two more files, delay_on and delay_off which set the on and off time in milliseconds:

```c
#include <stdio.h>
#include <unistd.h>
#include <fcntl.h>
int main(int argc, char **argv)
{
    int fd = open("/sys/class/leds/ACT/trigger", O_WRONLY);
    write(fd, "timer", 5);
    close(fd);
    fd = open("/sys/class/leds/ACT/delay_on", O_WRONLY);
    write(fd, "2000", 4);
    close(fd);
    fd = open("/sys/class/leds/ACT/delay_off", O_WRONLY);
    write(fd, "3000", 4);
    close(fd);
}
```

In this case the act LED flashes for two seconds on, three seconds off and doesn't need the program to keep going. Once set up, the trigger controls the LED until it is modified.

Finding Out About Drivers

All of this is very simple, but how do you find the information that you need to use the LED driver? The answer is that it can be challenging. You can look for documentation, but there usually isn't any and if there is then it generally is targeted at driver writers and explains how to make use of the driver's facilities in kernel mode, not user mode. This can be very confusing and can waste time if you try to use drivers in the way described in a user-mode program.

For example, if you look at the documentation for LEDs in the Linux source code tree for the Raspberry Pi, which you can find on the Raspberry Pi GitHub page, i.e. in `linux/Documentation/leds/`, you will see a lot of files, but which one has the information about basic LED operation is not clear.

There is usually a documentation file for the class or core driver, in this case `leds-class`. If you open this you will find some basic and very general information. It tells you that:

> *"In its simplest form, the LED class just allows control of LEDs from userspace. LEDs appear in /sys/class/leds/. The maximum brightness of the LED is defined in max_brightness file. The brightness file will set the brightness of the LED (taking a value 0-max_brightness). Most LEDs don't have hardware brightness support so will just be turned on for non-zero brightness settings."*

This is enough to get you started, but there is no information about what the actual LEDs in the `leds` folder are. That is, it doesn't help with what ACT and PWR actually are. The documentation does go on to explain the idea of triggers, but it doesn't tell you what triggers are available and there is no documentation for them. The best that you can do is read the source code for the triggers that are available in the `linux/drivers/leds/trigger/` folder:

```
cat trigger
[none] rc-feedback kbd-scrolllock kbd-numlock kbd-capslock kbd-
kanalock kbd-shiftlock kbd-altgrlock kbd-ctrllock kbd-altlock kbd-
shiftllock kbd-shiftrlock kbd-ctrlllock kbd-ctrlrlock timer oneshot
heartbeat backlight gpio cpu cpu0 default-on input panic mmc1 mmc0
rfkill-any rfkill-none rfkill0 rfkill1
```

Some of these are obvious, some less so, and working out how to use any of them is a matter of trial and error and reading the relevant driver code.

If you search the web you will find that other programmers have already investigated on your behalf:

```
none                No trigger
kbd-scrolllock      Keyboard scroll lock
kbd-numlock         Keyboard num lock
kbd-capslock        Keyboard caps lock
kbd-kanalock        Keyboard kana lock
kbd-shiftlock       Keyboard shift
kbd-altgrlock       Keyboard altgr
kbd-ctrllock        Keyboard ctrl
kbd-altlock         Keyboard alt
kbd-shiftllock      Keyboard left shift
kbd-shiftrlock      Keyboard right shift
kbd-ctrlllock       Keyboard left ctrl
kbd-ctrlrlock       Keyboard right ctrl
timer               Flash at 1 second intervals
oneshot             Flash only once
heartbeat           Flash like a heartbeat (1-0-1-00000)
backlight           Always on
gpio                Flash when a specified GPIO has an event
cpu0                Flash on cpu0 usage
cpu1                Flash on cpu1 usage
cpu2                Flash on cpu2 usage
cpu3                Flash on cpu3 usage
default-on          Always on
input               Default state
panic               Flash on kernel panic
mmc0                Flash on mmc0 (primary SD interface) activity
mmc1                Flash on mmc1 (secondary SD interface) activity
rfkill0             Flash on wifi activity
rfkill1             Flash on bluetooth activity
```

A lot more information about devices and drivers can be found via the device tree, which is the subject of Chapters 9 and 16.

Summary

- Blinky, flashing an LED, is the IoT's Hello World program and usually this involves wiring an LED and writing code to change the state of a GPIO line.

- Using the Linux LED driver you can create a Blinky program that flashes an onboard LED, so avoiding the need for extra hardware.

- A full Linux driver just to flash an LED may seem like overkill, but it has advantages in that you can connect it to any of a set of triggers that make it flash according to a range of sensors.

- The LED driver is typical of Linux drivers in general in that it creates a set of folders and files which you open and read and write to control the LED.

- The big problem with all drivers is finding documentation on how to use the driver and how to configure it.

Chapter 5

The GPIO Character Driver

As far as IoT goes, the fundamental Linux driver is the GPIO driver, which gives you access to the individual GPIO lines. This is another built-in driver and is like the LED driver introduced in the previous chapter, but it is a character driver and used in a slightly different way.

In most cases, when a device is connected via a set of GPIO lines, you usually use a specific device driver. In this way you can almost ignore the GPIO lines and what they are doing. However, there are still simple situations where a full driver would be overkill. If you want to interface a button or an LED, then direct control over the GPIO lines is the most direct way to do the job even if there are Linux LED drivers, see the previous chapter, and even an input driver.

The standard way to work with GPIO in Linux used to be via the sysfs interface. Although it was removed from the Linux kernel in 2020, having been deprecated in 2105, you will still encounter many programs making use of it and even find articles advocating its use. While you shouldn't use it for new projects, you may still need to know about it to cope with legacy software. If so consult GPIO Sysfx Interface which you will find on this book's page, https://iopress.info/

The replacement for the old sysfs interface is the GPIO character device and, while this looks superficially similar, it has many major differences. Although it has some advantages, it is slightly more complex and can no longer be used from the command line – it is a program-only interface. This said, there are some simple utility programs that are fairly standard and allow GPIO control from the command line. These are covered in the first part of the chapter, even though they are unlikely to be the main way that you work with the new interface.

There is also a wrapper library called libgpiod. Although it isn't necessary for simple access to the GPIO lines, it is described in this chapter.

GPIO Character Device

The new approach to working with GPIO comes pre-installed in Pi OS. If you look in the /dev directory you will find files corresponding to each GPIO controller installed. You will see at least:

/dev/gpiochip0

This represents the main GPIO controller and all of the GPIO lines it provides. Early versions of the CM5's OS used gpiochip4 for the user GPIO lines and this is still supported as a link to gpiochip0.

If you know how sysfs works you might well be expecting instructions on how to read and write to the file from the console. In this case, reading and writing to the file will do you little good as most of the work is carried out using ioctl(), the input/output control system call, which cannot be used from the command line. The use of ioctl is typical of a character driver, but it does mean that using the GPIO driver is very different from the other file-oriented drivers described later. The next chapter looks at the use of ioctl to directly control the GPIO character device.

If you want to explore the GPIO from the command line, you need to install some tools that have been created mainly as examples of using the new device interface. To do this you need to first install them and libgpiod. the gpiod library that you will use later:

sudo apt-get install gpiod libgpiod-dev libgpiod-doc

If you don't want to use the library to access the driver, you don't have to install it as the GPIO driver is loaded as part of the Linux kernel and is ready to use.

The Utilities

The standalone applications that are installed are:

 ♦ gpiodetect

   Lists all of the GPIO controllers that are installed:

```
pi@raspberrypi:~ $ gpiodetect
gpiochip0 [pinctrl-bcm2835] (54 lines)
pi@raspberrypi:~ $ ▮
```

◆ gpioinfo

Lists all of the GPIO lines provided by the named GPIO controller:

```
pi@raspberrypi:~ $ gpioinfo gpiochip0
gpiochip0 - 54 lines:
        line   0:      unnamed      unused   input    active-high
        line   1:      unnamed      unused   input    active-high
        line   2:      unnamed      unused   input    active-high
        line   3:      unnamed      unused   input    active-high
        line   4:      unnamed      unused   output   active-high
        line   5:      unnamed      unused   input    active-high
        line   6:      unnamed      unused   input    active-high
        line   7:      unnamed      unused   input    active-high
        line   8:      unnamed      unused   input    active-high
```

◆ gpiofind

You can give particular lines names by editing the device tree. If you do give them appropriate fixed names then gpiofind *name* returns the number of the GPIO line.

◆ gpioset

You can set any number of GPIO lines in one operation with:

gpioset *options chip name/number* <offset1>=<value1>

<offset2>=<value2> ...

where *options* are:

-l, --active-low	Sets the line's active state to low
-m, --mode =	Choice of what to do after setting values:
exit	Exit immediately, the default
wait	Wait for user to press ENTER
time	Sleep for a specified amount of time
signal	Wait for SIGINT or SIGTERM
-s, --sec = *SEC*	Number of seconds to wait
-u, --usec = *USEC*	Number of microseconds to wait
-b, --background	Detaches from the controlling terminal

The change in the line's state only persists while the command is executing. This means you have to use wait or time to see the effect. For example:

gpioset -m wait 0 4=0 17=1

sets gpiochip 0 GPIO4 to 0 and GPIO17 to 1 and waits until the user presses ENTER.

◆ gpioget

The gpioget command returns the state of the lines specified as text:

gpioget *chip name/number* <offset 1> <offset 2>

For example:

gpioget 0 4 17

displays the current state of GPIO4 and GPIO17 on gpiochip0.

◆ gpiomon

The gpiomon command lets you monitor changes in input lines using a poll system call:

gpiomon *options chip name/number <offset 1> <offset 2> …*

where *options* are:

-n, --num-events = *NUM*	Exit after processing *NUM* events
-s, --silent	Don't print event info
-r, --rising-edge	Only process rising edge events
-f, --falling-edge	Only process falling edge events
-F, --format =	Specify custom output format

%o	GPIO line offset
%e	event type (0 - falling edge, 1 - rising edge)
%s	seconds part of the event timestamp
%n	nanoseconds part of the event timestamp

For example, to monitor GPIO4 and GPIO17 for any changes:

```
pi@raspberrypi:~ $ gpiomon 0 4 17
event:  RISING EDGE offset: 4 timestamp: [1589563313.974056272]
event:  RISING EDGE offset: 17 timestamp: [1589563313.974694285]
```

These utilities are useful and they can be used in scripts to control GPIO lines. For example, if you save:

```
while true
do
 gpioset -m time -s 1 0 4=0 17=1
 gpioset -m time -s 1 0 4=1 17=0
done
```

in a text file called binky.sh and set its execution permission to owner then you can run it in a console and flash a pair of LEDs connected to GPIO4 and GPIO17. If any of the GPIO lines are in use, the script will return an error message.

You also need to keep in mind that the GPIO line is only in use while the gpioset command is running, that is, the line is opened at the start of the command and closed when it ends, so returning the line to input.

You can get a long way with shell scripts and the GPIO utilities, but sooner or later you are going to want to work with something else.

Installing the gpiod Library

The gpiod library is installed along with the tools discussed at the start of the chapter, but you don't have to use it if you are happy with the ioctl system calls described in the next chapter.

The library splits into two parts, the context-less functions and the lower-level functions, which can be considered context-using. In nearly all cases you will want to use the lower-level functions as the contextless functions have some serious drawbacks. Let's take a look at each in turn.

To use the library you need to install it if you haven't already done so:

```
sudo apt-get install gpiod libgpiod-dev libgpiod-doc
```

You also need to add the header:

```
#include <gpiod.h>
```

and you will need to load a library file.

If you are using VS Code you will need to edit `tasks.json` to load the library:

```
"args": [
    "-fdiagnostics-color=always",
    "-g",
    "${file}",
    "-o",
    "${fileDirname}/${fileBasenameNoExtension}",
     "-lgpiod"
],
```

Contextless Functions

The contextless functions all have `ctxless` in their names and they work by opening the necessary files, performing the operation and then closing them again. This means you don't have to keep track of what files are open and what GPIO lines are in use, but you have the overhead and side effects of repeatedly opening and closing files.

There are two simple get/set functions:

- gpiod_ctxless_get_value("*device*", *offset*, active_low, "*consumer*")
- gpiod_ctxless_set_value("*device*", *offset*, value, active_low, "*consumer*", callback, param)

where *device* is the name, path, number or label of the `gpiochip`, usually just 0, and *offset* is the GPIO number of the line you want to use. Set `value` to 0 or 1 according to whether you want the GPIO line set high or low `active_low` sets the state of the line regarded as active, 1 sets the line low and vice versa. You usually want to set this to 0 so that 1 sets it high.

Replace *consumer* with the name of the `program/user/entity` using the GPIO line. The attributes `callback` and `param` work together to define a callback function and the parameters passed to it. The callback function is called immediately before the line is closed. The get version of the function returns the current state of the line as a 0 or 1 according to the line state and the setting of `active_low`.

As an example of using the contextless functions, simply toggle GPIO 4 as fast as possible:

```c
#include <gpiod.h>
#include <stdio.h>
#include <unistd.h>
#include <stdlib.h>
int res;
int main(int argc, char **argv) {
    for (;;) {
        res = gpiod_ctxless_set_value("0", 4, 1, 1,
                                "output test", NULL, NULL);
        res = gpiod_ctxless_set_value("0", 4, 0, 1,
                                "output test", NULL, NULL);
    }
}
```

If you inspect the output of this program you will see reasonably equal pulses, each around 23μs wide:

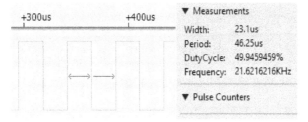

To set the pulse width you have to use a callback function to delay the closing of the file:

```c
#include <gpiod.h>
#include <stdio.h>
#include <unistd.h>
#include <stdlib.h>
#include <time.h>
int res;

int delayms(int ms) {
    struct timespec delay = {0, ms * 1000*1000};
    return nanosleep(&delay, NULL);
}

int main(int argc, char **argv) {

    for (;;) {
        res = gpiod_ctxless_set_value("0", 4, 1, 1, "output test",
                (gpiod_ctxless_set_value_cb) delayms, (void *) 100);
        res = gpiod_ctxless_set_value("0", 4, 0, 1, "output test",
                (gpiod_ctxless_set_value_cb) delayms, (void *) 100);
    }
}
```

Notice that the final parameter isn't actually being used as a pointer, instead it is just a way of passing an untyped value and the parameter isn't dereferenced in the callback.

This version of the program is more useful in that it produces pulses of around 100ms. Also notice the wrapper for `nanosleep`. This is because we can only pass a single parameter to the callback function. The first set makes the line go high and it stays high for the duration of the `nanosleep` and then the close operation resets it to input. The second set makes the line go low for the duration of the `nanosleep` and it stays low while the line is closed again. What this all means is that the time that the line is low is still longer than the `nanosleep` time because it includes the time to close and open the file.

You can see that the high time is around 100ms, but the low time is a little longer. You can either adjust the low timings or simply put up with it.

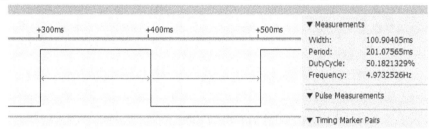

As well as single line get and set functions, there are also multiple line versions:

- `gpiod_ctxless_set_value_multiple(`*"device"*`,offsets[], values[],num_lines,active_low,` *"consumer"*`,callback,param)`
- `gpiod_ctxless_get_value_multiple(`*"device"*`,offsets[], values[],num_lines,active_low,` *"consumer"*`,callback,param)`

These work in the same way, but now you can specify a set of lines as an array of line structs and an array of values to get/set them to. Of course, you have to specify the number of lines and the arrays have to be the correct size.

For example, to pulse two lines out of phase you could use:

```
#include <gpiod.h>
#include <stdio.h>
#include <unistd.h>
#include <stdlib.h>
#include <time.h>
int res;
int delayms(int ms)
{
    struct timespec delay = {0, ms * 1000 * 1000};
    return nanosleep(&delay, NULL);
}
int main(int argc, char **argv)
{
    int offsets[] = {4, 17};
    int state1[] = {1, 0};
    int state2[] = {0, 1};
    for (;;) {
    gpiod_ctxless_set_value_multiple("0", offsets, state1, 2, 1,
    "output test", (gpiod_ctxless_set_value_cb)delayms, (void *)1);
    gpiod_ctxless_set_value_multiple("0", offsets, state2, 2, 1,
    "output test", (gpiod_ctxless_set_value_cb)delayms, (void *)2);
    }
}
```

This pulses lines 4 and 17 so that one is high while the other is low. Even though the function promises to change the lines at the same moment, there is about a 8μs delay between changing the state of lines, as can be seen in the logic analyzer display below:

If you are working in milliseconds, a delay of 8μs probably isn't important, but it is still necessary to know that the lines do not all change together and there are situations in which this matters.

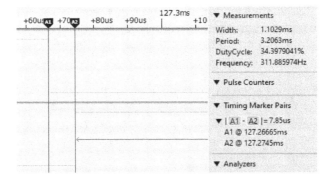

The context-less functions are rarely helpful and they are only slightly easier to use than the much more powerful context-using functions.

Context Functions

The only real difference in using the context functions is that you have to open the resources, use them and close them. This isn't difficult, it generally corresponds to what you actually want to do, and it follows the steps in using the ioctl system call directly as explained in the next chapter.

You have to:

1) Open the GPIO chip you want to use
2) Get the GPIO line or lines you want to use
3) Configure and use the lines
4) Close the GPIO chip

GPIO Chip

First you have to open the GPIO chip of your choice and there are various functions that allow you to specify the chip in different ways:

```
gpiod_chip_open("path")
gpiod_chip_open_by_name("name")
gpiod_chip_open_by_number(num)
gpiod_chip_open_by_label("label");
```

In each case NULL is returned if the open fails, otherwise a pointer is returned to a struct, gpiod_chip, which has the information about the chip. You can not access the fields of the struct directly. Instead there are a small number of access functions:

```
const char * name=gpiod_chip_name(chip)
const char * label=gpiod_chip_label(chip)
int number= gpiod_chip_num_lines(chip)
```

where chip is a pointer to struct gpiod_chip. Of course, when you are finished with the chip, you have to close it:

```
gpiod_chip_close(chip)
```

For example:

```
#include <gpiod.h>
#include <stdio.h>
#include <unistd.h>
#include <stdlib.h>
int main(int argc, char **argv) {
    int res;
    struct gpiod_chip *chip = gpiod_chip_open_by_number(0);
    const char *name = gpiod_chip_name(chip);
    int num = gpiod_chip_num_lines(chip);
    printf("%s %d", name, num);
    gpiod_chip_close(chip);
}
```

This displays the name and number of lines supported by GPIO chip 0.

Getting Lines

The main purpose of creating `gpiod_chip` structs is to access `gpiod_line` structs. There are different ways of doing this. First, there are two functions that return a pointer to a `gpiod_line` struct:

```
struct gpiod_line  *line = gpiod_chip_get_line(chip, offset)
struct gpiod_line  *line = gpiod_chip_find_line(chip,"name")
```

where `chip` is a pointer to struct `gpiod_chip` and the GPIO line is either specified by number or name.

You can also close the line:

```
void gpiod_line_release(struct gpiod_line *line);
```

There are three functions that work with groups of GPIO lines:

- `gpiod_chip_get_lines(chip, offsets[], num_offsets, bulk)`
- `gpiod_chip_find_lines(chip, names[], bulk)`
- `gpiod_chip_get_all_lines(chip, bulk)`

All three functions return a pointer to a `bulk` struct which contains an array of `gpiod_line` structs.

The fields of the `gpiod_line` structs are hidden from you, but there are a range of access functions:

- `int offset = gpiod_line_offset(line)`
- `const char *name = gpiod_line_name(line)`
- `const char *consumer = gpiod_line_consumer(line)`
- `int direction =  gpiod_line_direction(line)`
- `int active_state  = gpiod_line_active_state(line)`
- `bool used =  gpiod_line_is_used(line)`
- `bool open_drain = gpiod_line_is_open_drain(line)`
- `bool open_source = gpiod_line_is_open_source(line)`

where `line` is a pointer to a line struct.

There is also the small matter of whether a line is already in use. The old sysfs GPIO driver used `export` and `unexport` to reserve and release lines. The new driver simply reserves the line when you open it as a file or, using the gpiod library, when you get the line from the GPIO chip, and unreserves it when you release it. Notice that many other Linux drivers use the GPIO driver to access lines and hence using a device via a driver might well reserve the GPIO lines it uses.

You can test to see if a line is free using:

```
bool gpiod_line_is_used(line)
```

which returns `true` if the line is in use. Notice that while you cannot find out why a line is in use – it might be the operating system or another process – you do discover if it is being used and you can only use a line when it isn't already in use.

It could even be that the current process already has the line in use. You can check for this condition using:

```
bool gpiod_line_is_requested(struct gpiod_line *line)
```

If this returns true the current process has ownership of the line and can use it without first exporting it.

Using Lines

Once you have a struct gpiod_line you can use it to configure the line. There are two simple configuration functions:

- gpiod_line_request_input(line, "consumer")
- gpiod_line_request_output(line, "consumer", default_val)

where line is a pointer to struct gpiod_line and the second parameter assigns a label. For output, you can also set a default or initial value.

Once you have a line set to output you can set it using:

```
gpiod_line_set_value(line, value)
```

Once you have a line set to input you can read it using:

```
int value = gpiod_line_get_value(line)
```

For example, a simple program to toggle GPIO4 as fast as possible is:

```
#include <gpiod.h>
#include <stdio.h>
#include <unistd.h>
#include <stdlib.h>

int main(int argc, char **argv) {
    int res;
    struct gpiod_chip *chip = gpiod_chip_open_by_number(0);
    struct gpiod_line *line4 = gpiod_chip_get_line(chip, 4);
    res=gpiod_line_request_output(line4, "test output", 0);

    for(;;){
        res=gpiod_line_set_value(line4,  1);
        res=gpiod_line_set_value(line4,  0);
    };
}
```

The program opens the GPIO chip and retrieves GPIO 4, which is set to output and the infinite loop simply toggles the line. Notice that you cannot close the GPIO chip and continue to use the line. You can close or release the line and continue to use the chip.

For simplicity, in this case we didn't close the lines or the chip but in principle you always should and there is a combined line and chip close function:

```
gpiod_line_close_chip(line)
```

It is only when the line is closed does its status change from used to unused and another process can make use of it. In nearly all cases, however, the line is closed when your program ends.

If you try the program, you will discover that the pulses produced are around $0.6\mu s$, which is similar in speed to using ioctl system calls directly, see the next chapter.

You can also configure a line in more detail using:

```
gpiod_line_request(line, config, default_val)
```

where config is a pointer to a gpiod_line_request_config struct:

```
struct gpiod_line_request_config {
      const char *consumer;
      int request_type;
      int flags;
};
```

The request_type is any of:

- ◆ GPIOD_LINE_REQUEST_DIRECTION_AS_IS
- ◆ GPIOD_LINE_REQUEST_DIRECTION_INPUT
- ◆ GPIOD_LINE_REQUEST_DIRECTION_OUTPUT
- ◆ GPIOD_LINE_REQUEST_EVENT_FALLING_EDGE
- ◆ GPIOD_LINE_REQUEST_EVENT_RISING_EDGE
- ◆ GPIOD_LINE_REQUEST_EVENT_BOTH_EDGES

The event requests are discussed in more detail later and their flags are:

- ◆ GPIOD_LINE_REQUEST_FLAG_OPEN_DRAIN
- ◆ GPIOD_LINE_REQUEST_FLAG_OPEN_SOURCE
- ◆ GPIOD_LINE_REQUEST_FLAG_ACTIVE_LOW
- ◆ GPIOD_LINE_REQUEST_FLAG_BIAS_DISABLE
- ◆ GPIOD_LINE_REQUEST_FLAG_BIAS_PULL_DOWN
- ◆ GPIOD_LINE_REQUEST_FLAG_BIAS_PULL_UP

As discussed in Chapter 8, the open drain and open source flags don't work.

You will also find a set of functions which perform a request using only flags and a preset request type. Essentially these are just shortcuts that mean you don't have to fill in a gpiod_line_request_config struct:

- ◆ gpiod_line_request_input(struct gpiod_line *line,
                              const char *consumer);
- ◆ gpiod_line_request_output(struct gpiod_line *line,
                  const char *consumer, int default_val);
- ◆ gpiod_line_request_rising_edge_events
      (struct gpiod_line *line, const char *consumer);
- ◆ gpiod_line_request_falling_edge_events(
      struct gpiod_line *line, const char *consumer);
- ◆ gpiod_line_request_both_edges_events(
              struct gpiod_line *line,const char *consumer);

There is also a set of functions that do the same thing, but let you set the flags as well. Again, the only advantage is not having to create a gpiod_line_request_config struct:

- int gpiod_line_request_input_flags(struct gpiod_line *line, const char *consumer, int flags);
- int gpiod_line_request_output_flags(struct gpiod_line *line, const char *consumer, int flags,int default_val);
- int gpiod_line_request_rising_edge_events_flags(struct gpiod_line *line,const char *consumer,int flags);
- int gpiod_line_request_falling_edge_events_flags(struct gpiod_line *line,const char *consumer,int flags);
- int gpiod_line_request_both_edges_events_flags(struct gpiod_line *line,const char *consumer,int flags);

Working With More Than One Line

There are also "bulk" versions of the line functions which work with a set of lines at one time. The key to understanding these is the gpiod_line_bulk struct:

```
struct gpiod_line_bulk {
        struct gpiod_line *lines[GPIOD_LINE_BULK_MAX_LINES];
        unsigned int num_lines;
};
```

This is essentially an array of gpiod_line structs with the number of lines in use recorded in a separate field. Again a set of functions is provided to let you work with the struct:

- gpiod_line_bulk_init(struct gpiod_line_bulk *bulk)
- gpiod_line_bulk_add(struct gpiod_line_bulk *bulk, struct gpiod_line * line)
- gpiod_line* gpiod_line_bulk_get_line(struct gpiod_line_bulk *bulk,unsigned int offset)
- gpiod_line_bulk_num_lines(struct gpiod_line_bulk *bulk)

You can use these to initialize, add and retrieve line structs from the bulk struct.

The general initialization function:

```
int gpiod_line_request_bulk(struct gpiod_line_bulk *bulk,
            const struct gpiod_line_request_config *config,
                            const int *default_vals);
```

This configures each line according to the array of config structs and, for output, sets the initial values to the elements of the default_vals array.

As in the case of a single line, there are functions that set all of the lines to a particular configuration:

- ◆ int gpiod_line_request_bulk_input(
    struct gpiod_line_bulk *bulk,const char *consumer);
- ◆ int gpiod_line_request_bulk_output(
    struct gpiod_line_bulk *bulk,const char *consumer,
                            const int *default_vals);
- ◆ int gpiod_line_request_bulk_rising_edge_events(
    struct gpiod_line_bulk *bulk,const char *consumer);
- ◆ int gpiod_line_request_bulk_falling_edge_events(
    struct gpiod_line_bulk *bulk,const char *consumer);
- ◆ int gpiod_line_request_bulk_both_edges_events(
    struct gpiod_line_bulk *bulk,const char *consumer);

Likewise, there are extended functions that let you also set the flags:

- ◆ int gpiod_line_request_bulk_input_flags(
  struct gpiod_line_bulk *bulk,const char *consumer,int flags);
- ◆ int gpiod_line_request_bulk_output_flags(
  struct gpiod_line_bulk *bulk,const char *consumer,
                          int flags,const int *default_vals);
- ◆ int gpiod_line_request_bulk_rising_edge_events_flags(
  struct gpiod_line_bulk *bulk,const char *consumer,int flags);
- ◆ int gpiod_line_request_bulk_falling_edge_events_flags(
  struct gpiod_line_bulk *bulk,const char *consumer,int flags);
- ◆ int gpiod_line_request_bulk_both_edges_events_flags(
  struct gpiod_line_bulk *bulk,const char *consumer,int flags);

If you use any of these functions, all of the lines in the gpiod_line_bulk array are set to the same configuration.

There is also a function what will close all of the lines that you have been working with:

void gpiod_line_release_bulk(struct gpiod_line_bulk *bulk);

Once you have set up the bulk lines you can get and set them:

- ◆ int gpiod_line_get_value_bulk(struct gpiod_line_bulk
                                *bulk,int *values);
- ◆ int gpiod_line_set_value_bulk(struct gpiod_line_bulk
                                *bulk,const int *values);

For the get function, the values array is set to the state of all of the lines, including output lines and for the set function the values array is written to the lines.

How these functions all work is easy to understand after you see an example. In this case the program pulses two lines that are out of phase:

```
#include <gpiod.h>
#include <stdio.h>
#include <unistd.h>
#include <stdlib.h>

int main(int argc, char **argv) {
    int res;
    struct gpiod_chip *chip = gpiod_chip_open_by_number(0);

    struct gpiod_line_bulk bulk;
    gpiod_line_bulk_init(&bulk);
    gpiod_line_bulk_add(&bulk, gpiod_chip_get_line(chip, 4));
    gpiod_line_bulk_add(&bulk, gpiod_chip_get_line(chip, 17));

    res=gpiod_line_request_bulk_output(&bulk, "test", 0);
    for (;;) {
        gpiod_line_set_value_bulk(&bulk,(int[2]){0,1});
        gpiod_line_set_value_bulk(&bulk,(int[2]){1,0});

    };
}
```

The new steps are the creation of a gpio_line_bulk struct and the use of gpiod_line_bulk_add to add lines to it. Once we have the gpio_line_bulk struct set up, the gpiod_line_request_bulk_output is called to set the lines to output and finally the loop sets the lines to different values. The use of an array literal in the gpiod_line_set_value_bulk call only works in C99 and later. In earlier versions of C you need to create two separate arrays.

Overall, the gpiod library isn't a huge advance over using the raw ioctl calls. Use whichever approach you prefer. In Chapter 6 we will look at some of the interrupt-like features that the GPIO driver provides.

Using GPIO Lines – Measuring R and C

There is a simple way to measure either the resistance of a circuit or its capacitance. The idea is to set up a circuit with a capacitor and a resistor in series and a GPIO line:

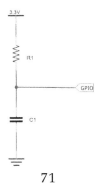

When the GPIO line is set to input the capacitor charges via R1 and eventually reaches 3.3V. In this state, the GPIO line reads the state as a high, i.e. a 1. If the GPIO line changes to an output and is set low, the capacitor discharges to 0V. The current through the GPIO line settles to 3.3/R1 and this should be less than 3mA, although the current when the capacitor first discharges will be much greater, it only flows for a short time. When the GPIO line reverts to input, the capacitor starts to charge again through the resistor R1. Eventually the capacitor reaches a high enough voltage for the GPIO line to read 1. The time it takes to read 1 is proportional to R1C1 and hence, if C1 is fixed, you can use the time to work out R1. If R1 is fixed, you can use the time to work out C1.

You can see that you can use time-to-charge to measure either the resistance or the capacitance. Any sensor that varies its resistance or capacitance in response to external conditions can be used with this arrangement. For example, a thermistor, a temperature-dependent resistor, and can be read and so can an LDR, a very common light-sensitive resistor.

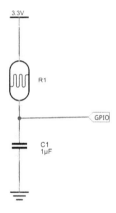

You can create a presence sensor by using a metal plate as one side of a capacitor. As people move closer, or further way, its capacitance changes. It is also possible to measure soil moisture content by measuring the resistance, or the capacitance, of two soil probes as both vary according to water content.

Using gpiod functions it is easy to create a program that measures resistance or capacitance:

```c
#define _POSIX_C_SOURCE 199309L
#include <gpiod.h>
#include <stdio.h>
#include <unistd.h>
#include <stdlib.h>
#include <time.h>

int main(int argc, char **argv)
{
    int res;
    struct timespec delay = {0, 10 * 1000 * 1000};
    struct timespec time1, time2;

    struct gpiod_chip *chip = gpiod_chip_open_by_number(0);
    struct gpiod_line *line4 = gpiod_chip_get_line(chip, 4);

    res = gpiod_line_request_input(line4, "RMeasure");
    nanosleep(&delay, NULL);
    gpiod_line_release(line4);

    res = gpiod_line_request_output(line4, "RMeasure", 0);
    nanosleep(&delay, NULL);
    gpiod_line_release(line4);

    clock_gettime(CLOCK_REALTIME, &time1);
    gpiod_line_request_input(line4, "RMeasure");
    while (gpiod_line_get_value(line4) == 0)
    {
    };
    clock_gettime(CLOCK_REALTIME, &time2);
    printf("Time=%d/n", (time2.tv_nsec - time1.tv_nsec) / 1000);
}
```

The program starts by setting up the GPIO chip on GPIO 4. Next we set the line to input and wait 10ms for things to settle. The line is then released and opened as an output set to 0. Again we wait 10ms for things to settle and then release the line again and set it to input. The time is recorded and we now wait till the line reads 1 and take the time again. The difference between the two times is the value we need.

If you try this out you will find the measurement is fairly noisy. This is probably due to the slow charging of the capacitor which causes the input to bounce:

Exactly when reading the line returns a **1** is a matter of chance. If you want to increase the accuracy, you could take ten or more measurements and average them.

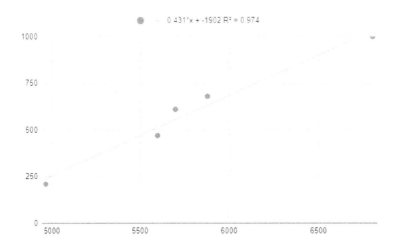

Typical result of measurements of resistors using a 1μF capacitor – resistance in ohms along the y-axis and time in ms on the x-axis.

If you want to use this approach, you can easily package the code into an easy-to-use function.

Summary

- The GPIO character driver replaces the sysfs GPIO driver and it is the one to use for all future projects.

- The gpiod library provides a higher level way of using the GPIO character driver, but if you don't want the overhead of using it then the direct ioctl interface is easy to use.

- After the library has been installed there are a number of utilities that are sometimes useful at the command line or in scripts.

- The library has two types of function, context-less and context-using. The contextless functions can be used in an ad-hoc fashion, but the context-using functions have to be used in an organized manner.

- The contextless functions set GPIO lines to input or output without opening them or reserving them in any way. This makes them slow and you need to use callback functions to control their output.

- The context-using functions require you to open the GPIO line and configure it before you use it. Once used you have to close the line to allow another process to make use of it.

- Context-using functions are not difficult to use and are much more flexible and fast.

- You can work with multiple GPIO lines in a single function call. However, there are still delays between setting lines to particular values.

- The context-using functions can create pulses as fast as $1\mu s$ to $2.0\mu s$.

- Using time-to-charge you can measure either the resistance or the capacitance of a circuit using a single GPIO line.

Chapter 6
GPIO Using I/O Control

The gpiod library is fairly easy to use, but so is the underlying ioctl, input/output control, interface. The main reasons for wanting to use it is that it is slightly faster and slightly more efficient in that you don't need to load a library. There is also the benefit of working directly with the ioctl driver and understanding what is going on.

Raw GPIO Character Device In C

You don't need anything special to work with a character device. All you need is the standard ioctl system call and for this you simply need to add:

```
#include <sys/ioctl.h>
```

The call varies according to the device it is being used with. Its general form is:

```
ioctl(fd, request, pstruct)
```

where `fd` is a file descriptor that returns the device being used and `request` is an unsigned long variable that specifies the request or operation to be performed. The third parameter is usually a pointer to a struct or an area of memory. Some ioctl calls have additional parameters.

The request number was never formalized and driver writers tended to invent their own, but there was an impromptu move to apply an organization and many request numbers follow a regular pattern. The most recent scheme uses two direction bits (`00`: none, `01`: write, `10`: read, `11`: read/write) followed by 14 size bits giving the size of the argument, followed by an 8-bit type which collects the ioctls in groups for a common purpose or a common driver, and an 8-bit serial number. A set of macros is provided so that the request number can be built up from its parts:

```
_IOR(type,nr,size)
_IOW(type,nr,size)
_IOWR(type,nr,size)
_IO(type,nr)
```

These are optional in that, if you know the request number, you can simply use it in the ioctl call.

The GPIO character device works entirely in terms of the ioctl system call – not by reading or writing the files. What you need to know to use the driver directly are the request codes and the structures that are passed. These are all defined in the gpio.h header:

```
#include <linux/gpio.h>
```

Working with the GPIO chip and the GPIO lines follows the same standard steps:

1. Find the request constant you need to use
2. Find the struct that is used with that constant
3. Open the appropriate file
4. Make an ioctl call using the constant and the struct.

Getting Chip Info

As a first simple example, let's get some information about the GPIO chip. If you look through the header file you will find:

```
GPIO_GET_CHIPINFO_IOCTL
```

which is the request constant. You will also find:

```
struct gpiochip_info {
      char name[32];
      char label[32];
      __u32 lines;
};
```

which is used to hold information about the GPIO chip.

With this information we can open the file and make the ioctl call:

```
#include <stdio.h>
#include <errno.h>
#include <unistd.h>
#include <fcntl.h>
#include <sys/ioctl.h>
#include <linux/gpio.h>
int main(int argc, char **argv) {
    int fd;
    struct gpiochip_info info;
    fd = open("/dev/gpiochip0", O_RDONLY);
    int ret = ioctl(fd, GPIO_GET_CHIPINFO_IOCTL, &info);
    close(fd);
    printf("label: %s\n name: %s\n number of lines: %u\n",
                        info.label,info.name,info.lines);
    return 0;
}
```

As with all good, easy-to-understand examples, error handling has been omitted. If you run this program you will see something like:

```
label: pinctrl-rp1
 name: gpiochip0
 number of lines: 54
```

GPIO Output

The next step is to set a GPIO line to output and use it. This involves only a few more ideas than the previous example. We need to go through the same steps, but in this case we first use the GPIO chip to make a GPIO handler device. This represents multiple GPIO lines, i.e. you can work with a group of lines, not just one line at a time. This is a two-stage process. First get the GPIO chip and then ask it to configure the GPIO lines and return a new file descriptor to the GPIO lines. The request constant for setting a line to a particular state and returning a new file descriptor that references the set line is:

```
GPIO_GET_LINEHANDLE_IOCTL
```

The appropriate struct is:

```
struct gpiohandle_request {
        __u32 lineoffsets[GPIOHANDLES_MAX];
        __u32 flags;
        __u8 default_values[GPIOHANDLES_MAX];
        char consumer_label[32];
        __u32 lines;
        int fd;
};
```

This has to be initialized to sensible values before the ioctl call. The lineoffsets array is simply a list of GPIO line numbers that you want to set.

The flags field is one of:

- GPIOHANDLE_REQUEST_OUTPUT
- GPIOHANDLE_REQUEST_INPUT
- GPIOHANDLE_REQUEST_ACTIVE_LOW
- GPIOHANDLE_REQUEST_OPEN_DRAIN
- GPIOHANDLE_REQUEST_OPEN_SOURCE

All of the lines specified in lineoffsets are set to the same state. Notice that you can OR the flags together where this makes sense, for example to request an active low output with an open drain. Two additional flags will be made available in the future:

- GPIOHANDLE_REQUEST_PULL_UP
- GPIOHANDLE_REQUEST_PULL_DOWN

The default_values array sets output lines to high or low, depending on whether you store 1 or 0 in each element.

The consumer_label assigns a label to each of the lines, which can be retrieved using a GPIO_GET_LINEINFO_IOCTL request and the struct:

```
struct gpioline_info {
        __u32 line_offset;
        __u32 flags;
        char name[32];
        char consumer[32];
};
```

Finally the lines field determines the number of lines being used, i.e. the number of elements of the lineoffsets array that contain meaningful data. The final fd field is used to return a file descriptor for the lines.

Now we are ready to write the program. First we set up the gpiohandle_request struct:

```
struct gpiohandle_request req;
req.lineoffsets[0] = 4;
req.lineoffsets[1] = 17;
req.flags = GPIOHANDLE_REQUEST_OUTPUT;
req.default_values[0] = 0;
req.default_values[1] = 0;
strcpy(req.consumer_label, "Output test");
req.lines = 2;
```

You can see that we are using GPIO4 and GPIO17 and setting both to output. They are also both set to start at 0 and are labeled Output test.

To actually set up these lines and get a file descriptor to them we need to call ioctl():

```
fd = open("/dev/gpiochip0", O_RDONLY);
ret = ioctl(fd, GPIO_GET_LINEHANDLE_IOCTL, &req);
close(fd);
```

Again, no error checking is included. Notice that we can close the GPIO chip as we now have the file descriptor to the lines that have been set up. Opening the line returns a file descriptor in the gpiohandle_request struct – in this case req.fd. You don't export or unexport a line, but you have ownership of the line until you close the file:

```
close(req.fd);
```

Notice that you have to close the file if you want to open the line in a different configuration.

Now we have the lines set up as outputs, we can use the request:

GPIOHANDLE_SET_LINE_VALUES_IOCTL

to set the line states.

It should come as no surprise that there is also a corresponding GET request and both use the struct:

```
struct gpiohandle_data {
        __u8 values[GPIOHANDLES_MAX];
};
```

When you use SET the values array specifies what the lines should be set to. When you use GET the values returned are the states of the lines.

Now we can write a loop that toggles the GPIO lines we have set up:

```
struct gpiohandle_data data;
data.values[0] = 0;
data.values[1] = 1;
while (1) {
  data.values[0] = !data.values[0];
  data.values[1] = !data.values[1];
  ret = ioctl(req.fd, GPIOHANDLE_SET_LINE_VALUES_IOCTL, &data);
}
```

Again, error handling has been ignored for the sake of simplicity.

Putting all this together gives:

```
#include <string.h>
#include <stdio.h>
#include <errno.h>
#include <unistd.h>
#include <fcntl.h>
#include <sys/ioctl.h>
#include <linux/gpio.h>

int main(int argc, char **argv) {
    int fd, ret;

    struct gpiohandle_request req;
    req.lineoffsets[0] = 4;
    req.lineoffsets[1] = 17;
    req.flags = GPIOHANDLE_REQUEST_OUTPUT;
    req.default_values[0] = 0;
    req.default_values[1] = 0;
    strcpy(req.consumer_label, "Output test");
    req.lines = 2;

    fd = open("/dev/gpiochip0", O_RDONLY);
    ret = ioctl(fd, GPIO_GET_LINEHANDLE_IOCTL, &req);
    close(fd);

    struct gpiohandle_data data;
    data.values[0] = 0;
    data.values[1] = 1;
    while (1) {
       data.values[0] = !data.values[0];
       data.values[1] = !data.values[1];
       ret = ioctl(req.fd, GPIOHANDLE_SET_LINE_VALUES_IOCTL,
                                                   &data);

    }
    return 0;
}
```

If you try this out you will discover that the pulses are $0.75\mu s$, but the switching of the two lines is not in sync. There is a 150ns lag between switching each line.

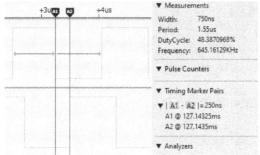

These figures should be compared to the performance of the obsolete sysfs approach, using gpiod is nearly twice as fast. However, compared to using the hardware directly from C, it is more than ten times slower.

GPIO Input

Reading data from GPIO lines follow the same steps as writing, but with obvious changes:

```
#include <string.h>
#include <stdio.h>
#include <errno.h>
#include <unistd.h>
#include <fcntl.h>
#include <sys/ioctl.h>
#include <linux/gpio.h>
int main(int argc, char **argv) {
    int fd, ret;
    struct gpiohandle_request req;
    req.lineoffsets[0] = 4;
    req.lineoffsets[1] = 17;
    req.flags = GPIOHANDLE_REQUEST_INPUT;
    strcpy(req.consumer_label, "Input test");
    req.lines = 2;
    fd = open("/dev/gpiochip0", O_RDONLY);
    ret = ioctl(fd, GPIO_GET_LINEHANDLE_IOCTL, &req);
    close(fd);
    struct gpiohandle_data data;
    ret = ioctl(req.fd, GPIOHANDLE_GET_LINE_VALUES_IOCTL, &data);
    printf("%hhu , %hhu",data.values[0],data.values[1]);
    close(req.fd);
    return 0;
}
```

You can see that now the request is to set an input line and the reading part of the program uses the GET and then displays the values in the data structure.

Measuring R and C Using I/O Control

The use of a gpio line to measure the time a capacitor took to charge implemented at the end of the previous chapter using gpiod is easy to implement using nothing but ioctl calls.

Using ioctl calls it is easy to create a program that measures resistance or capacitance:

```
#define _POSIX_C_SOURCE 199309L
#include <string.h>
#include <stdio.h>
#include <errno.h>
#include <unistd.h>
#include <fcntl.h>
#include <linux/gpio.h>
#include <sys/ioctl.h>
#include <time.h>

int main(int argc, char **argv){
    int fd, ret;
    struct timespec delay = {0, 10 * 1000 * 1000};
    struct timespec time1, time2;
    fd = open("/dev/gpiochip0", O_RDONLY);
    struct gpiohandle_request req;
    req.lineoffsets[0] = 4;
    strcpy(req.consumer_label, "RC Measure");
    req.lines = 1;

    req.flags = GPIOHANDLE_REQUEST_INPUT;
    ret = ioctl(fd, GPIO_GET_LINEHANDLE_IOCTL, &req);
    nanosleep(&delay, NULL);
    close(req.fd);

    req.flags = GPIOHANDLE_REQUEST_OUTPUT;
    struct gpiohandle_data data;
    data.values[0] = 0;
    ret = ioctl(fd, GPIO_GET_LINEHANDLE_IOCTL, &req);
    ret = ioctl(req.fd, GPIOHANDLE_SET_LINE_VALUES_IOCTL, &data);
    nanosleep(&delay, NULL);
    close(req.fd);

    req.flags = GPIOHANDLE_REQUEST_INPUT;
    clock_gettime(CLOCK_REALTIME,&time1);
    ret = ioctl(fd, GPIO_GET_LINEHANDLE_IOCTL, &req);
    ret = ioctl(req.fd, GPIOHANDLE_GET_LINE_VALUES_IOCTL, &data);
```

```
while (data.values[0] == 0){
    ret = ioctl(req.fd, GPIOHANDLE_GET_LINE_VALUES_IOCTL,&data);
}
clock_gettime(CLOCK_REALTIME,&time2);
printf("Time=%d",(time2.tv_nsec-time1.tv_nsec)/1000);
return 0;
}
```

The program opens the GPIO chip and uses its file descriptor to open GPIO4 for input. After 10ms it closes the line and opens it again for output and sets it to zero. After 10ms it closes the line and reopens it for input. It then reads the line waiting for it to go to 1. The times are taken and used to calculate the recharge time for the capacitor.

Summary

- The raw GPIO character driver is easy to use once you know the ioctl operations supported and their structs.

- The big problem with using ioctl is finding out the request numbers to use for any particular driver. Despite attempts to organize the allocation of values, this hasn't really worked.

- The GPIO lines have to remain open while you use them and you need to remember to close them when you have finished using them.

- You can set and read multiple GPIO lines in a single function call.

- The GPIO character driver is about twice as fast as the deprecated sysfs-based interface, but still ten times slower than direct access to the hardware using C.

Chapter 7

GPIO Events

The new GPIO character driver supports events and this is perhaps its biggest advantage over older and competing methods of working with the GPIO lines. Using it you can respond to events well after they have happened and determine the time they occurred more accurately than using a polling loop.

Something you quickly discover in an IoT, or any electronics-related, context, is that output is easy but input is difficult. The reason is that when working with output your program determines when something will happen. You can pulse a line every second by arranging for your program to do something every second using a timer. Input is quite different – when things happen is completely out of your control. When a line is set high all you can do is read its state as frequently as possible in an attempt to determine when it made the transition from low to high. The straightforward way of doing this is to set up a polling loop and test the line's state periodically. The problem with this approach is ensuring that the polling loop tests the line often enough and this becomes increasingly difficult as the other work the loop has to do increases.

The polling loop is a perfectly valid way to approach the input problem and it has the advantage of changing the problem from asynchronous to synchronous – your program determines when the input will be read. There are two important alternatives to the polling loop – events and interrupts. Many IoT programmers are convinced that interrupts are a really good idea. However, they are really only applicable to situations where things happen infrequently, but need to be dealt with quickly – events that are low frequency/low latency - and exactly what these terms mean varies according to the situation. In general, low frequency means a rate of occurring that gives time for the action needed to be completed before it happens again.

As interrupts are not available to user-mode programs, the GPIO character drivers implements a system of events, which if used carefully is more useful than an interrupt.

Events

An event is like a latch or a memory that something happened. Imagine that there is a flag that will be automatically set when an input line changes state. The flag is set without the involvement of software, or at least any software that you have control over. It is useful to imagine an entirely hardware-based setting of the flag, even if this is not always the case. With the help of an event, you can avoid missing an input because the polling loop was busy doing something else. Now the polling loop can read the state of the flag, rather than the actual state of the input line, and hence it can detect if the line has changed since it was last polled. The polling loop resets the event flag and processes the event. You can even arrange for the flag to store the time that the event happened and so increase the resolution of the polling loop.

A simple event can avoid the loss of a single input, but what if there is more than one input while the polling loop is unavailable? The most common solution is to create an event queue – that is, a FIFO (first in, first out) queue of events as they occur. The polling loop now reads the event at the front of the queue, processes it and reads the next. It continues like this until the queue is empty, when it simply waits for an event. As long as the queue is big enough, an event queue means you don't miss any input, but input events are not necessarily processed close to the time that they occurred.

Interrupts Considered Harmful?

As user-mode Linux programs have no access to interrupts, this is an important but academic discussion as far as most Linux IoT programs are concerned.

Interrupts are often confused with events, but they are very different. An interrupt is a hardware mechanism that stops the computer doing whatever it is currently doing and makes it transfer its attention to running an interrupt handler. You can think of an interrupt as an event flag that, when it is set, interrupts the current program to run the assigned interrupt handler.

Using interrupts means the outside world decides when the computer should pay attention to input and there is no need for a polling loop. Most hardware people think that interrupts are the solution to everything and polling is inelegant and only to be used when you can't use an interrupt. This is far from the reality.

There is a general feeling that real-time programming and interrupts go together and if you are not using an interrupt you are probably doing something wrong. The truth is that if you are using an interrupt you are probably doing something wrong. Indeed, some organizations are convinced that interrupts are so dangerous that they are banned from being used at all.

Interrupts are only really useful when you have a low frequency condition that needs to be dealt with on a high-priority basis. Interrupts can simplify the logic of your program, but rarely does using an interrupt speed things up because the overhead involved in interrupt handling is usually quite high.

If you have a polling loop that takes 100ms to poll all inputs and there is an input that demands attention in under 60ms, then clearly the polling loop is not going to be good enough. Using an interrupt allows the high-priority event to interrupt the polling loop and be processed in less than 100ms. However, if this happens very often the polling loop will cease to work as intended. Notice an alternative is to simply make the polling loop check the input twice per loop.

For a more real-world example, suppose you want to react to a doorbell push button. You could write a polling loop that simply checks the button status repeatedly and forever or you could write an interrupt service routine (ISR) to respond to the doorbell. The processor would be free to get on with other things until the doorbell was pushed, when it would stop what it was doing and transfer its attention to the ISR.

How good a design this is depends on how much the doorbell has to interact with the rest of the program and how many doorbell pushes you are expecting. It takes time to respond to the doorbell push and then the ISR has to run to completion. What is going to happen if another doorbell push happens while the first push is still being processed? Some processors have provision for forming a queue of interrupts, but it doesn't help with the fact that the process can only handle one interrupt at a time.

Despite their attraction, interrupts are usually a poor choice for anything other than low-frequency events that need to be dealt with quickly.

Events and the gpiod Library

The gpiod library provides a set of functions that wrap the lower-level interrupt handling provided by the GPIO character driver. These are marginally slower than using the ioctl system call directly, but they are slightly easier to use. There are two possible event types, rising or falling edge, and you can set a line to work with either or both.

You can set a line to respond to events using:

```
gpiod_line_request(line, config, default_val)
```

where config is a pointer to a gpiod_line_request_config struct:

```
struct gpiod_line_request_config {
        const char *consumer;
        int request_type;
        int flags;
};
```

The request_type is any of:
+ GPIOD_LINE_REQUEST_EVENT_FALLING_EDGE
+ GPIOD_LINE_REQUEST_EVENT_RISING_EDGE
+ GPIOD_LINE_REQUEST_EVENT_BOTH_EDGES

Each of these implies that the line is set to input. You can set pull-ups using the flags in the usual way.

There are also functions that will set event handling without needing a gpiod_line_request_config struct and a set of bulk functions, see Chapter 4 for a full list.

Once you have set a line to respond to events, there are some basic functions that let you handle the event:
+ gpiod_line_event_wait(line,timeout)
+ gpiod_line_event_wait_bulk(bulk,timeout, event_bulk)
+ gpiod_line_event_read(line, event)

where gpiod_line_event_wait and gpiod_line_event_wait_bulk wait for a single line to generate an event or a set of lines. The parameters are:

+ line   Pointer to a gpiod_line struct
+ event   Pointer to a gpiod_line_event struct
+ timeout   Pointer to a timespec struct
+ bulk   Pointer to a gpiod_line_bulk struct
+ event_bulk   Pointer to a second gpiod_line_bulk struct which holds the details of the lines that generated an event.

The gpiod_line_event_read function blocks until an event occurs and returns it in event, a pointer to a gpiod_line_event struct:

```
struct gpiod_line_event {
      struct timespec ts;
      int event_type;
};
```

Notice that this mechanism really does use an interrupt generated by the GPIO line which is handled by the kernel. For this to work, you have to make sure that the line:

dtoverlay=gpio-no-irq

isn't present in, or is commented out of, the /boot/firmware/config.txt file. The no-irq state used to be the default, but it was changed to accommodate the event handling of the gpiod library.

The simplest event program is:

```c
#include <gpiod.h>
#include <stdio.h>
#include <unistd.h>
#include <stdlib.h>

int main(int argc, char **argv) {
    int res;
    struct gpiod_chip *chip = gpiod_chip_open_by_number(0);
    struct gpiod_line *line4 = gpiod_chip_get_line(chip, 4);
    gpiod_line_request_both_edges_events(line4, "event test");
    gpiod_line_event_wait(line4, NULL);
    printf("Event on line 4");
}
```

This waits until an event, a rising or falling edge, occurs on GPIO4 and then prints a message. If you want details of the event, you can use:

```c
gpiod_line_event_read
```

which blocks until there is some event data to read:

```c
struct gpiod_line_event event;
gpiod_line_event_read(line4, &event);
printf("Event on line 4 %d,%d", event.event_type,event.ts.tv_nsec);
```

You can also read multiple events from the line, which have happened since the last read:

```c
int gpiod_line_event_read_multiple(struct gpiod_line *line,
        struct gpiod_line_event *events,unsigned int num_events)
```

You have to state the maximum number of items to read and you have to make sure that the `gpiod_line_event` struct array has enough elements. The system uses a 16-event ring buffer so if more events than this occur the earliest events are lost. You can also only read a maximum of 16 events at a time. This will block until there is at least one event to read.

Measuring R and C Using Events

To discover how events can improve the accuracy of a program, we can revisit the R/C measuring example introduced at the end of Chapter 4. The first part of the program is as before. We open the GPIO chip and GPIO4. Next we set GPIO4 to input and wait 100ms for things to settle and then set it to output with a value of zero and after a 100ms delay the line is released. This is where the program differs. Instead of polling the line waiting for a 1, we simply set a rising edge event and wait for it to occur. When it happens the read returns with the time it occurred.

Such an event-driven program is:

```c
#define _POSIX_C_SOURCE 199309L
#include <gpiod.h>
#include <stdio.h>
#include <unistd.h>
#include <stdlib.h>
#include <time.h>

int main(int argc, char **argv)
{
  int res;

  struct timespec delay = {0, 10 * 1000 * 1000};
  struct timespec time1;

  struct gpiod_chip *chip = gpiod_chip_open_by_number(0);
  struct gpiod_line *line4 = gpiod_chip_get_line(chip, 4);

  res = gpiod_line_request_input(line4, "RMeasure");
  nanosleep(&delay, NULL);
  gpiod_line_release(line4);

  res = gpiod_line_request_output(line4, "RMeasure", 0);
  nanosleep(&delay, NULL);
  gpiod_line_release(line4);
  clock_gettime(CLOCK_REALTIME, &time1);

  gpiod_line_request_rising_edge_events(line4, "RMeasuret");
  struct gpiod_line_event event;
  gpiod_line_event_read(line4, &event);
  printf("Event on line 4 %d, %d", event.event_type,
                    (event.ts.tv_nsec-time1.tv_nsec)/1000);
}
```

As the read is waiting for the first transition from 0 to 1, the timing is more accurate and not dependent on when the timing loop decides to read the line.

Measuring Pulses with Events

Now we have all of the functions, we are ready to implement a pulse measurement program using events. We can measure the width of any pulse as the distance between a rising and a falling edge or a falling and a rising edge and we need to make sure that we have a rising edge by waiting for one:

```c
do{
    res = gpiod_line_event_read(line4, &event);
  } while (event.event_type != GPIOD_LINE_EVENT_RISING_EDGE);
```

We then record the time of the event and wait for a falling edge:

```
do{
    res = gpiod_line_event_read(line4, &event);
  } while (event.event_type != GPIOD_LINE_EVENT_FALLING_EDGE);
```

and use both times to compute the pulse width.

The complete program is:

```
#include <gpiod.h>
#include <stdio.h>
#include <unistd.h>
#include <stdlib.h>
#include <time.h>

int main(int argc, char **argv)
{
  int res;
  struct timespec time1;
  struct gpiod_chip *chip = gpiod_chip_open_by_number(0);
  struct gpiod_line *line4 = gpiod_chip_get_line(chip, 4);
  res = gpiod_line_request_both_edges_events(line4, "Measure");
  struct gpiod_line_event event;
  while (true)
  {
    do
    {
      res = gpiod_line_event_read(line4, &event);
    } while (event.event_type != GPIOD_LINE_EVENT_RISING_EDGE);

    time1.tv_nsec = event.ts.tv_nsec;
    do
    {
      res = gpiod_line_event_read(line4, &event);
    } while (event.event_type != GPIOD_LINE_EVENT_FALLING_EDGE);

    printf("Pulse Width %d \r\n",
                    (event.ts.tv_nsec - time1.tv_nsec) / 1000);
    fflush(stdout);
  }
}
```

There are many variations on this program. You could set the line to respond only to a rising edge and then only to a falling edge, but this would mean closing the line and reopening it, which is potentially slow. If you are sure that a falling event always occurs after a rising event, you could remove the test for it and simply accept the next event as the one used to take the time.

How well this program works depends on how heavily the processor is loaded. As long as the program can run uninterrupted, it is accurate up to around 50kHz or higher. At 100kHz it misses edges and picks up following edges giving results that are too large.

An Edgy Button

To clarify the difference between reading the line to detect a change of state and using events, let's consider a simple non-event program that responds to the press of a button. In this case the GPIO line is set up for input and a message to press the button is printed. Then the program waits for 20s and finally tests the state of the line. Even if the user has pressed the button lots of times during the 20-second interval, all that matters is the final state of the line, read when the sleep(20) ends:

```
#include <gpiod.h>
#include <stdio.h>
#include <unistd.h>
#include <stdlib.h>
#include <time.h>


int main(int argc, char **argv)
{
    int res;
    struct gpiod_chip *chip = gpiod_chip_open_by_number(0);
    struct gpiod_line *line4 = gpiod_chip_get_line(chip, 4);
    res = gpiod_line_request_input(line4,"button");
    printf("Press button \n\r");
    fflush(stdout);
    sleep(20);

    if (gpiod_line_get_value(line4) == 1)
    {
        printf("button pressed");
    }
    else
    {
        printf("button not pressed");
    }
}
```

In other words, this program misses any button presses during the 20-second pause.

Now compare this to the same program using edge events:

```c
#include <gpiod.h>
#include <stdio.h>
#include <unistd.h>
#include <stdlib.h>
#include <time.h>


int main(int argc, char **argv)
{
    int res;
    struct timespec timeout = {0, 0};
    struct gpiod_chip *chip = gpiod_chip_open_by_number(0);
    struct gpiod_line *line4 = gpiod_chip_get_line(chip, 4);
    res = gpiod_line_request_both_edges_events(line4, "button");
    printf("Press button \n\r");
    fflush(stdout);
    sleep(20);
    struct gpiod_line_event event;

    res=gpiod_line_event_wait(line4,&timeout);
    if (res>0)
    {
        res = gpiod_line_event_read(line4, &event);
        printf("button pressed %d",event.ts.tv_nsec);
    }
    else
    {
        printf("button not pressed");
    }

}
```

In this case the GPIO line is set up as an input with a pull-up and it fires an event on the falling edge of a signal. The state of the event is discovered using gpiod_line_event_wait with a timeout of 0. This means the wait returns immediately and res is set to -1 if it timed out and 1 if at least one event occurs. Notice that now the if statement tests not the state of the line, but the state of the event. The difference is that if the user presses the button at any time during the 20-second sleep, the event occurs and is remembered and as a result the program registers the button press. The event occurs no matter what the program is doing, so instead of sleeping it could be getting on with some work, confident that it won't miss a button press. You can even know when the event occurred by calling gpiod_line_event_read which will return at once because you have already tested for an event.

Event Polling

Notice that the technique of calling gpiod_line_event_wait with a timeout of 0 used in the previous example, gives you a way of testing for events in a polling loop. In many cases, using an event within a polling loop means that you can get on with other tasks without the risk of missing an event that occurs while the program is otherwise occupied. Given that the system will keep multiple events, you could even rely on it to record more than one event and time, although it is better to try to handle one event at a time.

You can easily create an event-polling function:

```
int gpiod_line_event_poll(struct gpiod_line *line, struct
gpiod_line_event *event)
{
    struct timespec timeout = {0, 0};
    int res = gpiod_line_event_wait(line, &timeout);
    if (res > 0)
        res = gpiod_line_event_read(line, event);
    if (res == 0)
        res = -1;
    return res;
}
```

When you call this function, if it returns 1 then you can use the gpiod_line_event struct to determine when the event occurred. If it returns 0 then no event has occurred and the struct gpiod_line_event is unchanged and if it returns -1 there was an error.

A complete program that polls for an edge event is also easy:

```
#include <gpiod.h>
#include <stdio.h>
#include <unistd.h>
#include <stdlib.h>
#include <time.h>

int gpiod_line_event_poll(struct gpiod_line *line,
                          struct gpiod_line_event *event);

int main(int argc, char **argv)
{
    int res;

    struct gpiod_chip *chip = gpiod_chip_open_by_number(0);
    struct gpiod_line *line4 = gpiod_chip_get_line(chip, 4);

    res = gpiod_line_request_both_edges_events(line4, "button");

    struct gpiod_line_event event;
```

```
    while (true)
    {
        res = gpiod_line_event_poll(line4, &event);
        if (res > 0)
        {
            gpiod_line_event_read(line4, &event);
            printf("Event on line 4 %d,%d \n\r ",
                            event.event_type, event.ts);
            fflush(stdout);
        }
    }

}
int gpiod_line_event_poll(struct gpiod_line *line,
                            struct gpiod_line_event *event)
{
    struct timespec timeout = {0, 0};
    int res = gpiod_line_event_wait(line, &timeout);
    if (res > 0)
        res = gpiod_line_event_read(line, event);
    if (res == 0)
        res = 1;
    return res;
}
```

There are many other functions in the library, but we have covered the
different varieties and you should find it easy to make use of any that have
been ignored by reading the gpiod.h file for the function definitions.

Low-Level I/O Control Events

Advanced: Skip unless you need to use it.

It is worth knowing how the gpiod library wraps the lower-level ioctl
operation of the GPIO character driver and its events, as you will encounter
a general Linux principle that crops up in other places. Linux files can
generate interrupts to tell the kernel when they change state, for example by
having some data to read. User-mode programs often need to wait on files to
be ready and there are special commands, select, poll or epoll, that do the
job. Until recently, poll would have been the preferred way to wait for a file
to be ready, but today epoll is its more sophisticated replacement.

To be clear about what is happening - when your program waits on a file
using epoll it is suspended and other threads get to use the processor. When
the file is ready to be used, it fires an interrupt which the kernel handles and
the interrupt service routine that is called wakes up your suspended
program. Notice that, while this is a hardware interrupt, your program can't
do anything but wait for it to happen, so it is a little more restrictive than a
full interrupt. You can make it much more like a full interrupt by waiting for
the file to be ready on another thread, while allowing your main program's
thread to continue with other work.

What has all this got to do with the GPIO lines? The answer is that the GPIO character driver is a pseudo file and as such you can wait on it using `epoll`. As this makes use of an interrupt generated by the GPIO lines, you need to ensure that the line:

```
dtoverlay = gpio-no-irq
```

isn't present in, or is commented out of, the `/boot/config.txt` file.

To wait for an event on a GPIO line we have to use the `GPIO_GET_LINEEVENT_IOCTL` request to the GPIO character driver and the associated struct:

```
struct gpioevent_request {
        __u32 lineoffset;
        __u32 handleflags;
        __u32 eventflags;
        char consumer_label[32];
        int fd;
};
```

Notice that you can set only a single GPIO number as `lineoffset` isn't an array. The `handleflags` field is the same as the `flags` field and it is usually set to `GPIOHANDLE_REQUEST_INPUT`.

The `eventflags` field determines what causes an event:

- ◆ `GPIOEVENT_REQUEST_RISING_EDGE`
- ◆ `GPIOEVENT_REQUEST_FALLING_EDGE`
- ◆ `GPIOEVENT_REQUEST_BOTH_EDGES`

When the ioctl call returns the file descriptor in the `fd` field, it can be used to wait for an event to occur. For example, first we set up the `gpioevent` struct and make the `GPIO_GET_LINEEVENT_IOCTL` request:

```
int fd, ret;

struct gpioevent_request req;
req.lineoffset = 4;
req.handleflags = GPIOHANDLE_REQUEST_INPUT;
req.eventflags = GPIOEVENT_REQUEST_BOTH_EDGES;
strcpy(req.consumer_label, "Event test");

fd = open("/dev/gpiochip0", O_RDONLY);
ret = ioctl(fd, GPIO_GET_LINEEVENT_IOCTL, &req);
close(fd);
```

Now we can use `epoll` to wait on the file having something to read. The `epoll` system call accepts an array of `epoll_event` structs that tells it what it is waiting for and how to return the results.

In this case, we have only a single file descriptor and we are waiting for the file to have something to read:

```
static struct epoll_event ev;
ev.events = EPOLLIN;
ev.data.fd = req.fd;
```

The `events` field specifies what the poll is waiting for and `EPOLLIN` means that the file is ready to read. The `data.fd` field specifies the file that the event is associated with.

Once the array of structs, or just the single element in our example, is set up we can add it to an epoll instance, which also just happens to be a file:

```
int epfd = epoll_create(1);
int res = epoll_ctl(epfd, EPOLL_CTL_ADD, req.fd, &ev);
```

The first instruction creates the epoll entity, which lives in the kernel and returns a file descriptor to it. The single parameter specifies the number of events it will monitor. The second instruction adds the array of structs that specify the events. As well as `EPOLL_CTL_ADD`, you can also use `EPOLL_CTL_MOD` and `EPOLL_CTL_DEL` to modify and delete the elements in the array of structs. In this case, the file descriptor is used to identify which element to modify or delete. Finally, we can wait for the file, or files, to have something ready to read or attend to:

```
int nfds = epoll_wait(epfd, &ev,1,20000);
```

The first parameter specifies the epoll entity to use, the second is an array of `epoll_event` structs used to return the results, the third is the size of the array, and hence the number of events returned at any time, and the final parameter is the timeout in milliseconds. The `epoll_wait` suspends the thread that it is in and waits for an interrupt from the file or files it is waiting for. If the interrupt corresponds to one of the events being waited for, the epoll function restarts its user-mode thread and returns the number of file descriptors that have fired an event, `nfds` in this case. You can test to detect a timeout when `nfds` is 0. If it is greater than 0 you have to process each of the `epoll_event` structs returned. In this case, we have only one file so we can ignore the returned `epoll_event` struct and read the GPIO line to retrieve the event data in a `gpioevent_data` struct, which gives you an event id and a timestamp:

```
struct gpioevent_data edata;
read(req.fd,&edata,sizeof edata);
printf("%u,%llu",edata.id,edata.timestamp);
```

The complete program is:

```c
#include <string.h>
#include <stdio.h>
#include <errno.h>
#include <unistd.h>
#include <fcntl.h>
#include <sys/ioctl.h>
#include <linux/gpio.h>
#include <sys/epoll.h>

int main(int argc, char **argv) {
    int fd, ret;

    struct gpioevent_request req;
    req.lineoffset = 4;
    req.handleflags = GPIOHANDLE_REQUEST_INPUT;
    req.eventflags = GPIOEVENT_REQUEST_RISING_EDGE;
    strcpy(req.consumer_label, "Event test");

    fd = open("/dev/gpiochip0", O_RDONLY);
    ret = ioctl(fd, GPIO_GET_LINEEVENT_IOCTL, &req);
    close(fd);

    static struct epoll_event ev;
    ev.events = EPOLLIN;
    ev.data.fd = req.fd;
    int epfd = epoll_create(1);
    int res = epoll_ctl(epfd, EPOLL_CTL_ADD, req.fd, &ev);

    int nfds = epoll_wait(epfd, &ev, 1, 20000);
    if (nfds != 0) {
        struct gpioevent_data edata;
        read(req.fd, &edata, sizeof edata);
        printf("%u,%llu", edata.id, edata.timestamp);
    }
}
```

You can set up multiple GPIO lines to generate events. Also notice that the file that triggered the event might have more than one gpioevent_data struct ready to read. You have to read the data that is ready to clear the event.

One of the advantages of the new interface is that events are not lost and they are timestamped so you know when they happened.

gpiod and File Descriptors

Advanced: Skip unless you need to use it.

The gpiod library uses the ioctl calls to handle events in exactly the way described above. You can get the file descriptor of the file that gpiod opens using:

```
int gpiod_line_event_get_fd(struct gpiod_line *line)
```

You can also use gpiod to read an event from a file descriptor:

```
int gpiod_line_event_read_fd(int fd,
                          struct gpiod_line_event *event)
```

The event is returned in a gpiod event struct.

To illustrate this, the previous example using epoll can be rewritten using gpiod to set up the GPIO line and then use the file descriptor and epoll to wait for the event:

```
#include <string.h>
#include <stdio.h>
#include <errno.h>
#include <unistd.h>
#include <fcntl.h>
#include <sys/ioctl.h>
#include <linux/gpio.h>
#include <sys/epoll.h>
#include <gpiod.h>

int main(int argc, char **argv)
{
    int res;
    struct gpiod_chip *chip = gpiod_chip_open_by_number(0);
    struct gpiod_line *line4 = gpiod_chip_get_line(chip, 4);
    res = gpiod_line_request_rising_edge_events(line4, "button");
    int fd = gpiod_line_event_get_fd(line4);
    static struct epoll_event ev;
    ev.events = EPOLLIN;
    ev.data.fd = fd;
    int epfd = epoll_create(1);
    res = epoll_ctl(epfd, EPOLL_CTL_ADD, fd, &ev);

    int nfds = epoll_wait(epfd, &ev, 1, 20000);
    if (nfds != 0)
    {
        struct gpioevent_data edata;
        read(fd, &edata, sizeof edata);
        printf("%u,%llu", edata.id, edata.timestamp);
    }
}
```

If you want to read an event that you have waited for using `epoll` then you need to use `gpiod_line_event_read_fd`.

For example, the final `if` statement in the previous example can be rewritten as:

```
if (nfds != 0)
{
    struct gpiod_line_event event;
    gpiod_line_event_read_fd(fd, &event);
    printf("%d", event.ts.tv_nsec);
}
```

Simulating Interrupts

Advanced: Skip unless you need to use it.

The `epoll` function, or the gpiod `wait` function, gets you as close to handling interrupts as you can get in user-mode, but there is one thing missing - the thread is suspended while waiting for the interrupt. This is generally not what you want to happen.

You can create a better approximation to a true interrupt by running the `epoll` function, or `wait`, on another thread. That is, if the main program wants to work with an interrupt you have to define an interrupt-handling function that will be called when the interrupt occurs. Next you have to wait on the event using either `epoll` or `wait`. This causes your new thread to be suspended, but you don't care because its only purpose is to wait for the interrupt and meanwhile your program's main thread continues to run and do useful work. When the interrupt occurs, the new thread is restarted and it checks that the interrupt was correct and then calls your interrupt handler. When the interrupt handler completes, the thread cleans up and calls `epoll` again to wait for another interrupt. If you want to know more about threads, see Chapter 12 of *Applying C for the IoT with Linux*, ISBN: 9781871962611.

This is all very straightforward conceptually, but it does mean using threads, which is an advanced technique that tends to make programs prone to esoteric errors and more difficult to debug.

The following program provides the basic skeleton of using a thread to simulate a user-mode interrupt using gpiod, without error checking, error recovery or locking for simplicity. If you are going to use this sort of approach in the real world you would have to add code that handles what happens when something goes wrong, whereas this code simply assumes that everything goes right.

First we need to include the pthreads library. This isn't just a matter of adding #include <pthread.h>, you also have to specify the name of the library that you want the linker to add to your program.

The simplest way of implementing this is to create a function `waitInterrupt` that we can run on another thread:

```
void *waitInterrupt(void *arg)
{
    intVec *intData = (intVec *)arg;
    struct gpiod_line_event event;
    while (true)
    {
        int res = gpiod_line_event_read(intData->line, &event);
        if (res == 0)
            intData->func(&event);
    }
}
```

This casts the input `arg` to the correct type for use in the function. Then it repeatedly calls `gpiod_line_event_read`, which suspends the thread until the interrupt occurs. Then it wakes up and checks that it was the interrupt and not an error. If so it calls the interrupt routine which processes the event data and returns as soon as possible, so that the next event can be caught.

The `waitInterrupt` function accepts a pointer to a struct that contains all of the information about what the call has to wait for and the function to call when an event occurs:

```
typedef struct
{
    struct gpiod_line *line;
    eventHandler func;
} intVec;
```

The `line` field is just a pointer to a line that has been opened to respond to an event and `func` is the interrupt handler you want to call when the event occurs.

The `eventHandler`, the function called when the event occurs, receives a single parameter which is the event struct that informs it of the event. To create and pass a pointer to such a function we need a to define a type:

```
typedef void (*eventHandler)(struct gpiod_line_event *);
```

To try this out we need a main program and an event-handling function.

The interrupt function simply reports the data in the event struct passed to it:

```
void myHandler(struct gpiod_line_event *event)
{
    printf("%d,%d \n\r", event→event_type,
                                event->ts.tv_nsec / 1000);
    fflush(stdout);
}
```

The main program to test this is something like:

```c
int main(int argc, char **argv)
{
    int fd, ret, res;
    struct gpiod_chip *chip = gpiod_chip_open_by_number(0);
    struct gpiod_line *line4 = gpiod_chip_get_line(chip, 4);
    res = gpiod_line_request_rising_edge_events(line4, "button");
    intVec intData;
    intData.line = line4;
    intData.func = &myHandler;
    pthread_t intThread;
    if (pthread_create(&intThread, NULL, waitInterrupt,
                                        (void *)&intData))
    {
        fprintf(stderr, "Error creating thread\n");
        return 1;
    }
    for (;;)
    {
        printf("Working\n\r");
        fflush(stdout);
        sleep(2);
    }
}
```

This opens the GPIO line for an event on a rising edge, sets up the intData struct and then runs the waitInterrupt on a new thread. The main program then prints a message every two seconds to show it is still working. When you run the program, you will see the event details, including a timestamp, in milliseconds, every time there is an interrupt.

It is often argued that this approach to interrupts is second class, but if you think about how this threaded use of polling works, you have to conclude that it provides all of the features of an interrupt. The interrupt routine is idle and not consuming resources until the interrupt happens, when it is activated and starts running. This is how a true interrupt routine behaves.

There might even be advantages in a multi-core system, as the interrupt thread could be scheduled on a different core from the main program and hence run concurrently. This might, however, be a disadvantage if you are unsure as to whether the result is well behaved. There are some other disadvantages of this approach. The main one is that the interrupt routine is run on a different thread and this can cause problems with code that isn't thread-safe - UI components, for example.

In our example, the use of printf in both threads is certainly not thread-safe and if you run it often enough you will see some strange output. There are standard library functions that you can use in different threads listed in the documentation. You can make functions thread-safe by using locks, but this introduces another level of complexity.

It is also more difficult to organize interrupts on multiple GPIO lines. It is generally said that you need one thread per GPIO line, but in practice a single thread can wait on any number of GPIO lines using epoll or a bulk read function. If you plan to use this within a real application, you would also need to add functions to pause and remove the interrupt.

The complete program is:

```c
#include <string.h>
#include <stdio.h>
#include <errno.h>
#include <unistd.h>
#include <fcntl.h>
#include <sys/ioctl.h>
#include <gpiod.h>
#include <sys/epoll.h>
#include <pthread.h>

typedef void (*eventHandler)(struct gpiod_line_event *);

typedef struct
{
    struct gpiod_line *line;
    eventHandler func;
} intVec;

void myHandler(struct gpiod_line_event *event)
{
    printf("%d,%d \n\r", event->event_type,
                                event->ts.tv_nsec / 1000);
    fflush(stdout);
}

void *waitInterrupt(void *arg)
{
    intVec *intData = (intVec *)arg;
    struct gpiod_line_event event;
    while (true)
    {
        int res = gpiod_line_event_read(intData->line, &event);
        if (res == 0)
            intData->func(&event);
    }
}
```

```
int main(int argc, char **argv)
{
    int fd, ret, res;

    struct gpiod_chip *chip = gpiod_chip_open_by_number(0);
    struct gpiod_line *line4 = gpiod_chip_get_line(chip, 4);

    res = gpiod_line_request_rising_edge_events(line4, "button");

    intVec intData;
    intData.line = line4;
    intData.func = &myHandler;

    pthread_t intThread;
    if (pthread_create(&intThread, NULL, waitInterrupt,
                                        (void *)&intData))
    {
        fprintf(stderr, "Error creating thread\n");
        return 1;
    }
    for (;;)
    {
        printf("Working\n\r");
        fflush(stdout);
        sleep(2);
    }
}
```

The Contextless Event Functions

There are also some contextless functions which you probably won't need to use as they are very slow.

You can specify a monitor with:

```
gpiod_ctxless_event_monitor("device", event_type, offset,
    active_low,"consumer",*timeout, pollcallback, event_cb, data)
```

and its multiple line counterpart:

```
gpiod_ctxless_event_monitor_multiple("device",event_type,
offsets[],num_lines, active_low, "consumer",*timeout,
                                pollcallback, event_cb, data)
```

The *pollcallback* is used in the polling loop. If you set it to NULL the default poll, or more accurately ppoll, another version of epoll, is used to wait for the file descriptor to be ready. The *event_cb* is a function that is called when an event occurs. Notice that a call to gpiod_ctxless_event_monitor is blocking.

Monitoring a line is easy. If you want to set a timeout you need a `timespec` struct filled in correctly:

```
int main(int argc, char **argv) {
    int res;
    struct timespec time;
    time.tv_nsec=0;
    time.tv_sec=20;
    res = gpiod_ctxless_event_monitor("0",
            GPIOD_CTXLESS_EVENT_BOTH_EDGES,
            4, 0, "monitor test", &time, NULL, event_cb, NULL);
}
```

This waits for either a rising or falling edge on GPIO4 and calls `event_cb` when it occurs.

A demonstration `event_cb` could be:

```
int event_cb(int event, unsigned int offset,
            const struct timespec *timestamp, void *unused)
{
  printf("[%ld.%09ld] %s\n",
      timestamp->tv_sec, timestamp->tv_nsec,
      (event == GPIOD_CTXLESS_EVENT_CB_RISING_EDGE)? "rising":
      (event == GPIOD_CTXLESS_EVENT_CB_FALLING_EDGE)? "falling":
      (event == GPIOD_CTXLESS_EVENT_CB_TIMEOUT) ? "timeout":"??");
 fflush(stdout);
 return GPIOD_CTXLESS_EVENT_CB_RET_OK;
}
```

Notice that the polling loop only comes to an end if there is a timeout. You can also write a custom *pollcallback* which returns `GPIOD_CTXLESS_EVENT_POLL_RET_STOP` to stop the loop for any reason.

The complete program is:

```
#include <gpiod.h>
#include <stdio.h>
#include <unistd.h>
#include <stdlib.h>

int event_cb(int event, unsigned int offset,
            const struct timespec *timestamp, void *unused)
{
    printf("[%ld.%09ld] %s\n",
      timestamp->tv_sec, timestamp->tv_nsec,
      (event == GPIOD_CTXLESS_EVENT_CB_RISING_EDGE)? "rising" :
      (event == GPIOD_CTXLESS_EVENT_CB_FALLING_EDGE)? "falling" :
      (event == GPIOD_CTXLESS_EVENT_CB_TIMEOUT) ? "timeout" : "??");
      fflush(stdout);
      return GPIOD_CTXLESS_EVENT_CB_RET_OK;
}
```

```
int main(int argc, char **argv) {
    int res;
    struct timespec time;
    time.tv_nsec=0;
    time.tv_sec=20;
    res = gpiod_ctxless_event_monitor("0",
            GPIOD_CTXLESS_EVENT_BOTH_EDGES, 4, 0, "monitor test",
                &time, NULL, event_cb, NULL);
}
```

There are more contextless functions, but they are all fairly straightforward and obvious once you have seen the few described here. In most cases, it isn't worth using the contextless functions as they are slow and, if you are doing almost anything complicated with GPIO lines, it is worth explicitly opening the lines you want to use and closing them once you have finished.

Responding to Input

This look at methods of dealing with the problems of input isn't exhaustive – there are always new ways of doing things, but it does cover the most general ways of implementing input. As already mentioned, the problem with input is that you don't know when it is going to happen. What generally matters is speed of response.

For low-frequency inputs using interrupts, even Linux user-mode interrupt simulation using threads, is worthwhile. It can leave your program free to get on with other tasks and simplify its overall structure. For high-frequency inputs that need to be serviced regularly, a polling loop is still the best option for maximum throughput. How quickly you can respond to an input depends on how long the polling loop is and how many times you test for it per loop.

Finally, there is the operating system to consider. In all of the examples and measurements of input speeds, the samples were taken when the program had uninterrupted use of the processor. In all cases there were times when the program was suspended by the operating system and then no input occurred for tens of microseconds or more.

Summary

- Events are a stored indication that something has happened.

- Interrupts are events that cause something to happen.

- You can use an event with a polling loop to protect against missing input because the program is busy doing something else.

- If an event occurs before the current event has been cleared then it might be missed. To avoid missing events, you can use an event queue which stores events in the order they happened until they are processed.

- The gpiod library supports GPIO events. You can configure an event if the GPIO line goes high or low – a rising or falling edge.

- If you use events then you have to turn on GPIO generated event handling or the system will crash.

- Using events in a polling loop hardly slows things down at all.

- You can use events to generate an interrupt that you can wait for using an epoll. To do this you need to use the GPIO character driver to provide the file that the epoll waits on.

- The use of the GPIO character driver slows things down a lot.

- When using epolls, the thread simply waits for the interrupt to occur. If you want to continue processing until the interrupt occurs then you have to wait for the interrupt on a new thread. This is slow, but it is the closest approach to a true interrupt that user-mode allows.

- The gpiod library has some commands that will wait for an event to occur and report the timestamp of the event.

- Overall, events are useful, but interrupts are not. Neither increases the throughput of a polling loop and an interrupt only decreases response time if the event is infrequent.

Chapter 8
GPIO Hardware With Gpio5

The CM5 uses a custom RP1 chip to provide the connection to all of the peripherals. This is very different from the bcm2835 which is used in the earlier versions of the Pi. The RP1 may be new, but it is essentially a modified RP2040, the chip that powers the Pico. What this means is that the Pico SDK contains software that, with some modification, can be used with the Pi 5's peripherals. In this chapter, we look at how to get started with the GPIO hardware, which is very different from the implemented simple concept of on/off GPIO lines and its complexity can be something of a shock. Then we use this knowledge to implement Gpio5, a library of GPIO functions implemented for the purpose of this book that is modeled on the Pico SDK. With its help you can write fast GPIO programs and even port Pico GPIO programs with little change. This is an open-source project that you can fork and modify and can be found at Github https://github.com/IOPress/Gpio5. A full listing can also be found on the book's web page at www.iopress.info.

Accessing Memory

The CM5 has a huge peripheral area starting at `0x40000000`. This is the physical address which is translated to `0x1f00000000` in the 40-bit address space. The usual way of accessing memory under Linux is a strange roundabout way of sticking with the "everything is a file" idea. There are drivers that make memory look like a file and you can, in principle, read and write memory locations by reading and writing the file. In practice the files are provided, but you generally cannot use them by reading and writing to them.

What you have to do instead is use another Linux feature, memory mapping, to make the file accessible in memory. This allows you to take any file, load it into memory and then access it directly without needing to read and write the actual physical file. This is implemented mainly for efficiency. If you have a file that needs to be worked with as fast as possible you can memory-map it and work with it at the speed of main memory. Putting this together with the fact that we have files that represent memory we can access areas of memory directly by first opening a memory file and then mapping it into an address space so we can access it.

This seems like a silly idea at first – take memory, convert it into a file and then take that file and convert it back into memory – but it has security advantages and you can map the memory to a new address range.

The CM5 has a memory file called mem in the dev directory. The /dev/mem file can be used in the usual way, but you have to be running with root privileges. The /dev/gpiomem0 file only maps the GPIO area starting at 0x400d0000, or 0x1f000d0000, but it doesn't need root privileges. To use the GPIO file all you need is to be a member of the gpio user group. In the examples that follow, the mem file is used with root privileges because it works with peripherals other than the GPIO lines. If you want to use the gpiomem0 file you will be restricted to only accessing the GPIO lines. Gpio5 tries to access mem and if this fails falls back to gpiomem0.

To access the GPIO area of memory you can map the entire peripherals area into user space using:

```
int memfd = open("/dev/mem", O_RDWR | O_SYNC);
    uint32_t *map = (uint32_t *)mmap(
        NULL,
         64 * 1024* 1024,
        (PROT_READ | PROT_WRITE),
        MAP_SHARED,
        memfd,
        0x1f00000000
);
    if (map == MAP_FAILED)
    {
        printf("mmap failed: %s\n", strerror(errno));
        return (-1);
    };
    close(memfd);
```

This maps the entire 64MByte area. If you only want to use the GPIO lines then you can make this smaller, but there is no problem accommodating it in the 4,096MByte, 32-bit address space. Also notice that we only load the entire memory starting from 0x1f00000000, i.e. the start of the peripheral area. This means we can use the offsets from the start of the peripheral area as offsets from the return value of map.

For example, the GPIO control registers have an address of 0x400d0000, which gives an offset of 0xd0000 from the start of the peripherals area. As the pointers are to uint32_t we have to remember to divide by 4 so that the correct offset is added. That is, the GPIO registers are located at:

```
    uint32_t *PERIBase = map;
    uint32_t *GPIOBase = PERIBase + 0xd0000 / 4;
```

You can check that GPIOBase references a location in user space 0xd000 higher than PERIBase.

With this information we can now start to work with the GPIO registers:

Offset	Register Name	Description
0x000	GPIO0_STATUS	GPIO status
0x004	GPIO0_CTRL	GPIO control including function select and overrides
0x008	GPIO1_STATUS	GPIO status
0x00c	GPIO1_CTRL	GPIO control including function select and overrides
	... and so on down to	
0x0dc	GPIO29_CTRL	GPIO control including function select and overrides

You can see that there are two registers for each GPIO line from GPIO 0 to GPIO 27, one control register and one status register.

Each register has the same format for each GPIO line. For example, the status register is:

Bits	Name	Description	Type	Reset
31:30	Reserved		-	-
29	IRQTOPROC	Interrupt to processors, after override applied	RO	0x0
28	IRQCOMBINED	Interrupt to processors, after masking	RO	0x0
27	EVENT_DB_LEVEL_HIGH	Debounced input pin is high	RO	0x0
26	EVENT_DB_LEVEL_LOW	Debounced input pin is low	RO	0x0
25	EVENT_F_EDGE_HIGH	Input pin has seen a filtered rising edge. Clear with ctrl_irqreset	RO	0x0
24	EVENT_F_EDGE_LOW	Input pin has seen a filtered falling edge. Clear with ctrl_irqreset	RO	0x0
23	EVENT_LEVEL_HIGH	Input pin is high	RO	0x0
22	EVENT_LEVEL_LOW	Input pin is low	RO	0x0
21	EVENT_EDGE_HIGH	Input pin has seen rising edge. Clear with ctrl_irqreset	RO	0x0
20	EVENT_EDGE_LOW	Input pin has seen falling edge. Clear with ctrl_irqreset	RO	0x0
19	INTOPERI	Input signal to peripheral, after override applied	RO	0x0
18	INFILTERED	Input signal from PAD, after filtering is applied but before override. Not valid if inisdirect=1	RO	0x0
17	INFROMPAD	Input signal from PAD before override applied	RO	0x0

16	INISDIRECT	Input signal from PAD without filtering or override	RO	0x0
15:14	Reserved		-	-
13	OETOPAD	Output enable to PAD, after override applied	RO	0x0
12	OEFROMPERI	Output enable from selected peripheral, before override applied	RO	0x0
11:10	Reserved		-	-
9	OUTTOPAD	Output signal to PAD after override applied	RO	0x0
8	OUTFROMPERI	Output signal from selected peripheral, before override applied	RO	0x0
7:0	Reserved		-	-

You can see that many of the 32 bits in the register are not used, but bit 9 is OUTTOPAD which is the final state of the GPIO line after register overrides have been applied.

PAD stands for Pin Attenuation/Drive, sometimes referred to as "Pad Driver" You can read its current value using:

```
uint32_t *PERIBase = map;
uint32_t *GPIOBase = PERIBase + 0xd0000 / 4;

int pin = 0;
volatile uint32_t *addrGP0Status = GPIOBase + pin * 8 / 4;
uint32_t value = *addrGP0Status;
printf("status   10987654321098765432109876543210\n");
printf("status   %032b\n", value);
```

This prints the current status of GPIO 0 in binary. You can read the value of the bits to check that they correspond to what you would expect from the known status of the line.

Registers as Structs

In most cases it is better to associate more familiar C data types with the memory area referenced. For example, the set of GPIO registers in which each status register is followed by the corresponding control register like an array of structs, for example:

```
typedef struct{
    uint32_t status;
    uint32_t ctrl;
}GPIOregs;
#define GPIO ((GPIOregs*)GPIOBase)
```

This first defines the repeating pattern of a `status` register followed by a `ctrl` register as the `GPIOregs` struct. This allows you to treat `GPIO` as an array of register structs, i.e. `GPIO` type which is a pointer to `GPIOregs` defined to be `GPIOBase`. Using this the previous program to be written as:

```
uint32_t *PERIBase = map;
uint32_t *GPIOBase = PERIBase + 0xD0000 / 4;
int pin=2;
printf("status  10987654321098765432109876543210\n");
printf("status  %032b\n", GPIO[pin].status);
```

The expression:

`GPIO[pin].status`

expands to:

`((GPIOregs*)GPIOBase)[pin].status`

This is the general way you work with peripheral devices such as the PWM units or I2C hardware, but the GPIO is special in that it has another set of registers that control it.

Registered IO Block RIO

At this point you might think that we are ready to access the state of the GPIO lines for general input and output. This isn't quite the whole story. To accommodate the fact that the processor has two cores, and to make access to important devices faster, there is a special connection between the cores and the GPIO, the RIO or Registered IO Block.

Notice that the GPIO lines are multipurpose and to use a GPIO line via the RIO you have to set its mode to RIO via direct access to its control register. The low-order five bits of the GPIO control register set the function of the GPIO line. You can see the values needed for any given function in the documentation, but to assign the GPIO line to RIO control you have to set it to function `0x05`. In this sense the RIO is just another peripheral that can take control of a GPIO line.

The RIO provides a set of registers that makes using the GPIO much faster and much easier to use. The basic registers are:

0x00	OUT	Sets GPIO lines to high or low
0x04	OE	Sets GPIO line to output driver or high impedance
0x08	IN	Reads GPIO lines
0x0C	INSYNC	Reads GPIO lines synchronized to `clk_sys`

Each register holds a bit pattern such that bit n relates to `GPIOn`. For example, the first bit of `OUT` sets the level of GPIO 0, the fifth bit of `IN` reflects the current state of GPIO 4 and so on.

There is also a general principle that every register has a set of four aliases. If the register is at address X then:

X+0x0000	Normal read/write access
X+0x1000	Atomic XOR on write and reads have no side effects
X+0x2000	Atomic SET on write and normal read access
X+0x3000	Atomic CLR on write and normal read access

It is difficult to know from the documentation if there are any exceptions to this, but it does seem to be a general mechanism.

For the RIO registers the availability of XOR, SET and CLR registers is a great simplification. For example, if you want to set GPIO 0 to a high output without modifying any of the other GPIO lines then you would need to first read OUT, OR the value with 0x01 and then store the resulting bit pattern in OUT. Using SET you would simply store 0x01 in SET as the only line to be set is GPIO 0.

The RIO registers are at 0x400e0000, which makes its offset 0xe0000. We can use the same technique of defining a struct to allow access to the registers:

```
typedef struct
{
    uint32_t Out;
    uint32_t OE;
    uint32_t In;
    uint32_t InSync;
} rioregs;
```

```
#define rio ((rioregs *)RIOBase)
```

where RIOBase is:

```
uint32_t *RIOBase = PERIBase + 0xe0000 / 4;
```

We can use the same technique to access the XOR, SET and CLR registers:

```
#define rioXOR ((rioregs *)(RIOBase + 0x1000 / 4))
#define rioSET ((rioregs *)(RIOBase + 0x2000 / 4))
#define rioCLR ((rioregs *)(RIOBase + 0x3000 / 4))
```

PAD Control

Using the RIO we can read and write the GPIO lines, but there is a further step we have to complete before we can actually make use of them. Each GPIO line has its own PAD which is a set of components that control the physical connection of the line to the outside world. To make a GPIO line work you have to configure the pad to act as input or output and set its electrical characteristics. You can see the CM5's PAD structure in the diagram below:

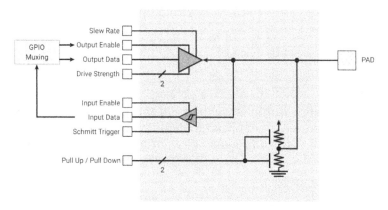

This is very similar to the PAD design found in other members of the Pi family. The PAD registers for the GPIO bank we are using is at `0x400f0000` which means its offset is `0xf0000`:

`uint32_t *PADBase = PERIBase + 0xf0000 / 4;`

The only complication is that the first register is a `VOLTAGE_SELECT` register which sets the voltage that all of the GPIO lines in bank 0 work with. A zero sets 3.3V and a one sets 1.8V. The default is 3.3V and you can ignore this register unless you need to work at 1.8V.

After the `VOLTAGE_SELECT` register there is a PAD register for each GPIO line:

Bits	Name	Description	Type	Reset
31:8	Reserved			
7	OD	Output disable. Has priority over output enable from peripherals	RW	0x1
6	IE	Input enable	RW	0x0
5:4	DRIVE	Drive strength. 0x0 → 2mA 0x1 → 4mA 0x2 → 8mA 0x3 → 12mA	RW	0x1

3	PUE	Pull-up enable	RW	Varies
2	PDE	Pull-down enable	RW	Varies
1	SCHMITT	Enable Schmitt trigger	RW	0x1
0	SLEWFAST	Slew rate control. 1 = Fast, 0 = Slow	RW	0x0

We can access the PAD registers using:

```
uint32_t *pad = PADBase + 1;
```

For example, if we want to set the PAD to output with a default drive, no pull-up/down, no Schmitt trigger and slow slew rate we would use:

```
pad[pin]= 0x10;
```

Notice that output is set by not enabling input.

A Fast Pulse

Now we can re-write a Blinky-style program to find out how fast the CM5 can toggle a GPIO line. We first have to map the peripherals area into user space and set up all of the addresses we want to use. Next we configure the pin as an output and start a loop that toggles the line using the XOR register:

The complete program is:

```
#include <stdio.h>
#include <stdlib.h>
#include <sys/mman.h>
#include <fcntl.h>
#include <errno.h>
#include <string.h>
#include <unistd.h>
#include <stdint.h>

typedef struct{
    uint32_t status;
    uint32_t ctrl;
}GPIOregs;
#define GPIO ((GPIOregs*)GPIOBase)

typedef struct
{
    uint32_t Out;
    uint32_t OE;
    uint32_t In;
    uint32_t InSync;
} rioregs;
#define rio ((rioregs *)RIOBase)
#define rioXOR ((rioregs *)(RIOBase + 0x1000 / 4))
#define rioSET ((rioregs *)(RIOBase + 0x2000 / 4))
#define rioCLR ((rioregs *)(RIOBase + 0x3000 / 4))
```

```
int main(int argc, char **argv)
{
    int memfd = open("/dev/mem", O_RDWR | O_SYNC);
    uint32_t *map = (uint32_t *)mmap(
        NULL,
        64 * 1024 * 1024,
        (PROT_READ | PROT_WRITE),
        MAP_SHARED,
        memfd,
        0x1f00000000
    );
    if (map == MAP_FAILED)
    {
        printf("mmap failed: %s\n", strerror(errno));
        return (-1);
    };
    close(memfd);

    uint32_t *PERIBase = map;
    uint32_t *GPIOBase = PERIBase + 0xD0000 / 4;
    uint32_t *RIOBase = PERIBase + 0xe0000 / 4;
    uint32_t *PADBase = PERIBase + 0xf0000 / 4;
    uint32_t *pad = PADBase + 1;

    uint32_t pin = 2;
    uint32_t fn = 5;

    GPIO[pin].ctrl=fn;
    pad[pin] = 0x10;
    rioSET->OE = 0x01<<pin;
    rioSET->Out = 0x01<<pin;

    for (;;)
    {
        rioXOR->Out = 0x04;
    }
    return (EXIT_SUCCESS);
}
```

If you try this out you will find that it produces 24ns pulses.

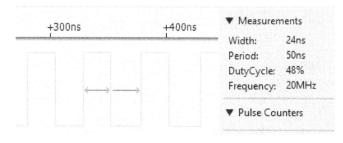

119

The Gpio5 Library

If you are going to use direct access to the GPIO registers it makes sense to build a library. The Gpio5 library is modeled on the Pico SDK and is close enough that it is possible to run Pico GPIO programs on the CM5 with only minor changes. You can find the complete Gpio5 at Github https://github.com/IOPress/Gpio5, at the book's web page at iopress.info or as a listing in Appendix I. The library is built up step by step in subsequent chapters but if you want to go directly to the finished code you can simply download and use it.

Initializing Memory

The first function we need, however, is not part of the Pico SDK. Before we can start working with the registers we have to map them into Linux user space. To make the library more useful it makes sense to first try to use mem as this gives complete access to the entire peripheral area. However, it needs to be run with root privileges. If an attempt at opening mem fails then it makes sense to fall back to gpiomem0 which only needs to be run by a member of the gpio user group and the default use is automatically a member of this group:

```
int rp1_Init()
{
    int memfd = open("/dev/mem", O_RDWR | O_SYNC);
    uint32_t *map = (uint32_t *)mmap(
        NULL,
        64 * 1024 * 1024,
        (PROT_READ | PROT_WRITE),
        MAP_SHARED,
        memfd,
        0x1f00000000);
    close(memfd);
    PERIBase = map;
    if (map == MAP_FAILED)
    {
        int memfd = open("/dev/gpiomem0", O_RDWR | O_SYNC);
        uint32_t *map = (uint32_t *)mmap(
            NULL,
            576 * 1024,
            (PROT_READ | PROT_WRITE),
            MAP_SHARED,
            memfd,
            0x0);
        close(memfd);
```

```
if (map == MAP_FAILED)
        {
              printf("mmap failed: %s\n", strerror(errno));
              return (-1);
        };
        PERIBase = map - 0xD0000 / 4;
    };

    GPIOBase = PERIBase + 0xD0000 / 4;
    RIOBase = PERIBase + 0xe0000 / 4;
    PADBase = PERIBase + 0xf0000 / 4;
    pad = PADBase + 1;
    return 0;
}
```

Notice that if we succeed in opening mem then the start of the block of memory is PERIBase. If we fail to open mem, usually because the program is not running as root, then gpiomem0 is tried and if it works the block of memory starts at GPIOBase and hence PERIBase is set to 0xD0000 "below" that and inaccessible. In either case the values of GPIOBase, RIOBase and PADBase are correct and are accessible.

Initializing GPIO

Before we can use a GPIO line it has to be initialized and connected to the RIO:

```
void gpio_init(uint32_t gpio)
{
    gpio_set_dir(gpio, GPIO_IN);
    gpio_put(gpio, 0);
    gpio_set_function(gpio, GPIO_FUNC_RIO);
}
```

This is almost identical to the corresponding function in the Pico SDK. The GPIO line is set to input and a zero output before connecting to the RIO, which is called SIO in Pico jargon. To make this work we need to define the functions called but, these are also standard Pico SDK functions and will be defined later.

All of the error detection code included in the Pico SDK is omitted from Gpio5. The reason is that in nearly all cases the errors being tested for can be detected at compile time and hence there is little point in slowing down the code at runtime. For example the Pico SDK usually checks that the GPIO line specified is a valid line but the number of the line to be used is usually selected and set by the programmer and a runtime check is usually not required. If you do need to use a runtime check then make it before calling the Gpio5 function.

The Pico SDK also provides a masked version of the function where you can set bits in the mask corresponding to lines that you want to set to RIO operation:

```
void gpio_init_mask(uint32_t gpio_mask)
{
    for (int i = 0; i < 29; i++)
    {
        if (gpio_mask & 1)
        {
            gpio_init(i);
        }
        gpio_mask >>= 1;
    }
}
```

The set_function function is:

```
void gpio_set_function(uint32_t gpio, enum gpio_function_rp1 fn)
{
    pad[gpio] = 0x50;
    GPIO[gpio].ctrl = fn;
}
```

This not only sets the function to RIO it also puts the line into input mode with output enabled so that other functions can change the direction.

A deinit function now easy:

```
void gpio_deinit(uint gpio) {
    gpio_set_function(gpio, GPIO_FUNC_NULL);
}
```

Next we need to set the line direction and the SDK has three functions to do the job. The first sets the direction of a single line by constructing a mask and then calling one of the two mask functions:

```
void gpio_set_dir(uint32_t gpio, bool out)
{
    uint32_t mask = 1ul << gpio;
    if (out)
        gpio_set_dir_out_masked(mask);
    else
        gpio_set_dir_in_masked(mask);
}
```

The `mask` functions do the actual job of setting the direction by accessing the RIO registers:

```
void gpio_set_dir_in_masked(uint32_t mask)
{
    rioCLR->OE = mask;
}
void gpio_set_dir_out_masked(uint32_t mask)
{
    rioSET->OE = mask;
}
```

The third function is a "bulk" setting function which only sets the direction of the lines specified in the `mask` to the direction specified by the corresponding bit in the `value`:

```
void gpio_set_dir_masked(uint32_t mask, uint32_t value)
{
    rioXOR->OE = (rio->OE ^ value) & mask;
}
```

This makes use of the XOR register and implements the well-known formula:

```
data XOR ( (data XOR value) AND mask)
```

to set the bits in `data` specified by `mask` to the values of the corresponding bits in `value`. An alternative expression that does the same job and is sometimes useful is:

```
data & ~mask | value & mask
```

Get and Set

Now we have the GPIO lines of our choice initialized and set to a direction we can start using them as input or output lines. There are two output functions that simply set or clear the GPIO lines specified in the mask:

```
void gpio_set_mask(uint32_t mask)
{
    rioSET->Out = mask;
}

void gpio_clr_mask(uint32_t mask)
{
    rioCLR->Out = mask;
}
```

An XOR function along the same lines is also often useful as this toggles the state of the lines specified in the mask:

```
void gpio_xor_mask(uint32_t mask)
{
    rioXOR->Out = mask;
}
```

Using these two functions we can now create a simple function to set a single GPIO line to a value:

```
void gpio_put(uint32_t gpio, bool value)
{
    uint32_t mask = 1ul << gpio;
    if (value)
        gpio_set_mask(mask);
    else
        gpio_clr_mask(mask);
}
```

A masked version of the function is also useful:

```
void gpio_put_masked(uint32_t mask, uint32_t value)
{
    rioXOR->Out = (rio->Out ^ value) & mask;
}
```

This sets the GPIO lines specified in mask to the states defined by the corresponding bits in value.

Finally we have a simple function that reads the state of a specific GPIO line:

```
bool gpio_get(uint32_t gpio)
{
    return rio->In & (1u << gpio);
}
```

and a function to read all of the lines in one go:

```
uint32_t gpio_get_all(void)
{
    return rio->In;
}
```

PAD Configuration

Often the default setting of the PAD is good enough but occasionally we need to fine tune the settings – pull mode, skew rate. Drive strength and hysteresis. There are PAD simple configuration set/get functions that make use of the bits in the control register:

- ◆ void gpio_set_pulls(uint32_t gpio, bool up, bool down);
- ◆ void gpio_pull_down(uint32_t gpio);
- ◆ void gpio_pull_up(uint32_t gpio);
- ◆ void gpio_disable_pulls(uint32_t gpio);
- ◆ bool gpio_is_pulled_up(uint32_t gpio);
- ◆ bool gpio_is_pulled_down(uint32_t gpio);
- ◆ void gpio_set_input_hysteresis_enabled (uint32_t gpio,
                                              bool enabled);
- ◆ bool gpio_is_input_hysteresis_enabled (uint32_t gpio);
- ◆ void gpio_set_slew_rate (uint32_t gpio,
                               enum gpio_slew_rate slew);
- ◆ enum gpio_slew_rate gpio_get_slew_rate (uint32_t gpio);

124

- ◆ void gpio_set_drive_strength (uint32_t gpio,
                           enum gpio_drive_strength drive);
- ◆ enum gpio_drive_strength gpio_get_drive_strength (uint32_t
  gpio);

These are all easy to implement. For example:

```
void gpio_set_pulls(uint32_t gpio, bool up, bool down)
{
    pad[gpio] = pad[gpio] & ~0xC;
    if (up)
    {
        pad[gpio] = pad[gpio] | 0x8;
    };
    if (down)
    {
        pad[gpio] = pad[gpio] | 0x4;
    }
}
```

and so on. You can see the details for the other functions in the Gpio5 listing in Appendix I.

The problems of using pull-up, pull-down and open source/drain modes is discussed in Chapter 8.

Working with Gpio5

As outlined in Appendix I, the library is divided into a .c file and a .h file. If you want to use it as a stable production version then the obvious thing to do is compile the two files into a library file and include the .h file into your program and then link to the library file. This allows you to treat all of the Gpio5 functions as if they were built in and so more or less ignore them.

Of course if you are developing something novel you might want to be able to change or add to the functions in the library and a better solution is to add both files to the project and modify the tasks.json file to compile and link your main program. Assuming that Gpio5 is stored in a directory called Gpio5 same directory as the current directory. i.e. in ../Gpio5, you can add it to the build by changing the args section to read:

```
"args": [
    "-fdiagnostics-color=always",
    "-g",
    "-I../Gpio5",
    "${file}",
    "../Gpio5/Gpio5.c",
    "-o",
    "${fileDirname}/${fileBasenameNoExtension}",
     "-lgpiod"
],
```

If you store Gpio5.c or Gpio5.h in a different folder you will need to modify the paths used.

Now when you compile the current program, Gpio5.c will be compiled and linked and if the program is correct it should run.

You can download Gpio5 from GitHub as a zip file and simply copy its contents into a Gpio5 folder.

Examples

With Gpio5 available it is very easy to write blinky by typing in a program targeting the Pico:

```c
#include <stdio.h>
#include <stdlib.h>
#include "Gpio5.h"

int main(int argc, char **argv)
{
    rp1_Init();
    gpio_init(2);
    gpio_set_dir(2, true);
    while (true)
    {
        gpio_put(2, 1);
        sleep(1);
        gpio_put(2, 0);
        sleep(1);
    }
    return (EXIT_SUCCESS);
}
```

The only change that was required was adding the call to rp1_Init().

If you remove the sleep function calls then you will discover that the fastest pulses you can create using Gpio5 is 24ns which is comparable to the direct approach given earlier:

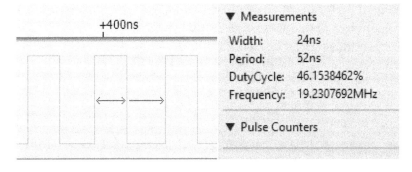

Another Pico program that runs without modification is to produce two pulses out of phase:

```c
#include <stdio.h>
#include <stdlib.h>

#include "Gpio5.h"

int main(int argc, char **argv)
{
  int pin1 = 4;
  int pin2 = 2;
  rp1_Init();
  gpio_init(pin1);
  gpio_set_dir(pin1, true);
  gpio_init(pin2);
  gpio_set_dir(pin2, true);

  uint32_t mask = (1 << pin1) | (1 << pin2);
  uint32_t value1 = 1 << pin1;
  uint32_t value2 = 1 << pin2;
  while (true)
  {
    gpio_put_masked(mask, value1);
    gpio_put_masked(mask, value2);
  }
  return (EXIT_SUCCESS);

}
```

The only change needed was the addition of the call to `rp1_Init()`. However, if you look at the output:

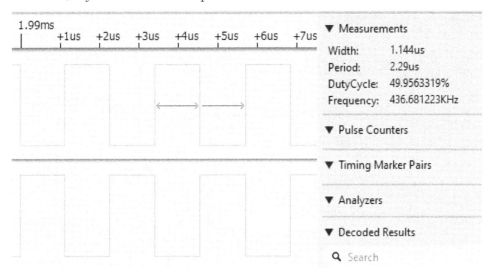

127

you will notice that the speed has reduced to $1.14\mu s$. This is because of setting the state of the two lines at the same time without changing the other lines. The slowdown is due to the need to read the RIO. If you set the lines without worrying about reading the state of the other lines then you get back to 24ns pulses.

Finally, here's an example of using a GPIO line as input:

```
#include <stdio.h>
#include <stdlib.h>
#include "Gpio5.h"

int main(int argc, char **argv)
{
  int pin1 = 4;
  int pin2 = 2;
  rp1_Init();
  gpio_init(pin1);
  gpio_set_dir(pin1, false);
  gpio_pull_up(pin1);
  gpio_init(pin2);
  gpio_set_dir(pin2, true);
  while (true)
  {
    if (gpio_get(pin1))
    {
      gpio_put(pin2, 0);
    }
    else
    {
      gpio_put(pin2, 1);
    }
  }
  return (EXIT_SUCCESS);
}
```

Again, the program is unchanged from a Pico program, except for the addition of `rp1_Init()`.

As the internal pull-up resistor is used, the switch can be connected to the line and ground without any external resistors:

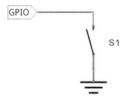

The program simply tests for the line, GPIO4, to be pulled low by the switch being closed and then sets GPIO2 high. If you connect GPIO2 to an LED or a logic analyzer you will see the effect of the button being closed – the LED will light up while it is pressed. That is, GPIO2 is set high when GPIO4 is pulled low by the switch.

If you change `gpio_pull_up(pin1)` to `gpio_pull_down(pin1)`, the way the switch is connected becomes:

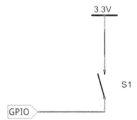

The program still works, but now GPIO2 is only high when the switch is pressed and hence, with no other changes to the program, the LED is on when the switch is not pressed.

Interrupts?

You may be wondering why the extensive list of Pico GPIO interrupt functions have not been added to Gpio5? The reason is that interrupts in Linux user space are not a good idea. It is part of the cost of using a complete operating system like Linux that things like raw interrupts are not allowed. In particular, the Linux kernel isn't re-entrant and so a hardware interrupt that Linux knows nothing about, and could occur when the Linux kernel is running, is a very bad idea.

The proper way to implement GPIO interrupts so as to integrate with Linux is to write a kernel driver that allows you to use epolling to wait on a file handle, as is done in gpiod. This is a fairly large task and raises the question, why not simply use gpiod? Another alternative to using interrupts is simply to create a thread to monitor by polling a GPIO line and then use this to call an event function as needed.

Having said all of this, it is possible to work with raw GPIO interrupts, but there are some important restrictions. The first is that any interrupt handler should run for as short a time as possible and should not make any Linux system calls. This generally means that the interrupt routine cannot call any library functions that in turn make Linux system calls. Overall, this makes working with raw GPIO interrupts error prone and generally not very useful.

Summary

- The CM5 has its peripherals implemented by the custom RP1 chip and this makes it incompatible with all previous versions of the Raspberry Pi.

- The memory map and the register configurations are different to other Pis and more like those found in the Pico.

- You can still work with the CM5's registers using the standard memory-mapping techniques.

- The /dev/mem device accesses all of the memory, but needs root privileges.

- The /dev/gpiomem0 device only provides the GPIO registers, but it can be used without root privileges.

- The CM5 uses the same RIO-based GPIO implementation as the Pico. To use the GPIO lines you first have to select RIO mode.

- Each GPIO line also has a PAD and a PAD control register.

- The RIO registers are used to control and read the state of the GPIO line.

- Using direct register access, the CM5 can produce well-formed 25ns pulses

- Although using the registers directly is a good way to get started, creating functions, and hence a library to do the same job, is a good idea.

- The Gpio5 library is based on the Pico SDK GPIO functions and it allows you to run Pico GPIO programs with little modification.

- Working with raw interrupts under Linux is not easy and best avoided.

Now that we have looked at some simple I/O, it is worth spending a little time on the electronics of output and input. We cover the electronics of input before looking at how the software handles input because we need to understand some of the problems that the software has to deal with.

First some basic electronics – how transistors can be used as switches. The approach is very simple, but it is enough for the simple circuits that digital electronics makes use of. It isn't enough to design a high-quality audio amplifier or similar analog device, but it might be all you need.

How to Think About Circuits

For a beginner electronics can seem very abstract, but that's not how old hands think about it. Most understand what is going on in terms of a hydraulic model, even if they don't admit it. The basic idea is that an electric current running in a wire is very much like a flow of water in a pipe. The source of the electricity plays the role of a pump and the wires, the pipe. The flow of electricity is measured in Amps and this is just the amount of electricity that flows per second. The flow is governed by how hard the pump is pumping, which is measured by voltage and how restrictive the pipe is, the resistance which is measured in Ohms.

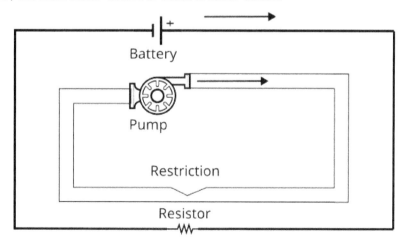

It is true that when you are doing electronics you are basically doing plumbing with a fluid that you generally can't see that flows in pipes called wires.

The only difficult one of these three ideas is the idea of pumping force. We tend to think of a pump providing a flow at the location of the pump but there is something, "a pumping force" that keeps the water flowing around every part of the circuit. In your imagination you have to think of the water being forced ever onward at every point in the pipe. In particular when there is constriction in the pipe then you might need more pumping force to get the water through. In a sense the pump provides the total pressure available and this distributes itself around the circuit as needed to push the flow through each restriction.

In electric circuits the pumping force is called EMF or ElectroMotive Force or just voltage. We also assume that the force needed to push electricity through wires is negligible and resistors are the only place that a voltage is needed to make the current flow.

The relationship between these quantities is characterized by Ohm's Law:

$V = IR$ or $I = V/R$ or $R = V/I$

where V is the voltage in volts, I is the current in amps and R is the resistance in ohms.

It is worth pointing out that in Ohm's Law we generally work in volts (V) and milliamps (mA), a milliamp being one thousandth of an amp, and this automatically gives resistance in kiloohms (kΩ).

You can see that if you increase the voltage, the flow, then the current increases. If you increase the resistance then the current decreases. Slightly more difficult is the idea that for a given resistance you need particular pumping force to achieve a given flow. If you know the actual flow and the resistance then you can work out the pumping force needed to get that flow.

The following points should be obvious. The flow through a pipe has to be the same at each point in the pipe – otherwise water would backup or need to be introduced. The total pressure that the pump provides has to be distributed across each of the resistances in the pipe to ensure the same flow. These pressures have to add up to the total pressure that the pump provides.

Slightly less obvious, but you can still understand them in terms of water flow, pressures add, currents add and resistances to flow in the same pipe add.

One of the main reasons for understanding electrical flow is that you can use Ohm's Law to avoid damaging things. As a current flows through a resistor it gets hot. The rule here is that the energy produced is proportional to VI. If you double the current, you double the heating effect. Most electronic devices have current limits beyond which they are liable to fail. One of the basic tasks in designing any electronic circuit is to work out what the current is and, if it is too high, add a resistor or lower the voltage to reduce it. To do this you need a good understanding of the hydraulic model and be able to use Ohm's Law. There are examples later in this chapter.

It is also worth pointing out that there are devices which do not obey Ohm's law – so-called non-Ohmic devices. These are the interesting elements in a circuit – LEDs, diodes, transistors and so on, but even these devices can be understood in terms of the flow of a fluid.

This is a lightning introduction to electronics, pun intended, and there is much to learn and many mistakes to make, most of which result in blue smoke.

Electrical Drive Characteristics

The basis of all electronics is Ohm's Law, $V = IR$, and this prerequisite implies an understanding of voltage, current and resistance. If you are not very familiar with electronics, the important things to know are what voltages are being worked with and how much current can flow. The most important thing to know about the Raspberry Pi is that it works with two voltage levels, 0V and 3.3V. If you have worked with other logic devices you might be more familiar with 0V and 5V as being the low and high levels. The Pi uses a lower output voltage to reduce its power consumption, which is good, but you need to keep in mind that you may have to use some electronics to change the 3.3V to other values. The same is true of inputs, which must not exceed 3.3V or you risk damaging the Pi.

In output mode a single GPIO line can source and sink 16mA, but the situation is a little more complicated than this suggests. Unfortunately, the Pi power supply can only supply enough power for all of the GPIO lines working at around 3mA each. If you use too much current then the 3.3V supply will fail. The safe limit is usually stated as 50mA in total, i.e all of the GPIO lines have to keep their current consumption below a total of 50mA. When you get close to this limit you might find that current spikes cause strange behavior. In addition, no single GPIO line should supply or sink more than 8mA, or 16mA if you configure a high drive current, see later.

In practice, if you are planning to use more than 3mA from multiple GPIO lines, consider using a transistor. If your circuits draw more than 50mA from the 3.3V supply rail, consider a separate power supply. You can use the 5V supply with a regulator if you need even more than the 3.3V supply can source. How much current the 5V pin can source is a difficult question that depends on the USB power supply in use, but 2A is a reasonable estimate if there are no other USB devices connected. The total of all USB, HDMI, Camera, and 5V pin demands has to be less than 2.5A. If in doubt use a separate power supply. Notice that the 16mA limit means that you cannot safely drive a standard 20mA red LED without restricting the current to below 16mA. A better solution is to use a low-power 2mA LED or use a transistor driver.

Driving an LED

One of the first things you need to know how to do is compute the value of a current-limiting resistor. For example, if you just connect an LED across a GPIO line and ground then no current will flow when the line is low and the LED is off, but when the line is high at 3.3V it is highly likely that the current will exceed the safe limit. In most cases nothing terrible will happen as the Pi's GPIO lines are rated very conservatively, but if you keep doing it eventually something will fail. The correct thing to do is to use a current-limiting resistor. Although this is an essential part of using an LED, it is also something you need to keep in mind when connecting any output device. You need to discover the voltage that the device needs and the current it uses and calculate a current-limiting resistor to make sure that is indeed the current it draws from the GPIO line.

An LED is a non-linear electronic component – the voltage across it stays more or less the same irrespective of the current passing through the device. Compare this to a more normal linear, or "Ohmic", device where the current and voltage vary together according to Ohm's Law, V = IR, which means that if the current doubles, so does the voltage and vice versa. This is not how an LED behaves. It has a fairly constant voltage drop irrespective of the current. (If you are curious, the relationship between current and voltage for an LED is exponential, meaning that big changes in the current hardly change the voltage across the LED.) When you use an LED you need to look up its forward voltage drop, about 1.7V to 2V for a red LED and about 3V for a blue LED, and the maximum current, usually 20mA for small LEDs. You don't have to use the current specified, this is the maximum current and maximum brightness.

To work out the current-limiting resistor you simply calculate the voltage across the resistor and then use Ohm's law to give you the resistor you need for the current required. The LED determines the voltage and the resistor sets the current.

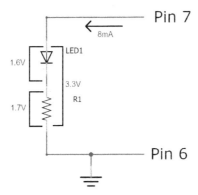

A GPIO line supplies 3.3V and if you assume 1.6V as its forward voltage across the LED that leaves 1.7V across the current-limiting resistor since voltage distributes itself across components connected in series. If we restrict the current to 8mA, which is very conservative, then the resistor we need is given by:

R = V/I = 1.7/8 = 0.212

The result is in kilo ohms, kΩ, because the current is in milliamps, mA. So we need at least a 212Ω resistor. In practice, you can use a range of values as long as the resistor is around 200 ohms – the bigger the resistor the smaller the current, but the dimmer the LED. If you were using multiple GPIO lines then keeping the current down to 3mA would be better, but that would need a transistor.

You need to do this sort of calculation when driving other types of output device. The steps are always the same. The 3.3V distributes itself across the output device and the resistor in some proportion and we know the maximum current. From these values we can compute the resistor needed to keep the actual current below this value.

LED BJT Drive

Often you need to reduce the current drawn from a GPIO line. The Bipolar Junction Transistor (BJT) may be relatively old technology, but it is a current amplifier, low in cost and easy to use. A BJT is a three-terminal device - base, emitter and collector - in which the current that flows through the emitter/collector is controlled by the current in the base:

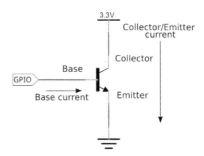

The diagram shows an NPN transistor, which is the most common. This diagram is a simplification in that, in reality, the current in the emitter is slightly larger than that in the collector because you have to add the current flowing in the base.

In most cases, all you have to know are two additional facts. Firstly, the voltage on the base is approximately 0.6V, no matter how much current flows since the base is a diode, a nonlinear device just like the LED in the previous section. Secondly, the current in the collector/emitter is hfe or ß (beta) times the current in the base. That is, hfe or beta is the current gain of the transistor and you look it up for any transistor you want to use. While you are consulting the datasheets, you also need to check the maximum currents and voltages the device will tolerate. In most cases, the beta is between 100 and 200 and hence you can use a transistor to amplify the GPIO current by at least a factor of 100.

Notice that, for the emitter/collector current to be non-zero, the base has to have a current flowing into it. If the base is connected to ground then the transistor is "cut off", i.e. no current flows. What this means is that when the GPIO line is high the transistor is "on" and current is flowing and when the GPIO line is low the transistor is "off" and no current flows.

This high-on/low-off behavior is typical of an NPN transistor. A PNP transistor works the other way round:

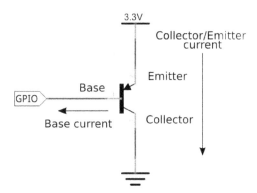

The 0.6V is between the base and the emitter and the current flows out of the base. What this means is that the transistor is off when the GPIO line is high and on when it is low.

This complementary behavior of NPN and PNP BJTs is very useful and means that we can use such transistors in pairs. It is also worth knowing that the diagram given above is usually drawn with 0V at the top of the diagram, i.e. flipped vertically, to make it look the same as the NPN diagram. You need to always make sure you know where the +V line is.

A BJT Example

For a simple example we need to connect a standard LED to a GPIO line with a full 20mA drive. Given that all of the Pi's GPIO lines work at 3.3V and ideally only supply a few milliamps, we need a transistor to drive the LED which typically draws 20mA. You could use a Field Effect Transistor (FET) of some sort, but for this type of application an old-fashioned BJT (Bipolar Junction Transistor) works very well and is cheap and available in a thru-hole mount, i.e. it comes with wires.

Almost any general purpose NPN transistor will work, but the 2N2222 is very common. From its datasheet, you can discover that the max collector current is 800mA and beta is at least 50, which makes it suitable for driving a 20mA LED with a GPIO current of at most 20/50mA = 0.4mA.

The circuit is simple but we need two current-limiting resistors:

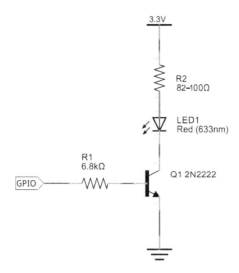

If you connect the base to the GPIO line directly then the current flowing in the base would be unrestricted – it would be similar to connecting the GPIO line to ground. R1 restricts the current to 0.39mA, which is very low and, assuming that the transistor has a minimum gain (hfe) of 50, this provides just short of 20mA to power it. The calculation is that the GPIO supplies 3.3V and the base has 0.6V across it, so the voltage across R1 is 3.3 - 0.6V = 2.7V. To limit the current to 0.4mA would need a resistor of 2.7/0.4kΩ = 6.7kΩ.

The closest preferred value is 6.8kΩ, which gives a slightly smaller current. Without R2 the LED would draw a very large current and burn out. R2 limits the current to 20mA. Assuming a forward voltage drop of 1.6V and a current of 20mA, the resistor is given by (3.3-1.6)/20kΩ = 85Ω. In practice, we could use anything in the range 82Ω to 100Ω.

The calculation just given assumes that the voltage between the collector and emitter is zero, but of course in practice it isn't. Ignoring this results in a current less than 20mA, which is erring on the safe side. The datasheet indicates that the collector emitter voltage is less than 200mV. The point is that you rarely make exact calculations for circuits such as this, you simply arrive at acceptable and safe operating conditions.

You can also use this design to drive something that needs a higher voltage. For example, to drive a 5V dip relay, which needs 10mA to activate it, you would use something like:

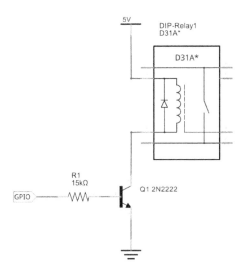

Notice that in this case the transistor isn't needed to increase the drive current – the GPIO line could provide the 10mA directly. Its purpose is to change the voltage from 3.3V to 5V. The same idea works with any larger voltage. If you are using the 2N2222 then the pinouts are:

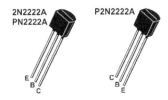

As always, the positive terminal on the LED is the long pin.

MOSFET Driver

There are many who think that the FET (Field Effect Transistor), or more precisely the MOSFET (Metal Oxide Semiconductor FET), is the perfect amplification device and we should ignore BJTs. They are simpler to understand and use, but it can be more difficult to find one with the characteristics you require.

Like the BJT, a MOSFET has three terminals called the gate, drain and source. The current that you want to control flows between the source and drain and it is controlled by the gate. This is analogous to the BJT's base, collector and emitter, but the difference is that it is the voltage on the gate that controls the current between the source and drain.

The gate is essentially a high resistance input and very little current flows in it. This makes it an ideal way to connect a GPIO line to a device that needs more current or a different voltage. When the gate voltage is low the source drain current is very small. When the gate voltage reaches the threshold voltage $V_{GS(th)}$, which is different for different MOSFETs, the source drain current starts to increase exponentially. Basically when the gate is connected to 0V or below $V_{GS(th)}$ the MOSFET is off and when it is above $V_{GS(th)}$ the MOSFET starts to turn on. Don't think of $V_{GS(th)}$ as the gate voltage at which the MOSFET turns on, but as the voltage below which it is turned off. The problem is that the gate voltage to turn a typical MOSFET fully on is in the region of 10V. Special "logic" MOSFETs need a gate voltage around 5V to fully turn on and this makes the 3.3V at which the Raspberry Pi's GPIO lines work a problem. The datasheets usually give the fully on resistance and the minimum gate voltage that produces it, usually listed as Drain-Source On-State Resistance. For digital work this is a more important parameter than the gate threshold voltage.

You can deal with this problem in one of two ways – ignore it or find a MOSFET with a very small $V_{GS(th)}$. In practice, MOSFETs with thresholds low enough to work at 3.3V are hard to find and when you do find them they are generally only available as surface mounts. Ignoring the problem sometimes works if you can tolerate the MOSFET not being fully on. If the current is kept low then, even though the MOSFET might have a resistance of a few ohms, the power loss and voltage drop may be acceptable.

What MOSFETs are useful for is in connecting higher voltages to a GPIO line used as an input, see later.

Also notice that this discussion has been in terms of an N-channel MOSFET. A P-channel works in the same way, but with all polarities reversed. It is cut off when the gate is at the positive voltage and turns on when the gate is grounded. This is exactly the same as the NPN versus PNP for the BJT.

MOSFET LED

A BJT is the easiest way to drive an LED, but as an example of using a common MOSFET we can arrange to drive one using a 2N7000, a low-cost, N-channel device available in a standard TO92 form factor suitable for experimentation:

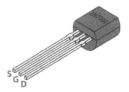

Its datasheet states that it has a $V_{GS(th)}$ of typically 2V, but it could be as low as 0.8V or as high as 3V. Given we are trying to work with a gate voltage of 3.3V you can see that in the worst case this is hardly going to work – the device will only just turn on. The best you can do is to buy a batch of 2N7000 and measure their $V_{GS(th)}$ to weed out any that are too high. This said, the circuit given below does generally work.

Assuming a $V_{GS(th)}$ of 2V and a current of 20mA for the LED, the datasheet gives a rough value of 6Ω for the on resistance with a gate voltage of 3V. The calculation for the current-limiting resistor is the same as in the BJT case and the final circuit is:

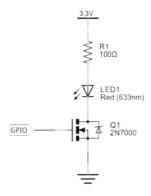

Notice that we don't need a current-limiting resistor for the GPIO line as the gate connection is high impedance and doesn't draw much current. In practice, it is usually a good idea to include a current-limiting resistor in the GPIO line if you plan to switch it on and off rapidly. The problem is that the gate looks like a capacitor and fast changes in voltage can produce high currents.

While there could be devices labeled 2N7000 that will not work in this circuit due to the threshold gate voltage being too high, encountering one is rare. A logic-level MOSFET like the IRLZ44 has a resistance of 0.028Ω at 5V compared to the 2N2222's of 6Ω. It also has a $V_{GS(th)}$ guaranteed to be between 1V and 2V.

Setting Drive Type

The GPIO output can be configured into one of a number of modes, but the most important is pull-up/down. Before we get to the code to do the job, it is worth spending a moment explaining the three basic output modes, push-pull, pull-up and pull-down.

Push-Pull Mode

In push-pull mode two transistors of opposite polarity, one PNP and one NPN, are used:

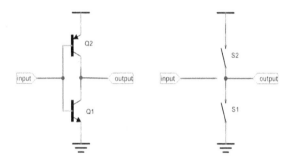

The circuit behaves like the two-switch equivalent shown on the right. Only one of the transistors, or switches, is "closed" at any time. If the input is high then Q1 is saturated and the output is connected to ground - exactly as if S1 was closed. If the input is low then Q2 is saturated, as if S2 was closed, and the output is connected to 3.3V. You can see that this pushes the output line high with the same "force" as it pulls it low. This is the standard configuration for a GPIO output.

Pull-Up Mode

In pull-up mode one of the transistors is replaced by a resistor:

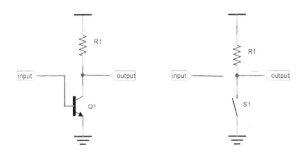

In this case the circuit is equivalent to having a single switch. When the switch is closed, the output line is connected to ground and hence driven low. When the switch is open, the output line is pulled high by the resistor. You can see that in this case the degree of pull-down is greater than the pull-up, where the current is limited by the resistor. The advantage of this mode is that it can be used in an AND configuration. If multiple GPIO or other lines are connected to the output, then any one of them being low will pull the output line low. Only when all of them are off does the resistor succeed in pulling the line high. This is used, for example, in a serial bus configuration like the SPI bus.

Pull-Down Mode

Finally, pull-down mode, which is the best mode for driving general loads, motors, LEDs, etc, is exactly the same as pull-up, only now the resistor is used to pull the output line low.

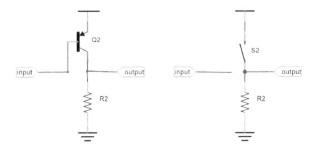

The line is held high by the transistor and pulled low by the resistor only when all the switches are open. Putting this the other way round, the line is high if any one switch is closed. This is the OR version of the shared bus idea.

143

Open Collector

There is one final output configuration – open collector or, when referring to a MOSFET, open drain. The idea is simple, you don't connect the collector or the drain to anything at all – you simply use it as the output:

There is no pull-up resistor, but you can supply one as an external pull-up if needed. You can also drive a device that needs a current flow through it rather than just a voltage – a coil is the standard example. However, a GPIO line usually cannot supply enough current for such devices.

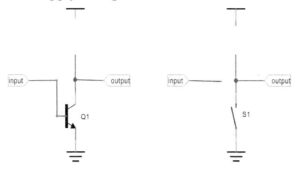

The real use of the open collector arrangement is to implement a shared data line:

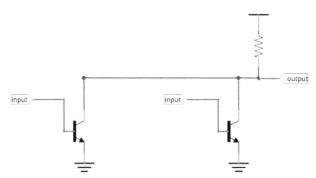

In this case two inputs control one output. If the first transistor is on then the output is low, irrespective of the state of the second transistor. The same is true if the second transistor is on. If you work through the possible combinations we have:

Input 1	Input 2	Output
Off	Off	High
Off	On	Low
On	Off	Low
On	On	Low

You might recognize this as the truth table for a NOR gate. This is exactly what an open collector output used in this way implements. Early integrated circuits referred to as RTL (Resistor Transistor Logic) implemented logic in this way. This was soon replaced by TTL (Transistor Transistor Logic) because transistors are easier to implement in an integrated circuit.

In IoT applications, open collector connections are used to allow any number of devices to share a line. If all of the devices are configured to be open collectors then any one of them can pull the line low. In most cases only one device will be active and sending data at any one time.

There is a corresponding configuration were the emitter of a BJT or the source of a MOSFET is left open – open emitter or open source.

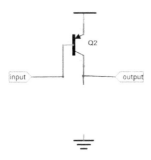

In this case the line is pulled low using a resistor and the line goes high when the transistor is turned on and the table for the two inputs is:

Input 1	Input 2	Output
Off	Off	Low
Off	On	High
On	Off	High
On	On	High

You can see that this is the table for an OR gate. Again this is useful if you want to share a line between multiple communicating devices.

The open collector/drain is the most commonly encountered configuration.

Basic Input Circuit - The Switch

Now it is time to turn our attention to the electrical characteristics of GPIO lines as inputs. One of the most common input circuits is the switch or button. Many beginners make the mistake of wiring a GPIO line to a switch something like:

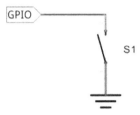

The problem with this is that, if the switch is pressed, the GPIO line is connected to ground and will read as zero. The question is, what does it read when the switch is open? A GPIO line configured as an input has a very high resistance. It isn't connected to any particular voltage and the voltage on it varies due to the static it picks up. The jargon is that the unconnected line is "floating". When the switch is open the line is floating and, if you read it, the result, zero or one, depends on whatever noise it has picked up.

The correct way to do the job is to tie the input line either high or low when the switch is open using a resistor. A pull-up arrangement would be something like:

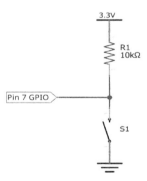

The value of the resistor used isn't critical. It simply pulls the GPIO line high when the switch isn't pressed. When it is pressed a current of a little more than 0.3mA flows in the resistor. If this is too much, increase the resistance to 100kΩ or even more, but notice that the higher the resistor value the noisier the input to the GPIO and the more it is susceptible to RF interference. This circuit gives a zero when the switch is pressed.

If you want a switch that pulls the line high instead of low, reverse the logic by swapping the positions of the resistor and the switch in the diagram to create a pull-down:

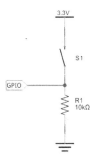

This gives a one when the switch is pressed.

The good news is that the Raspberry Pi has built-in pull-up and pull-down resistors which you can enable in software. This means that you can connect a switch directly to the GPIO and set a pull-up or pull-down configuration in software.

Setting Pull Mode

You can enable the builtin resistors via the gpiod driver using:

- GPIOD_LINE_REQUEST_FLAG_BIAS_DISABLE
- GPIOD_LINE_REQUEST_FLAG_BIAS_PULL_DOWN
- GPIOD_LINE_REQUEST_FLAG_BIAS_PULL_UP

in the flag field of the gpiod_line_request_config struct as outlined in Chapter 4.

To set pull-up/pull-down resistors using Gpio5 you can call:

```
void gpio_set_pulls(uint32_t gpio, bool up, bool down);
void gpio_pull_down(uint32_t gpio);
void gpio_pull_up(uint32_t gpio);
void gpio_disable_pulls(uint32_t gpio);
```

Notice that it generally only makes sense to enable pull-up/pull-down resistors when the GPIO line is set to input. Then the GPIO line is in a high impedance state and the resistor is capable of pulling the line high or low in the absence of another connected device overriding this. If you enable the resistors in output mode then the only result is that the line is more loaded than it would be without them and the current needed is greater.

You can enable both pull-up and pull-down resistors at the same time, but this isn't really useful. In principle, what should happen is that in input mode the line should settle to a voltage half way between the ground and working voltage. This is, of course, little use in a digital system that works in terms of ground, or full working, voltage. If you do enable both resistors then the system uses "bus keeper" mode, which is pulled up when input is high and pulled down when input is low. This is rarely useful.

There are no functions that set open source or open drain and a general GPIO line does not support either mode of operation. Other functions such as I2C do offer open drain/collector but a general GPIO line is always in push-pull mode. If you need to drive an open source or open drain connection then one solution is to connect a MOSFET or BJT to the output and configure it to be open source or drain.

An alternative that is usually good enough is to dynamically switch from input to output. When the GPIO line is in input mode it is high impedance and the line state is controlled by the pull-up/pull-down resistors and any other devices connected to the line.

That is, it behaves like a standard open collector:

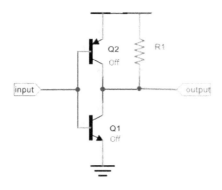

In input mode the CM5 can read the bus and collect any data that another device sends it. If the CM5 wants to take over the bus and send some data it can change to output mode.

If it drives the line low then only the "bottom" transistor is on and we have the standard configuration of an open collector bus being driven to a zero:

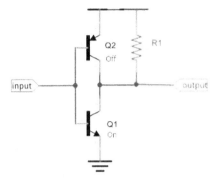

If the CM5 wants to send a one on the bus it can simply switch back to input mode when the bus will be pulled up by the resistor. Of course, if anything else on the bus drives it low then the data will be incorrect but this is true of a correctly implemented open collector bus.

To summarize:

- Set things up by writing a zero to the output register and selecting input mode.
- To receive data on the bus set input mode and read the line
- To send a zero switch to output mode which will pull the line low as long as there is a zero in the output register.
- To send a one switch to input mode.

To provide an example:

```
#include <stdio.h>
#include <stdlib.h>
#include "Gpio5.h"
int main(int argc, char **argv)
{
  int pin1 = 4;
  rp1_Init();
  gpio_init(pin1);
  gpio_pull_up(pin1);
  gpio_set_dir(pin1, false);
  gpio_put(pin1, false);
  volatile int temp;
  while (true)
  {
    gpio_set_dir(pin1, true);
    for(temp=0;temp<2000;temp++){};
    gpio_set_dir(pin1, false);
    for(temp=0;temp<2000;temp++){};
  }
  return (EXIT_SUCCESS);
}
```

Notice that we set the pin to input and its output register to zero. In the main loop all we have to do is change the line from input to output and back again to send a train of $3\mu s$ pulses. If you try to go faster the line doesn't have time to be completely pulled up before the GPIO line goes low again. In practice, how fast an open collector bus can run depends mainly on the size of the pull-up resistor - the lower the faster.

Debounce

Although the switch is the simplest input device, it is very difficult to get right. When a user clicks a switch of any sort, the action isn't clean - the switch bounces. What this means is that the logic level on the GPIO line goes high then low and high again and bounces between the two until it settles down. There are electronic ways of debouncing switches, but software does the job much better. All you have to do is insert a delay of a millisecond or so after detecting a switch press and read the line again. If it is still low then record a switch press. Similarly, when the switch is released, read the state twice with a delay. You can vary the delay to modify the perceived characteristics of the switch.

A more sophisticated algorithm for debouncing a switch is based on the idea of integration. All you have to do is read the state multiple times, every few milliseconds say, and keep a running sum of values. If you sum ten values each time then a total of between 6 and 10 can be taken as an indication that the switch is high. A total less than this indicates that the switch is low. You can think of this as a majority vote in the time period for the switch being high or low.

The Potential Divider

If you have an input that is outside of the range of 0V to 3.3V you can reduce it using a simple potential divider. In the diagram V is the input from the external logic and Vout is the connection to the GPIO input line:

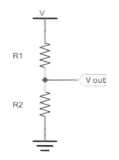

Vout = V R2/(R1+R2)

You can spend a lot of time working out good values of R1 and R2. For loads that take a lot of current you need R1+R2 to be small and divided in the same ratio as the voltages. For example, for a 5V device R1=18 or 20KΩ and R2=33KΩ work well to drop the voltage to 3.3V.

A simpler approach that works for a 5V signal is to notice that the ratio R1:R2 has to be the same as (5-3.3):3.3, i.e. the voltage divides itself across the resistors in proportion to their value, which is roughly 1:2. What this means is that you can take any resistor and use it for R1 and use two of the same value in series for R2 and the Vout will be 3.33333V.

The problem with a resistive divider is that it can round off fast pulses due to the small capacitive effects. This usually isn't a problem, but if it is then the solution is to use a FET or a BJT as an active buffer:

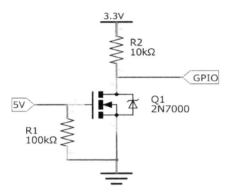

Notice that this is an inverting buffer, the output is low when the input is high, but you can usually ignore this and simply correct it in software, i.e. read a 1 as a low state and a 0 as a high state. The role of R1 is to make sure the FET is off when the 5V signal is absent and R2 limits the current in the FET to about 0.3mA. In most cases you should try the simple voltage divider and only move to an active buffer if it doesn't work.

This very basic look at electronics isn't all that you need to know, but it is enough for you to see some of the problems and find some answers. In general, this sort of electronics is all about making sure that voltages and currents are within limits. As switching speeds increase you have additional problems, which are mainly concerned with making sure that your circuits aren't slowing things down. This is where things get more subtle.

Summary

- You can get a long way with only a small understanding of electronics, but you do need to know enough to protect the Pi and things you connect to it.

- The maximum current from any GPIO line should be less than 16mA and the total current should be less than 50mA.

- All of the GPIO lines work at 3.3V and you should avoid directly connecting any other voltage.

- You can drive an LED directly from a GPIO line, but only at 16mA rather than the nominal 20mA needed for full brightness.

- Calculating a current-limiting resistor always follows the same steps – find out the current in the device, find out the voltage across the device, and work out the resistor that supplies that current when the remainder of the voltage is applied to it.

- For any load you connect to a GPIO output you generally need a current-limiting resistor.

- In many cases you need a transistor, a BJT, to increase the current supplied by the GPIO line.

- To use a BJT you need to calculate a current-limiting resistor in the base and, generally, one in the collector.

- MOSFETs are popular alternatives to BJTs, but it is difficult to find a MOSFET that works reliably at 3.3V.

- GPIO output lines can be set to active push-pull mode, where a transistor is used to pull the line high or low, or passive pull-up or pull-down mode, where one transistor is used and a resistor pulls the line high or low when the transistor is inactive.

- GPIO lines have built-in pull-up and pull-down resistors which can be selected or disabled under software control and can be used in input or output mode.

- When used as inputs, GPIO lines have a very high resistance and in most cases you need pull-up or pull-down resistors to stop the line floating. The built-in pull-up or pull-down resistors can be used in input mode.

- Mechanical input devices have to be debounced to stop spurious input.

- If you need to connect an input to something bigger than 3.3V, you need a potential divider to reduce the voltage back to 3.3V. You can also use a transistor.

Chapter 10

The Device Tree

Up to this point we have been using drivers that are installed and configured. In most cases you will at least need to configure the driver or some aspect of the system. The device tree is the modern way to install and configure drivers and is the subject of this chapter. This is an introduction to the device tree from the point of view of someone wanting to use ready made drivers and ready made driver configurations with minimal customization. Most introductions to the device tree go into much more detail and are often written from the point of view of the device driver writer. This one is about understanding enough about the device tree to use supplied overlays. Chapter 16 picks up this subject again and extends it so that you can write your own overlays.

The Device Tree and Overlays

Linux makes use of a data structure known as the device tree (DT) to describe the hardware it is running on. With the help of the device tree a single Linux kernel can configure itself to run on different hardware. There is some truth in the idea that the device tree was invented to take care of the many small variations found in different ARM processors and when the machine boots up it reads the device tree and modifies its configuration to suit the machine. Device tree files end in .dtbo and they are not human readable. To create a .dtbo file you create a text specification using an XML-like language and then compile it. Exactly how to do this is described in Chapter 16.

From our point of view, what is important about the device tree is that it selects which drivers are loaded and the parameters supplied to the drivers. Some drivers are compiled into the kernel and to remove them or add to them you have to edit the source code and compile the kernel. Most drivers, however, take the form of Linux kernel modules or Loadable Kernel Modules LKMs, which can be linked into the kernel at any point after the system has booted. The device tree determines which drivers are loaded and how they are configured. The original way of doing this is via a set of commands, `modprobe`, `lsmod` and so on, which are discussed in Chapter 16. For the moment let's concentrate on the use of the device tree.

There is a "master" device tree which is processed by the firmware loader, start.elf. The device trees appropriate for the hardware of each model of Pi are stored in /boot. The loader determines which of the available device trees should be loaded for the particular model of Pi in use. By selecting a device tree that is right for the hardware, the same Linux Kernel can be used to boot any model of Pi.

The master device tree sets a typical configuration for the machine and any customization is performed by using overlays. An overlay is a fragment of a device tree that the loader reads and merges with the master device tree to add or configure drivers. You can think of it as an editing process where the master device tree is merged with the updates provided by the overlays. There are a lot of overlay files stored in /boot/firmware/overlays and not all of them are used to modify the device tree. The file config.txt in the /boot/firmware folder has a list of commands that load the overlays you want to use.

The command to load an overlay is dtoverlay. For example:

```
dtoverlay=myoverlay
```

will load myoverlay.dtbo from the boot/firmware/overlays folder. All of the overlays in config.txt are loaded and merged with the master device tree to produce a final device tree which is passed to the kernel.

To make overlays even more flexible, you can define parameters which can be set using the dtparam command. For example, if myoverlay has a gpiopin parameter you could set it to a particular GPIO line using:

```
dtoverlay=myoverlay
dtparam=gpiopin=4
```

If there are multiple parameters you can repeat the dtparam command:

```
dtoverlay=myoverlay
dtparam=gpiopin=4
dtparam=gpio_in_pull=down
```

or you can put the parameters into a single dtparam command:

```
dtoverlay=myoverlay
dtparam=gpiopin=4,gpio_in_pull=down
```

You can also simply put the parameters in the dtoverlay command:

```
dtoverlay=myoverlay,gpiopin=4,gpio_in_pull=down
```

This is a lot of detail but the essentials are:

1) A device tree describes the hardware that the operating system is running on so that it can configure itself and load and configure any drivers required to use the hardware.
2) The loader selects the appropriate device tree for the Pi model that is booting.
3) The loader merges the device tree with the overlays listed in `config.txt` to produce a customized final device tree used to boot the system.
4) Overlays can themselves be customized by specifying parameters.
5) The final device tree determines what drivers are loaded and how they are configured.

Working with Overlays

Most of the time, using a particular piece of hardware is just a matter of using a presupplied overlay to load and configure a driver. For example, in the previous chapter we used the LED driver from C, but you can configure the driver using standard overlays. If you consult the list of overlays in `https://github.com/raspberrypi/firmware/blob/master/boot/overlays/README` or in the file `/boot/firmware/overlays/README` you will find:

```
Name:   act-led
Info:   Pi 3B, 3B+, 3A+ and 4B use a GPIO expander to drive the LEDs which can
        only be accessed from the VPU. There is a special driver for this with a
        separate DT node, which has the unfortunate consequence of breaking the
        act_led_gpio and act_led_activelow dtparams.
        This overlay changes the GPIO controller back to the standard one and
        restores the dtparams.
Load:   dtoverlay=act-led,<param>=<val>
Params: activelow                Set to "on" to invert the sense of the LED
                                 (default "off")

        gpio                     Set which GPIO to use for the activity LED
                                 (in case you want to connect it to an external
                                 device)
                                 REQUIRED
```

The important information here is that there is an overlay called `act-led.dtbo` and you can use it with `dtoverlay` as indicated. You have to use this overlay to return control of the LEDs back to the processor so that other overlays have an effect. To load it you simply add:

```
dtoverlay=act-led
```

to the `config.txt` file.

As an example of setting a parameter you can now change the trigger for the act LED using:

```
dtoverlay=act-led
dtparam=act_led_trigger=heartbeat
```

in the `config.txt` file. The changes only take effect after a reboot.

Finding Out About The Device Tree

When the loader parses the device tree and applies all of the overlays that you have specified, the final device tree is represented by the folders in /proc/device-tree/. There is a folder for each driver and within that folder, a folder for each device the driver is providing. For example, within /proc/device-tree/ you will find the leds folder which contains at least the act folder and possibly more if there are additional LEDs. Within the act folder you will see a number of files that contain the values specified as parameters in the device tree:

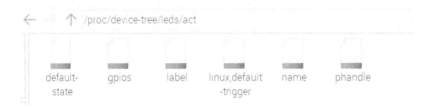

If you examine the contents you will find gpios empty, label contains act, linux, default-trigger contains heartbeat and name contains led0. This information is also repeated in the directory:
/sys/class/leds/ACT/device/of_node/led-act

The of_node folder shows you the information relating to that particular node in the device tree whereas the /proc/device-tree is a complete representation of the active device tree. If you move one level up to /sys/class/leds/ACT/device/of_node you will see another useful file – compatible. This gives the name of the driver that is used to implement the device. For example, in the case of act you will see gpio-leds and you can use this information to find the code of the driver in the GitHub repository.

A Driver Example - DHT22

As an example of the stages you have to go through in using a driver targeting a single device, we can do no better than the DHT22 Humidity/Temperature sensor, a more accurate version of the DHT11. It is very easy to use, low in cost and hence very popular. It makes use of a custom protocol which means you can't interface it using I2C or the SPI bus – you need something that will work with its unique characteristics.

The good news is that there is a driver that is easy to use and, while named DHT11, works well with both versions and also with the AM2302, which is equivalent to the DHT22. Notice that the DHT11 is not software compatible with the DHT22 but the driver solves this problem for us.

```
Model AM2302/DHT22
Power supply 3.3-5.5V DC
Output signal digital signal via 1-wire bus
Sensing element Polymer humidity capacitor
Operating range
  humidity 0-100%RH;
  temperature -40~80Celsius
Accuracy
  humidity +-2%RH(Max +-5%RH);
  temperature +-0.5Celsius
Resolution or sensitivity
  humidity 0.1%RH;
  temperature 0.1Celsius
Repeatability
  humidity +-1%RH;
  temperature +-0.2Celsius
```

The device will work at 3.3V and it makes use of a 1-wire open collector-style bus, which makes it very easy to make the physical connection to the Pi.

The 1-Wire bus used isn't standard, being used only by this family of devices, so we have little choice but to implement the protocol in C – or use a driver.

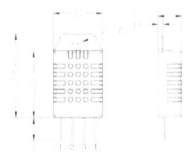

The pinouts are:

1. VDD
2. SDA serial data
3. not used
4. GND

The standard way of connecting the device is:

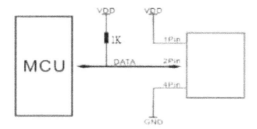

Although the recommended pull-up resistor is 1K, a higher value, typically 4.7K, works and so do even larger values.

Exactly how you build the circuit is a matter of preference. The basic layout can be seen below.

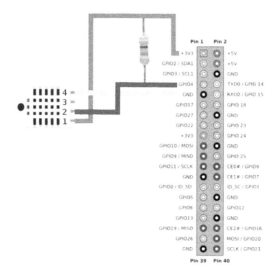

It is very easy to create this circuit using a prototyping board and some jumper wires. You can also put the resistor close to the DHT22 to make a sensor package connected to the Pi using three cables.

If you lookup the details of the dht11 overlay in the ReadMe you will find:

```
Name:    dht11
Info:    Overlay for the DHT11/DHT21/DHT22 humidity/temperature sensors
         Also sometimes found with the part number(s) AM230x.
Load:    dtoverlay=dht11,<param>=<val>
Params:  gpiopin                  GPIO connected to the sensor's DATA output.
                                  (default 4)
```

This is all very straightforward.

If you add:

```
dtoverlay=dht11 gpiopin=4
```

to the `config.txt` file then when you reboot, the driver will be loaded and configured to use GPIO4. Change the `gpiopin` parameter to whichever GPIO line you are using. After a reboot the driver will be ready to use – but where are the device folders? If you look in `/sys/class` you won't find any new or obvious folders, but examining the device tree listed in `/proc/device-tree` you will find a new device, `/proc/device-tree/dht11@0`. However, looking through the information listed there gives you no clue how to find and use the device folders. This is very typical of using a new device driver – its use is more than obvious to its creators, but a potential user is left out in the cold.

The key to using the dht11 device driver is to discover that it is stored in the Pi OS GitHub repository at `/linux/drivers/iio/humidity/dht11.c`. The `iio` folder is where drivers written to the Industrial I/O standard are stored. This is covered in more detail in Chapter 14, but for now we can ignore this fact and simply use it to find the device folders.

All IIO devices are stored in `/sys/bus/iio/devices/` and if you look you will find `/sys/bus/iio/devices/iio:device0`. This corresponds to the dht11 device you have just added. Of course, `iio:device0` isn't a name that is going to ensure that you have the dht11 device. A partial solution is to read the name file to discover the device name. To read the actual data you read `in_temp_input` for the temperature in millidegree Celsius and `in_humidityrelative_input` for the percentage humidity times 1000. There is no easy way to find the names of these files in the documentation, but once you have found the correct folder they are fairly obvious.

A program to read the name, temperature and humidity is:

```c
#include <stdio.h>
#include <errno.h>
#include <unistd.h>
#include <fcntl.h>
int main(int argc, char **argv)
{
    char buffer[25];
    int fd = open("/sys/bus/iio/devices/iio:device0/name",
                                              O_RDONLY);
    read(fd, buffer, 25);
    close(fd);
    printf("%s",buffer);
    fd = open("/sys/bus/iio/devices/iio:device0/in_temp_input",
                                              O_RDONLY);
    read(fd, buffer, 25);
    close(fd);
    int temp;
    sscanf(buffer, "%d", &temp);

    printf("%f\n\r", temp / 1000.0);
    fd=open("/sys/bus/iio/devices/iio:device0/
                        in_humidityrelative_input",O_RDONLY);
    read(fd, buffer, 25);
    close(fd);
    int hum;
    sscanf(buffer, "%d", &hum);
    printf("%f\n\r", hum / 1000.0);
}
```

If you run the program you will see the name dht11@0 and the temperature and humidity. In a more complete program you would check the name to make sure that it is the device you want and if there are multiple devices you would search through the top-level folder to find the device with the correct name.

Dynamic Loading Drivers

There are many problems with using drivers as part of an application and one big one is the need to configure the system to install the driver. The simplest solution is to ask the user to edit the config.txt file, but this could be a roadblock to your app being installed at all and then there is the possibility of user error. A better solution is to include the change in an install script. This is simple, but doesn't allow for the user or some other program changing the config.txt file so that your app no longer works. A good solution in some cases is to make use of the new dynamic overlay loading feature. This is fairly recent, but it works with the latest versions of Pi OS.

Instead of having to load drivers at boot time you can use the `dtoverlay` or `dtparam` commands to install and configure drivers. The only problem is that there are some cases where it doesn't work. Essentially you have to try it out to see if it works. The overlays that are dynamically loaded form a stack and, in theory, you can only remove the overlay on the top of the stack. In practice, removing any overlay often results in a memory leak at best and a crashed system at worst.

The `dtoverlay` command is described in the documentation as

```
Usage:
  dtoverlay <overlay> [<param>=<val>...]
                          Add an overlay (with parameters)
  dtoverlay -D            Dry-run (prepare overlay, but don't apply -
                          save it as dry-run.dtbo)
  dtoverlay -r [<overlay>] Remove an overlay (by name, index or the last)
  dtoverlay -R [<overlay>] Remove from an overlay (by name, index or all)
  dtoverlay -l            List active overlays/params
  dtoverlay -a            List all overlays (marking the active)
  dtoverlay -h            Show this usage message
  dtoverlay -h <overlay>  Display help on an overlay
  dtoverlay -h <overlay> <param>..  Or its parameters
     where <overlay> is the name of an overlay or 'dtparam' for dtparams
Options applicable to most variants:
    -d <dir>        Specify an alternate location for the overlays
                    (defaults to /boot/overlays or /flash/overlays)
    -p <string>     Force a compatible string for the platform
    -v              Verbose operation

Adding or removing overlays and parameters requires root privileges.
```

The `dtparam` command is:

```
dtparam <param>=<val>…   Add an overlay (with parameters)
dtparam -D               Dry-run (prepare overlay, but don't
                         apply -  save it as dry-run.dtbo)
dtparam -r [<idx>]       Remove an overlay (by index, or the
                         last)
dtparam -R [<idx>]       Remove from an overlay (by index, or
                         all)
dtparam -l               List active overlays/dtparams
dtparam -a               List all overlays/dtparams (marking
                         the active)
dtparam -h               Show this usage message
dtparam -h <param>...    Display help on the listed parameters
```

Options applicable to most variants:

```
-d <dir>        Specify an alternate location for the overlays
                (defaults to /boot/overlays or /flash/overlays)
-p <string>     Force a compatible string for the platform
-v              Verbose operation
```

161

The important thing is that you can use the -l option to discover what overlays are already loaded and hence avoid loading the same overlay again.

A function to check for the dht11 overlay and only load it if it isn't already loaded is easy enough with just some string handling and the use of the popen function:

```c
#include <stdio.h>
#include <stdlib.h>
#include <errno.h>
#include <unistd.h>
#include <string.h>
#include <fcntl.h>

FILE *doCommand(char *cmd)
{
    FILE *fp = popen(cmd, "r");
    if (fp == NULL)
    {
        printf("Failed to run command %s \n\r", cmd);
        exit(1);
    }
    return fp;
}
void checkDht11()
{
    FILE *fd = doCommand("sudo  dtparam -l");
    char output[1024];
    int txfound = 0;

    char indicator[] = "dht11  gpiopin=4";
    char command[] = "sudo dtoverlay dht11 gpiopin=4";
    while (fgets(output, sizeof(output), fd) != NULL)
    {
        printf("%s\n\r", output);
        fflush(stdout);
        if (strstr(output, indicator) != NULL)
        {
            txfound = 1;
        }
    }
    if (txfound == 0)
    {
        fd = doCommand(command);
    }

    pclose(fd);
}
```

```
int main(int argc, char **argv)
{
    char buffer[25];
    checkDht11();
    int fd = open(
               "/sys/bus/iio/devices/iio:device0/name", O_RDONLY);
    read(fd, buffer, 25);
    close(fd);
    printf("%s", buffer);

    fd = open(
      "/sys/bus/iio/devices/iio:device0/in_temp_input", O_RDONLY);
    read(fd, buffer, 25);
    close(fd);
    int temp;
    sscanf(buffer, "%d", &temp);

    printf("%f\n\r", temp / 1000.0);

    fd = open("/sys/bus/iio/devices/iio:device0/
                          in_humidityrelative_input", O_RDONLY);
    read(fd, buffer, 25);
    close(fd);
    int hum;
    sscanf(buffer, "%d", &hum);
    printf("%f\n\r", hum / 1000.0);
}
```

The indicator string is used to specify the string that is in the overlay listing when the driver is loaded and this isn't necessarily the same as the string in the command string, which is the command to install the driver with any parameters that are needed.

You can run this program without having to change the config.txt file. The driver remains loaded until the next reboot and is reinstalled when you next run the program. Notice that the program has to have root permissions to be able to run sudo, even if the program isn't being run as root.

Using Gpoi5 to Read DHT22

If is surprisingly easy to read the data from the DHT22 without the help of a driver using either the gpiod driver or Gpio5 to directly work with a GPIO line.

The serial protocol used by the DHT22 is also fairly simple:

1. The host pulls the line low for between 0.8ms and 29ms, usually 1ms.

2. It then releases the bus which is pulled high.

3. After between 20μs and 200μs, usually 30μs, the device starts to send data by pulling the line down for around 80μs and then lets it float high for another 80μs.

4. Next 40 bits of data are sent using a 70μs high for a 1μs and a 26μs high for a 0 with the high pluses separated by around 50μs low periods.

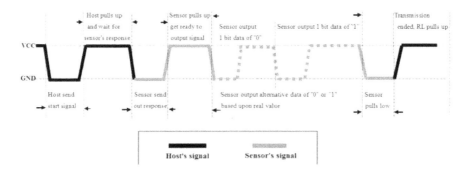

What we have to do is pull the line low for 1ms or so to start the device sending data and this is very easy. Then we have to wait for the device to pull the line down and let it pull up again for about 160μs and then read the time that the line is high 80 times. Some devices don't respond to a start pulse as short as 1ms. Increase its length if the device you are using seems not to work.

A 1 corresponds to 70μs and a 0 corresponds to 26μs. This is within the range of pulse measurement that can be achieved using standard library functions. There is also a 50μs low period between each data bit and this can be used to do some limited processing. Notice that we are only interested in the time that the line is held high.

When trying to work out how to decode a new protocol it often helps to try to answer the question, "how can I tell the difference between a 0 and a 1?"

If you have a logic analyzer it can help to look at the waveform and see how you work it out manually. In this case, despite the complex looking timing diagram, the difference comes down to a short versus a long pulse!

To get started all we do is to pull the line down for 1ms and see if the device responds with a stream of pulses. These can be seen on a logic analyzer or an oscilloscope, both are indispensable tools. If you don't have access to either tool then you will just have to skip to the next stage and see if you can read in some data.

The simplest code that will do the job is:

```
#include <stdio.h>
#include <stdlib.h>
#include "Gpio5.h"

int main()
{
    gpio_init(gpio);
    gpio_init(4);
    gpio_set_dir(4, GPIO_OUT);
    gpio_put(4, 1);
    sleep_ms(1);
    gpio_put(4, 0);
    sleep_ms(1);
    gpio_set_dir(4, GPIO_IN);
    return 0;
}
```

Setting the line initially high, to ensure that it is configured as an output, we then set it low, wait for around 1ms and then change its direction to input and so allow the line to be pulled high. Some DHT22 devices need a longer start pulse – try 20 ms if things don't work.

There is no need to set the line's pull-up mode because the Pi is the only device driving the line until it releases the line by changing direction to input. When a line is in input mode it is high impedance and this is why we need an external pull-up resistor in the circuit. See the discussion of open collector mode in Chapter 8.

As long as the circuit has been correctly assembled and you have a working device, you should see something like:

Reading the Data

With preliminary flight checks complete, it is time to read the 40-bit data stream. The first thing to do is wait for the low that the device sends before the start bit and then wait for the start bit:

```
for (int i = 0; i < 2; i++)
{
    while (gpio_get(4) == 1){};
    while (gpio_get(4) == 0){};
}
```

The for loop waits for two falling edges.

Next we can start to read in the data. A total of 40 bits, i.e. 5 bytes, is difficult to work with in standard variable types. A good compromise is to read in the first 32 bits into a 32-bit unsigned integer and then read the final byte into a byte variable. The reason is that the fifth byte is a checksum, so we have separated out the data and the checksum, but there are many different ways to organize this task.

First we read the 32 data bits:

```
uint32_t t2;
uint32_t data = 0;
uint32_t t1 = time_us_32();
for (int i = 0; i < 32; i++)
{
    while (gpio_get(4) == 1){};
    while (gpio_get(4) == 0){};
    t2 = time_us_32();
    data = data << 1;
    data = data | ((t2 - t1) > 100);
    t1 = t2;
}
```

You can see the general idea is to simply find the time between falling edges and then treat anything bigger than 100μs as a 1. In practice, the measured times between falling edges is 80μs for a 0 and 120μs and 100 is a threshold halfway between the two. The bits are shifted into the variable data so that the first byte transmitted is the high-order byte.

Next we need to read the checksum byte:

```
uint8_t checksum = 0;
for (int i = 0; i < 8; i++)
{
    while (gpio_get(4) == 1){};
    while (gpio_get(4) == 0){};
    t2 = time_us_32();
    checksum = checksum << 1;
    checksum = checksum | (t2 - t1) > 100;
    t1 = t2;
}
```

This works in the same way. At the end of this we have 32 data bits in data and eight checksum bits in checksum and all we have to do is process the data to get the temperature and humidity.

Extracting the Data

You can process the data without unpacking it into individual bytes, but it is easier to see what is happening if we do:

```
uint8_t byte1 = (data >> 24 & 0xFF);
uint8_t byte2 = (data >> 16 & 0xFF);
uint8_t byte3 = (data >> 8 & 0xFF);
uint8_t byte4 = (data & 0xFF);
```

The first two bytes are the humidity measurement and the second two the temperature.

The checksum is just the sum of the first four bytes reduced to eight bits and we can test it using:

```
printf("Checksum %X %X\n",checksum,(byte1+byte2+byte3+byte4)&0xFF);
```

If you don't want to unpack the data then you can use:

```
printf("Checksum %X %X\n", checksum, ((data & 0xFF) +
                (data >> 8 & 0xFF) + (data >> 16 & 0xFF) +
                                (data >> 24 & 0xFF)) & 0xFF);
```

If the two values are different, there has been a transmission error. The addition of the bytes is done as a full integer and then it is reduced back to a single byte by the AND operation. If there is a checksum error, the simplest thing to do is get another reading from the device. Notice, however, that you shouldn't read the device more than once every two seconds.

The humidity and temperature data are also easy to reconstruct as they are transmitted high byte first and 10 times the actual value.

Extracting the humidity data is easy:

```
float humidity = (float)((byte1 <<8)| byte2) / 10.0;
printf("Humidity= %f %%\n", humidity);
```

The temperature data is slightly more difficult in that the topmost bit is used to indicate a negative temperature. This means we have to test for the most significant bit and flip the sign of the temperature if it is set:

```
float temperature;
int neg = byte3 & 0x80;
byte3 = byte3 & 0x7F;
temperature = (float)(byte3 << 8 | byte4) / 10.0;
if (neg > 0)
    temperature = -temperature;
printf("Temperature= %f C\n", temperature);
```

This completes the data processing.

The program as presented works, but it would benefit from refactoring into functions. A complete, refactored, listing including a main program can be seen below. This is just one way to break the program down into functions and exactly how to do it depends on many factors.

```c
#include <stdio.h>
#include <stdlib.h>
#include "Gpio5.h"

static inline void WaitFallingEdge(int gpio)
{
    while (gpio_get(gpio) == 1)
    {
    };
    while (gpio_get(gpio) == 0)
    {
    };
}

uint32_t getData(int gpio)
{
    uint32_t t2;
    uint32_t data = 0;
    uint32_t t1 = time_us_32();
    for (int i = 0; i < 32; i++)
    {
        WaitFallingEdge(gpio);
        t2 = time_us_32();
        data = data << 1;
        data = data | ((t2 - t1) > 100);
        t1 = t2;
    }
    return data;
}

uint8_t getCheck(int gpio)
{
    uint8_t checksum = 0;
    uint32_t t2;
    uint32_t t1 = time_us_32();
    for (int i = 0; i < 8; i++)
    {
        WaitFallingEdge(gpio);
        t2 = time_us_32();
        checksum = checksum << 1;
        checksum = checksum | (t2 - t1) > 100;
        t1 = t2;
    }
    return checksum;
}
```

```c
void dhtInitalize(int gpio)
{
    gpio_init(gpio);
    gpio_set_dir(gpio, GPIO_OUT);
    gpio_put(gpio, 1);
    sleep_ms(1);
    gpio_put(gpio, 0);
    sleep_ms(1);
    gpio_set_dir(gpio, GPIO_IN);
    for (int i = 0; i < 2; i++)
    {
        WaitFallingEdge(gpio);
    }
}

typedef struct
{
    float temperature;
    float humidity;
    bool error;
} dhtData;

void dhtread(uint32_t gpio, dhtData *reading)
{
    dhtInitalize(gpio);
    uint32_t data = getData(gpio);
    uint8_t checksum = getCheck(gpio);
    uint8_t byte1 = (data >> 24 & 0xFF);
    uint8_t byte2 = (data >> 16 & 0xFF);
    uint8_t byte3 = (data >> 8 & 0xFF);
    uint8_t byte4 = (data & 0xFF);

    reading->error = (checksum !=
            ((byte1 + byte2 + byte3 + byte4) & 0xFF));
    reading->humidity = (float)((byte1 << 8) | byte2) / 10.0;
    int neg = byte3 & 0x80;
    byte3 = byte3 & 0x7F;
    reading->temperature = (float)(byte3 << 8 | byte4) / 10.0;
    if (neg > 0)
        reading->temperature = -reading->temperature;
}
int main()
{
    rp1_Init();
    printf("data\n");
    dhtData reading;
    dhtread(4, &reading);
    printf("Humidity= %f %\n", reading.humidity);
    printf("Temperature= %f C\n", reading.temperature);
    return 0;
}
```

Summary

- The Device Tree is the modern way to specify the hardware configuration of a machine and to load and configure drivers.

- The boot disk contains device trees for each of the different versions of the Pi and the loader selects the appropriate device tree for the Pi model that is booting.

- The loader merges the device tree with the overlays listed in the config.txt file to produce a customized final device tree used to boot the system.

- Overlays are fragments of the device tree which can be used to modify and add to the basic device tree.

- Overlays can themselves be customized by specifying parameters.

- When the loader parses the device tree and applies all the overlays you have specified, the final device tree is represented by the folders in /proc/device-tree.

- A fairly recent innovation is the ability to load and customize drivers after the system has booted using the dtoverlay and dtparam commands.

- You can easily write a program to load and configure missing drivers at runtime.

- Dynamic loading of overlays doesn't always work and unloading overlays, while possible, isn't a good idea.

- The DHT22 is a low-cost temperature and humidity sensor which provides an example of loading a driver to make use of it.

- It uses a custom single wire bus which is not compatible with the 1-Wire bus. Its asynchronous protocol is easy to implement directly in user space.

- An alternative to using a driver is to implement a direct measurement using a GPIO line and Gpio5.

Chapter 11

Pulse Width Modulation

One way around the problem of getting a fast response from a microcontroller is to move the problem away from the processor. In the case of the Pi there are some built-in devices, provided by the RP1 chip, that can use GPIO lines to implement protocols without the CPU being involved. In this chapter we take a close look at pulse width modulation (PWM) including generating sound and driving LEDs.

When performing their most basic function, i.e. output, the GPIO lines can be set high or low by the processor. How quickly they can be set high or low depends on the speed of the processor.

Using the GPIO line in its Pulse Width Modulation (PWM) mode you can generate pulse trains up to 25MHz, i.e. pulses just a little more than 40ns. The reason for the increase in speed, a factor of at least 100, is that the GPIO is connected to a pulse generator and, once set to generate pulses of a specific type, the pulse generator just gets on with it without needing any intervention from the GPIO line or the processor. In fact, the pulse output can continue after your program has ended if you forget to reset it.

Of course, even though the PWM line can generate pulses as short as a few nanoseconds it can only change the pulses it produces each time that the processor can modify them. For example, you can't use PWM to produce a single 16ns pulse because you can't disable the PWM generator in just $0.1\mu s$.

Some Basic Pi PWM Facts

There are some facts worth getting clear right from the start, although their full significance will only become clear as we progress.

First, what is PWM? The simple answer is that a Pulse Width Modulated signal has pulses that repeat at a fixed rate, say, one pulse every millisecond, but the width of the pulse can be changed.

There are two basic things to specify about the pulse train that is generated, its repetition rate and the width of each pulse. Usually the repetition rate is set as a simple repeat period and the width of each pulse is specified as a percentage of the repeat period, referred to as the duty cycle. So, for example, a 1ms repeat and a 50% duty cycle specifies a 1ms period, which is high for 50% of the time, i.e. a pulse width of 0.5ms.

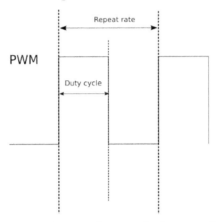

The two extremes are 100% duty cycle, i.e. the line is always high, and 0% duty cycle, i.e. the line is always low. The duty cycle is simply the proportion of time the line is set high. Notice it is the duty cycle that carries the information in PWM and not the frequency. What this means is that, generally, you select a repeat rate and stick to it and what you change as the program runs is the duty cycle.

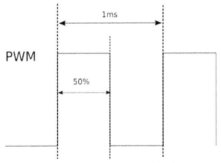

There are many ways to specify a PWM signal – frequency and duty cycle, time high and time low and so on. It is easy to convert between these different representations.

As you can guess, there are no PWM inputs, just output. If for some reason you need to decode, or respond to, a PWM input then you need to program it using the GPIO input lines and the pulse measuring techniques introduced in previous chapters.

Software PWM

The alternative to dedicated PWM hardware is to implement it in software. You can quite easily work out how to do this. All you need is to set a timing loop to set the line high at the repetition rate and then set it low again according to the duty cycle. You can easily implement software PWM using the GPIO character driver:

```c
#include <gpiod.h>
#include <stdio.h>
#include <unistd.h>
#include <stdlib.h>
#include <time.h>

void pwm(struct gpiod_line *line, int);

int main(int argc, char **argv)
{
    int period = 20;
    int duty = 25;
    int res;
    struct gpiod_chip *chip = gpiod_chip_open_by_number(0);
    struct gpiod_line *line4 = gpiod_chip_get_line(chip, 4);
    res = gpiod_line_request_output(line4, "test output", 0);

    struct timespec ontime = {0, 0};
    struct timespec offtime = {0, 0};
    ontime.tv_nsec = period * duty * 10 * 1000;
    offtime.tv_nsec = (period - period * duty / 100) * 1000 * 1000;

    for (;;)
    {
        res = gpiod_line_set_value(line4, 1);
        nanosleep(&ontime, NULL);
        res = gpiod_line_set_value(line4, 0);
        nanosleep(&offtime, NULL);
    };
}
```

The basic idea is to take the period in ms and the duty cycle as a percentage and work out the on and off time.

A more advanced version of the same program makes use of a thread to implement the toggling of the PWM line.

To understand how this works you need to be happy with threads and you have to compile with the pthreads library:

```c
#include <gpiod.h>
#include <stdio.h>
#include <unistd.h>
#include <stdlib.h>
#include <time.h>
#include <pthread.h>

struct pwmargs
{
    struct gpiod_line *line;
    int ontime;
    int offtime;
};

void *pwmrun(void *arg)
{
    struct pwmargs *pwmdata = (struct pwmargs *)arg;
    volatile int i;
    int res;
    for (;;)
    {
        res = gpiod_line_set_value(pwmdata->line, 1);
        for (i = 0; i < pwmdata->ontime; i++)
        {
        };
        res = gpiod_line_set_value(pwmdata->line, 0);
        for (i = 0; i < pwmdata->offtime; i++)
        {
        };
    };
}
```

```
static struct pwmargs pwmdata;
int main(int argc, char **argv)
{

  int period = 10;
  int duty = 25;
  int scale = 385;
  pwmdata.ontime = (period * duty / 100) * scale;
  pwmdata.offtime = (period - period * duty / 100) * scale;
  int res;
  struct gpiod_chip *chip = gpiod_chip_open_by_number(0);
  pwmdata.line = gpiod_chip_get_line(chip, 4);
  res = gpiod_line_request_output(pwmdata.line, "test output", 0);

    pthread_t pwmThread;
    if (pthread_create(&pwmThread, NULL, pwmrun, (void *)&pwmdata))
    {
        fprintf(stderr, "Error creating thread\n");
        return 1;
    }
    for (;;)
    {
    };
}
```

This will generate the PWM signal on the specified gpio line independent of the main program. If you want to use this in production you would need to add error handling and some functions to pause and stop the thread.

The thread-based method is much faster than the non-thread-based alternative simply because we don't have to rely on nanosleep for the delays. We can use a blocking loop for timing because it is in a thread that doesn't stop the main program running. Using nanosleep the accuracy falls until it becomes unusable at around 2kHz. The interrupt approach works well to more than 20kHz although the duty cycle is biased low and would need adjustment if accuracy was important.

As well as using gpiod you can also use Gpio5 and work directly with the hardware:

```
#include <gpiod.h>
#include <stdio.h>
#include <unistd.h>
#include <stdlib.h>
#include <time.h>
#include <pthread.h>
#include "Gpio5.h"

struct pwmargs
{
    int ontime;
    int offtime;
};
void *pwmrun(void *arg)
{
    struct pwmargs *pwmdata = (struct pwmargs *)arg;
    volatile int i;
    for (;;)
    {
        gpio_put(4, true);
        for(i=0;i<pwmdata->ontime;i++){};
        gpio_put(4, false);
        for(i=0;i<pwmdata->offtime;i++){};
    };
}

static struct pwmargs pwmdata;
int main(int argc, char **argv)
{
    int period = 50;
    int duty = 25;
    int scale=435;
    pwmdata.ontime=(period*duty*scale)/100;
    pwmdata.offtime=(period*scale*100 - period * duty*scale )/ 100;
    rp1_Init();
    gpio_init(4);
    gpio_set_dir(4, true);
    pthread_t pwmThread;
    if (pthread_create(&pwmThread, NULL, pwmrun, (void *)&pwmdata))
    {
        fprintf(stderr, "Error creating thread\n");
        return 1;
    }
    while(true){};
    return 0;
}
```

This has performance comparable to the gpiod driver approach. This is surprising as direct register access should be faster.

The PWM Driver

The Linux driver approach to PWM has the advantage of some machine independence, but it doesn't make full use of the PWM hardware available. The CM5 has four PWM channels, but only two can be used via the driver.

The two PWM hardware modules can be configured to drive different GPIO lines. The standard configuration is to have PWM0 drive either GPIO18 or GPIO12 and PWM1 drive either GPIO13 or GPIO19.

There are two PWM drivers available. One that activates a single PWM channel and one that activates both the available channels. The documentation for both is:

```
Name:    pwm
Info:    Configures a single PWM channel
         Legal pin,function combinations for each channel:
           PWM0: 12,4(Alt0) 18,2(Alt5) 40,4(Alt0)          52,5(Alt1)
           PWM1: 13,4(Alt0) 19,2(Alt5) 41,4(Alt0) 45,4(Alt0) 53,5(Alt1)
         N.B.:
           1) Pin 18 is the only one available on all platforms, and
              it is the one used by the I2S audio interface.
              Pins 12 and 13 might be better choices on an A+, B+ or Pi2.
           2) The onboard analogue audio output uses both PWM channels.
           3) So be careful mixing audio and PWM.
           4) Currently the clock must have been enabled and configured
              by other means.
Load:    dtoverlay=pwm,<param>=<val>
Params:  pin                     Output pin (default 18) - see table
         func                    Pin function (default 2 = Alt5) - see above
         clock                   PWM clock frequency (informational)



Name:    pwm-2chan
Info:    Configures both PWM channels
         Legal pin,function combinations for each channel:
           PWM0: 12,4(Alt0) 18,2(Alt5) 40,4(Alt0)          52,5(Alt1)
           PWM1: 13,4(Alt0) 19,2(Alt5) 41,4(Alt0) 45,4(Alt0) 53,5(Alt1)
         N.B.:
           1) Pin 18 is the only one available on all platforms, and
              it is the one used by the I2S audio interface.
              Pins 12 and 13 might be better choices on an A+, B+ or Pi2.
           2) The onboard analogue audio output uses both PWM channels.
           3) So be careful mixing audio and PWM.
           4) Currently the clock must have been enabled and configured
              by other means.
Load:    dtoverlay=pwm-2chan,<param>=<val>
Params:  pin                     Output pin (default 18) - see table
         pin2                    Output pin for other channel (default 19)
         func                    Pin function (default 2 = Alt5) - see above
         func2                   Function for pin2 (default 2 = Alt5)
         clock                   PWM clock frequency (informational)
```

Notice that you cannot currently use the driver to set the frequency of the PWM clock, but this is automatically enabled at a default frequency. You can find what the frequency is using:

`vcgencmd measure_clock pwm`

at the command prompt. It only reports an accurate value if the PWM driver is loaded and enabled.

If you load either driver by adding:

`dtoverlay=pwm`

or:

`dtoverlay=pwm-2chan`

to `boot/config.txt`, you will discover that on reboot you have a new `pwmchip2` folder in the `/sys/class/pwm` folder.

The CM5 has four PWM channels `pwm0` to `pwm3`. You can use either the `pwm` or the `pwm-2chan` overlay and the channels are selected by the number that you write to `export`. The GPIO lines and function modes associated with each channel are:

`pwm0` GPIO12 Mode 4
`pwm1` GPIO13 Mode 4
`pwm2` GPIO18 Mode 2
`pwm3` GPIO19 Mode 2

Notice that on a CM5 the indicated modes are the legacy GPIO modes used in other versions of the Pi, not the GPIO functions specified for the CM5. There are alternative choices that can be used for the GPIO lines, as listed above.

The driver is configured to see the PWM hardware as a single PWM "chip". To work with either PWM channel you have to export it. In this context exporting means that you claim sole use of the channel. To do this you have to write "0" or "1" to the `export` file in the `pwmchip0` folder. To unexport you do the same to the `unexport` file in the `pwmchip0` folder.

After you have exported the channel you will see new folders, `pwm0` and `pwm1` in the `pwmchip0` folder. Of course you only see the folders you have exported and you can only export `pwm0`, i.e. a single channel, if you have used the `PWM` driver.

Within the `pwmx` folder you will find the following important files:

- `period`   Period in nanoseconds
- `duty_cycle` Duty cycle in nanoseconds
- `enable`   Write "1" to enable, "0" to disable

So all you have to do is:

1. Export the channel by writing its number to `export`.
2. Write to `period`
3. Write to `duty_cycle`
4. Write "1" to `enable`

Notice that as this is hardware PWM, once you have set and enabled the channel, the PWM generation continues after the program ends.

For example, to use GPIO12 and GPIO13 you would use:

```c
#include <stdio.h>
#include <stdlib.h>
#include <errno.h>
#include <unistd.h>
#include <fcntl.h>
#include <string.h>
#include <fcntl.h>
FILE *doCommand(char *cmd)
{
    FILE *fp = popen(cmd, "r");
    if (fp == NULL)
    {
        printf("Failed to run command %s \n\r", cmd);
        exit(1);
    }
    return fp;
}
void checkPWM()
{
    FILE *fd = doCommand("sudo  dtparam -l");
    char output[1024];
    int txfound = 0;

    char indicator[] = "pwm";
    char command[] = "sudo dtoverlay pwm-2chan,
                            pin=13 func=4 pin2=12 func2=4";
    while (fgets(output, sizeof(output), fd) != NULL)
    {
        printf("%s\n\r", output);
        fflush(stdout);
        if (strstr(output, indicator) != NULL)
        {
            txfound = 1;
            printf("Overlay already loaded\n\r");
        }
    }
    if (txfound == 0)
    {
        fd = doCommand(command);
        sleep(2);
    }
    pclose(fd);
}
```

```
int main(int argc, char **argv)
{
    checkPWM();
    int fd = open("/sys/class/pwm/pwmchip2/export", O_WRONLY);
    write(fd, "0", 1);
    close(fd);
    sleep(3);
    fd = open("/sys/class/pwm/pwmchip2/pwm0/period", O_WRONLY);
    write(fd, "10000000", 8);
    close(fd);
    fd = open("/sys/class/pwm/pwmchip2/pwm0/duty_cycle", O_WRONLY);
    write(fd, "8000000", 7);
    close(fd);
    fd = open("/sys/class/pwm/pwmchip2/pwm0/enable", O_WRONLY);
    write(fd, "1", 1);
    close(fd);
    fd = open("/sys/class/pwm/pwmchip2/export", O_WRONLY);
    write(fd, "1", 1);
    close(fd);
    sleep(3);
    fd = open("/sys/class/pwm/pwmchip2/pwm1/period", O_WRONLY);
    write(fd, "10000000", 8);
    close(fd);
    fd = open("/sys/class/pwm/pwmchip2/pwm1/duty_cycle", O_WRONLY);
    write(fd, "5000000", 7);
    close(fd);
    fd = open("/sys/class/pwm/pwmchip2/pwm1/enable", O_WRONLY);
    write(fd, "1", 1);
    close(fd);
}
```

Notice that the two blocks of file commands differ only by the use of "0" and "1" for pwm0 and pwm1 respectively. Notice that the channels that you select use the GPIO lines indicated earlier.

As long as the overlay isn't already loaded, this will generate a PWM signal on GPIO12 and GPIO13. Otherwise nothing will happen. You can remove the overlay, before running the program, using:

```
sudo dtoverlay -R pwm-2chan
```

either at the command line or as part of the program.

The checkPWM function dynamically loads the pwm-2chan driver – you can change it to pwm if you only need one channel. It exports the channel and then sets the period to 100Hz with an 80% duty cycle. A delay of 1 second is included after the export to allow the system to create the folders and files. A better solution is to test for an error on the first open and keep looping until it works. This program doesn't need root permissions to run, only to dynamically install the driver. You can use the other channel in the same way.

It seems relatively safe to dynamically remove the pwm and pwm-2wchan overlays.

Simple PWM Functions

The big problem in using the PWM driver is in avoiding opening and closing files, which is a slow operation. A better idea is to implement a function that can work with the driver without closing the frequency and duty cycle files until they are no longer needed.

The only complication is the amount of string handling you need to use to make sure that the paths to the directories are correct:

```c
#include <stdio.h>
#include <stdlib.h>
#include <errno.h>
#include <unistd.h>
#include <fcntl.h>
#include <string.h>

FILE *doCommand(char *cmd)
{
    FILE *fp = popen(cmd, "r");
    if (fp == NULL)
    {
        printf("Failed to run command %s \n\r", cmd);
        exit(1);
    }
    return fp;
}
void checkPWM()
{
    FILE *fd = doCommand("sudo  dtparam -l");
    char output[1024];
    int txfound = 0;

    char indicator[] = "pwm-2chan";
    char command[] = "sudo dtoverlay pwm-2chan pin=12
                                func=4 pin2=13 func2=4";
    while (fgets(output, sizeof(output), fd) != NULL)
    {
        printf("%s\n\r", output);
        fflush(stdout);
        if (strstr(output, indicator) != NULL)
        {
            txfound = 1;
        }
    }
    if (txfound == 0)
    {
        pclose(fd);
        fd = doCommand(command);
    }
    pclose(fd);
}
```

```
enum pwm
{
    OpenChan,
    SetFreq,
    SetDuty,
    EnableChan,
    DisableChan,
    CloseChan
};

int pwmAction(enum pwm action, int chan, int param)
{
    static int fdf[2];
    static int fdd[2];
    int fd;
    char buf[150];
    char schan[6];
    if (chan != 0 && chan != 1)
        return -1;
    char path[] = "/sys/class/pwm/pwmchip2/";
    char chanNum[2];
    snprintf(schan, 6, "%s%d","pwm",chan);
    snprintf(chanNum,2,"%d",chan);
    int L;
    switch (action)
    {
    case OpenChan:
        checkPWM();
        snprintf(buf, 150, "%s%s", path, "export");
        fd = open(buf, O_WRONLY);
        write(fd,chanNum , 1);
        close(fd);
        sleep(2);
        snprintf(buf, 150, "%s%s%s", path, schan, "/period");
        fdf[chan] = open(buf, O_WRONLY);
        snprintf(buf, 150, "%s%s%s", path, schan, "/duty_cycle");
        fdd[chan] = open(buf, O_WRONLY);
        break;
    case SetFreq:
        L = snprintf(buf, 150, "%d", param);
        write(fdf[chan], buf, L);
        break;
    case SetDuty:
        L = snprintf(buf, 150, "%d", param);
        write(fdd[chan], buf, L);
        break;
    case EnableChan:
        snprintf(buf, 150, "%s%s%s", path, schan, "/enable");
        fd = open(buf, O_WRONLY);
        write(fd, "1", 1);
        close(fd);
        break;
```

```
            case DisableChan:
                snprintf(buf, 150, "%s%s%s", path, schan, "/enable");
                fd = open(buf, O_WRONLY);
                write(fd, "0", 1);
                close(fd);
                break;
            case CloseChan:
                close(fdf[chan]);
                close(fdd[chan]);
                snprintf(buf, 150, "%s%s%s", path, "/unexport");
                printf("%s\n",buf);
                fd = open(buf, O_WRONLY);
                write(fd, chanNum, 1);
                close(fd);
                break;
        }
        return 0;
}
```

The pwmAction function accepts an initial command parameter which controls what it does. The command can be one of:

```
enum pwm
{
    OpenChan,
    SetFreq,
    SetDuty,
    EnableChan,
    DisableChan,
    CloseChan
};
```

If you open a channel then the frequency and duty cycle files are opened and the file descriptors saved for the other commands to use. After opening a channel you can set the frequency and the duty cycle and then enable the channel. Using the function is easy, you simply supply the action as the first parameter, the channel 0 or 1 as the second, and the third is either the frequency or the duty cycle or is ignored.

For example:

```
int main(int argc, char **argv)
{
    pwmAction(OpenChan, 1, 0);
    pwmAction(SetFreq, 1, 10000000);
    pwmAction(SetDuty, 1, 8000000);
    pwmAction(EnableChan, 1, 0);

    pwmAction(OpenChan, 0, 0);
    pwmAction(SetFreq, 0, 10000000);
    pwmAction(SetDuty, 0, 2000000);
    pwmAction(EnableChan, 0, 0);
}
```

Using PWM Hardware – Extending Gpio5

The Linux drivers are easy enough to use, but they don't allow you to use all four channels, to set the clock frequency or to use any of the additional modes that the hardware supports. An attractive alternative is to access the PWM hardware directly via an extension to the Gpio5 library which takes it beyond just controlling the GPIO lines directly.

The CM5 has four PWM channels which correspond to GPIO lines:

```
      function 0   function 3
PWM 0  GPIO12
PWM 1  GPIO13
PWM 2  GPIO14        GPIO18
PWM 3  GPIO15        GPIO19
```

It is easier to use GPIO12 to GPIO15 as they can be enabled using the same function code.

All GPIO lines set to PWM expect the PAD to be correctly configured by additional code.

PWM Modes

The CM5's PWM hardware is more sophisticated than other hardware you might have encountered before. The first big difference is that it can work in a number of modes that generate different types of signal.

The basic PWM signal is generated using a 32-bit counter that rolls over at Range, the range boundary, or at zero depending on whether it is counting up or down. The value of Duty determines when the signal is high.

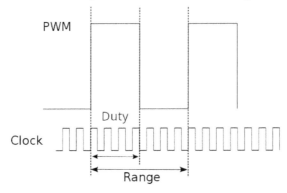

trailing-edge mode the counter starts at zero and counts up to range before rolling over. The output is a one when the count is less than the value of Duty and a zero when it is greater.

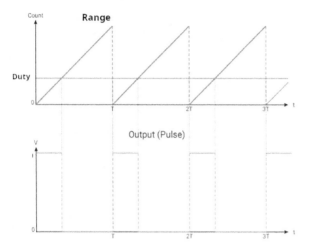

In leading-edge mode the count starts at Range and counts down to zero before rolling over. The output is a one when count is less than Duty. This produces a signal 180 degrees out of phase with trailing-edge mode.

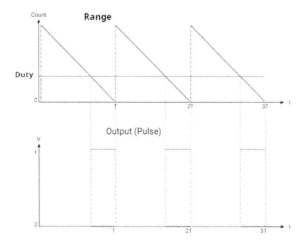

In double-edge mode the count starts at Range and counts down to zero and then starts to count up to Range before repeating. The output is high when the count is less than Duty. This produces a "phase-corrected" signal with the pulse at the center of the time slot:

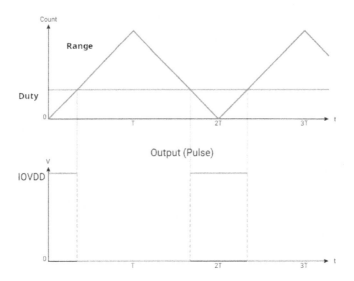

Pulse Density Mode

Simple PWM isn't so good for some power control tasks because the frequency is often low. This makes the filtering problem and hence creating a smooth output voltage, more difficult. For example, suppose you want a 1kHz pulse train with a 50% duty cycle to deliver half power or voltage to a device. The mark/space way of doing this switches the GPIO line on for 500μs and off for 500μs. The fluctuations in voltage are very slow and this causes problems for the driven device.

A better way would be to spread the high time across all of the clock cycles. For example, if the clock is 1μs then instead of setting the line high for the first 500 clock pulses and then low for the final 500 clock pulses it might be better to distribute 500 high clock pulses throughout the 1000 clock pulses:

blocks and spread the on and off times throughout the block to give the overall desired duty cycle. In this case the device would be high for 1μs and low for 1μs and the filtering problems would be much easier to solve.

You can see this for a lower clock rate in the diagram below. The top figure shows a standard PWM 50% duty cycle and the bottom image shows the same duty cycle spread across the entire repeat period:

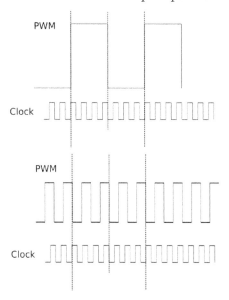

The algorithm for achieving the distribution of the "high" time across the full range period is given in the ARM manual as:

```
context = 0;
for(i=0;i<range;i++) {
        context = context + data;
        if(context >= range){
                context = context - range;
                set line high
        }else{
                set line low
}
```

Suppose Range is 8 and Duty is 4, giving a 50% duty cycle, then the algorithm generates:

```
clock            1 2 3 4 5 6 7 8
context          4 8 4 8 4 8 4 8
line             0 1 0 1 0 1 0 1
mark/space mode  1 1 1 1 0 0 0 0
```

Notice that each output pulse is the same width as the clock time rather than the time to count up to Range.

Pulse Position Mode

In pulse position mode the counter runs from 0 to Range and the output is only high when the count equals Duty. In this case the output is a single pulse, the width of the clock, at a position determined by Duty. That is, changing Duty changes where the pulse occurs.

There are also two serializer modes which allow you to output an arbitrary pulse train. Both modes make use of the duty register as a shift register and the output is composed of either the most significant, Serializer_MSB, or least significant, Serializer_LSB. bit in the shift register.

To summarize:

- There are three "proper" PWM modes – leading-edge, trailing-edge and double-edge mode which only differ in the phase of the signal they generate.

- The value of Range and the clock frequency set the PWM frequency.

- In the proper PWM modes, duty sets the time that the output is high for each PWM cycle.

- The pulse density and pulse position modes generate pulses that are the width of the clock pulse and vary in density or position based on the value of Duty.

- The serializer modes let you send a 32-bit bit stream stored in Duty as the output of the PWM.

In addition to these modes, the PWM channels can be configured to share a common range and duty register. There is also a shared 32-bit FIFO register, a "first-in, first out" queue with storage for 128 32-bit values that can be used to set the duty of enabled channels.

Notice that all four of the PWM channels are fed by a single clock which can be set to a frequency via a programmable divider. The only way that the PWM channels can produce different frequencies is by having different values of range.

Clocks and Duty Cycle Resolution

If you just take the PWM driver at face value then you might believe that you can set any frequency and any duty cycle – this is not the case. Due to hardware limitations, the resolution of the duty cycle depends on the PWM clock frequency and this also governs the highest frequency PWM signal you can create. 25MHz

The PWM clock is set to 50MHz and the PWM signal can only change once per clock pulse. What this means is that the highest frequency that you can use is 25MHz with a 50% duty cycle:

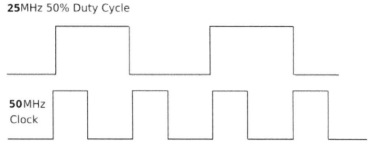

What happens is that two clock pulses are needed to change the state of the line twice – once high and once low. This corresponds to range=1 and duty=1. You can also see that 50% is the only possible duty cycle apart from 0% and 100%.

The number of different duty cycles you can achieve depends on the number of clock pulses in the total PWM period.

You can easily work out the number of duty cycles available at any given frequency:

PWM Frequency	Number of clock pulses	Number of different duty cycles	Resolution in bits
25MHz	2	3	1.6
12.5MHz	4	5	2.3
6.25MHz	8	9	3.2
3.125MHz	16	17	4.1
781kHz	32	33	5.0
390kHz	64	65	6.0
195kHz	128	129	7.0
nkHz	50000/n	50000/n + 1	$\log_2(50000/n + 1)$

In many applications 8-bit resolution for the duty cycle is considered the minimum acceptable and this sets the highest frequency to about 195kHz, which is high enough for most things. For example, if you want to control a servo motor, see later, then you need a PWM signal with a frequency of 50Hz and at this frequency you can specify the duty cycle down to about 25 bits or around 40 million increments, more than enough for any real servo motor.

The PWM Registers

The PWM registers start at 0x40098000, which gives them an offset of 0x9800. Each PWM channel has two fundamental registers, RANGE and DUTY.

The first register in the set is GLOBAL_CTRL in which the first four bits enable the corresponding PWM channel and the topmost bit triggers the setting of new values in the PWM hardware from the registers.

Bits	Name	Access	Reset
31	SET_UPDATE	SC	0x0
30:4	Reserved		
3	CHAN3_EN	RW	0x0
2	CHAN2_EN	RW	0x0
1	CHAN1_EN	RW	0x0
0	CHAN0_EN	RW	0x0

That is, if you write 0x1 to the GLOBAL_CTRL register then PWM0 is enabled. You can then set its control registers, but these have no effect until you write 080000000 to the GLOBAL_CTRL register to set bit 31, SET_UPDATE, when all of the new parameters are transferred to the PWM hardware. This ensures that all of the PWM settings are changed on the same clock pulse.

After this come the FIFO control register for modes that use the FIFO:

0x04	FIFO_CTRL
0x08	COMMON_RANGE
0x0c	COMMON_DUTY
0x10	DUTY_FIFO

The FIFO_CTRL configures the FIFO register at DUTY_FIFO. The COMMON_RANGE and COMMON_DUTY registers set the range and duty for channels that are set to channel binding.

From here we have a control, range, phase and duty register for each of the channels. This can be converted into a C array of structs:

```
typedef struct
{
    uint32_t Ctrl;
    uint32_t Range;
    uint32_t Phase;
    uint32_t Duty;
} PWMregs;
#define PWM ((PWMregs *)(PWMBase + 0x14 / 4))
```

The only register that hasn't been discussed is the phase register. This can be used to initialize the counter so as to cause an offset between the different channels i.e. a phase shift.

The channel control registers have a simple structure:

Bits	Name	Access	Reset
31:16	SDM_BIAS	RW	0x0000
15:12	SDM_BITWIDTH	RW	0x0
11:9	Reserved		
8	FIFO_POP_MASK	RW	0x1
7	SDM_DITHER	RW	0x0
6	SDM	RW	0x0
5	USEFIFO	RW	0x0
4	BIND	RW	0x0
3	INVERT	RW	0x0
2:0	MODE	RW	0x0

The fields starting SDM control a Sigma Delta filter so that the PWM output can be used to create analog signals, something that is beyond the scope of this book. The fields with FIFO in their name control the way that the first-in, first out buffer is used in generating custom bit sequences. For the standard PWM modes of operation, the fields that are useful are in the first five bits. Bit 4 can be set to 1 to force the channel to use the global RANGE and DUTY registers – note that each channel still controls its own phase. Bit 3 can be set to invert the output and the low three bits set the PWM mode as described earlier.

You can see the correspondence between the bit values and the modes along with an enum to make it easier to use in the following table:

	Action	enum pwm_mode_rp1
0x0	Generates 0	`Zero`
0x1	Trailing-edge mark-space PWM modulation	`TrailingEdge`
0x2	Phase-correct mark-space PWM modulation	`PhaseCorrect`
0x3	Pulse-density encoded output	`PDE`
0x4	MSB Serializer output	`MSBSerial`
0x5	Pulse position modulated output	`PPM`
0x6	Leading-edge mark-space PWM modulation	`LeadingEdge`
0x7	LSB Serialiser output	`LSBSerial`

There are also some registers at higher locations concerned with PWM interrupts.

PWM Clock Registers

As well as working with the PWM registers, we also have to set the PWM clock. The problem is that the details of the registers are not well documented so we need to resort to reverse engineering. The PWM clock has four registers:

```
typedef struct
{
    uint32_t PWM0_CTRL;
    uint32_t PWM0_DIV_INT;
    uint32_t PWM0_DIV_FRAC;
    uint32_t PWM0_SEL;
} pwmclockregs;
#define PWMCLK ((pwmclockregs *)ClockBase)
```

The CTRL and SEL registers are used to setup the clock and the DIV_INT and DIV_FRAC registers set the integer and fractional part of the clock division factors.

The PWM clock registers are at:

```
#define PWMCLK ((pwmclockregs *)(ClockBase+0x74/4))
```

To set the PWM clock we need to add two functions to Gpio5:

```
void pwm_init_clock(void)
{
    PWMCLK->PWM0_CTRL = 0x11000840;
    PWMCLK->PWM0_SEL = 1;
}
```

and:

```
void pwm_set_clock(uint32_t div,uint32_t frac)
{
    PWMCLK->PWM0_DIV_INT = div;
    PWMCLK->PWM0_DIV_FRAC = frac;
}
```

The init_clock function is called to configure the PWM clock and the set_clock function is called to set the frequency divider to get the frequency you actually want.

Working with PWM

Extending Gpio5 to work with PWM is fairly easy but there is no point in trying to follow the Pico SDK as its PWM hardware is very different from the CM5.

Now we have the functions to set the clock running we can set the GPIO lines we want to use into PWM mode:

```
int pwm_setup(uint32_t gpio, enum pwm_mode_rp1 mode)
{
    int pwm = getPWM(gpio);
    if (pwm < 0)
        return -1;
    pwm_init_clock();
    if (gpio == 18 | gpio == 19){
        gpio_set_function(gpio, GPIO_FUNC_PWM2);
    }
    else{
        gpio_set_function(gpio, GPIO_FUNC_PWM1);
    }
    PWM[pwm].Ctrl = mode;
    pwm_disable(gpio);
}
enum pwm_mode_rp1
{
    Zero = 0x0,
    TrailingEdge = 0x1,
    PhaseCorrect = 0x2,
    PDE = 0x3,
    MSBSerial = 0x4,
    PPM = 0x5,
    LeadingEdge = 0x6,
    LSBSerial = 0x7
};
```

This allows you to setup a GPIO line to use PWM, but of course not all GPIO lines support PWM and the ones that do use particular pwm channels. The getPWM function returns the channel used or -1 if the GPIO line isn't PWM compatible:

```
int getPWM(uint32_t gpio)
{
    switch (gpio)
    {
    case 12:
        return 0;
    case 13:
        return 1;
    case 14:
        return 2;
    case 15:
        return 3;
    case 18:
        return 2;
    case 19:
        return 3;
    }
    return -1;
}
```

Notice that this returns the correct PWM channels for GPIO18 and GPIO19 and the setup function uses the correct GPIO mode for this selection.

The PWM line is set to a disabled state so that it can have its range, duty and phase set before being enabled:

```
int pwm_enable(uint32_t gpio)
{
    int pwm = getPWM(gpio);
    if (pwm < 0)
        return -1;
    uint32_t temp = 1 << pwm;
    *PWMBase = *PWMBase | temp | 0x80000000;
}
int pwm_disable(uint32_t gpio)
{
    int pwm = getPWM(gpio);
    if (pwm < 0)
        return -1;
    uint32_t temp = 1 << pwm;
    temp = ~temp & 0xf;
    *PWMBase = (*PWMBase & temp) | 0x80000000;
}
```

Notice that no check is made to see if the PWM line has been configured. A check is made that the GPIO line is a valid PWM line. After this the GLOBAL_CTRL register is used to enable the PWM channel and set the top most bit to commit the change. Notice that this update is done so as not to change any other settings in the register.

Now all we need is a function that sets the range, duty and phase:

```
int pwm_set_range_duty_phase(int32_t gpio, uint32_t range,
                                     uint32_t duty, uint32_t phase)
{
    int pwm = getPWM(gpio);
    if (pwm < 0)
        return -1;
    PWM[pwm].Range = range;
    PWM[pwm].Duty = duty;
    PWM[pwm].Phase = phase;
    *PWMBase = *PWMBase | 0x80000000;
}
```

Notice that the high bit of the GLOBAL_CTRL register is set to commit the changes. Only the phase register actually needs this as the DUTY and RANGE registers update automatically at the end of the PWM cycle.

The set_range_duty_phase function works, but in many cases we would like to set a frequency and a duty cycle as a percentage:

```
int pwm_set_frequency_duty(int32_t gpio, int32_t freq,
                                     int dutyPercent)
{
    int32_t div = PWMCLK->PWM0_DIV_INT;
    int32_t frac = PWMCLK->PWM0_DIV_FRAC;
    int32_t pwmf = PWMClock / div;
    int32_t range = pwmf / freq-1;
    int32_t duty = range * dutyPercent / 1000+1;
    pwm_set_range_duty_phase(gpio, range, duty, 0);
}
```

The duty cycle is specified as a percentage*10 to allow it to specify a decimal part. For example setting duty to 25 sets the duty cycle to 2.5%

Notice that this function assumes that you have set the correct clock rate to give a good duty cycle resolution.

Controlling an LED

You can use PWM to generate physical quantities such as the brightness of an LED or the rotation rate of a DC motor. The only differences required by these applications are to do with the voltage and current you need and the way the duty cycle relates to whatever the physical effect is. In other words, if you want to change some effect by 50%, how much do you need to change the duty cycle?

For example, how do we "dim" an LED?

By changing the duty cycle of the PWM pulse train you can set the amount of power delivered to an LED, or any other device, and hence change its brightness. In the case of an LED, the connection between duty cycle and brightness is a complicated matter, but the simplest approach uses the fact that the perceived brightness is roughly proportional to the cube of the input power. The exact relationship is more complicated, but this is good enough for most applications.

As the power supplied to the LED is proportional to the duty cycle we have:

$$b = kd^3$$

where b is the perceived brightness and d is the duty cycle. The constant k depends on the LED.

Notice that, as the LED when powered by a PWM signal is either full on or full off, there is no effect of the change in LED light output with current - the LED is always run at the same current.

What all of this means is that if you want an LED to fade in a linear fashion you need to change the duty cycle in a non-linear fashion. Intuitively it means that changes when the duty cycle is small produce bigger changes in brightness than when the duty cycle is large.

For a simple example, let's connect a standard LED to the PWM line and then use the BJT driver circuit introduced in Chapter 5.

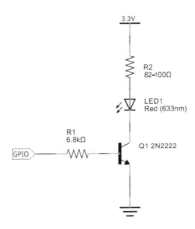

Assuming that you have this circuit constructed, then a simple PWM program to modify its brightness from low to high and back to low in a loop is:

```c
int main(int argc, char **argv)
{
    pwmAction(OpenChan, 0, 0);
    int t = 1000000;
    pwmAction(SetFreq, 0, t);
    int d = 0;
    pwmAction(SetDuty, 0, d);
    pwmAction(EnableChan, 0, 0);

    struct timespec delay = {0, 50000 * 1000};

    int inc = 100000;
    for (;;)
    {
        pwmAction(SetDuty, 0, d);
        d = d + inc;
        if (d > t)
        {
            d = t;
            inc = -inc;
        }

        if (d <= 0)
        {
            d = 0;
            inc = -inc;
        }
        nanosleep(&delay, NULL);
    }
}
```

Note: This program is to be used with the pwmAction function given earlier. The basic idea is to set up a pulse train with a period of 1ms. Next, in the for loop, the duty cycle is set to 0% to 100% and then back down to 0%. If you watch the flashing you will see that it changes brightness very quickly and then seems to spend a long time "stuck" at almost full brightness and then suddenly starts to dim rapidly. This is a consequence of the way the human eye perceives light output as a function of input power. For a linear change you have to vary the duty cycle as a cubic power, but in most cases a simple flash works just as well.

Using Gpio5 we can implement a cubic power dimming of the LED:

```c
#include <stdio.h>
#include <stdlib.h>
#include <time.h>
#include "Gpio5.h"

int main(int argc, char **argv)
{
    struct timespec delay = {0, 10000 * 1000};
    rp1_Init();
    gpio_init(12);
    pwm_set_clock(2, 0);
    pwm_setup(12, TrailingEdge);
    pwm_set_frequency_duty(12, 2000, 0);
    pwm_enable(12);
    int w = 0;
    int inc = 1;
    for (;;)
    {
        pwm_set_frequency_duty(12, 2000, w * w * w / (10 * 100));
        w = w + inc;
        if (w >= 100 || w <= 0)
            inc = -inc;
        nanosleep(&delay, NULL);
    }
    return (EXIT_SUCCESS);
}
```

If you try this out you should see the LED fade more smoothly than a simple linear fade.

How Fast Can You Modulate?

For reasons that will be discussed later, the whole point of using PWM is to vary the duty cycle, or the period, of the pulse train. This means that the next question is how fast can you change the characteristic of a PWM line? In other words, how fast can you change the duty cycle? There is no easy way to give an exact answer and, in most applications, an exact answer isn't of much value. The reason is that for a PWM signal to convey information it generally has to deliver a number of complete cycles with a given duty cycle. This is because of the way pulses are often averaged in applications.

We also have another problem, synchronization. There is no way to swap from one duty cycle to another exactly when a complete duty cycle has just finished. All you can do is use a timer to estimate when the pulse is high or low. What this means is that there is going to be a glitch when you switch from one duty cycle to another. Of course, this glitch becomes less important as you slow the rate of duty cycle change and exactly what is usable depends on the application.

For example, having set the period to 150kHz, which provides an 8-bit duty cycle resolution, we can change the duty cycle from 25% to 75% as quickly as possible with:

```
int main(int argc, char **argv)
{
    pwmAction(OpenChan, 0, 0);
    int freqkHz = 150;
    int dutyPc = 75;

    int t = 1000000000 / (freqkHz * 1000);
    pwmAction(SetFreq, 0, t);

    int d1 = t * 75 / 100;
    int d2 = t * 25 / 100;

    pwmAction(EnableChan, 0, 0);

    for (;;)
    {
        pwmAction(SetDuty, 0, d1);
        pwmAction(SetDuty, 0, d2);
    }
}
```

The result looks fairly good, but notice that the changeover time is around two pulses. It is sometimes too short and then you only get a single pulse before the duty cycle changes.

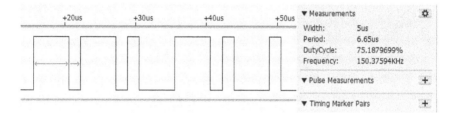

The fastest PWM repetition rate that you can use is 26.6μs for an 8-bit resolution and you can change the duty cycle as frequently as once per pulse.

Using Gpio5 to do the same job produces the same result:

```
#include <stdio.h>
#include <stdlib.h>
#include <time.h>
#include "Gpio5.h"
int main(int argc, char **argv)
{
    rp1_Init();
    gpio_init(12);
    pwm_set_clock(1, 0);
    pwm_setup(12, TrailingEdge);

    pwm_set_frequency_duty(12, 150000, 0);
    pwm_enable(12);

    for (;;)
    {
        pwm_set_frequency_duty(12, 150000, 250);
        pwm_set_frequency_duty(12, 150000, 750);
    }
}
```

Controlling a Servo

Hobby servos, the sort used in radio control models, are very cheap and easy to use and the Pi has enough PWM lines to control two of them without much in the way of extras.

A basic servo has just three connections, ground, a power line and a signal line. The colors used vary, but the power line is usually red, ground is usually black or brown and the signal line is white, yellow or orange.

The power wire has to be connected to a 5V supply capable of providing enough current to run the motor - anything up to 500mA or more depending on the servo. In general, you cannot power a full-size servo from the Pi's 5V pin, you need a separate power supply.

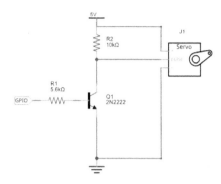

You can power some micro servos directly from the Pi's 5V line but you need to check the specifications. The good news is that the servo signal line generally needs very little current, although it does, in theory, need to be switched between 0 and 5V using a PWM signal.

This is the correct way to drive a servo, but in nearly all cases you can connect the servo to a 5V supply and the pulse line directly to the 3.3V GPIO line. In other words, in most cases you don't need a transistor driver and the circuit shown below will work:

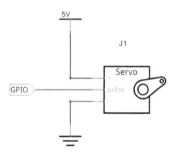

Now all we have to do is set the PWM line to produce 20ms pulses with pulse widths ranging from 0.5ms to 2.5ms or a duty cycle of 2.5% to 12.5%, but this varies quite a lot according to the servo.

The simplest servo program you can write is something like:

```
int main(int argc, char **argv)
{
    pwmAction(OpenChan, 0, 0);
    int t = 20 * 1000000;
    pwmAction(SetFreq, 0, t);
    int d1 = t * 2.5 / 100;
    int d2 = t * 12 / 100;
    pwmAction(EnableChan, 0, 0);
    for (;;)
    {
        pwmAction(SetDuty, 0, d1);
        sleep(1);
        pwmAction(SetDuty, 0, d2);
        sleep(1);
    }
}
```

This moves the servo to two extreme positions, pausing between them.

The Gpio5 version is:

```
#include <stdio.h>
#include <stdlib.h>
#include <time.h>
#include "Gpio5.h"
int main(int argc, char **argv)
{
    rp1_Init();
    gpio_init(12);
    pwm_set_clock(1, 0);
    pwm_setup(12, TrailingEdge);

    pwm_set_frequency_duty(12, 50, 0);
    pwm_enable(12);

    for (;;)
    {
        pwm_set_frequency_duty(12, 50, 25);
        pwm_set_frequency_duty(12, 50, 120);
    }
}
```

This works with the direct drive servo circuit, but not with the transistor drive circuit. The reason is that the transistor voltage driver is an inverter. When the PWM line is high the transistor is fully on and the servo's pulse line is effectively grounded. When the PWM line is low the transistor is fully off and the servo's pulse line is pulled high by the resistor.

The standard solution in this case is to use two transistors to generate a non-inverted pulse. The simplest solution of all is to ignore the problem in hardware and solve the problem in software. This is generally a good approach - before you consider modifying the hardware, always see if there is an easier software fix. Instead of generating 20ms pulses with pulse widths 0.5ms to 2.5ms, you can generate an inverted pulse with 20ms pulses with widths in the range 17.5ms to 19.5ms. The principle is that, if the servo needs a 10% duty cycle, we supply it with a 90% duty cycle, which the transistor inverter converts back to a 10% duty cycle. The range of duty cycles we need goes from 17.5ms to 19.5ms, which in percentages is 87.5% to 97.5%.

Fortunately we have a simpler solution than having to manually invert the duty cycles. Each PWM channel has a polarity file, which if you write inversed results in the PWM signal polarity being flipped. Writing normal returns it to active high rather than active low. We can add another case to our pwmAction function to set the polarity:

```
    case InvertChan:
        snprintf(buf, 150, "%s%s%s",
          "/sys/class/pwm/pwmchip0/pwm", schan, "/polarity");
        fd = open(buf, O_WRONLY);
        if (param == 0)
        {
            L = snprintf(buf, 150, "%s", "normal");
            write(fd, buf, L);
        }
        if (param == 1)
        {
            L = snprintf(buf, 150, "%s", "inversed");
            write(fd, buf, L);
        }
        close(fd);
        break;
    }
```

We also need to modify the enumeration to read:

```
enum pwm
{
    OpenChan,
    SetFreq,
    SetDuty,
    EnableChan,
    DisableChan,
    CloseChan,
    InvertChan
};
```

The final parameter is 0 for normal and 1 for inverted.

To drive the servo with a transistor buffer you can use:

```
int main(int argc, char **argv)
{
    pwmAction(OpenChan, 0,0);
    int t = 20 * 1000000;
    pwmAction(SetFreq, 0, t);
    int d1 = t * 2.5 / 100;
    int d2 = t * 12 / 100;
    pwmAction(InvertChan,0,1);
    pwmAction(EnableChan, 0,0);

    for (;;)
    {
        pwmAction(SetDuty, 0, d1);
        sleep(1);
        pwmAction(SetDuty, 0, d2);
        sleep(1);
    }
}
```

We can add invert set and clear functions to Gpio5:

```
int pwm_set_invert(int32_t gpio)
{
    int pwm = getPWM(gpio);
    if (pwm < 0)
        return -1;
    PWM[pwm].Ctrl = PWM[pwm].Ctrl | 0x8;
    *PWMBase = *PWMBase | 0x80000000;
}

int pwm_clr_invert(int32_t gpio)
{
    int pwm = getPWM(gpio);
    if (pwm < 0)
        return -1;
    PWM[pwm].Ctrl = PWM[pwm].Ctrl & ~0x8ul;
    *PWMBase = *PWMBase | 0x80000000;
}
```

Using this the Gpio5 version of driving the transistor is:

```
#include <stdio.h>
#include <stdlib.h>
#include <time.h>
#include "Gpio5.h"
int main(int argc, char **argv)
{
    rp1_Init();
    gpio_init(12);
    pwm_set_clock(1, 0);
    pwm_setup(12, TrailingEdge);
    pwm_set_frequency_duty(12, 50, 0);
    pwm_enable(12);
    pwm_set_invert(12);
    for (;;)
    {
        pwm_set_frequency_duty(12, 50, 25);
        pwm_set_frequency_duty(12, 50, 120);
    }
}
```

These methods may work, but in either case the servo might not reach its limits of movement. Servos differ in how they respond to the input signal and you might need to calibrate the pulse widths. Many robot implementations, for example, calibrate the servos to find their maximum movement using either mechanical switches to detect when the servo is at the end of its range or a vision sensor. Hence you will often see a robot apparently doing a "warm up" before moving. What is happening is that each servo is being moved until it activates the limit switch giving the duty cycle needed to move it to that position. Low-cost servos are particularly hard to pin down in terms of specification and variations in behavior generally have to be taken account of in software.

What Else Can You Use PWM For?

PWM lines are incredibly versatile and it is always worth asking the question "could I use PWM?" when you are considering almost any problem. The LED example shows how you can use PWM as a power controller. You can extend this idea to a computer-controlled switch-mode power supply. All you need is a capacitor to smooth out the voltage and perhaps a transformer to change the voltage. You can also use PWM to control the speed of a DC motor and if you add a simple bridge circuit you can control its direction and speed.

The amount of power delivered to a device by a pulse train is proportional to the duty cycle. A pulse train that has a 50% duty cycle is delivering current to the load only 50% of the time and this is irrespective of the pulse repetition rate. So the duty cycle controls the power, but the period still matters in many situations because you want to avoid any flashing or other effects. A higher frequency smooths out the power flow at any duty cycle.

With a sufficiently fast period you can also use PWM as a digital to analog converter. Simply add a low-pass filter to remove the pulsing and you have a steady voltage proportional to the duty cycle. This can be used to create an audio signal if the clock is fast enough.

Finally, you can use a PWM signal as a modulated carrier for data communications. For example, most infrared controllers make use of a 38kHz carrier, which is roughly a $26\mu s$ pulse. This is switched on and off for 1ms and this is well within the range that the PWM can manage. So all you have to do is replace the red LED in the previous circuit with an infrared LED and you have the start of a remote control, or data transmission, link.

Summary

- PWM, Pulse Width Modulation, has a fixed repetition rate but a variable duty cycle, i.e. the amount of time the signal is high or low changes.

- PWM can be generated by software simply by changing the state of a GPIO line correctly, but it can also be generated in hardware, so relieving the processor of some work.

- Hardware PWM can generate high speed pulses, but how quickly you can change the duty cycle is still software-limited.

- All versions of the Pi have two hardware PWM channels which can be used and configured using Linux drivers.

- The CM5 has two additional channels which cannot be easily used via the driver. The PWM chip has also changed from `pwmchip0` to `pwmchip2`.

- The PWM drivers do not provide control over the PWM clock frequency which determines how accurately you can set the duty cycle.

- A typical use of PWM is to control a servo and this only requires a PWM frequency of 50Hz. The position of the servo depends on the duty cycle.

- You can easily invert the sense of the PWM signal, which is useful when the device is being driven by a single transistor.

- As well as being a way of signaling, PWM can also be used to vary the amount of power or voltage transferred. The higher the duty cycle, the more power/voltage.

- In the same way, by varying the duty cycle, you can dim an LED. As the brightness of an LED is not linear with applied voltage, you have to modify the output using a cubic law to get linear changes in brightness.

Chapter 12
SPI Devices

The CM5 offers two standard ways of connecting more sophisticated devices in hardware – the Serial Peripheral Interface or SPI bus and the I2C or I-squared-C bus. In addition there is a Linux driver which supports the non-standard 1-Wire bus in software. The following chapters focus on these buses rather than specific devices. The advantage of a bus is that, once you know how to use it, connecting compatible devices is more or less the same task, irrespective of device.

There are drivers for some specific SPI devices and if such a driver exists you should use it. More information on how to do this is given later. However, if a driver doesn't exist it isn't difficult to interface to an SPI device at a lower level via the Linux SPI driver. First, however, we need to know something about how SPI works. If you just want to use a device driver, skip this section until you need it.

SPI Bus Basics

In the hardware configuration most used for the Pi, there is a single master and, at most, two slaves.

The signal lines are:

- MOSI (Master Output Slave Input), i.e. data to the slave
- MISO (Master Input Slave Output), i.e. data to the master
- SCLK (Serial Clock), which is always generated by the master

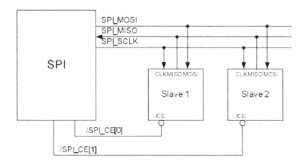

In general, there can also be any number of SS (Slave Select), CE (Chip Enable) or CS (Chip Select) lines, which are usually set low to select which slave is being addressed. Notice that unlike other buses, I2C for example, there are no SPI standard commands or addresses, only bytes of data. However, slave devices do interpret some of the data as commands to do something or send some particular data.

SPI Interfaces

The CM5 has six SPI interfaces that can be accessed via the exposed GPIO lines.

SPI0 GPIO Mode 0		
Function	Pin	**GPIO**
MOSI	19	GPIO10
MISO	21	GPIO09
SCLK	23	GPIO11
CE0	24	GPIO08
CE1	26	GPIO07
CE2	5	GPIO03
CE3	7	GPIO04

SPI1 GPIO Mode 0		
Function	Pin	**GPIO**
MOSI	38	GPIO20
MISO	35	GPIO19
SCLK	40	GPIO21
CE0	12	GPIO18
CE1	11	GPIO17
CE2	36	GPIO16
CE3	13	GPIO27 (mode 8)

SPI2 GPIO Mode 8		
Function	Pin	**GPIO**
MOSI	3	GPIO02
MISO	28	GPIO01
SCLK	5	GPIO03
CE0	27	GPIO00
CE1	18	GPIO24

SPI3 GPIO Mode 8		
Function	Pin	**GPIO**
MOSI	3	GPIO02
MISO	28	GPIO01
SCLK	5	GPIO03
CE0	27	GPIO00
CE1	22	GPIO25

SPI4 GPIO Mode 8		
Function	Pin	**GPIO**
MOSI	19	GPIO10
MISO	21	GPIO09
SCLK	23	GPIO11
CE0	24	GPIO08

SPI5 GPIO Mode 8		
Function	Pin	**GPIO**
MOSI	8	GPIO14
MISO	33	GPIO13
SCLK	10	GPIO15
CE0	32	GPIO12
CE1	37	GPIO26

Notice that some SPI controllers share GPIO lines and therefore cannot be used at the same time, e.g SPI2 and SPI3, SPI4 and SPI0. For these and other reasons it is better to use SPI0 and SPI1 if at all possible.

SPI Protocol

The data transfer on the SPI bus is slightly odd. What happens is that the master pulls one of the chip selects low, which activates a slave. Then the master toggles the clock SCLK and both the master and the slave send a single bit on their respective data lines. After eight clock pulses a byte has been transferred from the master to the slave and from the slave to the master. You can think of this as being implemented as a circular buffer, although it doesn't have to be.

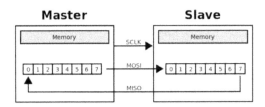

This full-duplex data transfer is often hidden by the software and the protocol used. For example, there is a read function that reads data from the slave and sends zeros or data that is ignored by the slave. Similarly, there is a write function that sends valid data, but ignores whatever the slave sends. The transfer is typically in groups of eight bits, usually most significant bit first, but this isn't always the case. In general, as long as the master supplies clock pulses, data is transferred.

Notice this circular buffer arrangement allows for slaves to be daisy-chained with the output of one going to the input of the next. This makes the entire chain one big circular shift register. This can make it possible to have multiple devices with only a single chip select, but it also means any commands sent to the slaves are received by each one in turn. For example, you could send a convert command to each A to D converter in turn and receive back results from each one.

The final odd thing about the SPI bus is that there are four modes which define the relationship between the data timing and the clock pulse. The clock can be either active high or low, which is referred to as clock polarity (CPOL), and data can be sampled on the rising or falling edge of the clock, which is clock phase (CPHA).

All combinations of these two possibilities gives the four modes:

SPI Mode*	Clock Polarity CPOL	Clock Phase CPHA	Characteristics
0	0	0	Clock active high data output on falling edge and sampled on rising
1	0	1	Clock active high data output on rising edge and sampled on falling
2	1	0	Clock active low data output on falling edge and sampled on rising
3	1	1	Clock active low data output on rising edge and sampled on falling

*The way that the SPI modes are labeled is common but not universal.

There is often a problem trying to work out what mode a slave device uses. The clock polarity is usually easy and the clock phase can sometimes be worked out from the data transfer timing diagrams by noting that:

♦ First clock transition in the middle of a data bit means CPHA=0

♦ First clock transition at the start of a data bit means CPHA=1

So to configure the SPI bus to work with a particular slave device:

1) Select the clock frequency - anything from 125MHz to 3.8kHz

2) Set the CS polarity - active high or low

3) Set the clock mode – to one of mode0 to mode3

SPI Driver

Before you can use the SPI bus you have to load its driver. You can do this by adding:

dtparam=spi=on

to the /boot/firmware/config.txt file. This loads a driver for SPI0 using two chip select lines. To find out how to activate other SPI channels see later. For the rest of this section we will be using SPI0.

Alternatively you can activate the driver dynamically:

```
FILE *doCommand(char *cmd)
{
    FILE *fp = popen(cmd, "r");
    if (fp == NULL)
    {
        printf("Failed to run command %s \n\r", cmd);
        exit(1);
    }
    return fp;
}
```

```
void checkSPI0()
{
    FILE *fd = doCommand("sudo  dtparam -l");
    char output[1024];
    int txfound = 0;

    char indicator[] = "spi=on";
    char command[] = "sudo dtparam spi=on";
    while (fgets(output, sizeof(output), fd) != NULL)
    {
        printf("%s\n\r", output);
        fflush(stdout);
        if (strstr(output, indicator) != NULL)
        {
            txfound = 1;
        }
    }
    if (txfound == 0)
    {
        fd = doCommand(command);
        sleep(2);
    }

    pclose(fd);
}
```

This works by first using the `dtparam -l` command to list the loaded overlays. If the `spi` overlay is already loaded nothing is done. If it isn't then it runs the command:

```
dtparam spi = on
```

SPIDev

The interface to the SPI driver is generally referred to as SPIdev and there is a header file, `spidev.h`, which provides all of the definitions you need to make use of it. When you load the SPI driver to install SPI Channel n a number of character devices are created in `/dev` of the general form `spidevn.m` where n is the channel number and m is the chip select line used to control the device. For example, the basic SPI driver uses channel 0, i.e. SPI0 with two chip select lines, and thus you will find `spidev0.0` and `spidev0.1` which control the SPI device connected to SPI0 on chip select 0 and 1 respectively. By default, `spidev0.0` uses GPIO8 pin 26 and `spidev0.1` uses GPIO7 pin 28 for chip selects.

To work with an SPI device all you have to do is use `ioctl` to send requests to the relevant file. If you want to know more about `ioctl` see Chapter 4.

There are a range of configuration requests:

- ◆ `SPI_IOC_WR_MODE`   Sets mode
- ◆ `SPI_IOC_WR_LSB_FIRST`   Sets LSB first or last
- ◆ `SPI_IOC_WR_BITS_PER_WORD` Sets number of bits per word
- ◆ `SPI_IOC_WR_MAX_SPEED_HZ` Sets SPI clock if possible

There are also requests with `WR` replaced by `RD` which read, rather than write, the configuration.

Note: `SPI_IOC_WR_LSB_FIRST` and `SPI_IOC_RD_LSB_FIRST` are not supported on Pi OS.

Once you have the SPI interface set up, you can send and receive data using the `SPI_IOC_MESSAGE` request. This is slightly different from other requests in that a macro is used to construct a request that also specifies the number of operations needed.

Each operation is defined by a struct:

```
struct spi_ioc_transfer {
        __u64       tx_buf;
        __u64       rx_buf;

        __u32       len;
        __u32       speed_hz;

        __u16       delay_usecs;
        __u8        bits_per_word;
        __u8        cs_change;
}
```

The fields are fairly obvious. The `tx_buf` and `rx_buf` are byte arrays used for the transmitted and received data and they can be the same array. The `len` field specifies the number of bytes in each array. The `speed_hz` field modifies the SPI clock. The `delay_usecs` field sets a delay before the chip select is deselected after the transfer. The `cs_change` field is true if you want the chip select to be deselected between each transfer.

The best way to find out how this all works is to write the simplest possible example.

A Loopback Example

Because of the way that data is transferred on the SPI bus, it is very easy to test that everything is working without having to add any components. All you have to do is connect MOSI to MISO so that anything sent is also received in a loopback mode. There is an official example program to implement a loopback, but it is complicated for a first example and has a bug. Our version will be the simplest possible and, hopefully, without bugs.

First connect GPIO9 to GPIO10 using a jumper wire and start a new project. The program is very simple. First we check that the SPI bus is loaded:

```
checkSPI0();
```

and next we open spdev0.0:

```
int fd = open("/dev/spidev0.0", O_RDWR);
```

As this is a loopback test we really don't need to configure the bus as all that matters is that the transmit and receive channels have the same configuration. However, we do need some data to send:

```
uint8_t tx[] = {0xAA};
uint8_t rx[] = {0};
```

The hex value AA is useful in testing because it generates the bit sequence 10101010, which is easy to see on a logic analyzer.

To send the data we need an spi_ioc_transfer struct:

```
struct spi_ioc_transfer tr =
    {
        .tx_buf = (unsigned long)tx,
        .rx_buf = (unsigned long)rx,
        .len = 1,
        .delay_usecs = 0,
        .speed_hz = 500000,
        .bits_per_word = 8,
    };
```

We can now use the ioctl call to send and receive the data:

```
int status = ioctl(fd, SPI_IOC_MESSAGE(1), &tr);
if (status < 0)
        printf("can't send data");
```

Finally we can check that the send and received data match and close the file.

Putting all of this together gives us the complete program:

```
#include <stdio.h>
#include <stdlib.h>
#include <string.h>
#include <fcntl.h>
#include <unistd.h>
#include <sys/ioctl.h>
#include <linux/spi/spidev.h>
#include <stdint.h>
```

```
int main(int argc, char **argv)
{
    checkSPI0();

    uint8_t tx[] = {0xAA};
    uint8_t rx[] = {0};

    struct spi_ioc_transfer tr =
        {
            .tx_buf = (unsigned long)tx,
            .rx_buf = (unsigned long)rx,
            .len = 1,
            .delay_usecs = 0,
            .speed_hz = 500000,
            .bits_per_word = 8,
        };

    int fd = open("/dev/spidev0.0", O_RDWR);
    int status = ioctl(fd, SPI_IOC_MESSAGE(1), &tr);
    if (status < 0)
        printf("can't send data");
    printf("%X,%X", tx[0],rx[0]);
    close(fd);
}
```

Note: The checkSPI0 function needs to be added to this listing.

If you run the program and don't get any data, or receive the wrong data, then the most likely reason is that you have connected the wrong two pins, or not connected them at all. If you connect a logic analyzer to the four pins involved you will see the data transfer:

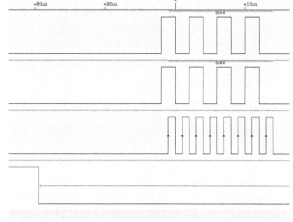

If you look carefully you will see the CS0 line go low before the master places the first data bit on the MOSI, and hence on the MISO line. Notice that the clock rises in the middle of each data bit, making this a mode 0 transfer.

217

If you need to configure the SPI interface you can use the ioctl calls. For example:

```
static uint8_t mode = 1;
int ret = ioctl(fd, SPI_IOC_WR_MODE, &mode);
if (ret == -1)
    printf("can't set spi mode");
static uint8_t bits = 8;
ret = ioctl(fd, SPI_IOC_WR_BITS_PER_WORD, &bits);
if (ret == -1)
    printf("can't set bits per word");
static uint32_t speed = 500000;
ret = ioctl(fd, SPI_IOC_WR_MAX_SPEED_HZ, &speed);
if (ret == -1)
    printf("can't set max speed hz");
```

After this you should see mode 1 selected and the clock going high at the start of each bit.

All of the SPI interfaces all have a set of drivers that follow a standard pattern, where *n* is the port number. They use one or two chips selects respectively:

- spi*n*-1cs, cs0_pin = pin

- spi*n*-2cs, cs0_pin = pin1,cs1_pin = pin2

If you don't specify a pin to be used for the chip select then the default used is the pin shown above.

SPI1 also has the possibility of using three chip selects:

- spi1-3cs, cs0_pin = pin1,cs1_pin = pin2,cs2_pin = pin3

It is also worth knowing that the drivers do not use the SPI hardware's chip select implementation. Instead they use a general GPIO line and set it high and low under software control. This means you can use any GPIO line as a chip select, not just the ones supported by the hardware.

You can also use the `csm_spidev` parameter to prevent the creation of an SPI driver node for the mth chip select.

SPI0 is the same on all models of Pi and this is the one you should consider as first choice if you value compatibility.

SPI with Gpio5

You can avoid the use of a driver by working directly with the SPI hardware directly via an extended Gpio5. The only problem is that this is not well documented by Raspberry Pi. The hardware is based on the Synopsys DW_apb_ssi SPI implementation and the registers and other details are described in the company's databook, which you can find by searching the web or as a download from this book's web page at www.iopress.info. This document details all of the registers and their detailed function. The only problem is that there are a lot of registers and it is intimidating to getting started. Fortunately, most of the registers are set to a reasonable configuration on system reset for an SPI master and so the number of registers you actually have to interact with at first is much smaller than you might expect. It is easy to construct a struct to access the registers:

```
volatile typedef struct{
int32_t CTRLR0;// frame format, clock polarity, phase
int32_t CTRLR1;
int32_t SSIENR;   //enable/disable
int32_t MWCR;
int32_t SER;      // slave CS enable
int32_t BAUDR;   // baud rate - clock divisor
int32_t TXFTLR;
int32_t RXFTLR;
int32_t TXFLR;
int32_t RXFLR;
int32_t SR;       // status register
int32_t IMR;      // interrupt mask register
int32_t ISR;
int32_t RISR;
int32_t TXOICR;
int32_t RXOICR;
int32_t RXUICR;
int32_t MSTICR;
int32_t ICR;
int32_t DMACR;
int32_t DMATDLR;
int32_t DMARDLR;
int32_t IDR;
int32_t SSI_VERSION_ID;
int32_t DR;  // data register
int32_t DRx[35];
int32_t RX_SAMPLE_DLY;
int32_t SPI_CTRLR0 ;
int32_t TXD_DRIVE_EDGE;
}SPIregs;
```

The registers that are most useful have comments indicating what they do. It is worth mentioning that the data register DR is duplicated in DRx 35 times and you can use any of these registers to read or write the next data value in the FIFO buffers.

The addresses of each block of SPI registers is given in the documentation:

```
typedef SPIregs  *SPI;

#define RP1_SPI0_BASE 0x050000
#define RP1_SPI1_BASE 0x054000
#define RP1_SPI2_BASE 0x058000
#define RP1_SPI3_BASE 0x05c000
#define RP1_SPI4_BASE 0x060000
#define RP1_SPI5_BASE 0x064000
#define SPI0  ((SPI)( PERIBase+RP1_SPI0_BASE/4))
#define SPI1  ((SPI)( PERIBase+RP1_SPI1_BASE/4))
#define SPI2  ((SPI)( PERIBase+RP1_SPI2_BASE/4))
#define SPI3  ((SPI)( PERIBase+RP1_SPI3_BASE/4))
#define SPI4  ((SPI)( PERIBase+RP1_SPI4_BASE/4))
#define SPI5  ((SPI)( PERIBase+RP1_SPI5_BASE/4))

#define SPIClock 200000000
```

Following the Pico SDK, the constants SPI*n* have been defined and these are used as pointers to the registers for each SPI channel.

The first function we need is something to initialize the SPI channel we are about to use:

```
void spi_init(SPI spi, int32_t baudrate)
{
    spi_set_baudrate(spi, baudrate);
    spi->BAUDR = SPIClock / baudrate;
    spi_enable(spi, false);
// set CPOL and CHPA
    spi_set_format(spi, 8, SPI_CPOL_0, SPI_CPHA_0, SPI_MSB_FIRST);
    spi_enable(spi, false);
// set CE to stay active (bit 24 set low)
    spi->CTRLR0 = (spi->CTRLR0) & 0xFFFFFFFFFEFFFFFF;
// set CE0 as default
    spi->SER = 1;
//  clear interrupts
    uint32_t reg_icr = spi->ICR;
    spi_enable(spi, true);
}
```

This is based on the Pico SDK function and it uses other functions to set the baud rate and format. It sets defaults of 8-bit data frames and mode 0. Notice that the SPI_MSB_FIRST is ignored in both the Pico and the CM5 and is included for compatibility.

The CM5's SPI implementation automatically controls the chip selects and it can either lower the select between each transmission or keep it asserted until the FIFO buffer is empty. The default is set to keep it asserted until the transfer is complete and a function to set this value is listed later.

Each SPI controller has a different possible number of chip selects and which one is used depends on which bit is set in the SER register. The default is set to be CE0 but it is easy to change using a function given later.

The function to set the baudrate is only complicated by the fact that the divisor has to be even:

```
void spi_set_baudrate(SPI spi, int32_t baudrate)
{
    int32_t div= SPIClock / baudrate;
    if(div%2!=0) div=div-1;
    spi_enable(spi, false);
    spi->BAUDR = div;
    spi_enable(spi, true);
}
```

The SPI clock is fixed at 200MHz and the register can only be changed when the SPI controller is not enabled. The set baud rate function can be used after the SPI controller has been initialized and a function to get the baud rate is useful for discovering what the clock speed actually is:

```
int32_t spi_get_baudrate(SPI spi)
{
    return SPIClock / (spi->BAUDR);
}
```

Most of the configuration is done by set_format and this can be called after the SPI channel has been initialized to change the defaults:

```
void spi_set_format(SPI spi, uint32_t data_bits, spi_cpol_t cpol,
                            spi_cpha_t cpha, spi_order_t order)
{
    spi_enable(spi, false);
    uint32_t mask = 0x1F00C0;
    data_bits = (data_bits - 1) & 0x1F;
    uint32_t value = data_bits << 16 | cpol << 7 | cpha << 6;
    int32_t data = spi->CTRLR0;
    spi->CTRLR0 = (data & ~mask) | (value & mask);
    spi_enable(spi, true);
}
```

Bits 16 to 20 set the number of databits used in a data frame and bits 6 and 7 control CPHA and CPOL.

There are a number of utility functions that are simple enough to not need additional explanation: To enable or disable the SPI channel

```
void spi_enable(SPI spi, bool enable)
{
    if (enable)     {
        spi->SSIENR = 0x1;
    }else{
        spi->SSIENR = 0x0;
    }
}
```

Can you write to the SPI tx FIFO buffer

```
bool spi_is_writable(SPI spi)
{
    return (spi->SR) & 0x2;
}
```

This is the same as `tx` FIFO is not full.

Is there data ready to be read in the Rx FIFO buffer.

```
bool spi_is_readable(SPI spi)
{
    return spi->SR & 0x8;
}
```

This is the same as `Rx` FIFO is not empty.

Is the SPI channel busy

```
bool spi_is_busy(SPI spi)
{
    return spi->SR & 0x1;
}
```

Is the Rx FIFO full

```
bool spi_rx_full(SPI spi)
{
    return spi->SR & 0x10;
}
```

How many items in the Rx FIFO.

```
int spi_rx_num(SPI spi)
{
    return spi->RXFLR;
}
```

How many items in the Tx FIFO.

```
int spi_tx_num(SPI spi)
{
    return spi->TXFLR;
}
```

The status functions are needed to implement read/write functions and they are generally useful in user programs.

SPI Read/Write Function

The basic read/write function first writes a set of bytes and reads the same number back. This sounds simple, but achieving maximum throughput and automatic control of the CS lines makes it more complicated. A simple approach would be to set up a loop that writes a byte to the FIFO buffer and then attempts to read one. You would need to check that the Tx FIFO had space before writing and you would need to check that the Rx FIFO had something to read each time through the loop. This works well at clock speeds less than about 10MHz. At higher clock speeds what happens is that the FIFO transmits the frame before the next frame has been stored and so it spends time between frames empty. This slows things down and it resets the CS line which is automatically active when there is data in the Tx FIFO and set to inactive when it is empty. At lower clock speeds, the Tx FIFO stays full and the CS line stays active until all of the frames have been sent.

A better but more complicated algorithm first places as many items of data in the Tx FIFO as it can hold and then starts a loop that reads data from the Rx FIFO while keeping the Tx FIFO fed with data. The only subtle point is that we have avoid filling the Rx FIFO buffer as well as the Tx FIFO buffer:

```
int spi_write_read_blocking(SPI spi, const uint8_t *src,
                                     uint8_t *dst, size_t len)
{
    const size_t fifo_depth = 64;
    size_t rx_remaining = len, tx_remaining = len;
    for (int i = 0; i < (fifo_depth < len ? fifo_depth : len)-1;
                                                            i++)
    {
        spi->DR = (uint32_t)*src++;
        --tx_remaining;
    }
    while (rx_remaining || tx_remaining)
    {
        if (tx_remaining && spi_is_writable(spi) &&
                            spi_rx_num(spi) < fifo_depth)
        {
            spi->DR = (uint32_t)*src++;
            --tx_remaining;
        }
        if (rx_remaining && spi_is_readable(spi))
        {
            *dst++ = (uint8_t)spi->DR;
            --rx_remaining;
        }
    }
    return (int)len;
}
```

This function is a modification of the same one in the Pico SDK.

This works up to about 6MHz. After this the Tx FIFO eventually empties and the CS line is deactivated until another frame is read to transmit. At 10MHz it takes 82Bytes to empty the Tx FIFO and the first 82Bytes are transmitted at 1250 KBytes per second and following bytes at 300KBytes per second. A more serious problem in some cases is the toggling of the CS line which some slaves cannot work with.

If the CS line toggling is a problem then you have no choice but to take control of the GPIO line manually. Simply reset the CS line into GPIO mode, set its direction to output and change it from high to low and back again around the call to write_read_blocking. This doesn't speed things up, it simply ensures that the CS line is active for the entire transfer.

If you want to go faster than this then DMA is required and this is beyond the scope of this book.

You can create the spi_write16_read16_blocking which is in the Pico SDK simply by changing all occurrences of uint8_t to uint16_t. You can also create an spi_write32_read32_blocking, which isn't in the Pico SDK, by changing uint8_t to uint32_t. Notice that you have to change the frame size to 16 bits or 32 bits to make these functions work. If you don't then only the number of bits specified are transferred.

It is also trivial to create read_blocking and write_blocking functions in each frame size by discarding received data and by sending dummy data.

Two functions that are not in the Pico SDK can be used to set the CS line to activate and how the CS line should behave between data frames:

```
void spi_set_slave(SPI spi, int slave)
{
    spi_enable(spi, false);
    spi->SER = 1ul << slave;
    spi_enable(spi, true);
}
```

and

```
void spi_set_CS_toggle(SPI spi, bool enable)
{
    spi_enable(spi, false);
    if (enable)
    {
        spi->CTRLR0 = (spi->CTRLR0) | 0x1000000;
    }
    else
    {
        spi->CTRLR0 = (spi->CTRLR0) & 0xFFFFFFFFFEFFFFFF;
    }
    spi_enable(spi, true);
}
```

Notice that the number of CS lines varies according to the SPI channel in use and it is up to you to initialize all of the GPIO lines in use, including the CS lines.

Loopback Example Using GPIO5

Using the functions listed above it is easy to implement the loopback example given earlier:

```
#include <stdio.h>
#include <stdlib.h>
#include <time.h>
#include "Gpio5.h"

int main(int argc, char **argv)
{
    rp1_Init();

    gpio_set_function(8, GPIO_FUNC_SPI);   // CS0
    gpio_set_function(7, GPIO_FUNC_SPI);   // CS1
    gpio_set_function(3, GPIO_FUNC_SPI);   // CS2
    gpio_set_function(4, GPIO_FUNC_SPI);   // CS3
    gpio_set_function(9, GPIO_FUNC_SPI);   // MISO
    gpio_set_function(10, GPIO_FUNC_SPI);  // MOSI
    gpio_set_function(11, GPIO_FUNC_SPI);  // SCLK

    spi_init(SPI0, 5000000);
    spi_set_format(SPI0, 8, SPI_CPOL_0, SPI_CPHA_0,
                                        SPI_MSB_FIRST);
    spi_set_slave(SPI0, 0);
    uint8_t wBuff[1] = {0xAA};
    uint8_t rBuff[1];
    int n = spi_write_read_blocking(SPI0, wBuff, rBuff, 1);
    printf(" %X %X %d \n ", wBuff[0], rBuff[0], n);
    return (EXIT_SUCCESS);
}
```

Notice that we set all of the CS lines that SPI0 supports but only use CS0. We could include the setting up of the GPIO lines in the spi_init function, but doing it this way allows the selection of which CS lines to initialize within the user program.

The MCP3008

The SPI bus can be difficult to make work at first, but once you know what to look for about how the slave claims to work it gets easier. To demonstrate how its done, let's add eight channels of 12-bit A to D using the MCP3008. There is a full driver for the MCP3008, but working with it directly via the SPI driver is also very easy.

The MCP3008 is available in a number of different packages, but the standard 16-pin PDIP is the easiest to work with using a prototyping board. You can buy it from the usual sources including Amazon. Its pinouts are fairly self-explanatory:

```
        CHO ▯1      ⌣   16▯ V_DD
        CH1 ▯2          15▯ V_REF
        CH2 ▯3      M   14▯ AGND
        CH3 ▯4      C   13▯ CLK
        CH4 ▯5      P   12▯ D_OUT
        CH5 ▯6      3   11▯ D_IN
        CH6 ▯7      0   10▯ CS/SHDN
        CH7 ▯8      0    9▯ DGND
                    8
```

You can see that the analog inputs are on the left and the power and SPI bus connections are on the right. The conversion accuracy is claimed to be 10 bits, but how many of these bits correspond to reality and how many are noise depends on how you design the layout of the circuit.

You need to take great care if you need high accuracy. For example, you will notice that there are two voltage inputs V_{DD} and V_{REF}. V_{DD} is the supply voltage that runs the chip and V_{REF} is the reference voltage that is used to compare the input voltage. Obviously, if you want highest accuracy, V_{REF} which has to be lower than or equal to V_{DD}, should be set by an accurate low-noise voltage source. However, in most applications V_{REF} and V_{DD} are simply connected together and the usual, low- quality, supply voltage is used as the reference. If this isn't good enough then you can use anything from a Zener diode to a precision voltage reference chip such as the TL431. At the very least, however, you should add a $1\mu F$ capacitor to ground connected to the V_{DD} pin and the V_{REF} pin.

The MC3000 family is a type of A-to-D converter (ADC) called a successive approximation converter. You don't need to know how it works to use it, but it isn't difficult to understand. The idea is that first a voltage equal to $V_{REF}/2$ is generated and the input voltage is compared to this. If it is lower then the most significant bit is a 0 and if it is greater than or equal then it is a 1. At the next step the voltage generated is $V_{REF}/2 + V_{REF}/4$ and the comparison is repeated to generate the next bit.

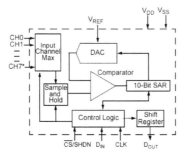

You can see that successive approximation fits in well with a serial bus as each bit can be obtained in the time needed to transmit the previous bit. However, the conversion is relatively slow and a sample-and-hold circuit has to be used to keep the input to the converter stage fixed. The sample-and-hold takes the form of a 20pF capacitor and a switch. The only reason you need to know about this is that the conversion has to be completed in a time that is short compared to the discharge time of the capacitor. So, for accuracy, there is a minimum SPI clock rate as well as a maximum.

Also, to charge the capacitor quickly enough for it to follow a changing voltage, it needs to be connected to a low-impedance source. In most cases this isn't a problem, but if it is you need to include an op amp.

If you are using an op amp buffer then you might as well implement an anti-aliasing filter to remove frequencies from the signal that are too fast for the A-to-D to respond to. How all this works takes us into the realm of analog electronics and signal processing and well beyond the core subject matter of this book.

You can also use the A-to-D channels in pairs, i.e. in differential mode, to measure the voltage difference between them. For example, in differential mode you measure the difference between CH0 and CH1, i.e. what you measure is CH1-CH0. In most cases you want to use all eight channels in single-ended mode. In principle, you can take 200k samples per second, but only at the upper limit of the supply voltage, i.e. V_{DD}=5V, falling to 75k samples per second at its lower limit of V_{DD}=2.7V.

The SPI clock limits are a maximum of 3.6MHz at 5V and 1.35MHz at 2.7V. The clock can go slower, but because of the problem with the sample-and-hold mentioned earlier, it shouldn't go below 10kHz. How fast we can take samples is discussed later.

Connecting to the CM5

The connection from the MCP3008 to the CM5's SPI bus is very simple and can be seen in the diagram below.

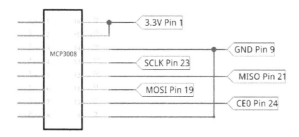

The only additional component that is recommended is a 1μF capacitor connected between pins 15 and 16 to ground, which is mounted as close to the chip as possible. As discussed in the previous section, you might want a separate voltage reference for pin 15, rather than just using the 3.3V supply.

Basic Configuration

From the datasheet, the chip select has to be active low and, by default, data is sent most significant bit first for both the master and the slave. The only puzzle is what mode to use? This is listed in the datasheet as mode 0 0 with clock active high or mode 1 1 with clock active low. For simplicity, we will use mode 0 0, which is mode0 in SPIdev.

We now have enough information to initialize the SPI bus:

```
int fd = open("/dev/spidev0.0", O_RDWR);
 printf("%d\n\r", fd);

static uint8_t mode = 0;
int status = ioctl(fd, SPI_IOC_WR_MODE, &mode);
if (status == -1)
    printf("can't set spi mode");
static uint8_t bits = 8;
status = ioctl(fd, SPI_IOC_WR_BITS_PER_WORD, &bits);
if (status == -1)
    printf("can't set bits per word");
static uint32_t speed = 100000;
status = ioctl(fd, SPI_IOC_WR_MAX_SPEED_HZ, &speed);
if (status == -1)
    printf("can't set max speed hz");
```

The Protocol

Now we have the SPI initialized and ready to transfer data, but what data do we transfer? The SPI bus doesn't have any standard commands or addressing structure. Each device responds to data sent in different ways and sends data back in different ways. You simply have to read the datasheet to find out what the commands and responses are.

Reading the datasheet might be initially confusing because it says that you have to send five bits to the slave - a start bit, a bit that selects its operating mode single or differential, and a 3-bit channel number. The operating mode is 1 for single-ended and 0 for differential.

So to read Channel 3, i.e. 011, in single-ended mode you would send the slave:

```
11011xxx
```

where an x can take either value. The response from the slave is that it holds its output in a high impedance state until the sixth clock pulse, then sends a zero bit on the seventh followed by bit 9 of the data on the eighth clock pulse. That is, the slave sends back:

```
xxxxxx0b9
```

where x means indeterminate. The remaining nine bits are sent back in response to the next nine clock pulses. This means you have to transfer three bytes to get all ten bits of data. This all makes reading the data in 8-bit chunks confusing.

The datasheet also suggests a different way of doing the job that delivers the data more neatly packed into three bytes. What it suggests to send a single byte is:

```
00000001
```

At the same time, the slave transfers random data, which is ignored. The final 1 is treated as the start bit. If you now transfer a second byte with the most significant bit indicating single or differential mode, then a 3-bit channel address and the remaining bits set to 0, the slave will respond with the null and the top two bits of the conversion. Now all you have to do to get the final eight bits of data is to read a third byte:

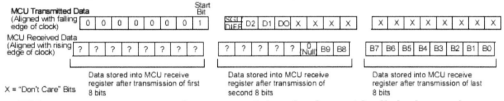

This way you get two neat bytes containing the data with all the low-order bits in their correct positions.

Using this information we can now write some instructions that read a given channel. For example, to read Channel 0 we first send a byte set to 0x01 as the start bit and ignore the byte the slave transfers. Next we send 0x80 to select single-ended and Channel 0 and keep the byte the slave sends back as the two high-order bits.

Finally, we send a zero byte (0x00) so that we get the low-order bits from the slave i.e.

```c
uint8_t tx[] = {0x01,0x80,0x00};
uint8_t rx[3] ;
struct spi_ioc_transfer tr =
    {
        .tx_buf = (unsigned long)tx,
        .rx_buf = (unsigned long)rx,
        .len = 3,
        .delay_usecs = 0,
        .speed_hz = 0,
        .bits_per_word = 0,
    };
int status = ioctl(fd, SPI_IOC_MESSAGE(1), &tr);
printf("%d\n\r", status);
if (status < 0)
    printf("can't send data");
```

Notice you cannot send the three bytes one at a time using transfer because that results in the CS line being deactivated between the transfer of each byte.

To get the data out of rx we need to do some bit manipulation:

```
int data = ((int) rx[1] & 0x03) << 8 | (int) rx[2];
```

The first part of the expression extracts the low three bits from the first byte the slave sent and, as these are the most significant bits, they are shifted up eight places. The rest of the bits are then ORed with them to give the full 10-bit result. To convert to volts we use:

```
float volts = (float) data * 3.3f / 1023.0f;
```

assuming that V_{REF} is 3.3V.

In a real application you would also need to convert the voltage to some other quantity, like temperature or light level.

If you connect a logic analyzer to the SPI bus you will see something like:

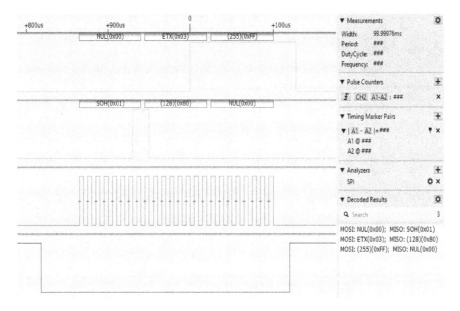

You can see the commands and the response, in this case a reading of 3.3V.

The complete program is:

```c
#include <stdio.h>
#include <stdlib.h>
#include <string.h>
#include <fcntl.h>
#include <unistd.h>
#include <sys/ioctl.h>
#include <linux/spi/spidev.h>
#include <stdint.h>

FILE *doCommand(char *cmd)
{
    FILE *fp = popen(cmd, "r");
    if (fp == NULL)
    {
        printf("Failed to run command %s \n\r", cmd);
        exit(1);
    }
    return fp;
}

void checkSPI0()
{
    FILE *fd = doCommand("sudo  dtparam -l");
    char output[1024];
    int txfound = 0;
    char indicator[] = "spi=on";
    char command[] = "sudo dtparam spi=on";
    while (fgets(output, sizeof(output), fd) != NULL)
    {
        printf("%s\n\r", output);
        fflush(stdout);
        if (strstr(output, indicator) != NULL)
        {
            txfound = 1;
        }
    }
    if (txfound == 0)
    {
        fd = doCommand(command);
        sleep(2);
    }
    pclose(fd);
}
```

```c
int main(int argc, char **argv)
{
    checkSPI0();

    uint8_t tx[] = {0x01, 0x80, 0x00};
    uint8_t rx[3];

    struct spi_ioc_transfer tr =
        {
            .tx_buf = (unsigned long)tx,
            .rx_buf = (unsigned long)rx,
            .len = 3,
            .delay_usecs = 0,
            .speed_hz = 0,
            .bits_per_word = 0,
        };

    int fd = open("/dev/spidev0.0", O_RDWR);

    static uint8_t mode = 0;
    int status = ioctl(fd, SPI_IOC_WR_MODE, &mode);
    if (status == -1)
        printf("can't set spi mode");

    static uint8_t bits = 8;
    status = ioctl(fd, SPI_IOC_WR_BITS_PER_WORD, &bits);
    if (status == -1)
        printf("can't set bits per word");

    static uint32_t speed = 100000;
    status = ioctl(fd, SPI_IOC_WR_MAX_SPEED_HZ, &speed);
    if (status == -1)
        printf("can't set max speed hz");

    status = ioctl(fd, SPI_IOC_MESSAGE(1), &tr);
    if (status < 0)
        printf("can't send data");

    int data = ((int)rx[1] & 0x03) << 8 | (int)rx[2];
    float volts = (((float)data) * 3.3f) / 1023.0f;
    printf("%f V\n\r", volts);

    close(fd);
}
```

MCP3008 in Gpio5

The same program is easy to implement in Gpio5 using its SPI functions:

```
#include <stdio.h>
#include <stdlib.h>
#include <time.h>
#include "Gpio5.h"
int main(int argc, char **argv)
{
    rp1_Init();
    gpio_set_function(8, GPIO_FUNC_SPI);  // CS0
    gpio_set_function(9, GPIO_FUNC_SPI);  // MISO
    gpio_set_function(10, GPIO_FUNC_SPI); // MOSI
    gpio_set_function(11, GPIO_FUNC_SPI); // SCLK
    spi_init(SPI0, 3 * 1000 * 1000);
    spi_set_format(SPI0, 8, SPI_CPOL_0, SPI_CPHA_0, SPI_MSB_FIRST);
    uint8_t wBuff[3] = {0x01, 0x80, 0x00};
    uint8_t rBuff[3];
    spi_set_slave(SPI0, 0);
    spi_set_CS_toggle(SPI0, false);
    int n = spi_write_read_blocking(SPI0, wBuff, rBuff, 3);
    int data = ((int)rBuff[1] & 0x03) << 8 | (int)rBuff[2];
    float volts = (float)data * 3.3f / 1023.0f;
    printf("%f V\n", volts);
    return (EXIT_SUCCESS);
}
```

The clock speed is set to 3MHz and the CS line is set to CS0 with no toggle.

How Fast

Once you have the basic facilities working, the next question is always how fast does something work. In this case we need to know what sort of data rates we can achieve using this A-to-D converter. The simplest way of finding this out is to use the fastest read loop for Channel 0:

```
for (;;)
{
    status = ioctl(fd, SPI_IOC_MESSAGE(1), &tr);
    if (status < 0)
        printf("can't send data");
}
```

With the clock set at 100K, the sampling rate is measured to be 3.6kHz. This is perfectly reasonable as it takes at least 24 clock pulses to read the data. Most of the time in the loop is due to the 24 clock pulses, so there is little to be gained from optimization. Increasing the clock rate to the maximum of 3MHz increases the sampling rate to 34kHz,

The same test using Gpio5 gives a repeat rate of 89KHz for a clock rate of 3MHz.

The MCP3008 Driver

Although there are some advantages in dealing with the MCP2008 ADC using `spidev`, you can also use a driver that works directly with it and avoid dealing with SPI and the device commands altogether.

To do this you need to add:

```
dtparam=spi=on
dtoverlay=mcp3008:spi0-0-present,spi0-0-speed=1000000
```

to the `/boot/firmware/config.txt` file. At the time of writing you can't enable the driver dynamically. You have to specify the SPIdev node that the device is on, `spi0.0` in this case, and the speed of the clock, 1MHz in this case. If you want to use another SPI interface, you have to load a driver for it and change the SPIdev node specified.

Once you have the driver loaded, reboot after editing `/boot/config.txt`, you will discover that there are some new folders and files in `/sys/bus/`. The reason that they are in this different location is that the driver is an IIO (Industrial I/O) driver. These are described in detail in Chapter 14, but all that really matters is that the pseudo files relating to the device are in a different location. All IIO devices live in the `/sys/bus/iio/devices/` directory and a folder of the form `iio:devicex` is created for each device. In our case there is only one IIO device and so the folder we are interested in is `/sys/bus/iio/devices/iio:device0`.

If you list this folder you will find files with names that indicate their function:

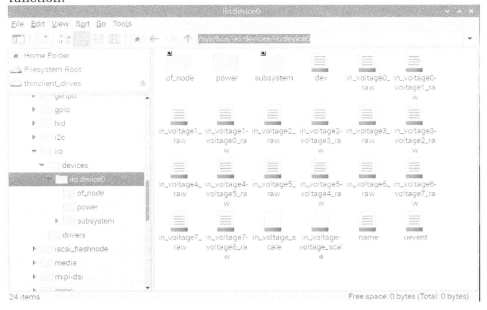

For example in_voltage0_raw is the raw reading from channel 0 of the device. Similarly in_voltage0-voltage1_raw is the differential voltage using input 0 and input 1 as a differential input.

A program to read channel 0, given that the drivers are loaded, is very simple:

```c
#include <stdio.h>
#include <stdlib.h>
#include <string.h>
#include <fcntl.h>
#include <unistd.h>
#include <sys/ioctl.h>
#include <linux/spi/spidev.h>
#include <stdint.h>
int main(int argc, char **argv)
{
    char buf[100];
    int fd =open("/sys/bus/iio/devices/iio:device0/
                           in_voltage0_raw",O_RDONLY);

    int n = read(fd, buf, 100);

    int data;
    sscanf(buf, "%d", &data);

    printf("%d\n\r", data);
    float volts = (((float)data) * 3.3f) / 1023.0f;
    printf("%f V\n\r", volts);
}
```

The act of opening the file starts the conversion.

To read the device a second time you either have to close the file and reopen it or reposition it to the start:

```c
    for (;;)
    {
        int n = read(fd, buf, 100);
        int data;
        sscanf(buf, "%d", &data);
        printf("%d\n\r", data);
        float volts = (((float)data) * 3.3f) / 1023.0f;
        printf("%f V\n\r", volts);
        lseek(fd, SEEK_SET, 0);
    }
```

Without any processing of the data, you can read data at around 17kHz.

Problems

The SPI bus is often a real headache because of the lack of a definitive standard, but in most cases you can make it work. The first problem is in discovering the characteristics of the slave device you want to work with. In general, this is solved by a careful reading of the datasheet or perhaps some trial and error, see the next chapter for an example.

If you are working with a single slave then generally things work once you have the SPI bus configuration set correctly. Things are more difficult when there are multiple devices on the same bus. Typically you will find SPI devices that don't switch off properly when they are not being addressed. In principle, all SPI devices should present high impedance outputs (i.e. tristate buffers) when not being addressed, but some don't. If you encounter a problem you need to check that the selected slave is able to control the MISO line properly.

Another problem, which is particularly bad for the Pi, is noise. If you are using a USB, or some other power supply that isn't able to supply sufficient instantaneous current draw to the Pi, you will see noise on any or all of the data lines - the CS0/1 lines seem to be particularly sensitive. The solution is to get a better power supply.

If there is a full driver for the device then it is a good idea to give it a try, but many SPI device drivers are poorly supported and documentation is usually non-existent. If you can get a direct driver to work then it will usually be faster and easier, but it might not be as stable as hand-coding your own user-side interaction with the device with the help of SPIdev or Gpio5.

Notice that some of the SPI controllers support multiple data lines. SPI0 will work in quad mode, SP1,2,3 and 5 will work in dual mode. SPI4 will only work with a single data line. It is not difficult to add these transfer modes to Gpio5 by writing the appropriate register – see CTRLR0 SPI_FRF SPI Frame Format.

Summary

- The CM5 has six SPI controllers but not all can be used at the same time.

- Making SPI work with any particular device has four steps:

  1. Discover how to connect the device to the SPI pins. This is a matter of identifying pinouts and what chip selects are supported.

  2. Find out how to configure the Pi's SPI bus to work with the device. This is mostly a matter of clock speed and mode.

  3. Identify the commands that you need to send to the device to get it to do something and what data it sends back as a response.

  4. Find, or work out, the relationship between the raw reading, the voltage, and the quantity the voltage represents.

- The Linux SPI driver can be used to interface to any SPI device as long as you know what commands to send and what the data sent back means.

- The SPI driver is supported by the SPIdev header which provides the basic tools to work with the ioctl interface.

- The SPI driver uses general GPIO lines as chip select lines and not the built-in hardware.

- The hardware SPI controllers are based on Synopsys DW_apb_ssi and this is well documented.

- It is easy to extend Gpio5 to work with SPI with many advantages.

- Using the other SPI interfaces on the CM5 is just a matter of selecting the appropriate driver.

- The MCP3000 range of A-to-D converters is very easy to use via SPI. It can be used directly from the SPI bus by sending commands and reading the data generated.

- There is also a specific MCP3008 driver which allows you to work with the device without having to know anything about SPI or the commands that have to be sent to read the data.

- The MCP3008 driver is an example of an IIO device.

Chapter 13

I2C Driver and Gpio5

The I2C, standing for Inter-Integrated Circuit and pronounced I-Squared-C, bus, is one of the most useful ways of connecting moderately sophisticated sensors and peripherals to any processor. The only problem is that it can seem like a nightmarish confusion of hardware, low-level interaction and high-level software. There are few general introductions to the subject because at first sight every I2C device is different, but there are shared principles that can help you work out how to connect and talk to a new device.

The I2C bus is a serial bus that can be used to connect multiple devices to a controller. It is a simple bus that uses two active wires: one for data and one for a clock. Despite there being lots of problems in using the I2C bus, because it isn't well standardized and devices can conflict and generally do things in their own way, it is still commonly used and is too useful to ignore.

The big problem in getting started with the I2C bus is that you will find it described at many different levels of detail, from the physical bus characteristics and protocol to the details of individual devices. It can be difficult to tie all of this together and produce a working project. In fact, you only need to know the general workings of the I2C bus, some general features of the protocol, and know the addresses and commands used by any particular device.

To explain and illustrate these ideas, we really do have to work with a particular device to make things concrete. However, the basic stages of getting things to work, the steps, the testing and verification, are more or less the same irrespective of the device.

I2C Hardware Basics

The I2C bus is very simple from the hardware point of view. It has just two signal lines, SDA and SCL, the data and clock lines respectively. Each of these lines is pulled up by a suitable resistor to the supply line at whatever voltage the devices are working - 3.3V and 5V are common choices. The size of the pull-up resistors isn't critical, but 4.7K is typical as shown in the circuit diagram:

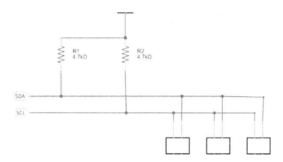

You simply connect the SDA and SCL pins of each of the devices to the pull-up resistors. Of course, if any of the devices have built-in pull-up resistors you can omit the external resistors. More of a problem is if multiple devices each have pull-ups. In this case you need to disable all but one.

The I2C bus is an open collector bus. This means that it is actively pulled down by a transistor set to on. When the transistor is off, however, the bus returns to the high voltage state via the pull-up resistor. The advantage of this approach is that multiple devices can pull the bus low at the same time. That is, an open collector bus is low when one or more devices pull it low and high when none of the devices is active.

The SCL line provides a clock which is used to set the speed of data transfer, one data bit is presented on the SDA line for each pulse on the SCL line. In all cases, the master drives the clock line to control how fast bits are transferred. The slave can, however, hold the clock line low if it needs to slow down the data transfer. In most cases the I2C bus has a single master device, the Pi in our case, which drives the clock and invites the slaves to receive or transmit data. Multiple masters are possible, but this is advanced and usually not necessary.

At this point we could go into the details of how all of this works in terms of bits. All you really need to know is that all communication occurs in 8-bit packets. The master sends a packet, an address frame, which contains the address of the slave it wants to interact with. Every slave has to have a unique address, which is usually 7 bits, but it can be 11 bits, and the Pi does support this.

One of the problems in using the I2C bus is that manufacturers often use the same address, or same set of selectable addresses, and this can make using particular combinations of devices on the same bus difficult or impossible.

The 7-bit address is set as the high-order 7 bits in the byte and this can be confusing as an address that is stated as 0x40 in the datasheet results in 0x80 being sent to the device. The low-order bit of the address signals a write or a read operation depending on whether it is a 0 or a 1 respectively. After sending an address frame, it then sends or receives data frames back from the slave. There are also special signals used to mark the start and end of an exchange of packets, but the library functions take care of these.

This is really all you need to know about I2C in general to get started, but it is worth finding out more of the details as you need them. You almost certainly will need them as you debug I2C programs using a logic analyzer.

The clock SCL and data SDA lines rest high. The master signals a Start bit by pulling the SDA line down – S in the diagram below. The clock is then pulled low by the master, during which time the SDA line can change state. The state of the bit is read in the middle of the following high period of the clock pulse B1, B2 and so on in the diagram. This continues until the last bit has been sent, when the data line is allowed to rise while the clock is high, so sending a stoP bit – P in the diagram. Notice that when data is being transmitted the data line doesn't change while the clock is high. Any change in the data line when the clock is high sends a start or a stop bit, i.e. clock high and falling data line is a start bit and clock high and rising data line is a stop bit:

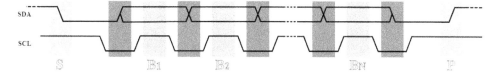

The clock speed was originally set at 100kHz, standard mode, but then increased to 400kHz in fast mode. In practice, devices usually specify a maximum clock speed that they will work with.

Data Transfer

Now that we know the low-level details of how the I2C bus works it is time to look at the detailed interaction between the master and the slave. To make use of I2C you often don't need this deeper knowledge, but as soon as something goes wrong you most definitely do.

In most cases the clock line is controlled by the master – the exception to this rule is during clock stretching, see later. Whichever entity is transmitting data, i.e. controlling the data line, the last bit is set by the other entity to signal a success – ACK, data line low, or failure – NAK, data line high.

Let's start by examining what happens when the master writes data to the slave. In all cases, first an address frame, a byte containing the address of the device you specified, is transmitted. Notice that the 7-bit address has to be shifted into the topmost bits and the first bit has to be zeroed for a write operation. So when you write to a device with an address of 0x40 you will see 0x80 on a logic analyzer, i.e. 0x40<<1.

Having sent the address frame, the master can send as many bytes as it wants to. The slave responds with an ACK or a NAK bit after each byte.

That is, the usual block write transaction sending n bytes is:

```
START|ADDR|ACK|DATA0|ACK|
            DATA1|ACK|
               . . . .
            DATAn|ACK|STOP
```

Notice that it is the slave that sends the ACK bit and if the data is not received correctly it can send NAK instead and a write error will be reported.

A multibyte transfer is quite different from sending n single bytes one at a time.

```
START|  ADDR  |ACK|DATA0|ACK|STOP
START|  ADDR  |ACK|DATA1|ACK|STOP
        . . .
START|  ADDR  |ACK|DATAn|ACK|STOP
```

Notice that there are now multiple ADDR frames sent as well as multiple START and STOP bits. What this means in practice is that you have to look at a device's datasheet and send however many bytes it needs as a single operation. You cannot send the same number of bytes broken into chunks. The Linux driver naturally provides a block write.

Reading works in much the same way - the master sends an address frame and then reads as many bytes from the slave as specified. As in the case of write, the address supplied is shifted up one bit and the lower order bit set to 1 to indicate a read operation. So if the current slave is at address 0x40, the read address is 0x41 and the master sends a read address of 0x81.

The read transaction is:

```
START|ADDR|ACK|DATA0|ACK|
              |DATA1|ACK|
        . . .
              |DATAn|NAK|STOP
```

The master sends the address frame and the slave sends the ACK after the address to acknowledge that it has been received and it is ready to send data. Then the slave sends bytes one at a time and the master sends ACK in response to each byte. Finally the master sends a NAK to indicate that the last byte has been read and then a STOP bit. That is, the master controls how many bytes are transferred.

As in the case of the write functions, a block transfer of n bytes is different from transferring n bytes one at a time because of the additional stop bits.

Using a Register

A very standard interaction between master and slave is writing or reading data to and from a register. This isn't anything special and, as far as the I2C bus is concerned, you are simply writing raw data. However, datasheets and users tend to think in terms of reading and writing internal storage locations, i.e. registers in the device. In fact, many devices have lots of internal storage. Indeed, some I2C devices, for example I2C EPROMS, are nothing but internal storage. In this case a standard transaction to write to a register is:

1) Send address frame
2) Send a data frame with the command to select the register
3) Send a data frame containing the byte or word to be written to the register

Notice the command that has to be sent depends on the device and you have to look it up in its datasheet. Also notice that there is a single START and STOP bit at the beginning and end of the transaction. Sometimes just the register address is sufficient, i.e. no following data. In this case you can think of the register address as a command if you like.

Reading from a register is a very standard operation, but it is slightly more complicated in that you need a combined write and read operation. That is, to read a register you need a write operation to send the address of the register to the device and then a read operation to get the data that the device sends as the contents of the register. This write/read combination is so common that I2C libraries often provide a single function to do the job.

In theory, and mostly in practice, a register read of this sort can work with a stop-start separating the write and read operations, which is what you get if you use separate write and read function calls:

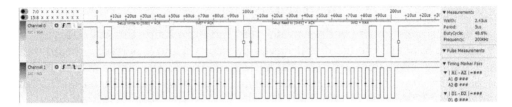

That is, the transfer sequence is:

```
START|ADDR|ACK|REGADDR|ACK|STOP|
START|ADDR|ACK|DATA1|ACK|
              |DATA2|ACK|
          . . .
              |DATAn|NAK|STOP
```

If you look at the end of the write and the start of the read you will see that there is both a STOP and a START bit between them. For some devices this is a problem. A STOP bit is a signal that another transaction can start and this might allow another master to take over the bus. To avoid this, some devices demand a repeated START bit between the write and the read and no STOP bit. This is referred to as a repeated start bit transaction. That is, the sequence for a repeated start bit register read is:

```
START|ADDR|ACK|REGADDR|ACK|
START|ADDR|ACK|DATA0|ACK|
              |DATA1|ACK|
          . . .
              |DATAn|NAK|STOP
```

Notice that there is only one STOP bit and it does mark the true end of the data transfer.

In theory, either form of transaction should work but in practice you will find that some slave devices state that they need a repeated start bit and no stop bits in continued transactions. In this case you need to be careful how you send and receive data.

Slow Read – Clock Stretching v Polling

The I2C clock is mostly controlled by the master and this raises the question of how we cope with the speed that a slave can or cannot respond to a request for data. There are two broad approaches to waiting for data on the I2C bus. The first is simply to request the data and then perform reads in a polling loop. If the device isn't ready with the data, then it sends a data frame with a NAK bit set. So all we have to do is test for an NAK response. Of course, the polling loop doesn't have to be "tight". The response time is often long enough to do other things and you can use the I2C bus to work with other slave devices while the one you activated gets on with trying to get the data you requested. All you have to do is to remember to read its data at some later time.

The second way is to allow the slave to hold the clock line low after the master has released it – so called clock stretching. In most cases the master will simply wait before moving on to the next frame while the clock line is held low. This is very simple and it means you don't have to implement a polling loop, but also notice that your program is frozen until the slave releases the clock line. The Raspberry Pi's implementation of I2C clock stretching has a flaw in that it fails if the clock stretching is very short, and as a result polling is the preferred option.

Basic I2C Hardware

The CM5 uses an implementation of I2C based on the Synopsys DW_apb_i2c (v2.02) which provides seven I2C controllers, but only four are available on external GPIO lines:

I2C0

Function	Pin	GPIO
SDA	27 or 24	GPIO0 or 8
SCL	28 or 21	GPIO1 or 9

I2C1

Function	Pin	GPIO
SDA	3 or 19	GPIO2 or 10
SCL	5 or 23	GPIO3 or 11

I2C2

Function	Pin	GPIO
SDA	3 or 32	GPIO4 or 12
SCL	5 or 33	GPIO5 or 13

I2C3

Function	Pin	GPIO
SDA	3 or 8	GPIO6 or 14
SCL	5 or 10	GPIO7 or 15

All use GPIO mode 3 to set the GPIO lines to the I2C function. The first two I2C channels are also available on other Pi models. I2C 0 is used by the system to detect installed HATs – this can be disabled, but it is simpler to use one of the alternative I2C controllers.

Enabling the Driver

There are many specific device drivers which make use of the I2C bus and, as in the case of the SPI bus, there is usually a choice of hand-coding the interaction using the basic I2C driver or using the specific device driver.

To make use of the Linux I2C driver you have to enable it by adding dtparam=i2c_arm=on to the /boot/config.txt file. Alternatively you can load it dynamically:

```
FILE * doCommand(char *cmd) {
    FILE *fp = popen(cmd, "r");
    if (fp == NULL) {
        printf("Failed to run command %s \n\r", cmd);
        exit(1);
    }
    return fp;
}

void checkI2CBus() {
    FILE *fd = doCommand("sudo dtparam -l");
    char output[1024];
    int txfound = 0;
    while (fgets(output, sizeof (output), fd) != NULL) {
        printf("%s\n\r", output);
        fflush(stdout);
        if (strstr(output, "i2c_arm=on") != NULL) {
            txfound = 1;
        }
        if (strstr(output, "i2c_arm=off") != NULL) {
            txfound = 0;
        }
    }
    pclose(fd);
    if (txfound == 0) {
        fd = doCommand("sudo dtparam i2c_arm=on");
        pclose(fd);
    }
}
```

This is slightly different to the earlier driver loading functions. The first part of the function uses dtparam -l to get a list of loaded overlays. If it finds ic2_arm=on as the last ic2_arm overlay then it does nothing. If it doesn't find it then it activates the overlay. As you can also use ic2_arm=off and it is the last overlay that controls the state of the system we need to find the last occurrence of ic2_arm and make sure it is "=on".

Both actions create a device file:

```
/dev/i2c-1
```

You can check that the driver has been installed using:

```
ls /dev/i2c*
```

which will return a list of I2C devices.

Using the I2C Driver From C

As is the case for all Linux devices, the I2C device /dev/i2c-x, where x is the I2C bus number, looks like a file. You can do a block read by simply opening the file for reading and reading an array of bytes:

```
int i2cfd = open("/dev/i2c-1", O_RDWR);
read(i2cfd,buf,n);
```

This reads a maximum of *n* bytes of data and returns it as an array of bytes. The only problem is how do you specify the address of the device? Opening the file only opens the I2C channel and there might be multiple devices connected to it. As in the case of other /dev character devices we need to use the standard Linux ioctl function to send a command to it.

In the case of the I2C driver the most important ioctl command is:

```
I2C_SLAVE
```

This is used to set the address of the slave that subsequent read and writes apply to. So to set the address of the device you want to read from to 0x40 you would use:

```
#include <linux/i2c-dev.h>

ioctl(i2cfd, I2C_SLAVE, 0x40);
```

Finally to reset the hardware and return all GPIO lines to their default modes you have to close the file:

```
close(i2cfd);
```

Putting all of the together a block read/write is:

```
#include <stdio.h>
#include <stdlib.h>
#include <sys/ioctl.h>
#include <unistd.h>
#include <string.h>
#include <fcntl.h>
#include <linux/i2c-dev.h>

void checkI2CBus();
FILE * doCommand(char *cmd);

int main(int argc, char** argv) {
    checkI2CBus();
    int i2cfd = open("/dev/i2c-1", O_RDWR);
    ioctl(i2cfd, I2C_SLAVE, 0x40);
    char buf[4] = {0xE7};
    write(i2cfd,buf,1);
    read(i2cfd,buf,1);
    close(i2cfd);
    return (EXIT_SUCCESS);
}
```

By default stop bits are not sent between each byte read, a stop bit is only sent at the end of the block of data that is written.

If you try these programs out you will discover that the I2C clock frequency is the default 100KHz. You can't change the clock frequency dynamically, but you can add:

```
dtparam=i2c_arm=on,i2c_arm_baudrate=10000
```

to the `/boot/firmware/config.txt` file and after a reboot the I2C clock will be set to the frequency specified by `baudrate`. The baud rate is simply the clock speed in Hz.

A Real Device - HTU21D

Using an I2C device has two problems - the physical connection between master and slave and figuring out what the software has to do to make it work. Here we'll work with the SparkFun HTU21D/Si7021 and the information in its datasheet to make a working temperature and humidity sensor using the I2C functions we've just met.

First the hardware. The HTU21D Humidity and Temperature sensor is one of the easiest of I2C devices to use. Its only problem is that it is only available in a surface-mount package. To overcome this you could solder some wires onto the pads or buy a general breakout board. However, it is much simpler to buy the SparkFun HTU21D breakout board because this has easy connections and built-in pull-up resistors. The HTU21D has been replaced by the Si7021, which is more robust than the original and works in the same way although the HTU21D is still available from many sources. If you decide to work with some other I2C device you can still follow the steps given, modifying what you do to suit it. In particular, if you select a device that only works at 5V you might need a level converter.

It is worth noting that there is a specific Linux driver for the HTU21D. This is described in Chapter 14 and in most cases is the preferred way to use the device. To provide a generalizable example, here we look at exactly how the device works on the I2C bus and a program that interfaces with it at a low level is described.

Wiring the HTU21D

Given that the HTU21D has pull-up resistors, we really should disable them for use on the Pi's internal I2C bus which already has pull-ups. In practice, the additional pull-ups don't seem to make much difference to the waveforms and you can leave them in place while testing. You can use a prototype board to make the connections and this makes it easier to connect other instruments such as a logic analyzer. As we are using I2C1 we need to connect to GPIO2 and GPIO3.

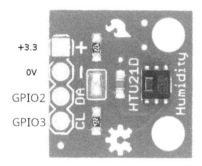 

A First Program

After wiring up any i2C device the first question that needs to be answered is, does it work? Unfortunately for most complex devices finding out if it works is a multi-step process. Our first program aims to read some data back from the HTU21D - any data will do.

If you look at the datasheet you will find that the device address is 0x40 and its supports the following commands/registers:

Command	Code	Comment
Trigger Temperature Measurement	0xE3	Hold master
Trigger Humidity Measurement	0xE5	Hold master
Trigger Temperature Measurement	0xF3	No Hold master
Trigger Humidity Measurement	0xF5	No Hold master
Write user register	0xE6	
Read user register	0xE7	
Soft Reset	0xFE	

The easiest of these to get started with is the Read user register command, which gives the current setup of the device and can be used to set the resolution of the measurement.

Notice that the codes that you send to the device can often be considered addresses or commands. In this case you can think of sending 0xE7 as a command to read the register or the read address of the register, it makes no difference. In most cases the term command is used when sending the code makes the device do something, and the term address is used when it simply makes the device read or write specific data.

To read the user register we have to write a byte containing 0xE7 and then read the byte the device sends back. This involves sending an address frame, a data frame, and then another address frame and reading a data frame. The device seems to be happy if you send a stop bit between each transaction or just a new start bit.

A program to read the user register is fairly easy to put together. The address of the device is 0x40 so its write address is 0x80 and its read address is 0x81. As the I2C functions adjust the address as needed, we simply use 0x40 as the device's address, but it does affect what you see if you sample the data being exchanged:

```c
#include <stdio.h>
#include <stdlib.h>
#include <string.h>
#include <sys/ioctl.h>
#include <unistd.h>
#include <fcntl.h>
#include <linux/i2c-dev.h>

void checkI2CBus();
FILE * doCommand(char *cmd);


int main(int argc, char** argv) {

    checkI2CBus();

    int i2cfd = open("/dev/i2c-1", O_RDWR);
    ioctl(i2cfd, I2C_SLAVE, 0x40);
    char buf[4] = {0xE7};
    write(i2cfd,buf,1);
    read(i2cfd,buf,1);
    printf("%x\n\r",buf[0]);
    close(i2cfd);
    return (EXIT_SUCCESS);
}
```

This sends the address frame 0x80 and then the data byte 0xE7 to select the user register. Next it sends an address frame 0x81 to read the data.

If you run the program you will see "2".

This is the default value of the register and it corresponds to a resolution of 12 and 14 bits for the humidity and temperature respectively and a supply voltage greater than 2.25V.

I2C Protocol In Action

If you have a logic analyzer that can interpret the I2C protocol connected what you will see is:

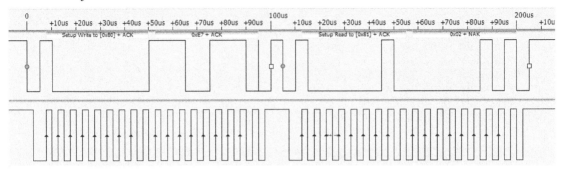

You can see that the `write_byte` function sends an address packet set to the device's 7-bit address `0x40` as the high order bits with the low order bit set to zero to indicate a write, i.e `0x80`. After this you get a data packet sent containing `0xE7`, the address of the register. After a few microseconds it sends the address frame again, only this time with the low order bit set to 1 to indicate a read, i.e. it sends `0x81`. It then receives back a single byte of data from the device, `0x02`. This demonstrates that the external device is working properly and we can move on to getting some data of interest.

Reading Raw Temperature Data

Now we come to reading one of the two quantities that the device measures – temperature. If you look back at the command table you will see that there are two possible commands for reading the temperature:

Command	Code	Comment
Trigger Temperature Measurement	0xE3	Hold master
Trigger Temperature Measurement	0xF3	No Hold master

What is the difference between Hold master and No Hold master? This was discussed earlier in a general context. The device cannot read the temperature instantaneously and the master can either opt to be held waiting for the data, i.e. hold master, or released to do something else and poll for the data until it is ready. The simplest thing to do is poll for the data. How to use the alternative approach of clock stretching is described later.

In this case we send F3 and then wait for there to be something to read. If the slave isn't ready it simply replies with a NAK and this causes the read to return -1. When the slave returns an ACK then three bytes are read and result is 3, bringing the loop to an end:

```
char buf[3] = {0xF3};
write(i2cfd, buf, 1);

while (1) {
    int result = read(i2cfd, buf, 3);
    if (result > 0) break;
    usleep(100*1000);

}
```

This polls repeatedly until the slave device returns an ACK, when the data is loaded into the data.

Putting this into a complete program gives:

```
int main(int argc, char** argv) {
    checkI2CBus();

    int i2cfd = open("/dev/i2c-1", O_RDWR);
    ioctl(i2cfd, I2C_SLAVE, 0x40);
    char buf[3] = {0xF3};
    write(i2cfd, buf, 1);

    while (1) {
        int result = read(i2cfd, buf, 3);
        if (result > 0) break;
        usleep(10*1000);

    }
    uint8_t msb = buf[0];
    uint8_t lsb = buf[1];
    uint8_t check = buf[2];
    printf("msb %d \n\rlsb %d \n\rchecksum %d \n\r",
                                            msb, lsb, check);
    close(i2cfd);
    return (EXIT_SUCCESS);
}
```

Where the checkI2CBus has been omitted as it was given earlier.

If you try this out you should find that it works and it prints something like:

```
msb 97
lsb 232
checksum 217
```

with the temperature in the 20C range.

253

If you look at what is happening using a logic analyzer then you will see the initial interaction:

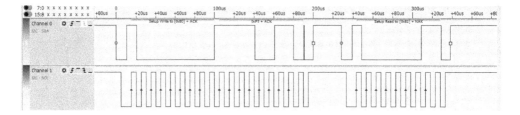

followed by repeated attempts to read the data:

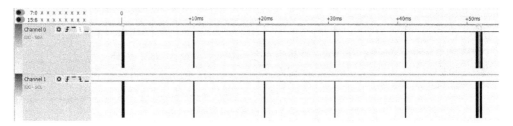

When the device is ready it responds with an ACK and the three data bytes are read:

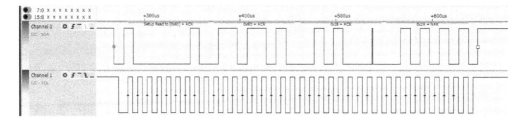

You can also see that only one start and one stop bit is used.

Processing The Data

Our next task isn't really directly related to the problem of using the I2C bus, but it is a very typical next step. The device returns the data in three bytes, but the way that this data relates to the temperature isn't simple.

If you read the datasheet you will discover that the temperature data is the 14-bit value that results from putting together the most and least significant byte and zeroing the bottom two bits. The bottom two bits are used as status bits, bit zero currently isn't used and bit one is 1 if the data is a humidity measurement and 0 if it is a temperature measurement.

To put the two bytes together we use:

```
unsigned int data16=((unsigned int) msb << 8) |
                          (unsigned int) (lsb & 0xFC);
```

This zeros the bottom two bits, shifts the `msb` up eight bits and ORs the two together. The result is a 16-bit temperature value with the bottom two bits zeroed.

Now we have raw temperature value but we still have to convert it to standard units. The datasheet gives the formula:

```
Temp in C = -46.85 + 175.72 * data16 / 216
```

The only problem in implementing this is working out 2^{16}. You can work out 2^x with the expression 1<<x, i.e. shift 1 x places to the left.

This gives:

```
float temp = (float)(-46.85 +(175.72 * data16 /(float)(1<<16)));
```

As 2^{16} is a constant that works out to 65536 it is more efficient to write:

```
float temp = (float)(-46.85 +(175.72 * data16 /(float)65536));
```

Now all we have to do is print the temperature:

```
printf("Temperature %f C \n\r", temp);
```

Reading The Humidity

The nice thing about I2C and using a particular I2C device is that it gets easier. Once you have seen how to do it with one device, the skill generalizes and once you know how to deal with a particular device other aspects of the device are usually similar. Reading the humidity using polling is exactly the same as reading the temperature - all that changes is the command code we send:

```
  buf[0] = 0xF5;
    write(i2cfd, buf, 1);
    while (1) {
        int result = read(i2cfd, buf, 3);
        if (result > 0) break;
        usleep(10 * 1000);
    }
    msb = buf[0];
    lsb = buf[1];
    check = buf[2];
```

Once we have the data, the formula to convert the 16-bit value to percentage humidity is:

```
RH= -6 + 125 * data16 / 2¹⁶
```

and the temperature in C is:

```
data16 = ((unsigned int) msb << 8) | (unsigned int) (lsb & 0xFC);
float hum = -6 + (125.0 * (float) data16) / 65536;
printf("Humidity %f %% \n\r", hum);
```

Checksum Calculation

Although computing a checksum isn't specific to I2C, it is another common task. The datasheet explains that the polynomial used is:

```
X8 + X5 + X4 + 1
```

Once you have this information you can work out the divisor by writing a binary number with a one in each location corresponding to a power of X in the polynomial. In this case the 8th, 5th, 4th and 1st bit. Hence the divisor is:

```
0x0131
```

What you do next is roughly the same for all CRCs. First you put the data that was used to compute the checksum together with the checksum value as the low order bits:

```
uint32_t data32 = ((uint32_t) msb << 16) | ((uint32_t) lsb << 8) |
                                            (uint32_t) check;
```

Now you have three bytes, i.e 24 bits in a 32-bit value. Next you adjust the divisor so that its most significant non-zero bit aligns with the most significant bit of the three bytes. As this divisor has a 1 at bit eight it needs to be shifted 15 places to the right to move it to be the 24th bit:

```
uint32_t divisor = 0x988000;
```

Now that you have both the data and the divisor aligned, you step through the top-most 16 bits, i.e. you don't process the low order eight bits which is the received checksum. For each bit you check to see if it is a 1 - if it is you replace the data with the data XOR divisor. In either case you shift the divisor one place to the right:

```
for (int i = 0; i < 16; i++) {
    if (data32 & (uint32_t) 1 << (23 - i)) data32 ^= divisor;
    divisor >>= 1;
};
```

When the loop ends, if there was no error, the data32 should be zeroed and the received checksum is correct and as computed on the data received.

A complete function to compute the checksum is:

```
uint8_t crcCheck(uint8_t msb, uint8_t lsb, uint8_t check) {
  uint32_t data32 = ((uint32_t) msb << 16) |
                    ((uint32_t) lsb << 8) | (uint32_t) check;
  uint32_t divisor = 0x988000;
  for (int i = 0; i < 16; i++) {
      if (data32 & (uint32_t) 1 << (23 - i)) data32 ^= divisor;
      divisor >>= 1;
  };
  return (uint8_t) data32;
}
```

It is rare to get a CRC error on an I2C bus unless it is overloaded or subject to a lot of noise.

The Complete Program

```c
#include <stdio.h>
#include <stdlib.h>
#include <stdint.h>
#include <string.h>
#include <sys/ioctl.h>
#include <unistd.h>
#include <fcntl.h>
#include <linux/i2c-dev.h>
void checkI2CBus();
FILE * doCommand(char *cmd);
uint8_t crcCheck(uint8_t msb, uint8_t lsb, uint8_t check);
int main(int argc, char** argv) {
    checkI2CBus();
    int i2cfd = open("/dev/i2c-1", O_RDWR);
    ioctl(i2cfd, I2C_SLAVE, 0x40);
    char buf[3] = {0xF3};
    write(i2cfd, buf, 1);
    while (1) {
        int result = read(i2cfd, buf, 3);
        if (result > 0) break;
        usleep(10 * 1000);

    }
    uint8_t msb = buf[0];
    uint8_t lsb = buf[1];
    uint8_t check = buf[2];
    printf("msb %d \n\rlsb %d \n\rchecksum %d \n\r", msb, lsb,
                                                    check);
    unsigned int data16 = ( (unsigned int) msb << 8) |
                                (unsigned int) (lsb & 0xFC);
    float temp = (float) (-46.85 + (175.72 * data16 /
                                        (float) 65536));
    printf("Temperature %f C \n\r", temp);
    printf("crc = %d\n\r", crcCheck(msb, lsb, check));
    buf[0] = 0xF5;
    write(i2cfd, buf, 1);
    while (1) {
        int result = read(i2cfd, buf, 3);
        if (result > 0) break;
        usleep(10 * 1000);
    }
    msb = buf[0];
    lsb = buf[1];
    check = buf[2];
    printf("crc = %d\n\r", crcCheck(msb, lsb, check));
    data16 = ((unsigned int) msb << 8) |
                                    (unsigned int) (lsb & 0xFC);
    float hum = -6 + (125.0 * (float) data16) / 65536;
    printf("Humidity %f %% \n\r", hum);
```

```
        close(i2cfd);
        return (EXIT_SUCCESS);
}
uint8_t crcCheck(uint8_t msb, uint8_t lsb, uint8_t check) {
    uint32_t data32 = ((uint32_t) msb << 16) |
                        ((uint32_t) lsb << 8) | (uint32_t) check;
    uint32_t divisor = 0x988000;
    for (int i = 0; i < 16; i++) {
        if (data32 & (uint32_t) 1 << (23 - i)) data32 ^= divisor;
        divisor >>= 1;
    };
    return (uint8_t) data32;
}
void checkI2CBus() {
    FILE *fd = doCommand("sudo dtparam -l");
    char output[1024];
    int txfound = 0;
    while (fgets(output, sizeof (output), fd) != NULL) {
        printf("%s\n\r", output);
        fflush(stdout);
        if (strstr(output, "i2c_arm=on") != NULL) {
            txfound = 1;
        }
        if (strstr(output, "i2c_arm=off") != NULL) {
            txfound = 0;
        }
    }
    pclose(fd);
    if (txfound == 0) {
        fd = doCommand("sudo dtparam i2c_arm=on");
        pclose(fd);
    }
}
FILE * doCommand(char *cmd) {
    FILE *fp = popen(cmd, "r");
    if (fp == NULL) {
        printf("Failed to run command %s \n\r", cmd);
        exit(1);
    }
    return fp;
}
```

Other I2C Interfaces

There are some additional I2C drivers that you can enable by simply using the appropriate overlay. To enable I2C bus *n*, where *n* goes from 3 to 6 you use:

```
dtoverlay=i2cn,<param>
```

where the parameters are:

- pins_x_y   Use pins x and y
- baudrate   Set the baud rate for the interface (default "100000")

258

For example, to enable i2c4 on GPIO 6 as SDA and GPIO 7 as SCL, with a clock of 50Khz, you would use:

```
dtoverlay=i2c4 pins_6_7 baudrate=50000
```

You can enable the I2C bus dynamically. To enable bus *n*, and pins pin1 and pin2 use:

```
void enableI2C(int n, int pin1, int pin2) {
    char cmd[100];
    snprintf(cmd, 100, "i2c%d  pins_%d_%d=true", n, pin1, pin2);
    FILE *fp = popen("sudo dtparam -l", "r");
    if (fp == NULL) {
        printf("Failed to run command\n\r");
        exit(1);
    }
    char output[1024];
    int txfound = 0;
    while (fgets(output, sizeof (output), fp) != NULL) {
        fflush(stdout);
        if (strstr(output, cmd) != NULL) {
            txfound = 1;
        }
    }
    pclose(fp);
    printf("%d",txfound);
    if (txfound == 0) {
        snprintf(cmd, 100, "sudo dtoverlay i2c%d  pins_%d_%d=true",
                                                n, pin1, pin2);
        fp = popen(cmd, "r");
        if (fp == NULL) {
            printf("Failed to run command\n\r");
            exit(1);
        }
        pclose(fp);
    }
}
```

Notice that you have to make sure that the GPIO lines you are using aren't already in use by something else.

Using any of these additional i2C interfaces is just a matter of changing the filename from i2c-1 to i2c-*n* where *n* is the number of the interface. So, you could use the HTU21D with i2c6 by connecting pin 15, GPIO22, to SDA and 16, GPIO23 to SCL and changing the start of the program to:

```
    enableI2C(6, 22, 23);
    int i2cfd = open("/dev/i2c-6", O_RDWR);
```

Software I2C

If you can use a hardware implementation of the I2C bus then it will provide much better performance. However, there are times when you need additional I2C interfaces and there is no free I2C hardware. One solution is to use a software emulation of I2C. This has the advantage of working on any pair of GPIO lines that aren't being used for anything else.

To enable software emulation use:

```
dtoverlay=i2c-bus=n, gpio,i2c_gpio_sda=pin1, i2c_gpio_scl=pin2,
                                        i2c_gpio_delay_us=t
```

where n is the bus number you want to use, pin1 and pin2 are the GPIO lines and delay is the width of the clock pulse in microseconds, μs.

For example:

```
dtoverlay=i2c-gpio,bus=8,i2c_gpio_sda=22, i2c_gpio_scl=23
```

creates /dev/i2c-8 using GPIO22 and GPIO23 with a default clock rate of 100KHz.

You can enable a software I2C bus dynamically:

```
void enableGPIOI2C(int n, int pin1, int pin2, int clock) {
    char cmd[100];
    snprintf(cmd, 100,
                    "i2c-gpio  bus=%d
                      i2c_gpio_sda=%d
                        i2c_gpio_scl=%d
                          i2c_gpio_delay_us=%d",
                          n, pin1, pin2, clock);

    FILE *fp = popen("sudo dtparam -l", "r");
    if (fp == NULL) {
        printf("Failed to run command\n\r");
        exit(1);
    }
    char output[1024];
    int txfound = 0;
    while (fgets(output, sizeof (output), fp) != NULL) {

        fflush(stdout);
        if (strstr(output, cmd) != NULL) {
            txfound = 1;
        }
    }
    pclose(fp);
    printf("%s", cmd);
```

```
    if (txfound == 0) {
        snprintf(cmd, 100, "sudo dtoverlay i2c-gpio  bus=%d
                                        i2c_gpio_sda=%d
                                        i2c_gpio_scl=%d
                                        i2c_gpio_delay_us=%d",
                                        n, pin1, pin2, clock);
        fp = popen(cmd, "r");
        if (fp == NULL) {
            printf("Failed to run command\n\r");
            exit(1);
        }
        pclose(fp);
    }
}
```

You can only enable a particular bus number once and a second attempt will
fail even if the parameters are different. As always, removing a dynamic
overlay isn't recommended

With this in place you could use the HTU21D with i2c8, working at 40KHz,
by connecting pin 15, GPIO22, to SDA and 16, GPIO23 to SCL and changing
the start of the program to:

```
    enableGPIOI2C(8, 22, 23, 10);
    int i2cfd = open("/dev/i2c-8", O_RDWR);
```

A Lower-Level I2C

The Linux I2C device driver supports a lower-level interface that works via
the ioctl function. Using this you can gain control over many different
aspects of data transfer, in particular you can use it to implement a register
read that removes the stop bit between the write of the register address and
the read of the data. Using the file interface a write followed by a read is
always separated by a stop bit. The ioctl commands currently supported are:

I2C_RETRIES	Number of times a device address should be polled when not acknowledging
I2C_TIMEOUT	Set timeout in units of 10 ms
I2C_SLAVE	Use this slave address in all read/write operations
I2C_SLAVE_FORCE	Use this slave address, even if it is already in use by a driver
I2C_TENBIT	0 for 7-bit addresses, !=0 for 10-bit addresses
I2C_FUNCS	Get the adapter functionality mask
I2C_RDWR	Combined R/W transfer (one stop bit)
I2C_PEC	!= 0 to use PEC (Packet Error Check) with SMBus

All of these are defined in i2c.h. We have already used I2C_SLAVE to specify
the slave address. The timeout and retry are useful if you have to work with

a slow device or one that transfers a lot of data, but notice that these do not control the clock stretch timeout. It is also worth knowing that 10-bit addressing isn't supported.

The I2C_FUNCS call, which takes a pointer to an unsigned long, returns a bit status which defines what the I2C interface is capable of. The following bit masks are available:

```
I2C_FUNC_I2C
I2C_FUNC_10BIT_ADDR
I2C_FUNC_PROTOCOL_MANGLING
I2C_FUNC_NOSTART
I2C_FUNC_SLAVE
```

If you try it out:

```
int i2cfd = open("/dev/i2c-1", O_RDWR);
uint32_t support;
ioctl(i2cfd, I2C_FUNCS, &support);
if(support & I2C_FUNC_I2C) printf("I2C Support\n\r");
if(support & I2C_FUNC_10BIT_ADDR)
                            printf("10 bit address Support\n\r");
if(support & I2C_FUNC_PROTOCOL_MANGLING)
                            printf("I2C Mangling Support\n\r");
if(support & I2C_FUNC_NOSTART) printf("I2C Nostart Support\n\r");
if(support & I2C_FUNC_SLAVE) printf("I2C Slave Support\n\r");
```

you will discover that the only feature supported is I2C and 10-bit addressing.

The most important of the new ioctl functions is I2C_RDWR, which allows you to send and receive any amount of data as a single transaction using just one stop bit. The way that you use it is via two structs defined in i2c.h. The first is used for the data you want to send or receive:

```
struct i2c_msg {
__u16 addr; /* slave address */
__u16 flags; /*control transfer */
__u16 len; /* msg length */
__u8 *buf; /* pointer to msg data */
};
```

The following flags control what happens:

I2C_M_RD	Read data, default is write
I2C_M_TEN	Use 10-bit chip address
I2C_M_RECV_LEN	Length will be first received byte
I2C_M_NO_RD_ACK	Don't use read acknowledgment
I2C_M_M_IGNORE_NAK	Treat NAK as it is was ACK

I2C_M_REV_DIR_ADDR	Swap read and write
I2C_M_NOSTART	Send only one start bit per transaction
I2C_M_STOP	Send a stop bit after the message

You can only use the flags that are supported by the I2C interface in question, which is only I2C_M_RD, but this is enough to write a combined transfer function.

The second struct provides the driver with information about how many message blocks there are:

```
struct i2c_rdwr_ioctl_data {
    struct i2c_msg *msgs;       /* pointers to i2c_msgs */
    __u32 nmsgs;                /* number of i2c_msgs */
};
```

Each message block is sent with a start bit, but a stop bit is only sent after all the message blocks have been processed. For example, to create a read register function all you need to do is send a write block followed by a read block:

```
int i2cReadRegister(int i2cfd, uint8_t slaveaddr, uint8_t reg,
                                    uint8_t *buf,int len) {

    struct i2c_msg msgs[2];
    struct i2c_rdwr_ioctl_data msgset[1];

    msgs[0].addr = slaveaddr;
    msgs[0].flags = 0;
    msgs[0].len = 1;
    msgs[0].buf = &reg;

    msgs[1].addr = slaveaddr;
    msgs[1].flags = I2C_M_RD;
    msgs[1].len = len;
    msgs[1].buf = buf;

    msgset[0].msgs = msgs;
    msgset[0].nmsgs = 2;

    if (ioctl(i2cfd, I2C_RDWR, &msgset) < 0) {
        return -1;
    }
    return 0;
}
```

The first block just sends the register number to the slave and the second block reads however many bytes the slave sends back.

If you look back at the first HTU21D program, it performed a register read using separate write and read file operations:

```
int i2cfd = open("/dev/i2c-1", O_RDWR);
ioctl(i2cfd, I2C_SLAVE, 0x40);
char buf[4] = {0xE7};
write(i2cfd,buf,1);
read(i2cfd,buf,1);
printf("%x\n\r",buf[0]);
close(i2cfd)
```

This works, but it is strictly incorrect as it puts a stop bit after the write:

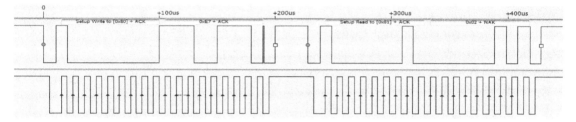

If you use the i2cReadRegister function:

```
#include <stdio.h>
#include <stdlib.h>
#include <sys/ioctl.h>
#include <unistd.h>
#include <fcntl.h>
#include <stdint.h>
#include <string.h>
#include <linux/i2c-dev.h>
#include <linux/i2c.h>

void checkI2CBus();
FILE * doCommand(char *cmd);
int i2cReadRegister(int i2cfd, uint8_t slaveaddr,
                    uint8_t reg, uint8_t *buf,int len);

int main(int argc, char** argv) {
    checkI2CBus();
    int i2cfd = open("/dev/i2c-1", O_RDWR);
    char buf2[1]={0};
    i2cReadRegister(i2cfd, 0x40, 0xE7,buf2,1);
    printf("%d \n\r",buf2[0]);
    return (EXIT_SUCCESS);
}
```

This works, but now sends no stop bit between the write and the read:

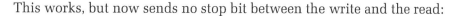
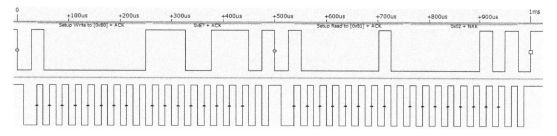

It is easy to create functions to read and write single blocks or any complex mix of read or writes as a single transaction with a single final stop bit.

I2C Tools

There is a package of tools designed to make I2C devices usable from the command line. This might be useful if you need to experiment or test something out and they can also be used within scripts. The main use case for these tools seems to be reading I2C memory devices and this means that the main objective is to provide simple bulk transfer. There are many I2C features that cannot be controlled. In most cases it is better to ignore them. The tools should already be installed, but if not use:

```
apt-get update
apt-get install i2c-tools
```

Let's deal with each tool in turn.

i2cdetect

This scans the I2C bus and tries each possible address and displays a map of what it has found:

```
pi@raspberrypi:~ $ i2cdetect 1
WARNING! This program can confuse your I2C bus, cause
I will probe file /dev/i2c-1.
I will probe address range 0x03-0x77.
Continue? [Y/n] y
     0  1  2  3  4  5  6  7  8  9  a  b  c  d  e  f
00:          -- -- -- -- -- -- -- -- -- -- -- --
10: -- -- -- -- -- -- -- -- -- -- -- -- -- -- -- --
20: -- -- -- -- -- -- -- -- -- -- -- -- -- -- -- --
30: -- -- -- -- -- -- -- -- -- -- -- -- -- -- -- --
40: 40 -- -- -- -- -- -- -- -- -- -- -- -- -- -- --
50: -- -- -- -- -- -- -- -- -- -- -- -- -- -- -- --
60: -- -- -- -- -- -- -- -- -- -- -- -- -- -- -- --
70: -- -- -- -- -- -- -- --
```

You do need to take notice of the warning if you are running any unusual devices. You can change which bus is scanned by specifying its number or name. It is also possible to disable interactive mode on all of these commands using -y.

i2cget

This will read an I2C register. For example to read the user register 0xE7 from the HTU21D at address 0x40 you would use:

```
pi@raspberrypi:~ $ i2cget 1 0x40 0xE7 b
WARNING! This program can confuse your I2C bus, cause data loss and worse!
I will read from device file /dev/i2c-1, chip address 0x40, data address
0xe7, using read byte data.
Continue? [Y/n] y
0x02
```

The general form is:

```
i2cget bus address register data
```

where *data* is one of b for byte, w for word, or c for write a byte/read a byte.

i2cdump

Use this to read a set of registers. Its general form is:

```
i2cdump bus address
```

This will transfer the values of all of the registers. You can limit the range of registers using rfirst – last, you can use b,w and c to signify byte or word transfer and I for I2C bus block transfer. You will also come across s for smbus (System Management bus), but this is to be avoided as it is a specific implementation of I2C used to control the setup of a PC.

i2cset

This works like i2cget and sets a register's value:

```
i2cset bus address register value data
```

In addition to data set to b or w you can also specify s or I for a smbus or I2C block write. Block writes are determined by the number of values specified.

It is also possible to specify a mask which determines which bits of the value are sent to the register. For example, to set the user register of the HTU21D at address 0x40 you would use:

```
pi@raspberrypi:~ $ i2cset 1 0x40 0xE6 02 b
WARNING! This program can confuse your I2C bus, cause data loss and worse!
I will write to device file /dev/i2c-1, chip address 0x40, data address
0xe6, data 0x02, mode byte.
Continue? [Y/n] y
```

i2ctransfer

This command lets you perform a block transfer read or write. Its general form is:

```
i2ctransfer bus blocks
```

The blocks are made up of individual blocks which start with r or w for read or write, the length of the data in bytes and @address which is the address of the device the block is sent to. You only need to specify the address once unless it changes. Each block is a single transaction with a single final stop bit. If you don't specify all of the data in the block you can use = to mean keep using the value, + to increment the value, - to decrement it and p to use random values. For example:

```
i2ctransfer 1 w1@0x40  0xE7 r1
```

will send 0xE7, read user register, to the device HTU21D at address 0x40 and then read a single byte back:

```
pi@raspberrypi:- $ i2ctransfer 1 w1@0x40  0xE7 r1
WARNING! This program can confuse your I2C bus, cause data loss and worse!
I will send the following messages to device file /dev/i2c-1:
msg 0: addr 0x40, write, len 1, buf 0xe7
msg 1: addr 0x40, read, len 1
Continue? [y/N] y
0x02
```

To perform a register write of the HTU21D at address 0x40 and return three bytes you would use:

```
i2ctransfer 1 w1@0x40  0xF3 r3
```

```
pi@raspberrypi:- $ i2ctransfer 1 w1@0x40  0xE3 r3
WARNING! This program can confuse your I2C bus, cause data loss and worse!
I will send the following messages to device file /dev/i2c-1:
msg 0: addr 0x40, write, len 1, buf 0xe3
msg 1: addr 0x40, read, len 3
Continue? [y/N] y
0x70 0xa4 0x03
```

This might seem very effective, but it doesn't work using a no-hold read as the command doesn't poll for the device to be ready. It does work with a clock-stretching-hold read, but only if the I2C time out has been set to be long enough for it to wait for the clock to go high and this is something that cannot be done from the command line.

I2C with Gpio5

There is very little documentation on the I2C controllers implemented in the CM5, but as they are based on the Synopsys DW_apb_i2c (v2.02) their details are described in the company's databook which you can find by searching the web or can download from this book's web page at www.iopress.info. This document details all of the registers and their functions. The only problem is that there are a lot of registers and it is intimidating when you are trying to get started. Fortunately, most of the registers are set to a reasonable configuration on system reset for an SPI master and so the number of registers you actually have to interact with at first is much smaller than you might expect.

It is easy to construct a struct to access the registers:

```
#define I2CClock 200000000
volatile typedef struct
{
    int32_t con;
    int32_t tar;
    int32_t sar;
    uint32_t _pad0;
    int32_t data_cmd;
    int32_t ss_scl_hcnt;
    int32_t ss_scl_lcnt;
    int32_t fs_scl_hcnt;
    int32_t fs_scl_lcnt;
    uint32_t _pad1[2];
    uint32_t intr_stat;
    int32_t intr_mask;
    int32_t raw_intr_stat;
    int32_t rx_tl;
    int32_t tx_tl;
    int32_t clr_intr;
    int32_t clr_rx_under;
    int32_t clr_rx_over;
    int32_t clr_tx_over;
    int32_t clr_rd_req;
    int32_t clr_tx_abrt;
    int32_t clr_rx_done;
    int32_t clr_activity;
    int32_t clr_stop_det;
    int32_t clr_start_det;
    int32_t clr_gen_call;
    int32_t enable;
    int32_t status;
    int32_t txflr;
    int32_t rxflr;
    int32_t sda_hold;
    int32_t tx_abrt_source;
```

```
    int32_t slv_data_nack_only;
    int32_t dma_cr;
    int32_t dma_tdlr;
    int32_t dma_rdlr;
    int32_t sda_setup;
    int32_t ack_general_call;
    int32_t enable_status;
    int32_t fs_spklen;
    uint32_t _pad2;
    int32_t clr_restart_det;
    int32_t scl_stuck_at_low_timeout;
    int32_t sda_stuck_at_low_timeout;
    uint32_t _pad3[16];
    uint32_t comp_param_1;
    uint32_t comp_version;
    uint32_t comp_type;
} i2cregs;
```

The addresses of each block of I2C registers is given in the documentation:

```
typedef i2cregs *I2C;
#define RP1_I2C0_BASE 0x070000
#define RP1_I2C1_BASE 0x074000
#define RP1_I2C2_BASE 0x078000
#define RP1_I2C3_BASE 0x07c000
#define RP1_I2C4_BASE 0x080000
#define RP1_I2C5_BASE 0x084000
#define RP1_I2C6_BASE 0x088000

#define I2C0 ((I2C)(PERIBase + RP1_I2C0_BASE / 4))
#define I2C1 ((I2C)(PERIBase + RP1_I2C1_BASE / 4))
#define I2C2 ((I2C)(PERIBase + RP1_I2C2_BASE / 4))
#define I2C3 ((I2C)(PERIBase + RP1_I2C3_BASE / 4))
#define I2C4 ((I2C)(PERIBase + RP1_I2C4_BASE / 4))
#define I2C5 ((I2C)(PERIBase + RP1_I2C5_BASE / 4))

#define I2CClock 200000000
```

Following the Pico SDK, the constants I2Cn have been defined and these are used as pointers to the registers for each I2C channel.

The first function we need is something to initialize the I2C channel we are about to use:

```
void i2c_enable(I2C i2c, bool enable)
{
   i2c->enable = enable?  1:  0;
}
```

```
uint32_t i2c_init(I2C i2c, uint32_t baudrate)
{
    i2c_enable(i2c, false);
    // Configure as a fast-mode master with
    // RepStart support, 7-bit addresses
    i2c->con = (0x2ul << 1) | 0x01 | 0x040 | 0x20 | 0x100;
    // Set FIFO watermarks to 1
    i2c->tx_tl = 0;
    i2c->rx_tl = 0;
    return i2c_set_baudrate(i2c, baudrate);
}
```

This is based on the Pico SDK function and it uses other functions to set the baud rate and format.

The set_baudrate function is complicated by the intricacies of the I2C clock format:

```
int32_t i2c_set_baudrate(I2C i2c, int32_t baudrate)
{
  i2c_enable(i2c, false);
  // use "fast" mode
  i2c->con = (i2c->con & ~0x06ul) | (0x02 << 1 & 0x06);
  // set frequency and duty
  uint32_t period = (I2CClock + baudrate / 2) / baudrate;
  i2c->fs_scl_lcnt = period * 3 / 5; // 40% duty cycle
  i2c->fs_scl_hcnt = period - period * 3 / 5;
  // set spike suppression
  i2c->fs_spklen = i2c->fs_scl_lcnt < 16 ? 1 :
                                    i2c->fs_scl_lcnt / 16;
  // set hold time
  uint32_t sda_tx_hold_count=(baudrate < 1000000)?
   ((I2CClock * 3) / 10000000) + 1:((I2CClock * 3) / 25000000) + 1;
  i2c->sda_hold = (i2c->sda_hold & ~0x0000ffff) |
                            (sda_tx_hold_count & 0x0000ffff);
  i2c_enable(i2c, true);
  return I2CClock / period;
}
```

For simplicity, fast mode is always used as it works at the lower speed 400kHz. The clock frequency is set by a count in hcnt which gives the high time and lcnt which gives the low time in terms of the main clock. For fast mode the duty cycle is around 40% and 2/5ths is a good approximation. Next we set some of the more subtle aspects of the clock. The spike suppression sets a threshold for noise pulses which are ignored. Finally the hold time for the data line is set – this is the time that the data line is held after the clock.

Once initialized, all we need is a write function and a read function. Following the Pico SDK, it is worth creating functions with timeouts:

```
int i2c_write_blocking_internal(I2C i2c, uint8_t addr,
         const uint8_t *src, size_t len, bool nostop, uint32_t
timeout_per_char_us)
{
    i2c_enable(i2c, false);
    i2c->tar = addr;
    i2c_enable(i2c, true);

    bool abort = false;
    bool timeout = false;
    uint32_t abort_reason = 0;

    int byte_ctr;
    int ilen = (int)len;
    for (byte_ctr = 0; byte_ctr < ilen; ++byte_ctr)
    {
        bool first = byte_ctr == 0;
        bool last = byte_ctr == ilen - 1;

        uint32_t startbitnext =
            ((uint32_t)!!(first && restart_on_next)) << 10;
        uint32_t stopbit = ((uint32_t)!!(last && !nostop)) << 9;
        uint64_t tm = micros() + timeout_per_char_us;
        i2c->data_cmd = startbitnext | stopbit | *src++;
        do
        {
            if (micros() > tm)
                timeout = true;
        } while (!timeout && !(i2c->raw_intr_stat & 0x10));

        if (timeout)
            break;

        // check for non-timeout abort
        abort_reason = i2c->tx_abrt_source;
        if (abort_reason)
        {
            int32_t temp = i2c->clr_tx_abrt;
            abort = true;
        }
    }
    restart_on_next = nostop;
    if (abort || timeout)
        return i2c_handleAbort(i2c, timeout, abort_reason);
    return byte_ctr;
}
```

First we set the address of the slave that the data is to be sent to – this does not start transmission and is not sent until the data is sent. The first and last byte of the data are special in that we need to send a start bit and perhaps a stop bit. The stop bit can be sent or suppressed. The instruction:

```
 i2c->data_cmd = startbitnext | stopbit | *src++;
```

sends the next item of data and a start bit and stop bit as appropriate. This is also where we start measuring the time for the transaction so as to implement a timeout. Next we loop until the Tx FIFO is empty or a timeout occurs. If a timeout occurs the send loop is exited and the error reported. If the Tx FIFO empties we still have to check for any errors the hardware reported and pass the error code back to the calling program:

```
int32_t i2c_handleAbort(I2C i2c, bool timeout, int32_t abortreason)
{
    if (timeout)
        return 1 << 31 | 1 << 30; // bit 30 set for timout
    return abortreason | 1 << 31;
}
```

In this case if there wasn't a timeout we return a negative value, by setting the high bit, and set the remaining bits of the abort register. If there was a timeout, we return a negative value with bit 30 set.

A read with timeout follows very similar lines:

```
int i2c_read_blocking_internal(I2C i2c, uint8_t addr, uint8_t *dst,
        size_t len, bool nostop, uint32_t timeout_per_char_us)
{

    i2c_enable(i2c, false);
    i2c->tar = addr;
    i2c_enable(i2c, true);

    bool abort = false;
    bool timeout = false;
    uint32_t abort_reason;

    int byte_ctr;
    int ilen = (int)len;

    for (byte_ctr = 0; byte_ctr < ilen; ++byte_ctr)
    {
        bool first = byte_ctr == 0;
        bool last = byte_ctr == ilen - 1;

        while (!i2c_get_write_available(i2c))
        {
        };
```

```
        uint32_t startbitnext =
            (uint32_t)!!(first && restart_on_next) << 10;
        uint32_t stopbit = (uint32_t)!!(last && !nostop) << 9;
        uint64_t tm = micros() + timeout_per_char_us;
        i2c->data_cmd = startbitnext | stopbit | 0x100;

        do
        {
            if (micros() > tm)
            {
                timeout = true;
                abort = true;
            }
            abort_reason = i2c->tx_abrt_source;
            // check tx abort bits
            if (i2c->raw_intr_stat & 0x40)
            {
                abort = true;
                i2c->clr_tx_abrt;
            }

        } while (!abort && !i2c_get_read_available(i2c));

        if (abort)
            break;

        *dst++ = (uint8_t)i2c->data_cmd;
    }
    restart_on_next = nostop;
    if (abort)
        return i2c_handleAbort(i2c, timeout, abort_reason);
    return byte_ctr;
}
```

The first thing we have to do is make sure that there is space in the Tx FIFO
buffer. Next we set the command register to the appropriate start and stop
bits and attempt a read. To do this we have to loop until there is data in the
FIFO – tested for by i2c_get_read_available. If this is successful then the
data is in the data_cmd register and can be transferred to the buffer. However
we still need to check for errors and timeout and report any status codes to
the calling program.

The functions used are:

```
size_t i2c_get_write_available(I2C i2c)
{
    return I2C_TX_BUFFER_DEPTH - (i2c->txflr);
}
size_t i2c_get_read_available(I2C i2c)
{
    return i2c->rxflr;
}
uint64_t micros()
{
    struct timespec ts;
    clock_gettime(CLOCK_MONOTONIC_RAW, &ts);
    uint64_t us = ts.tv_sec * 1000000 + ts.tv_nsec / 1000;
    return us;
}
```

We also need a global variable to keep track of when a stop bit needs to be sent:

```
bool restart_on_next = false;
```

This should be a per-controller variable, but for simplicity we assume that only one controller is active at any given time. If you need to break this rule then you need to store the state in an array with one location per I2C controller.

With all of this defined we can now create some end user-callable functions that are the same as the Pico SDK:

A blocking 8-bit read

```
int i2c_read_blocking(I2C i2c, uint8_t addr,
                      uint8_t *dst, size_t len, bool nostop)
{
    return i2c_read_blocking_internal(i2c, addr, dst,
                                      len, nostop, 0xFFFFFFFF);
}
```

A blocking 8-bit write

```
int i2c_write_blocking(I2C i2c, uint8_t addr,
                const uint8_t *src, size_t len, bool nostop)
{
    return i2c_write_blocking_internal(i2c, addr, src, len,
                                       nostop, 0xFFFFFFFF);
}
```

An 8-bit write with per character timeout

```
int i2c_write_timeout_per_char_us(I2C i2c, uint8_t addr,
        const uint8_t *src, size_t len, bool nostop,
                                uint32_t timeout_per_char_us)
{
    return i2c_write_blocking_internal(i2c, addr, src, len,
                                nostop, timeout_per_char_us);
}
```

An 8-bit read with per character timeout

```
int i2c_read_timeout_per_char_us(I2C i2c, uint8_t addr,
        uint8_t *dst, size_t len, bool nostop,
                                uint32_t timeout_per_char_us)
{

    return i2c_read_blocking_internal(i2c, addr, dst, len,
                                nostop, timeout_per_char_us);
}
```

These use the internal read/write functions in obvious ways.

The Gpio5 approach has the advantage that you can now add features that are supported by the hardware, such as 10-bit addresses and working as a slave, simply by writing to the appropriate registers.

HTU1D Using Gpio5

With the I2C functions defined in Gpio5 we can now take a Pico program that reads the HTU21D and run it with only minor modifications:

```
#include <stdio.h>
#include <stdlib.h>
#include <time.h>
#include "Gpio5.h"
uint8_t crcCheck(uint8_t msb, uint8_t lsb, uint8_t check)
{
    uint32_t data32 = ((uint32_t)msb << 16) |
                      ((uint32_t)lsb << 8) | (uint32_t)check;
    uint32_t divisor = 0x988000;
    for (int i = 0; i < 16; i++)
    {
        if (data32 & (uint32_t)1 << (23 - i))
            data32 ^= divisor;
        divisor >>= 1;
    };
    return (uint8_t)data32;
}
int main(int argc, char **argv)
{
    rp1_Init();
    gpio_set_function(2, GPIO_FUNC_I2C);
    gpio_set_function(3, GPIO_FUNC_I2C);
```

```
    i2c_init(I2C1, 100 * 1000);

    uint8_t buf[4] = {0xE3};
    i2c_write_blocking(I2C1, 0x40, buf, 1, true);
    i2c_read_blocking(I2C1, 0x40, buf, 3, false);
    uint8_t msb = buf[0];
    uint8_t lsb = buf[1];
    uint8_t check = buf[2];
    printf("msb %d \n\r lsb %d \n\r checksum %d \n\r",
                                        msb, lsb, check);
    unsigned int data16 = ((unsigned int)msb << 8) |
                                (unsigned int)(lsb & 0xFC);
    printf("crc = %d\n\r", crcCheck(msb, lsb, check));
    float temp = (float)(-46.85 + (175.72 *
                                data16 / (float)65536));
    printf("Temperature %f C \n\r", temp);
    buf[0] = 0xF5;
    i2c_write_blocking(I2C1, 0x40, buf, 1, true);

    while (i2c_read_blocking(I2C1, 0x40, buf, 3, false) & 0x1 )
    {
        sleep_ms(1);
    };

    msb = buf[0];
    lsb = buf[1];
    check = buf[2];
    printf("msb %d \n\r lsb %d \n\r checksum %d \n\r",
                                        msb, lsb, check);
    printf("crc = %d\n\r", crcCheck(msb, lsb, check));
    data16 = ((unsigned int)msb << 8) | (unsigned int)(lsb & 0xFC);
    float hum = -6 + (125.0 * (float)data16) / 65536;
    printf("Humidity %f %% \n\r", hum);
    return (EXIT_SUCCESS);
}
```

Reading the temperature is performed using clock stretching and works perfectly. Reading the humidity is performed using polling, just as an illustration of how this works. After performing the write, the master simply loops until it reads data without getting a NAK from the slave. Notice that we could simply test for a negative return value or the more specific NAK error indicated by bit one.

Summary

- Each I2C device has a built-in address or set of addresses that it can respond to. Address clashes are a particular problem if you want to mix devices on a single I2C bus.

- There are a few subtle variations on the data protocol that modify how multiple blocks of data are sent. Getting this exactly right is another common I2C problem.

- Slow devices are accommodated by either polling for the device to be ready or allowing the device to hold down the clock line, clock stretching, until it is ready.

- The CM5 has four I2C bus controllers of which the first two are the same as found in other Pis.

- The I2C driver can be loaded dynamically and it provides the basic facilities to interface with any I2C device.

- As an example of using the driver, the HTU21D is easy to set up and read. It also has a dedicated Linux driver which is discussed in Chapter 14.

- Without clock-stretching support, all we can do is to poll for data to be ready to read.

- Computing a CRC is something every IoT programmer needs to know how to do in the general case.

- There are a number of command line tools that let you work with I2C, but they need to be used with caution.

- Using the additional I2C interfaces that the CM5 supplies is just a matter of configuring the Linux driver and using appropriate pins.

- You can make use of clock stretching on all recent Pis running the latest OS.

- At the time of writing only a few ioctl operations are supported, but they can be used to write a register address and read the result with the correct stop bits.

- Adding I2C support to Gpio5 is fairly easy and, once you have the necessary functions, reading the HTU21D without the use of a driver is also easy.

Chapter 14

Sensor Drivers - Linux IIO & hwmon

There are a number of I2C device drivers that allow you to use I2C devices without worrying about the exact nature of the protocol in use. In general they conform to either one of two broader, protocol-independent way of implementing drivers, hwmon, standing for hardware monitoring system and IIO, for interfacing Linux Industrial I/O devices. These form a framework for creating, publishing and using drivers for devices irrespective of the protocol used to control them. At the time of writing the following are supported, the majority being I2C devices:

bme680	I2C or SPI	IIO	Bosch Sensortronic BME680 Temperature, Humidity and Pressure Sensor
bmp085	I2C or SPI	IIO	Bosch Sensortronic BMP085 superseded by the BMP180
bmp180	I2C	IIO	Bosch Sensortronic BMP180 Barometric Pressure Sensor
bme280	I2C	IIO	Bosch Sensortronic BME280 Temperature, Humidity and Pressure Sensor
ds1621	I2C	hwmon	Dallas Semiconductors Temperature Sensor range inc DS1621, DS1625, DS1631, DS1721, DS1731
hdc100x	I2C	IIO	Texas Instruments HDC100x Temperature Sensor range -only HDC1010 and HDC1080 are current
htu21	SPI	IIO	HTU21 Temperature and Humidity Sensor
lm75	I2C	hwmon	Maxim LM75 Temperature Sensor and compatible devices.
max17040	I2C	hwmon	Maxim Integrated MAX17040 Battery Monitor
sht3x	I2C	hwmon	Sensiron SHT3x Temperature and Humidity Sensor
Si7020	I2C	hwmon	Silicon Labs Si7013/20/21 Humidity/Temperature Sensor
sps30	I2C	IIO	Sensirion SPS30 Particulate Matter Sensor
tmp102	I2C	hwmon	Texas Instruments TMP102 Temperature Sensor
tsl4531	I2C	IIO	AMS TSL4531 Digital Ambient Light Sensor
veml6070	I2C	IIO	Vishay VEML6070 Ultraviolet Light Sensor

There are many more devices available as drivers that you have to build and install for yourself, but these are usually provided by the manufacturer of the device and you will find instructions on the relevant websites.

The majority of these devices are available at reasonable cost in either prototype-friendly DIL packages or as breakout boards. Of course, there are many sensors that are not supported by a Linux driver, but making a choice from this list can save you a lot of time and trouble.

These device drivers are either part of the Industrial I/O (IIO) subsystem project or the older hwmon subsystem, which was intended to be a way of reading and configuring built-in sensors and devices. For example, you can read the CPU temperature or the supply voltage of the Pi using the built-in sensors that are part of hwmon. However, you can also add drivers to the hwmon subsystem that aren't built in. This use of hwmon as a "home" for sensors is what led to the decision to create IIO as a better and more appropriate place for sensors.

There are some big differences between hwmon and IIO. In particular IIO only deals with input devices and, in principle, it can do so in much more sophisticated ways than hwmon. Hwmon has the advantage of dealing with input and output devices, but it is much simpler and makes a good starting point for seeing the general principles in action.

hwmon

Drivers that install into the hwmon system work in the same way as most Linux drivers by pretending to be folders and files. You will find all hwmon devices in:

`/sys/class/hwmon/`

and each device creates a `deviceX` folder where X is an integer. Within each folder you will find the files you need to work with the device. In particular, you will find a `name` file which gives the usual name of the device and often an `update_interval` file which gets and sets the update interval for the device. If you look at the `/sys/class/hwmon` folder you will see that there are already three device folders:

The first corresponds to the built-in temperature sensor, the second to the A-to-D converter that monitors CPU voltage and the third an undocummented ADC in the RP1. As an example, let's read the CPU temperature.

Inside the hwmon0 folder are a number of files and folders:

The ones that matter most are name, which gives the name of the sensor and temp1_input, the data file. The uevent file is present in all driver folders and it is used by the system to implement dynamic changes to the hardware, see udev in Chapter 16.

Reading the CPU temperature is just a matter of opening the file and reading:

```
#include <stdio.h>
#include <stdlib.h>
#include <string.h>
#include <unistd.h>
#include <fcntl.h>

int main(int argc, char** argv) {
    int fd = open("/sys/class/hwmon/hwmon0/temp1_input", O_RDONLY);
    char buf[100] = {0};
    read(fd, buf, 100);
    printf("%s\n\r", buf);
    float temp;
    sscanf(buf, "%f", &temp);
    temp = temp / 1000;
    printf("%f\n\r", temp);
}
```

Notice that the string returned from the file is terminated by /n and not by a zero, hence the need to initialize the buffer to all zeros.

You can use the same approach to read the CPU voltage, only the filename changes.

Installing an hwmon Device LM75

Installing an hwmon device is very straightforward, with no surprises if you have been following how things work. As an example, let's install an LM75 temperature device. This is a low-cost I2C temperature sensor with an accuracy of around 2 degrees Celsius and a resolution of 11 bits. You can buy a suitable LM75 module, complete with prototype board, from many sources. It has three pins that can be used to set the low three bits of the address, which means you can support up to eight devices on the same bus:

You can see the standard I2C pins plus power and ground. The final pin, OS, is a thermal shutdown output which goes high when the temperature is above a set value.

To use the device you generally have to solder either pins or wires to the connections. You also have to connect the address pads on the back of the device. This can be done with a solder bridge – a blob of solder connecting the pads together. You don't need pull-up resistors as they are in place on the other side of the board. Be careful not to create a solder blob so large that it shorts out the ground and power pads.

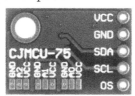

For this example, connect all of the address lines to ground, giving an address of 0x48. By connecting them differently you can use addresses from 0x48 to 0x4f. The chip has registers that can be read to discover the temperature and that can be written to set the critical temperature and the hysteresis. The over-temperature alarm is triggered when the temperature exceeds the critical temperature and it is untriggered when the temperature is lower than that set by the hysteresis.

The LM75 can be used via the raw I2C interface or you can make use of its Linux driver. The LM75 driver is implemented by a general i2c-sensor driver which can be set to work with a range of devices. In this case we need to add:

```
dtparam=i2c_arm=on
dtoverlay i2c-sensor,lm75,addr=0x48
```

to the /boot/firmware/config.txt file. If you don't specify an address parameter the default is 0x4F.

You can also load the drivers dynamically:

```c
FILE *doCommand(char *cmd)
{
    FILE *fp = popen(cmd, "r");
    if (fp == NULL)
    {
        printf("Failed to run command %s \n\r", cmd);
        exit(1);
    }
    return fp;
}
int findInd(FILE *fd, char *indicator)
{
    char output[1024];
    int txfound = 0;
    while (fgets(output, sizeof(output), fd) != NULL)
    {
        printf("%s\n\r", output);
        fflush(stdout);
        if (strstr(output, indicator) != NULL)
        {
            txfound = 1;
        }
    }
    return txfound;
}
void checkLM75()
{
    FILE *fd = doCommand("sudo  dtparam -l");
    char indicator1[] = "i2c_arm=on";
    char command1[] = "sudo dtparam i2c_arm=on";
    char indicator2[] = "lm75";
    char command2[] = "sudo dtoverlay i2c-sensor lm75 addr=0x48";

    int txfound = findInd(fd, indicator1);
    if (txfound == 0){
        pclose(fd);
        fd = doCommand(command1);
        sleep(2);
    }
    pclose(fd);
    fd = doCommand("sudo  dtparam -l");
    txfound = findInd(fd, indicator2);
    if (txfound == 0){
        pclose(fd);
        fd = doCommand(command2);
        sleep(2);
    }
    pclose(fd);
}
```

Once the drivers are loaded you will discover that there is a new directory in hwmon:

/sys/class/hwmon/hwmon3

device   of_node   power   subsystem   name   temp1_input

temp1_max temp1_max_hyst   uevent   update_interval

You can see that `temp1_input` is going to be the file to read to get the current temperature:

```
int main(int argc, char **argv)
{
    checkLM75();

    int fd = open("/sys/class/hwmon/hwmon3/temp1_input",
                                               O_RDONLY);
    char buf[100] = {0};
    read(fd, buf, 100);
    printf("%s\n\r", buf);
    float temp;
    sscanf(buf, "%f", &temp);
    temp = temp / 1000;
    printf("%f\n\r", temp);
    close(fd);
}
```

The temperature is returned as a string in millidegrees Celsius.

If you want to set the critical temperature and hysteresis you can use:

```
    fd = open("/sys/class/hwmon/hwmon3/temp1_max", O_RDWR);
    char max[] = "20000";
    write(fd, max, 5);
    close(fd);

    fd = open("/sys/class/hwmon/hwmon3/temp1_max_hyst", O_RDWR);
    char min[] = "190000";
    write(fd, max, 5);
    close(fd);
```

This sets the critical temperature to 20°C and the hysteresis to 19°C. After this, if the temperature goes above 20°C the LED on the board will come on and stay on until the temperature drops below 19°C. Notice that you need to run this program with root permissions as it is writing to files in /sys.

Industrial I/O

The hwmon system of drivers was never intended as a way of adding external sensors and this is why Industrial I/O (IIO) was created in 2015. It is a very ambitious system, intended to become the main way that programmers would create IoT type applications. To make this possible, the idea was that IIO devices would use a ring buffer to store readings taken independently of the user-space application. This would allow the user-space application to read the data when it was ready without loss of data and hence at sampling rates higher than could be achieved directly.

The documentation says:

> The main purpose of the Industrial I/O subsystem (IIO) is to provide support for devices that in some sense perform either analog-to-digital conversion (ADC) or digital-to-analog conversion (DAC) or both. The aim is to fill the gap between the somewhat similar hwmon and input subsystems. Hwmon is directed at low sample rate sensors used to monitor and control the system itself, like fan speed control or temperature measurement. Input is, as its name suggests, focused on human interaction input devices (keyboard, mouse, touchscreen).

The main innovation is the use of triggers to determine when readings will be taken, independent of when the data is read.

At the time of writing, IIO drivers are generally not full-featured and many don't support the more advanced functions such as triggers or buffering. However, it is difficult to know the current state of affairs because nearly all of the documentation is aimed at driver writers rather than driver users. This said, there is no reason not to use IIO device drivers as, at the very least, they provide the same facilities as other driver types.

You can load any of the IIO drivers using the usual `dtoverlay` line in `boot.txt` or you can dynamically load any of the drivers.

Once the driver has been loaded, there will be a new folder in `sys/bus/iio/devices`. The folder will be called `iio.deviceX` where X is the number of the device. Within the new folder are files and folders that relate to the new device and allow you to read its state and data:

For a driver conforming to IIO you should find:

- ◆ name   Description of the physical chip
- ◆ dev   Shows the major:minor pair associated with /dev/iio:deviceX node
- ◆ sampling_frequency_available The discrete set of sampling frequency values available for the device

Consult Documentation/ABI/testing/sysfs-bus-iio in the Linux kernel to discover what each device supports, but note that it is a very incomplete list. In general, you can work out what each file is for from its name. For example, in the case of the HTU21D sensor that we used earlier, you can see that:

in_temp_input is what you read to get the current temperature and in_humidityrelative_input is what you would read to get the humidity There is also a file called iio:deviceX in /dev/ which provides buffered I/O and event information. It is important to realize that not all devices implement the same range of features and basically you have to investigate what files have been created by the driver.

As well as providing the ability to read data from the device and write configuration data, the IIO bus also lets you do more sophisticated things. For example, you can set up triggers that take readings at set intervals and you can read a ring buffer of collected data. Such facilities allow user-mode programs to gather data at rates normally only possible for system-mode programs.

An Example - the HTU21

As an example of how much easier things are using a sensor driver, let's write a program to read the data from the HTU21D Temperature and Humidity Sensor.

First we need a function to load the driver:

```
void loadHTU21() {
    FILE *fd = doCommand("sudo dtparam -l");
    char output[1024];
    int txfound = 0;
    while (fgets(output, sizeof (output), fd) != NULL) {
        printf("%s\n\r", output);
        fflush(stdout);
        if (strstr(output, "i2c-sensor  htu21=true") != NULL) {
            txfound = 1;
        }
    }
    pclose(fd);
```

```
    if (txfound == 0) {
        fd = doCommand("sudo dtoverlay i2c-sensor htu21");
        pclose(fd);
    }
}
```

As always, unloading a driver isn't a good idea.

With the driver loaded we can simply read the temperature from the
appropriate file:

```
loadHTU21();
float temp;

char output[1024] = {0};
int fdtemp = open("/sys/bus/iio/devices/iio:device0/in_temp_input",
                                                         O_RDWR);
read(fdtemp, output, sizeof (output));
close(fdtemp);
printf("%s\n\r", output);
sscanf(output, "%f", &temp);
temp = temp / 1000;
fflush(stdout);
```

You can see that this is now a trivial operation. If you are wondering how
the driver reads data from the device, it simply initiates the read and waits
for around 50ms for the data to be read – no polling and no clock stretching.

The complete program to read both temperature and humidity is:

```
#include <stdio.h>
#include <stdlib.h>
#include <string.h>
#include <unistd.h>
#include <fcntl.h>
#include <stdint.h>
#include <linux/i2c-dev.h>
#include <linux/i2c.h>
void loadHTU21();
int main(int argc, char** argv) {
    loadHTU21();
    float temp;
    float hum;
    {
        char output[1024] = {0};
        int fdtemp = open("/sys/bus/iio/devices/iio:device0/
                                        in_temp_input", O_RDWR);
        read(fdtemp, output, sizeof (output));
        close(fdtemp);
        printf("%s\n\r", output);
        sscanf(output, "%f", &temp);
        temp = temp / 1000;
        fflush(stdout);
    }
```

```c
    {
        char output[1024] = {0};
        int fdhum = open("/sys/bus/iio/devices/iio:device0/
                         in_humidityrelative_input", O_RDWR);
        read(fdhum, output, sizeof (output));
        close(fdhum);
        printf("%s\n\r", output);
        sscanf(output, "%f", &hum);
        hum = hum / 1000;
        fflush(stdout);
    }
    printf("%f\n\r", temp);
    printf("%f\n\r", hum);

    return (EXIT_SUCCESS);
}

FILE *doCommand(char *cmd)
{
    FILE *fp = popen(cmd, "r");
    if (fp == NULL)
    {
        printf("Failed to run command %s \n\r", cmd);
        exit(1);
    }
    return fp;
}
void loadHTU21() {
    FILE *fd = doCommand("sudo dtparam -l");
    char output[1024];
    int txfound = 0;
    while (fgets(output, sizeof (output), fd) != NULL) {
        printf("%s\n\r", output);
        fflush(stdout);
        if (strstr(output, "i2c-sensor  htu21=true") != NULL) {
            txfound = 1;
        }
    }
    pclose(fd);
    if (txfound == 0) {
        fd = doCommand("sudo dtoverlay i2c-sensor htu21");
        pclose(fd);
    }
}
```

As the HTU21 driver doesn't support a buffer, you can't do buffered I/O or use a trigger to gather data. All you can do is read the temperature and humidity when you need to, but this is often enough.

If you look back to Chapter 11 you will find another example of using an IIO bus driver, for the MCP3008 A-to-D converter.

The IIO Utilities

There are some utilities that can sometimes help with finding out what is happening when you have installed an IIO device, but how useful they are is very variable. To install the IIO utilities the simplest thing to do is search for "iio" using the usual Pi software installer search:

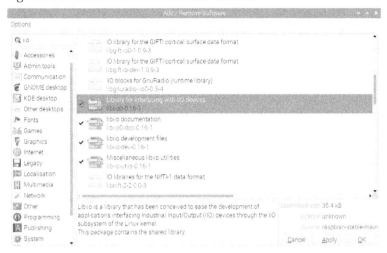

You might also want to install the libiio libraryfor use as an alternative way to connect to IIO devices, see the next section.

iio_info and iio_attr

`iio_info` provides a summary of installed devices, channels and attributes.

```
Library version: 0.16 (git tag: v0.16)
Compiled with backends: local xml ip usb serial
IIO context created with local backend.
Backend version: 0.16 (git tag: v0.16)
Backend description string: Linux raspberrypi 5.4.51-v7l+ #1325 SMP Mon Jul 13 1
3:47:17 BST 2020 armv7l
IIO context has 1 attributes:
        local,kernel: 5.4.51-v7l+
IIO context has 1 devices:
        iio:device0: htu21
        2 channels found:
                humidityrelative:  (input)
                1 channel-specific attributes found:
                        attr  0: input ERROR: Remote I/O error (-121)
                temp:  (input)
                1 channel-specific attributes found:
                        attr  0: input value: 30906
        4 device-specific attributes found:
                        attr  0: battery_low value: 0
                        attr  1: heater_enable value: 0
                        attr  2: sampling_frequency value: 20
                        attr  3: sampling_frequency_available value: 204070 120
```

`iio_attr` specifically lists device attributes:

```
pi@raspberrypi:~ $ iio_attr -d htu21
dev 'htu21', attr 'battery_low', value :'0'
dev 'htu21', attr 'heater_enable', value :'0'
dev 'htu21', attr 'sampling_frequency', value :'20'
dev 'htu21', attr 'sampling_frequency_available', value :'20 40 70 120'
```

It can also be used to write to an attribute by appending a value to the end of the command.

iio_readdev and iio_writedev

You can use these two to read and write to a device's buffer. The simplest form of the commands are:

`readdev` *device channel*   Sends data from the buffer to `stdout`
`writedev` *device channel* Sends data from `stdin` to the device/channel

Notice that if the device doesn't support a buffer then these two don't work. For example, they don't work with the HTU21.

The Libiio Library

The "standard" library for working with IIO devices is libiio, but at the time of writing it is not well supported on the Raspberry Pi. You can download and install it, but not by the usual methods. Its documentation is also very poor and aimed at the expert, not the beginner. It provides the basic facilities of finding and using IIO devices directly, but it also has many sophisticated features, including remote access to devices running on other machines via USB or networking. In most cases, trying to use it isn't worth the effort as the actual IIO drivers don't support its more sophisticated features. If you simply want to read data at the sort of rates that the basic drivers allow, there is little to be gained from using libiio and it is a steep learning curve.

Summary

- The IIO and hwmon systems are attempt to create drivers that present a standard interface, irrespective of the way that the devices are actually interfaced to the machine.

- Hwmon is the older system and was originally intended only for devices that are built into the system rather than discrete devices connected via external buses.

- The LM75 Temperature Sensor is often found built-in to monitor hardware operating conditions, but it can also be connected via I2C and interfaced using the hwmon driver.

- Industrial I/O (IIO) was invented as an extension of hwmon to create something that could support a wide range of sensors.

- IIO has many sophisticated features including triggers that can be used to make regular measurements in kernel space, something most other drivers don't support.

- The HTU21 introduced in Chapter 12 has an IIO driver.

- There are a set of IIO utilities that you can install, but again due to limited driver support many features don't work.

- There is also a more sophisticated library, libiio, which makes IIO devices easier to work with, but lack of driver support makes it less attractive than working directly with devices.

The 1-Wire bus is a proprietary protocol that is very easy to use and has a lot of useful devices you can connect to it, including the iButton security devices. However, probably the most popular of all 1-Wire devices is the DS18B20 Temperature Sensor - it is small, very cheap and very easy to use. This is the device that we are going to focus on in this chapter but the techniques generalize to working with any 1-Wire device you care to use.

The Hardware

1-Wire devices are very simple and only use a single wire, hence the name, to transmit data:

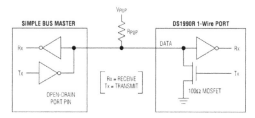

The 1-wire device can pull the bus low using its Tx (Transmit) line and can read the line using its Rx (Receive) line. The reason for the pull-up resistor is that both the bus master and the slave can pull the bus low and it will stay low until they both release the bus.

The device can even be powered from the bus line by drawing sufficient current through the pull-up resistor - so called parasitic mode. Low-power devices work well in parasitic mode, but some devices have such a heavy current draw that the master has to provide a way to connect them to the power line - so called strong pull-up. In practice parasitic mode can be difficult to make work reliably for high power devices.

In normal-powered mode there are just three connections - V power (usually 3.3V for the Pi), Ground, and Data:

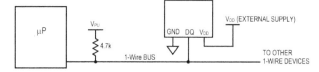

The pull-up resistor varies according to the device, but anything from 2.2K to 4.7kΩ works. The longer the bus the lower the pull-up resistor has to be to reduce "ringing". There can be multiple devices on the bus and each one has a unique 64-bit lasered ROM code, which can be used as an address to select the active devices.

The GPIO Driver

There are a number of drivers that implement the 1-Wire master, but the only one supported without extra work for the Raspberry Pi is the w1-gpio driver which implements the 1-Wire protocol on any GPIO pin that you aren't using for something else. There is also the w1-gpio-pullup variant of the driver, which is only needed if you are driving a 1-Wire device over a long wire connection.

You can enable the 1-Wire driver using:

```
dtoverlay=w1-gpio-pi5,gpiopin=n
```

where *n* is the GPIO line you want to use. The default is GPIO4, but you can use any GPIO line. Notice that the driver used here is specific to the CM5. You can add this dtoverlay line to the /config/boot.txt file or you can enable it dynamically using:

```
void load1w(int pin) {
    FILE *fd = doCommand("sudo dtparam -l");
    char output[1024];
    int txfound = 0;
    while (fgets(output, sizeof (output), fd) != NULL) {
      printf("%s\n\r", output);
      fflush(stdout);
      if (strstr(output, "w1-gpio-pi5") != NULL) {
        txfound = 1;
      }
    }
    pclose(fd);
    if (txfound == 0) {
      char cmd[100];
      snprintf(cmd, 100,
              "sudo dtoverlay w1-gpio-pi5 gpiopin=%d", pin);
      fd = doCommand(cmd);
      pclose(fd);
    }
}
```

This just checks to see if there is an overlay currently active and if not it sets the pin you specify to be the 1-Wire bus.

As with all dynamic overlays, removing it isn't a good idea and in the case of the 1-Wire driver. Once loaded, the overlay can stay active until the next reboot.

Listing Devices

When the driver is loaded it scans the 1-Wire bus for connected devices. It repeats the scan at intervals, so keeping the system up-to-date as you add new devices. For each device it finds, it creates a directory with the same name as the serial number of the device in /sys/bus/w1/devices/. Inside the folder are, among other things, files that let you work with the sensor. In particular, there is the w1_slave file that allows you to initiate a measurement and read the result.

We have read the names of the folders in /sys/bus/w1/devices/ and extract each one and use this to construct paths to each of the w1_slave files that have been created. Usually we know the class of device we are working with by the form of its serial number. Each device has a 64-bit number that is composed of a family code that tells you the type of the device and a unique serial number:

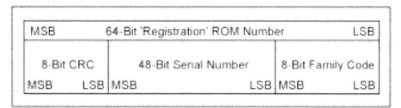

For example, all DS18B20 Temperature Sensors have a serial number that starts with 28-. Variations on the device have different family codes:

```
W1_THERM_DS18S20     0x10
W1_THERM_DS1822      0x22
W1_THERM_DS18B20     0x28
W1_THERM_DS1825      0x3B
W1_THERM_DS28EA00    0x42
```

All of these are supported by the Linux driver.

Working with directories in Linux isn't difficult, but if you need a refresher then see *Applying C for the IoT with Linux*, ISBN: 9781871962611. The following is the usual way to find out what devices are connected, but arguably there is a better way, see later.

First we open the devices directory:

```
int getDevices(char path[][100], int *num) {
    DIR *dirp;
    char name[10][50];
    struct dirent *direntp;
    if ((dirp = opendir("/sys/bus/w1/devices/")) == NULL) {
        return -1;
    }
```

Next we scan through all of the directories that this contains, looking for names that start with 28-:

```
*num = 0;
while ((direntp = readdir(dirp)) != NULL) {
    if (strstr(direntp->d_name, "28-")) {
        strncpy(name[*num], direntp->d_name, 50);
        (*num)++;
    }
}
closedir(dirp);
```

Each one found is copied to an element of the name string array. Notice that the name array only has space for 10 devices – you could make it bigger. Finally we construct a string array with the path to each of the w1_slave files that allow us to read each of the sensors:

```
for (int i = 0; i < *num; i++) {
  snprintf(path[i],100, "/sys/bus/w1/devices/%s/w1_slave",name[i]);
}
return 0;
}
```

Notice that when the getDevices function is called it has to be supplied with a path string array of the required dimensions.

The complete function is:

```
int getDevices(char path[][100], int *num)
{
    DIR *dirp;
    char name[10][50];
    struct dirent *direntp;
    if ((dirp = opendir("/sys/bus/w1/devices/")) == NULL)
    {
        return -1;
    }
    *num = 0;
    while ((direntp = readdir(dirp)) != NULL)
    {
        if (strstr(direntp->d_name, "28-"))
        {
            strncpy(name[*num], direntp->d_name, 50);
            (*num)++;
        }
    }
    closedir(dirp);
    for (int i = 0; i < *num; i++)
    {
        snprintf(path[i], 100, "/sys/bus/w1/devices/%s", name[i]);
    }
    return 0;
}
```

As outlined in Chapter 16 it is also possible to arrange for an action to occur when a new device is added.

The DS18B20

The DS18B20 is a good choice as an example of a 1-Wire bus device as it is almost the only device anyone makes significant use of. It is low-cost, easy to use and you can use multiple devices on a single GPIO line.

The DS18B20 is available in a number of formats, but the most common makes it look just like a standard BJT (Bipolar Junction Transistor) which can sometimes be a problem when you are trying to find one. You can also get them made up into waterproof sensors complete with cable.

No matter how packaged, they will work at 3.3V or 5V.

The basic specification of the DS18B20 is:

◆   Measures temperatures from -55°C to +125°C (-67°F to +257°F)
◆   ±0.5°C accuracy from -10°C to +85°C
◆   Thermometer resolution is user-selectable from 9 to 12 bits
◆   Converts temperature to 12-bit digital word in 750ms (max)

It can also be powered from the data line, making the bus physically need only two wires - data and ground. However, this "parasitic power" mode is difficult to make work reliably and best avoided in an initial design. To supply it with enough power during a conversion, the host has to connect it directly to the data line by providing a "strong pull-up" - essentially a transistor. In normal-powered mode there are just three connections:

Ground needs to be connected to the system ground, VDD to 3.3V, and DQ to the pull-up resistor of an open collector bus.

While you can have multiple devices on the same bus, for simplicity it is better to start off with a single device until you know that everything is working.

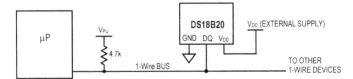

You can build the circuit in a variety of ways. You can solder the resistor to the temperature sensor and then use some longer wires with clips to connect to the Pi.

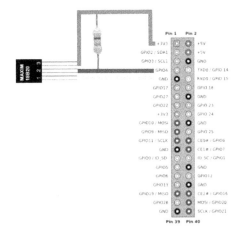

Once the driver is loaded and the device is recognized you will find a set of new folders in the w1/devices folder:

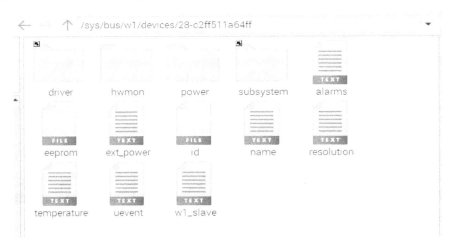

298

Most of the files have functions that are obvious from their names but there are some points of detail:

- **name** — Returns the name of the device which is the same as its serial number.

- **w1_slave** — uses the nine bytes that the device returns in a check sum - if the check sum is OK then the string ends with `t=` the temperature in millidegrees Celsius.

- **temperature** — Returns the temperature in millidegrees Celsius – the string is not null terminated.

- **resolution** — Returns the number of bits of resolution used. Writing a number to it sets the resolution if the device supports it.

- **ext_power** — Reads `0` if the device is parasitic powered and `1` if externally powered.

- **alarms** — Reads or writes the high and low temperatures, `TH` and `TL`, for the temperature alarm. The values are space separated and the lowest value is automatically used for `TL`.

- **eeprom** — Saves the current configuration if you write "`save`" to it and restores it if you write "`restore`". It supports a limited number of writes so should be used sparingly.

It is also worth knowing that the device is also added to the hwmon folder and that folder is replicated in the devices folder. The reason for this is to allow integration with any hwmon software you may have – there are no advantages over using the device directly.

The 1-Wire master also has some useful files in the w1_bus_master folder:

◆	`therm_bulk_read`	Takes a temperature from all devices
◆	`w1_master_add`	Manually registers a slave device
◆	`w1_master_attempts`	Number of times a search attempted
◆	`w1_master_max_slave_count`	Max number of slaves to search for
◆	`w1_master_name`	Name of the device (`w1_bus_masterX`)
◆	`w1_master_pullup`	5V strong pull-up 0 enabled/1 disabled
◆	`w1_master_remove`	Manually remove a slave device
◆	`w1_master_search`	Number of searches left to do
◆	`w1_master_slave_count`	Number of slaves found
◆	`w1_master_slaves`	Names of the slaves, one per line
◆	`w1_master_timeout`	Delay in seconds between searches
◆	`w1_master_timeout_us`	Delay in microsecs between searches

Normally a temperature conversion is triggered when you read the appropriate file but if you write trigger to the `therm_bulk_read` file all of the connected devices are read and the readings stored for the next time you read the device. Reading the file returns 0 if no bulk conversion is in progress, -1 if at least one device is still converting and 1 if conversion is complete but there is still data to be read from the devices.

You can set the `w1_master_search` to a small number if the attached devices rarely change. If your devices never change you could set it to zero and use `w1_master_add` to add the serial numbers.

The `w1_master_timeout` and `w1_master_timeout_us` determine the interval between searches for devices. Each time a search occurs `w1_master_search` is decremented and `w1_master_attempts` is incremented.

You can use the `w1_master_slave_count` and `w1_master_slaves` as an alternative way of discovering what devices are installed:

```
int getDevices(char path[][100], int *num)
{
    char buffer[500];
    int fd = open("/sys/bus/w1/drivers/w1_master_driver/
                    w1_bus_master1/w1_master_slaves", O_RDONLY);
    read(fd, buffer, 500);
    close(fd);
    *num = 0;
    for (char *p = strtok(buffer, "\n"); p != NULL;
                                        p = strtok(NULL, "\n"))
    {
        snprintf(path[(*num)++], 100, "/sys/bus/w1/devices/%s", p);
    }
    num--;
}
```

Notice that the names are separated by newline characters and the strtok function splits the string on "/n". You have to make sure that buffer is big enough to read all the names in one go.

A complete program that reads and displays the data of the first device
connected to the 1-Wire bus is:

```
#include <stdio.h>
#include <stdlib.h>
#include <string.h>
#include <unistd.h>
#include <sys/ioctl.h>
#include <fcntl.h>

FILE *doCommand(char *cmd)
{
    FILE *fp = popen(cmd, "r");
    if (fp == NULL)
    {
        printf("Failed to run command %s \n\r", cmd);
        exit(1);
    }
    return fp;
}

void load1w(int pin)
{
    FILE *fd = doCommand("sudo dtparam -l");
    char output[1024];
    int txfound = 0;
    while (fgets(output, sizeof(output), fd) != NULL)
    {
        printf("%s\n\r", output);
        fflush(stdout);
        if (strstr(output, "w1-gpio-pi5") != NULL)
        {
            txfound = 1;
        }
    }
    pclose(fd);
    if (txfound == 0)
    {
        char cmd[100];
        snprintf(cmd, 100, "sudo dtoverlay w1-gpio-pi5 gpiopin=%d",
                                                        pin);

        fd = doCommand(cmd);
        pclose(fd);
    }
}
```

```
int getDevices(char path[][100], int *num)
{
    char buffer[500];
    int fd = open("/sys/bus/w1/drivers/w1_master_driver/
                     w1_bus_master1/w1_master_slaves", O_RDONLY);
    read(fd, buffer, 500);
    close(fd);
    *num = 0;
    for (char *p = strtok(buffer, "\n"); p != NULL;
                                      p = strtok(NULL, "\n"))
    {
        snprintf(path[(*num)++], 100, "/sys/bus/w1/devices/%s", p);
    }
    num--;
}

int getData(char path[], char name[], char data[], int n)
{
    char file[100];
    snprintf(file, 100, "%s/%s", path, name);
    int fd = open(file, O_RDONLY);
    int c = read(fd, data, n);
    close(fd);
    data[c] = 0;
    return c;
}

int main(int argc, char **argv)
{
    load1w(4);
    char path[10][100];
    int num;
    getDevices(path, &num);
    printf("%d  %s\n\r", num, path[0]);
    if (num < 1)
        exit(-1);

    char output[1024] = {0};
    char file[100];

    getData(path[0], "name", output, 100);
    printf("Name %s\n\r", output);

    getData(path[0], "resolution", output, 100);
    printf("Resolution %s\n\r", output);

    getData(path[0], "w1_slave", output, 100);
    printf("w1_slave %s\n\r", output);
```

```
getData(path[0], "temperature", output, 100);
printf("temperature %s\n\r", output);
float temp;
sscanf(output, "%f", &temp);
temp = temp / 1000;
printf("temperature %f C\n\r",temp);

getData(path[0], "alarms", output, 100);
printf("alarms %s\n\r", output);
```

}

Active Pull-Up

The 1-Wire bus isn't very robust. Its use of pull-up resistors at such high
speeds means that it doesn't take much capacitance to make the pulses look
more like a capacitor charging up. Getting the wiring right for a 1-Wire bus
with multiple devices isn't easy. What is more, scanning the bus is the only
time, apart from the presence pulse, when multiple devices control the bus.
A setup that works perfectly well with a single device often has problems
when there is more than one device. In fact, a standard 1-Wire bus
debugging technique is to remove all but one device and see if what wasn't
working suddenly works.

You can get around some of the problems by lowering the value of the pull-
up resistor, but this does increase the load on the driving GPIO lines and the
slave devices. You can reduce the pull-up to 2kΩ, or even less to account for
the reduced working voltage of 3.3V. The 1-Wire bus works best at 5V when
the lines are long, but it is usually not worth the trouble to add a 3.3V to 5V
driver.

If you want to drive a very long line, or just need the highest possible
performance, there is a technique which, while it might not be worth using
in many situations, is worth knowing about. It is called by a number of
names but "controllable slew rate" is close enough. The idea is that when the
master releases the bus, we have to wait for it to be pulled up via the resistor
and this can be slow. We can make it faster by replacing resistors by active
devices.

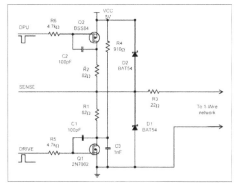

The principle used is that we can put a transistor in parallel with the pull-up resistor and use it to pull the line up faster when appropriate. For example, when the master pulls the line low for a presence pulse, it can trigger the pull-up transistor when the pulse ends to get the line back up faster than just via the resistor.

The fast pull-up transistor Q2, controlled by DPU, is switched off just before the slaves start to pull the line low. You can use the fast pull-up transistor when the master writes a 0 or reads or writes a 1. Of course, you don't need to use it when the master reads a 0 because the slave holds the line low for the whole time slot and there is no need for a fast pull-up. It is claimed that lines as long as 500m can work in this mode. Notice that you now need an additional GPIO line to drive the fast pull-up transistor. If you want to know more then refer to the Maxim design notes.

The fast pull-up is also recommended if you are planning to run a true 1-Wire device and power attached devices from the data line. A typical circuit is:

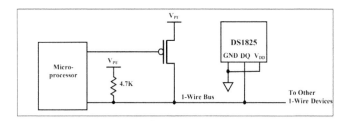

You can see that the device only needs a single wire if it can find a common ground connection. You can also see that the transistor is playing the role of a fast pull-up, but in this case the reason for it is to ensure that the device gets as much current as possible to keep it running.

The documentation says:

> The 1-Wire bus must be switched to the strong pullup within 10s (max) after a Convert T [44h] or Copy Scratchpad [48h] command is issued, and the bus must be held high by the pullup for the duration of the conversion (tconv) or data transfer (twr = 10ms). No other activity can take place on the 1-Wire bus while the pullup is enabled.

If you work with 1-Wire devices at a low level then it is up to you to drive the second pull-up GPIO line manually.

If you want to use a Linux driver then there is one that takes care of this for you:

Name: w1-gpio-pullup-pi5

Configures the w1-gpio-pi5 Onewire interface module

Load: dtoverlay=w1-gpio-pullup-pi5,<param>=<val>

Params: gpiopin   GPIO for I/O (default "4")

extpullup   GPIO for external pull-up (default "5")

pullup   Enabled by default (ignored)

This is used in exactly the same way as the w1-gpio driver, but now you have to specify an additional GPIO line to drive the active pull-up, the default being GPIO5.

In practice, you have to face up to the fact that you will get errors when working with the 1-Wire bus and especially so with multiple devices and parasitic power. The problem is particularly bad if you are testing a circuit using a prototype board. Things often work better when you move to properly soldered connections and cables, but you will still get errors.

The only way to live with errors is to detect them and attempt to re-read the device.

One Wire File System (OWFS)

If you are going to use a lot of 1-Wire devices then it might be worth looking into the One Wire File System, OWFS, which you can find out about at www.owfs.org. It is an open source project which supports a range of 1-Wire master and slaves. The downside is that it is more involved to install and get working, the pay off is that every device now has its own directory in a mountable file system and the range of devices supported is larger than the basic Linux drivers. How to use OWFS would take us a long way from the main topic of this book, but it is worth looking into if you want to use a mix of 1-Wire devices.

1-Wire Using Gpio5

It is fairly easy to read a 1-wire device without the help of a driver. The only problem is generating accurate signals at the 10 μs range.

Every transaction with a 1-wire device starts with an initialization handshake. First we have to work out how to configure the GPIO line. This example assumes that the 1-wire device is connected to GPIO4.

What we do in practice to simulate an open collector driver is to configure the GPIO line for output only when the master needs to drive the line. Once the master is finished the GPIO line is set back to input and the pull-up resistor is allowed to pull the line back up. After this, any slave wanting to send data is free to pull the line low.

The first transaction we need is the initialization pulse. This is simply a low pulse that lasts at least 480μs, a pause of 15μs to 60μs follows and then any and all of the devices on the bus pull the line low for 60μs to 240μs.

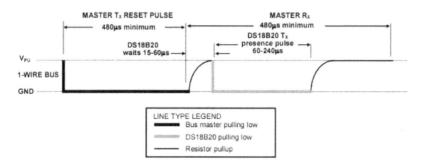

The suggested timings are set the line low for 480μs and read the line after 70μs followed by a pause of 410μs.

This is fairly easy to implement as a function:

```
int presence(uint8_t pin)
{
    gpio_set_dir(pin, GPIO_OUT);
    gpio_put(pin, 1);
    sleep_ms(1);
    gpio_put(pin, 0);
    sleep_us(500);
    gpio_set_dir(pin, GPIO_IN);
    sleep_us(70);
    int b = gpio_get(pin);
    sleep_us(410);
    return b;
}
```

We pull the line low for 500μs and then let it be pulled back up by changing the line to input, i.e. high impedance. After a 70μs wait, which is right at the start of the guaranteed period when the line should be low if there is an active device on the bus, we read the input line and then wait another 410μs to complete the data slot.

The timings in this case are not critical as long as the line is read while it is held low by the slaves, which is never less than 60μs and is typically as much as 100μs. If there is a device, the function should return a 0 and if there are no devices it should return a 1.

```c
#include <stdio.h>
#include <stdlib.h>
#include "Gpio5.h"
int main()
{
    rp1_Init();
    gpio_init(4);

    if (presence(4) == 1)
    {
        printf("No device \n");
    }
    else
    {
        printf("Device present \n");
    }
    return 0;
}
```

If you try this partial program and have a logic analyzer with a 1-wire protocol analyzer you will see something like:

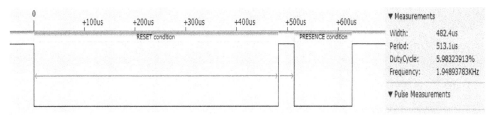

Seeing a presence pulse is the simplest and quickest way to be sure that your hardware is working.

Writing Bits

Our next task is to implement the sending of some data bits to the device. The 1-Wire bus has a very simple data protocol. All bits are sent using a minimum of 60μs for a read/write slot. Each slot must be separated from the next by a minimum of 1μs.

The good news is that timing is only critical within each slot. You can send the first bit in a time slot and then take your time before you send the next bit as the device will wait for you. This means you only have to worry about timing within the functions that read and write individual bits.

To send a 0 you have to hold the line low for most of the slot. To send a 1 you have to hold the line low for just between 1μs and 15μs and leave the line high for the rest of the slot. The exact timings can be seen below:

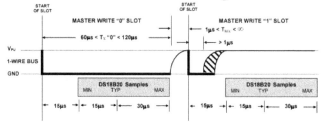

It seems reasonable to use the typical timings given in the datasheets. So for a 0 we hold the line low for 60μs then let it go high for the remainder of the slot, 10μs. To send a 1 we hold the line for 6μs and then let it go high for the remainder of the slot, 64μs. As the only time critical operations are the actual setting of the line low and then back to high, there is no need to worry too much about the speed of operation of the entire function so we might as well combine writing 0 and 1 into a single writeBit function:

```
void writeBit(uint8_t pin, int b)
{
    int delay1, delay2;
    if (b == 1)
    {
        delay1 = 6;
        delay2 = 64;
    }
    else
    {
        delay1 = 60;
        delay2 = 10;
    }
    gpio_set_dir(pin, GPIO_OUT);
    gpio_put(pin, 0);
    sleep_us(delay1);
    gpio_set_dir(pin, GPIO_IN);
    sleep_us(delay2);
}
```

The code at the start of the function simply increases the time between slots slightly. Notice that once again we return the GPIO line to input, i.e. high impedance, rather than driving the line high at the end of the transaction. This allows the line to be pulled high ready for any response from the slave. You can see two ones followed by two zeros in the following logic analyzer trace:

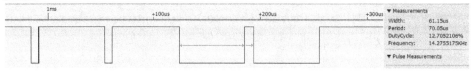

A First Command - Writing Bytes

After discovering that there is at least one device connected to the bus, the master has to issue a ROM command. In many cases the ROM command used first will be the Search ROM command, which enumerates the 64-bit codes of all of the devices on the bus. After collecting all of these codes, the master can use Match ROM commands with a specific 64-bit code to select the device the master wants to talk to.

While it is perfectly possible to implement the Search ROM procedure, it is simpler to work with the single device by using commands which ignore the 64-bit code and address all of the devices on the bus at the same time. Of course, this only works as long as there really is only one device on the bus. If there is only one device then we can use the Skip ROM command 0xCC to tell all the devices on the bus to be active.

We now need a function that can send a byte. The writeByte function will write the low eight bits of an int to the device:

```
void writeByte(uint8_t pin, int byte) {
    int i;
    for (i = 0; i < 8; i++) {
        if (byte & 1) {
            writeBit(pin, 1);
        } else {
            writeBit(pin, 0);
        }
        byte = byte >> 1;
    }
}
```

Using this we can send a Skip ROM command using:

```
writeByte(2, 0xCC);
```

You can see the pattern of bits sent on a logic analyzer:

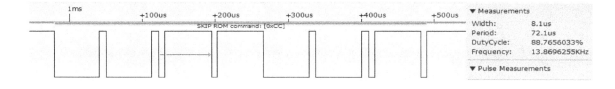

Reading Bits

We already know how the master sends a 1 and a 0. The protocol for the slave device is exactly the same except that the master still provides the slot's starting pulse. That is, the master starts a 60 μs slot by pulling the bus down for at least 1 μs. Then the slave device either holds the line down for a further 15 μs minimum or it simply allows the line to float high. See below for the exact timings:

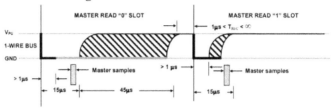

So all we have to do to read bits is to pull the line down for more than 1μs and then sample the bus after pausing long enough for the line to be pulled up or held low. The datasheet gives 6μs for the master's pulse and a 9μs pause.

In practice, a final delay of 2μs seems to work best and allows for the time to change the line's direction:

```
uint8_t readBit(uint8_t pin)
{
 gpio_set_dir(pin, GPIO_OUT);
 gpio_put(pin, 0);
 sleep_us(8);
 gpio_set_dir(pin, GPIO_IN);
 sleep_us(2);
 uint8_t b = gpio_get(pin);
 sleep_us(60);
 return b;
}
```

A logic analyzer shows the typical pattern of bits from the device:

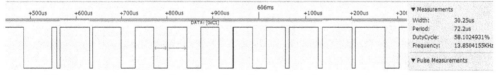

By adding some commands to toggle a line after the sample is taken, we can see how the timing works:

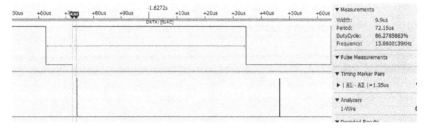

310

You might think that sampling so close to the rising edge of the timing pulse is a bad idea, but the timing of the sample tends to drift longer not shorter and this short timing reduces the error rate.

Finally, we need a function that will read a byte. As in the case of writing a byte, there is no time criticality in the time between reading bits so we don't need to take extra special care in constructing the function:

```
int readByte(uint8_t pin) {
    int byte = 0;
    int i;
    for (i = 0; i < 8; i++) {
        byte = byte | readBit(pin) << i;
    };
    return byte;
}
```

The only difficult part is to remember that the 1-Wire bus sends the least significant bit first and so this has to be shifted into the result from the right. The sequence is:

- Test to see if a device is present:
  `presence(uint8_t pin)`
- Write a byte:
  `void writeByte(uint8_t pin, int byte)`
- Read a byte:
  `int readByte(uint8_t pin)`

Computing the CRC

We have already encountered the idea and implementation of a CRC (Cyclic Redundancy Checksum) in Chapter 12. The 1-Wire bus uses the same CRC for all its devices and therefore we need to implement it just once. This is perhaps not in the most efficient way, but it will work. For low data rate applications high efficiency isn't needed and you can make use of a direct implementation. The 1-Wire datasheet specifies the CRC used in 1-wire devices as a shift register rather than as a polynomial equation:

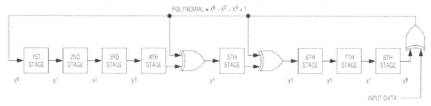

However, this is equivalent to a generator polynomial that defines the CRC as it is simply the hardware implementation of the calculation.
In this case it is:

$$X^8 + X^5 + X^4 + 1$$

The first question to answer is, what is the connection between binary values, polynomials and shift-registers? The answer is that you can treat a binary number as the coefficients of a polynomial, for example 101 is $1*X^2+0*X+1$. Each bit position corresponds to a power of X. Using this notation creates a very simple relationship between multiplying by X and a left-shift.

For example:

$(1*X^2 + 0*X+ 1)*X = 1*X^3 + 0*X^2 + 1X + 0$

corresponds to:

101 <<1 == 1010

You can see that this extends to multiplying one polynomial by another and even polynomial division, all accomplished by shifting and XOR (eXclusive OR).

The CRC is the remainder when you divide the polynomial that represents the data by the generator polynomial. The computation of the remainder is what the shift register specified on the datasheet does. The fact that the division can be implemented so simply in hardware is what makes this sort of CRC computation so common. All the hardware has to do is zero the shift register and feed the data into it. When all the data has been shifted in, what is left in the shift register is the CRC, i.e. the remainder.

To check the data you have received, all you have to do is run it through the shift register again and compare the computed CRC with the one received. A better trick is also to run the received CRC through the shift register. If there have been no errors, this will result in 0.

You can look into the theory of CRCs, bit sequences and polynomials further, it is interesting and practically useful, but we now know everything we need to if we want to implement the CRC used by1-Wire devices. All we have to do is implement the shift register in software.

From the diagram, what we have to do is take each bit of the input data and XOR it with the least significant bit of the current shift register. If the input bit is 0, the XORs in the shift register don't have any effect and the CRC just has to be moved one bit to the right. If the input bit is 1, we have to XOR the bits at positions 3 and 4 with 1 and put a 1 in at position 7 to simulate shifting a 1 into the register, i.e. XOR the shift register with 10001100.

So the algorithm for a single byte is:

```
for (j = 0; j < 8; j++) {
        temp = (crc ^ databyte) & 0x01;
        crc >>= 1;
        if (temp)
                crc ^= 0x8C;
                databyte>>= 1;
        }
}
```

First we XOR the data with the current CRC and extract the low-order bit into temp. Then we right-shift the CRC by one place. If the low-order result stored in temp was a 1, we have to XOR the CRC with 0x8C to simulate the XORs in the shift register and shift in a 1 at the most significant bit. Then shift the data one place right and repeat for the next data bit.

With this worked out, we can now write a crc8 function that computes the CRC for the entire eight bytes of data:

```
uint8_t crc8(uint8_t *data, uint8_t len) {
        uint8_t i;
        uint8_t j;
        uint8_t temp;
        uint8_t databyte;
        uint8_t crc = 0;
        for (i = 0; i < len; i++) {
                databyte = data[i];
                for (j = 0; j < 8; j++) {
                        temp = (crc ^ databyte) & 0x01;
                        crc >>= 1;
                        if (temp)
                        crc ^= 0x8C;
                        databyte >>= 1;
                }
        }
        return crc;
}
```

With this in place we can now check the CRC of any data a 1-Wire bus device sends us.

Reading the DS1820

So far everything we've met has been generic to the 1-Wire bus and if you use it to send the correct commands you can work with any 1-Wire device. As an example, we can read the temperature as measured by a single DS1820 connected to GPIO4.

As there is only one device on the 1-Wire bus, we can use the Skip ROM command (0xCC) to signal it to be active:

```
writeByte(2, 0xCC);
```

You can see the pattern of bits sent on a logic analyzer:

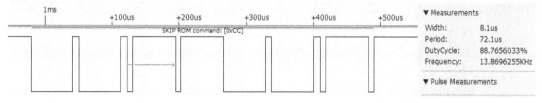

313

If there is more than one device connected to the bus you have to select it first.

Our next task is to send a Convert command, 0x44, to start the DS18B20 making a temperature measurement. Depending on the resolution selected, this can take as long as 750ms. How the device tells the master that the measurement has completed depends on the mode in which it is operating, but using an external power line, i.e. not using parasitic mode, the device sends a 0 bit in response to a bit read until it is completed when it sends a 1.

This is how 1-Wire devices that need time to get data ready slow down the master until they are ready. The master can read a single bit as often as it likes and the slave will respond with a 0 until it is ready with the data.

As we already have a readBit function this is easy. The software polls for the completion by reading the bus until it gets a 1 bit:

```
int convert(uint8_t pin)
{
    writeByte(pin, 0x44);
    int i;
    for (i = 0; i < 500; i++)
    {
        sleep_ms(10);
        if (readBit(pin) == 1)
            break;
    }
    return i;
}
```

You can of course test the return value to check that the result has been obtained. If convert returns 500 then the loop times out. When the function returns, the new temperature measurement is stored in the device's scratchpad memory and now all we have to do is read this.

Reading the Scratchpad

The scratchpad memory has nine bytes of storage in total and does things like control the accuracy of conversion and provide status information. In our simple example the only two bytes of any great interest are the first two, which hold the result of a temperature conversion. However, as we are going to check the CRC for error detection, we need to read all nine bytes.

All we have to do is issue a Read Scratchpad, 0xBE, command and then read the nine bytes that the device returns. To send the new command we have to issue a new initialization pulse and a Skip ROM, 0xCC, command followed by a Read Scratchpad command, 0xBE:

```
presence(2);
writeByte(2, 0xCC);
writeByte(2, 0xBE);
```

Now the data is ready to read. We can read all nine bytes of it or just the first two that we are interested in. The device will keep track of which bytes have been read. If you come back later and read more bytes you will continue the read from where you left off. If you issue another initialization pulse then the device aborts the data transmission.

As we do want to check the CRC for errors, we will read all nine bytes:

```
uint8_t data[9];
    for (int i = 0; i < 9; i++)
    {
        data[i] = readByte(2);
    }
```

Now we have all of the data stored in the scratchpad and the CRC byte, we can check for errors:

```
uint8_t crc = crc8(data, 9);
```

As before, `crc` will be 0 if there are no transmission errors. The `crc8` function was given earlier.

Getting the Temperature

To obtain the temperature measurement we need to work with the first two bytes, which are the least and most significant bytes of the 12-bit temperature reading:

```
int t1 = data[0];
int t2 = data[1];
```

`t1` holds the low-order bits and `t2` the high-order bits.

All we now have to do is to put the two bytes together as a 16-bit two's complement integer and we can do this very easily:

```
int16_t temp1 = (t2 << 8 | t1);
```

Notice that this only works because `int16_t` really is a 16-bit integer. If you were to use:

```
int temp1= (t2<<8 | t1);
```

`temp1` would be correct for positive temperatures but it would give the wrong answer for negative values because the sign bit isn't propagated into the top 16 bits. If you want to use a 32-bit integer, you will have to propagate the sign bit manually:

```
if(t2 & 0x80) temp1=temp1 | 0xFFFF0000;
```

Finally, we have to convert the temperature to a scaled floating-point value. As the returned data gives the temperature in centigrade with the low-order four bits giving the fractional part, it has to be scaled by a factor of 1/16:

```
float temp = (float) temp1 / 16;
```

Now we can print the `CRC` and the temperature:

```
printf("CRC %hho \n\r ", crc);
printf("temperature = %f C \n", temp);
```

A Temperature Function

Packaging all of this into a single function is easy:

```c
float getTemperature(uint8_t pin) {
    if (presence(pin) == 1) return -1000;
    writeByte(pin, 0xCC);
    if (convert(pin) == 500) return -3000;
    presence(pin);
    writeByte(pin, 0xCC);
    writeByte(pin, 0xBE);
    int i;
    uint8_t data[9];
    for (i = 0; i < 9; i++) {
        data[i] = readByte(pin);
    }
    uint8_t crc = crc8(data, 9);
    if(crc!=0) return -2000;
    int t1 = data[0];
    int t2 = data[1];
    int16_t temp1 = (t2 << 8 | t1);
    float temp = (float) temp1 / 16;
    return temp;
}
```

Notice that the function returns -1000 if there is no device, -2000 if there is a CRC error and -3000 if the device fails to provide data. These values are outside the range of temperatures that can be measured.

The Complete Program

The complete program to read and display the temperature is:

```c
#include <stdio.h>
#include <stdlib.h>
#include "Gpio5.h"

int presence(uint8_t pin)
{
    gpio_set_dir(pin, GPIO_OUT);
    gpio_put(pin, 1);
    sleep_ms(1);
    gpio_put(pin, 0);
    sleep_us(500);
    gpio_set_dir(pin, GPIO_IN);
    sleep_us(70);
    int b = gpio_get(pin);
    sleep_us(410);
    return b;
}
```

```c
void writeBit(uint8_t pin, int b)
{
    int delay1, delay2;
    if (b == 1)
    {
        delay1 = 6;
        delay2 = 64;
    }
    else
    {
        delay1 = 60;
        delay2 = 10;
    }
    gpio_set_dir(pin, GPIO_OUT);
    gpio_put(pin, 0);
    sleep_us(delay1);
    gpio_set_dir(pin, GPIO_IN);
    sleep_us(delay2);
}

void writeByte(uint8_t pin, int byte)
{
    for (int i = 0; i < 8; i++)
    {
        if (byte & 1)
        {
            writeBit(pin, 1);
        }
        else
        {
            writeBit(pin, 0);
        }
        byte = byte >> 1;
    }
}
uint8_t readBit(uint8_t pin)
{
    gpio_set_dir(pin, GPIO_OUT);
    gpio_put(pin, 0);
    sleep_us(8);
    gpio_set_dir(pin, GPIO_IN);
    sleep_us(2);
    uint8_t b = gpio_get(pin);
    sleep_us(70);
    return b;
}
```

```c
int readByte(uint8_t pin)
{
    int byte = 0;
    int i;
    for (i = 0; i < 8; i++)
    {
        byte = byte | readBit(pin) << i;
    };
    return byte;
}
int convert(uint8_t pin)
{
    writeByte(pin, 0x44);
    int i;
    for (i = 0; i < 500; i++)
    {
        sleep_ms(10);
        if (readBit(pin) == 1)
            break;
    }
    return i;
}

uint8_t crc8(uint8_t *data, uint8_t len)
{
    uint8_t i;
    uint8_t j;
    uint8_t temp;
    uint8_t databyte;
    uint8_t crc = 0;
    for (i = 0; i < len; i++)
    {
        databyte = data[i];
        for (j = 0; j < 8; j++)
        {
            temp = (crc ^ databyte) & 0x01;
            crc >>= 1;
            if (temp)
                crc ^= 0x8C;

            databyte >>= 1;
        }
    }

    return crc;
}
```

```c
float getTemperature(uint8_t pin)
{
    if (presence(pin) == 1)
        return -1000;
    writeByte(pin, 0xCC);
    if (convert(pin) == 500)
        return -3000;
    presence(pin);
    writeByte(pin, 0xCC);
    writeByte(pin, 0xBE);
    int i;
    uint8_t data[9];
    for (i = 0; i < 9; i++)
    {
        data[i] = readByte(pin);
    }
    uint8_t crc = crc8(data, 9);
    if (crc != 0)
        return -2000;
    int t1 = data[0];
    int t2 = data[1];
    int16_t temp1 = (t2 << 8 | t1);
    float temp = (float)temp1 / 16;
    return temp;
}

int main()
{
    rp1_Init();
    gpio_init(4);

    if (presence(4) == 1)
    {
        printf("No device \n");
    }
    float t;
    for (;;) {
        do {
            t = getTemperature(4);
        } while (t<-999);
        printf("%f\r\n",t);
        sleep(1);
    };

    return 0;
}
```

Summary

- The 1-Wire bus is easy to use and has good Linux support.

- The `w1-gpio` driver will use any GPIO pin to implement a 1-Wire bus in software.

- All 1-Wire devices have a unique serial number, which also codes for the type of the device.

- You can list devices using directory operations or you can use the driver to interrogate the master.

- The DS18B20 Temperature Sensor is a good example of a 1-Wire device.

- You can power a 1-Wire device over the line that is used for data. This only works if you use a strong pull-up in the form of a transistor.

- If you want to make extensive use of 1-Wire devices it might be worth looking into OWFS – the One Wire File System.

- Implementing the 1-Wire protocol is mostly a matter of getting the timing right.

- There are three types of interaction: presence pulse, read and write. The presence pulse simply asks any connected devices to reply and make themselves known.

- The 1-Wire protocol is easier to implement than you might think because each bit is sent as a "slot" and while timing is critical within the slot, how fast slots are sent isn't and the master is in control of when this happens.

- The DS18B20 temperature sensor is one of the most commonly encountered 1-Wire bus devices. It is small, low-cost and you can use multiple devices on a single bus.

- After a convert command is sent to the device, it can take 750ms before a reading is ready.

- To test for data ready you have to poll on a single bit. Reading a zero means data not ready and reading a one means data ready.

- When the data is ready you can read the scratchpad memory where the data is stored.

The traditional way to approach any custom or unsupported protocol is to use "bit banging". This is simply the act of writing a program which controls GPIO lines to simulate the hardware that might be used to implement the protocol. Basically what you have to do is set GPIO lines high and low as dictated by the timing of the protocol and then read data at set times. This is easy in theory, but getting the timings right is harder that it appears and synchronization between state changes is particularly challenging. In addition there is the problem that bit banging ties up the processor. In many cases this doesn't matter. In other cases you can use one core to implement the protocol and another to process the data. Even so with a multi-tasking operating system like Linux you always have the possibility that the task will be suspended and this generally ruins the timing of the protocol.

A good alternative to using the general purpose CPU to control the GPIO lines involved in a timing sensitive protocol is to build a special programmable subsystem that is sufficiently flexible to be used in generating and measuring pulses. The Raspberry Pi Pico introduced just such a device in the form of its Programmable Input Output, PIO . This allows custom implementation of protocols without the involvement of the CPU but at the price of having to learn how to use it.

Until recently, the big problem was that there was no easy way of using it without extensive reverse engineering. Now we have access to the PIO via a driver and a wrapper library PIOLib, written to emulate the Pico SDK along the same lines as Gpio5. This means you can take an existing Pico PIO program and run it on the CM5 with only minor modifications.

Setting up PIOLib

PIOLib needs the CM5 to be fully up-to-date and it is a good idea to follow the setup instructions exactly:

First update Linux and dependencies on the CM5:

```
sudo apt update
sudo apt upgrade
```

Make sure you have the latest EEPROM

```
sudo rpi-eeprom-update -a
```

Install CMake

```
sudo apt install build-essential cmake
```

Next you need to download PIOLib and this can be done in a number of ways. The simplest is to download the entire `utils` repo from GitHub:

```
https://github.com/raspberrypi/utils/tree/master
```

Use the Code button and select download ZIP. When you have the ZIP file open it in a compression tool and extract just the `piolib` directory into the location where you create CM5 programs. Of course, if you want other utilities you can extract these as well, but `piolib` is all you need to use the PIO.

Change directory to `piolib` and use the command:

```
cmake .
```

followed by

```
make
```

This will compile the library and the driver.

Finally reboot and you should see `pio0` in the /dev directory.

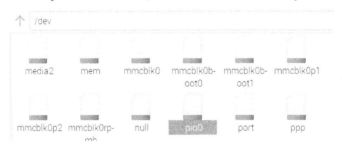

If `pio0` is owned by root and in group root you will also need to add the line:

```
SUBSYSTEM=="*-pio", GROUP="gpio", MODE="0660"
```

to the end of:

```
/etc/udev/rules.d/99-com.rules
```

and either restart or use:

```
sudo udevadm control --reload-rules && sudo udevadm trigger
```

If this procedure doesn't work repeat at least twice before you look for some more serious problem.

PIO Basic Concepts

The problem with getting to grips with the PIO is that there are two distinct views of it – inside and outside. You can also add to this the extra complication of setting up a project that makes use of it, but that is a one-time problem. The best way to think about the PIO is as a black box that performs some transaction using GPIO lines and presents and accepts data from the processor – exactly like other I/O subsystems PWM, SPI, I2C etc. The only difference is that the transaction it performs is programmable.

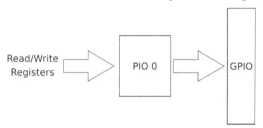

This is the same situation as for the I2C or SPI hardware – once set up you communicate with the PIO by reading and writing registers and it is associated with a number of GPIO lines.

Whereas the Pico has two PIO blocks, PIO 0 and PIO 1 the CM5 has a single PIO block, PIO 0. You communicate with the PIO by reading and writing registers, but, as with other hardware modules, the Pico SDK provides functions to do this for you on the Pico. The PIO driver for the CM5 implements the usual Linux file approach to drivers and it would be used directly via ioct calls – and these aren't documented. The PIOlib library works as a wrapper and implements the Pico SDK by converting calls to it into ioct calls. This allows you to run Pico PIO programs on the CM5 with minimal changes.

Configuring GPIO for PIO Output

The first and most important thing to master is that the PIO doesn't use instructions that work with particular GPIO lines. You don't write a PIO program that sets the output of GPIO 2, say. Instead you specify which GPIO lines are to be included in a number of groups. The PIO has four different "state machines" that can be set to run a program stored in the PIO. Each state machine has its own set of GPIO lines that it works with and at the simplest each state machine can perform the same sort of task on different GPIO pins. So for example, if you programmed the PIO to be an SPI controller then you could define four different SPI interfaces, each to a different set of pins. It is also possible to run each state machine from a different program, but more of this later.

Each state machine has two sets of output lines:

- ◆ OUT - Lines in the OUT group are specified by a base and a count, e.g. if base is GPIO 4 and count is 2 this gives GPIO 4 and GPIO 5. They are controlled by instructions that transfer data from the processor to the state machine, that is, they are lines you set by writing data to the state machine. Typically the lines in the OUT group are what you would think of as data lines.

You can set the OUT group using:

```
sm_config_set_out_pins (pio_sm_config *c, uint out_base,
                                           uint out_count)
```

which modifies a configuration struct c which you use later to configure the state machine using pio_sm_init. The out_base parameter gives the first GPIO line in the group and the out_count parameter gives you the number of lines in the group. By default all of the OUT pins are set to high impedance mode and have to be explicitly set to act as outputs.

- ◆ SET – Lines in the SET group are specified by a base and a count, e.g. if base is GPIO 4 and count is 2. this gives GPIO 4 and GPIO 5. They are controlled by instructions running on the state machine, that is they are lines you set within the PIO program. Typically the lines in the SET group are used for what you would think of as clock lines.

You can set the SET group using:

```
sm_config_set_set_pins (pio_sm_config *c, uint set_base,
                                           uint set_count)
```

which again modifies a configuration struct c which you use later to configure the state machine using pio_sm_init. The set_base parameter gives the first GPIO line in the group and the set_count parameter gives you the number of lines in the group. By default all of the SET pins are set to high impedance mode and have to be explicitly set to act as outputs.

A third group of output lines, SIDESET, is also available and while it turns out to be very useful it is slightly more difficult to understand. We will return to it later.

Notice that a PIO program doesn't write to a particular GPIO line but to one of the groups of lines and these are defined by using the SDK functions in your C program. Also notice that the groups of GPIO lines are associated with different PIO instructions. The OUT group is used by the out instruction and the SET group is used by the set instruction.

This might seem a complicated way to go about things but it allows you to write PIO programs that work with a general group of lines and then use a C program to determine which particular GPIO lines are used i.e. you can change which GPIO lines are used without changing the PIO program.

PIO Blinky

Now it is time to write and run our first PIO program and in the grand tradition we will, eventually, write a Blinky program – the Hello World of hardware.

The PIO is programmed using a special assembly language and we will return to its main features later, but for now you can most probably understand the meaning of our first simple program:

```
.program squarewave
    set pindirs, 1    ; Set pin to output
again:
    set pins, 1       ; Drive pin high
    set pins, 0       ; Drive pin low
    jmp again         ; Set PC to label `again`
```

This should be stored in `sqwave.pio` in the project folder that contains the C program that makes use of it.

The first instruction

```
set pindirs, 1
```

sets pin 1 in the SET group of pins to be an active output, i.e. it changes from a high impedance state to an output. This is more complicated than it seems. More of exactly how this works in the section on Output to the GPIO but essentially the value is used as a bit mask setting I/O lines to input or output e.g. 5 or 101 sets the first and third line in the SET group to output.

The loop that follows this repeatedly changes the first pin in the SET group of pins from high to low. Again the value is a bit mask that is used to set the pins in the SET group. Notice that from this program you cannot tell which pins are actually being used – this is set in your C program via the PIO registers or the equivalent SDK functions.

The PIO Assembler

The program is simple, but now we have to convert it into machine code by either hand-assembling it, which is possible but tedious, or passing it through an assembler. The Pico SDK has an assembler included, but this is not available as part of the Pi's software. The simplest solution is to install the Pico SDK to your Windows, Mac or Linux development machine. You can then navigate to the `~/.pico-sdk/tools/2.1.0/pioasm` directory and copy `pioasm` or `pioasm.exe` file to a development directory.

You can also find copies of `pioasm` and `pioasm.exe` in the Gpio5/PIOAsm directory on GitHub.

To make use of the assembler you need to copy it to a suitable directory and the .vscode directory is a reasonable choice and is the folder used to host the assembler in the rest of this chapter.

The assembler is a command line tool and its help tells you how to use it:

```
usage: pioasm <options> <input> (<output>)

Assemble file of PIO program(s) for use in applications.
   <input>              the input filename
   <output>             the output filename (or filename prefix if the output format produces multiple outputs).
                        if not specified, a single output will be written to stdout

options:
  -o <output_format>    select output_format (default 'c-sdk'); available options are:
                           c-sdk
                               C header suitable for use with the Raspberry Pi Pico SDK
                           python
                               Python file suitable for use with MicroPython
                           hex
                               Raw hex output (only valid for single program inputs)
                           json
                               Machine-formatted output for integrating with external tools
                           ada
                               Ada specification
                           go
                               Go file suitable for use with TinyGo. See https://github.com/tinygo-org/pio.
  -p <output_param>     add a parameter to be passed to the output format generator
  -v <version>          specify the default PIO version (0 or 1)
  -?, --help            print this help and exit
```

The defaults suit our purpose in generating a header file for use in a C program. For example:

```
pioasm sqwave.pio sqwave.pio.h
```

creates a header that can be included in a sqwave.c program to supply the assembled program in a usable form.

If you get a permissions error when you try to run pioasm you need to set its execute bit:

```
chmod +x .vscode/pioasm
```

To make it easier to create the header file from the PIO file we can create a VS Code task:

```
{
    "tasks": [
        {
            "label":"Build PIO header",
            "type":"process",
            "command":".vscode/pioasm",
            "args":[
                "${fileDirname}/${fileBasenameNoExtension}.pio",
                "${fileDirname}/${fileBasenameNoExtension}.pio.h"
            ]
        },
```

Add these lines to the task.json file and you can associate a shortcut key press to run the task more easily. Notice that it assumes that pioasm is stored in .vscode within the project directory and is executable.

The C Program

The `sqwave.pio` program contains the PIO program in PIO language. The `sqwave.pio.h` file contains the assembled program and some helper functions.

Now all we need is a C program to make use of the assembler to load it and set the state machine running. We have to include the header file that the assembler generated:

```
#include "sqwave.pio.h"
```

This adds the definition of the machine code to your program:

```
static const uint16_t squarewave_program_instructions[] = {
            //     .wrap_target
    0xe081, //  0: set     pindirs, 1
    0xe001, //  1: set     pins, 1
    0xe000, //  2: set     pins, 0
    0x0001, //  3: jmp     1
            //     .wrap
};
```

You could write some code to load the contents of the array into a PIO, but the header file also creates a struct that can be passed to an SDK function that will load the code for you:

```
static const struct pio_program squarewave_program = {
    .instructions = squarewave_program_instructions,
    .length = 4,
    .origin = -1,
};
```

To load the code all we have to do is use the standard function:

```
uint offset = pio_add_program(pio0, &squarewave_program);
```

Now we have the code loaded into `pio0`, the next job is to pick one of the four possible state machines to execute it and it is better to let the SDK select the first free machine:

```
uint sm = pio_claim_unused_sm(pio0, true);
```

The final parameter will cause the program to fail if there are no state machines available. Set the final parameter to false and the return value is negative rather than a state machine index in case of error.

With the state machine that we are going to use settled, we can now configure it. You could do this directly, but the simplest and best way to do the job is to use the SDK. This allows you to set up a struct with all of the configuration values set and then initialize the state machine in one go. First we need a default configuration and this is another utility function provided by the header file that the assembler creates:

```
pio_sm_config c = squarewave_program_get_default_config(offset);
```

Now we have to set the configuration as promised. We need to specify which pins are going to be in the SET group:

```
sm_config_set_set_pins(&c, 2, 1);
```

and in this case we have selected just one pin, GPIO 2, as the group starts at GPIO 2 and has just one pin. This means that our set instruction in the PIO program will toggle just pin GPIO 2. We also have to set the GPIO function to `GPIO_FUNC_PIO0` to let the processor know that the pin is being controlled by the PIO.

Instead of using the function from Gpio5:

```
gpio_set_function(2, GPIO_FUNC_PIO0);
```

you can use the specific PIO function to do the same job:

```
pio_gpio_init(pio0, 2);
```

Finally we can load the configuration into the state machine and start it running:

```
pio_sm_init(pio0, sm, offset, &c);
pio_sm_set_enabled(pio0, sm, true);
```

If you now look at the output of GPIO 2 you will see a square wave.

The complete program is listed below, but remember that it needs the PIO header that the assembler creates:

```
#include "pico/stdlib.h"
#include "hardware/pio.h"

#include "sqwave.pio.h"

int main()
{
 uint offset = pio_add_program(pio0, &squarewave_program);

 uint sm = pio_claim_unused_sm(pio0, true);
 pio_sm_config c =
 squarewave_program_get_default_config(offset);

 sm_config_set_set_pins(&c, 2, 1);
 pio_gpio_init(pio0, 2);

 pio_sm_init(pio0, sm, offset, &c);
 pio_sm_set_enabled(pio0, sm, true);
 while(true){};
 return 0;
}
```

The `pico/stdlib.h` and `hardware/pio.h` headers are supplied by the library. `stdlib.h` simply includes:

```
#include <stddef.h>
#include <stdio.h>
#include <stdlib.h>
#include "piolib.h"
```

`pio.h` header doesn't do anything and is only included for compatibility with Pico programs so it can be deleted.

To make this work you also need to let VS Code know where the PIO include files are. Add:

```
"args": [
    "-fdiagnostics-color=always",
    "-I../piolib/include",
    "-g",
    "${file}",
    "../piolib/piolib.c",
    "../piolib/pio_rp1.c",
    "-o",
    "${fileDirname}/${fileBasenameNoExtension}"
],
```

to the args section of the `C/C++: gcc build active file` task in tasks.json . This assumes that the header files and PIO C files are in a folder called `piolib` in the same folder as the project folder.

Note: At the time of writing you cannot use piolib at the same time as Gpio5 as some of the functions they define are in common and hence clash. The simplest solution is to add Gpio5_ to the start of each gpio function in the Gpio5 library – this works but it means you cannot run a Pico program without modification.

If you try this out you will find that the program does produce a square wave, but it isn't suitable as a Blinky example. At the moment the clock rate is set to produce a square wave at around 66 MHz and we need to bring down the frequency to something more reasonable so that we can see an LED blink on and off. Notice that the CM5's PIO runs at 200MHz and this is faster than the standard Pico PIO, which means that timings will change when you port a program from the Pico to the CM5.

Notice that the PIO program runs as fast as the PIO clock allows it to run, but the C program runs slower than in the case of the Pico due to the fact that the PIO isn't directly connected to the CPU running the C program. For programs that simply load the PIO with a program and some data this makes no difference, but for programs that interact with the running PIO program it can introduce timing problems.

Clock Division and Timing

There are a number of ways of controlling the speed at which things happen, the most direct and preferable is to change the clock frequency by specifying a divider. The PIO clock can be divided down using a 16-bit divider – 8-bit integer/8-bit fractional. In most cases, you should avoid using a fractional divider as it introduces extra periods to make the frequency average out to the fractional part. This can make the PIO subject to jitter, which decreases the reliability.

You can set the clock divider using either:

```
pio_sm_set_clkdiv (PIO pio, uint sm, float div)
```

or:

```
pio_sm_set_clkdiv_int_frac (PIO pio, uint sm,
                            uint16_t div_int, uint8_t div_frac)
```

If you add:

```
sm_config_set_clkdiv_int_frac(&c,255,0);
```

then you will get the lowest clock frequency using the default clock, i.e. roughly 260 kHz.

This brings us to another important idea. Most of the timing in PIO programs is linked to the time an instruction takes to complete and most instructions take one clock cycle. This can cause difficulties in that execution paths may not be equal in time when you want them to be. For example, consider our simple PIO program:

```
.program squarewave
    set pindirs, 1    ; Set pin to output
again:
    set pins, 1       ; Drive pin high
    set pins, 0       ; Drive pin low
    jmp again         ; Set PC to label `again`
```

The first set pins takes one clock cycle, the second takes one clock cycle, but the jmp instruction also takes one clock cycle meaning that the GPIO line is high for one clock cycle and low for two clock cycles. There are a number of ways of changing timings. For example, you could include a nop instruction which wastes a single clock cycle, but also uses one memory slot. Alternatively, you could specify a delay as part of the instruction – all PIO instructions can have a delay in clock cycles specified as [n] at the end of the instruction.

So our new program to hold the line high for two clock cycles and low for two clock cycles is:

```
.program squarewave
    set pindirs, 1   ; Set pin to output
again:
    set pins, 1 [1]  ; Drive pin high
    set pins, 0      ; Drive pin low
    jmp again        ; Set PC to label `again`
```

If you try this out you will find that the frequency drops to around 50Mhz, but with an approximately 50% duty cycle.

With the maximum clock divider this gives a square wave output at around 120 kHz, which is still too fast for flashing an LED. The maximum delay you can specify in any instruction is 31 clock cycles so even:

```
.program squarewave
    set pindirs, 1   ; Set pin to output
again:
    set pins, 1 [31] ; Drive pin high
    set pins, 0 [30] ; Drive pin low
    jmp again        ; Set PC to label `again`
```

only brings the clock down to around 12kHz.

In general, you should try to choose a clock frequency that makes timing of pulses using just per instruction delays to adjust the relative timings. Each instruction and delay takes one clock cycle so this is the natural unit of measurement to use.

In our case we need a much longer delay than can be produced by 32-clock cycle instructions. It calls instead for a spin wait loop.

Writing Loops

One of the things you will most likely have to do is write the equivalent of a for or while loop in PIO assembler and it might not be obvious how to do this because it doesn't have control structures like C. To write a loop you need to know that each state machine has two scratch 32-bit storage registers called x and y. You can store values and use values in these registers from various sources using the in, out, set or mov instructions. If you want to set a register, x say, to a constant value then you need to use:

set x,31

where 31 is the maximum value you can set because the instruction is limited to a 5-bit immediate value.

You can use the registers to implement a for loop with up to 32 repeats. The jmp instruction can test the value of a register for zero and auto-decrement it after the test. This means an n-repeat for loop can be constructed as:

```
set x,n
loop: nop
jmp x--, loop
```

The jump is taken if x is non-zero and is auto-decremented each time.

Using this you can slow the rate at which the GPIO line is toggled by repeating the nop 32 times. However, even if you use:

```
set x,n
loop: nop [31]
jmp x--, loop
```

the effective rate of toggling the GPIO line is still too great to see an LED flash. To slow it down even more you need two nested loops.

The complete PIO program is:

```
.program squarewave
    set pindirs, 1
again:
    set pins, 1
    set x, 31
 loop1:
    set y,31
    loop2:
       nop [31]
       jmp y--,loop2
    jmp x--,loop1
    set pins, 0
    set x, 31     loop3:
    set y,31
  loop4:
     nop [31]
     jmp y--,loop4
  jmp x--,loop3
  jmp again
```

You can see the two nested loops – loop1/loop2 and loop3/loop4.

This is not a good design, but it is a working Blinky program and there are many optimizations you can apply to reduce the size of the program. If you try it you will find it runs at about 11Hz, which is still fast but at least you can see the LED flash.

The need for a pair of nested loops to slow things down is due to the simple fact that we can only set the x or y register to a maximum of 31 because the PIO assembly instructions only have space for a 5-bit literal field. There is another way to set the x and y register using data transferred into the PIO program from the C program and this brings us to the subject of data input.

Data to the PIO

You can send data to the PIO from your C program in the same way as from any of the I/O subsystems. While there are more basic ways to do this job, the SDK provides easy-to-use functions. The PIO provides a 3-element, 32-bit FIFO buffer, the TX FIFO, for input to the state machine and, usually, output to the GPIO lines.

You can write data to the TX FIFO using:

```
pio_sm_put (PIO pio, uint sm, uint32_t data)
pio_sm_put_blocking (PIO pio, uint sm, uint32_t data)
```

The difference is that the first function doesn't wait for free space in the FIFO and returns without making any changes apart from setting the TXOVER flag if the FIFO is full. The second blocks until there is space to store the data.

You can discover the current state of the FIFO using:

```
static bool pio_sm_is_tx_fifo_full (PIO pio, uint sm)
static bool pio_sm_is_tx_fifo_empty (PIO pio, uint sm)
static uint pio_sm_get_tx_fifo_level (PIO pio, uint sm)
```

The PIO program can read data from the TX FIFO using the pull instruction which moves the first item of data from the FIFO into the Output Shift Register, OSR. Usually the OSR is then used to drive the OUT group of lines, more of this later. However, the mov instruction can be used to move the OSR to a range of destinations including the x and y registers. This means we can use the TX FIFO buffer to set the x or y register to a full 32-bit value.

To move a 32-bit word from the TX FIFO into the OSR you can use:

```
pull ifEmpty
```

or:

```
pull block
```

The difference is that ifEmpty only loads the OSR if it has emptied any data previously loaded and block waits until there is data in the TX FIFO.

Using this we can create a Blinky program that just uses one loop and can create time delays in excess of 30 minutes. The PIO program is:

```
.program squarewave
    set pindirs, 1
    pull block
again:
    set pins, 1
    mov x, osr
 loop1:
     jmp x--,loop1
    set pins, 0
    mov x, osr
 loop2:
   jmp x--,loop2
jmp again
```

Notice the way the OSR is used as a way of storing the loop count so that it can be used to reset the x register each time. If you needed to use the OSR for something else, this wouldn't be possible and you would have to use the y register or some other method. Also notice that the `pull block` instruction causes the PIO program to wait until there is some data in the TX FIFO to start things off.

The C program is:

```
#include "pico/stdlib.h"
#include "hardware/pio.h"

#include "sqwave.pio.h"

int main()
{
  uint offset = pio_add_program(pio0, &squarewave_program);
  uint sm = pio_claim_unused_sm(pio0, true);
  pio_sm_config c =
            squarewave_program_get_default_config(offset);
  sm_config_set_set_pins(&c, 2, 1);
  pio_gpio_init(pio0, 2);

  sm_config_set_clkdiv_int_frac(&c, 255, 0);
  pio_sm_init(pio0, sm, offset, &c);
  pio_sm_set_enabled(pio0, sm, true);

  pio_sm_put_blocking(pio0, sm, 0xFFFF);
  while(true){};
  return 0;
}
```

The only real difference is the `pio_sm_put_blocking` function at the end which stores 0xFFFF in the TX FIFO to start the PIO running. If you run this program you will find that the frequency is 6Hz and this is plenty slow enough to see an LED flash.

This is a way of passing a single parameter to a PIO program. Due to the way that the PIO is interfaced to the CPU it is slower than in the Pico, but as it is only a single transfer it is unlikely to cause a problem. If you want to pass two or more parameters then it can be done, but things become more complicated and there could be timing problems.

Sharing GPIO lines

The use of the Output Shift Register, OSR, to store a value that is moved to the x register is reasonable, but it isn't the usual role for the OSR. It normally acts as a link between values passed to the state machine and the state of the GPIO lines. We have already seen that the SET group of GPIO lines can be controlled using the `set` command, now we move on to consider how the OUT group of GPIO lines can be controlled using the `out` command.

There is a sense in which the SET and OUT groups of GPIO lines are just a programming construct rather than anything implemented in the hardware and it is worth looking at this in detail before moving on.

Each state machine has its own mapping of the SET and OUT groups to the physical GPIO pins. There are two 32-bit registers which control the GPIO direction and output and these are not mapped – bit zero always controls GPIO 0, bit one always controls GPIO 1 and so on. As the CM5 has only 28 usable GPIO lines not all of the bits are useful.

Which of these GPIO lines the state machine uses depends on the setting of the SET and OUT groups. These, as already explained, control a consecutive set of GPIO lines specified by *first GPIO line, number of GPIO lines*. For example, 4,3 specifies three lines starting at GPIO 4 i.e. GPIO 4, GPIO 5 and GPIO 6. The SET group can have up to five GPIO lines and the OUT group can have all 32 GPIO lines.

If you write a bit mask using either out or set then the bits are applied to the GPIO lines in the relevant OUT or SET group. For example, if the SET group is 4,3 then

```
set pins,0x5
```

will set GPIO 4 to 1, GPIO 5 to 0 and GPIO 6 to 1 as the bitmask is 101.

Notice that all of the state machines share the GPIO lines and the OUT group and SET group can overlap. You can use this method to set the GPIO outputs using pins as the destination or the directions using the pindir destination.

Out to the GPIO

The out instruction works in the same general way as the set instruction, but its data source is the OSR register.

Recall that the OUT group is a set of GPIO lines specified by a starting number and number of lines:

```
sm_config_set_out_pins (pio_sm_config *c, uint out_base,
                                          uint out_count)
```

The data in the OSR can be moved to the OUT group of pins using the out instruction:

```
out pins, n
```

where n is the number of bits shifted to the OUT group. The bits that are shifted out are used to set the first n GPIO lines in the OUT group and any remaining lines in the group are set to zero.

Although we use the term "shift" this applies only to what happens to the contents of the OSR register. The n bits are presented to the n GPIO lines in one operation, i.e. all of the GPIO lines change their state at the same time.

The "shift" simply means that the data in the OSR register is moved to remove the n bits used. You can set the direction of the shift so as to make either the most significant or least significant bits the ones that are used in the OSR register first:

```
sm_config_set_out_shift (pio_sm_config *c,  bool shift_right,
                              bool autopull, uint pull_threshold)
```

The last two parameters control the automatic loading of the OSR, see later.

If you repeat the out instruction the next n bits are used and so on until the shift register is empty when all 32 bits have been shifted out.

A simple PIO program example will help clarify this.

Here we send the bits from a 32-bit value to two GPIO pins just to show how things work:

```
.program squarewave
    set pindirs, 3
    pull block
again:
    out pins,2
    jmp again
```

The set pindirs command sets the first two lines in the SET group to be output. The out command sends two bits of data from the OSR to the first two lines of the OUT group. For this to work the SET and OUT group have to have the first two pins in common. You could use an out command to set the first two pins in the OUT group:

```
out pindir,2
```

but now the direction of each line would be set by two bits in the OSR register. Sometimes this approach is useful as it allows the C program to set the GPIO lines using the OSR to pass a single parameter.

Another solution is to configure the pindirs from the C program using:

```
pio_sm_set_consecutive_pindirs (PIO pio,  uint sm,
                    uint pin_base,  uint pin_count,  bool is_out)
```

or:

```
pio_sm_set_pindirs_with_mask (PIO pio, uint sm,
                    uint32_t pin_dirs,  uint32_t pin_mask)
```

The first sets the GPIO pins starting at GPpin_base and ending at GPpin_base+pin_count to high impedance or output according to is_out. The second uses a mask to set the directions of the pins corresponding to ones in the mask to the state specified in pin_dirs.

Notice that in both cases you are working with the entire 32 GPIO lines, not any of the PIO groups. These functions should be used to initialize the PIO before it is enabled.

Now we have the PIO program, all that remains is the C program which sends some "random" data to the OUT group of GPIO lines:

```c
#include "pico/stdlib.h"
#include "hardware/pio.h"
#include "sqwave.pio.h"

int main()
{

    uint offset = pio_add_program(pio0, &squarewave_program);

    uint sm = pio_claim_unused_sm(pio0, true);
    pio_sm_config c =
                squarewave_program_get_default_config(offset);
    sm_config_set_set_pins(&c, 2, 2);
    sm_config_set_out_pins(&c, 2, 2);
    pio_gpio_init(pio0, 2);
    pio_gpio_init(pio0, 3);

    sm_config_set_clkdiv_int_frac(&c, 255, 0);
    pio_sm_init(pio0, sm, offset, &c);
    pio_sm_set_enabled(pio0, sm, true);

    pio_sm_put_blocking(pio0, sm, 0xFEDCBA98);
    return 0;
}
```

Notice that we need to set the SET and the OUT pins to be the same as we use both set and out instructions in the PIO program. The final instruction sends some arbitrary data to the TX FIFO and this is output two bits at a time to the two GPIO lines, GPIO 2 and GPIO 3:

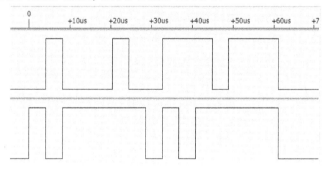

The output stops when the OSR is empty, but the out instruction keeps sending zeros to the GPIO lines.

337

If you want to keep the data flowing, you have to keep refilling the OSR. For example, you could change the C program to send data to the buffer whenever there was a free space:

```
while (true)
{
    pio_sm_put_blocking(pio0, sm, 0xFEDCBA98);
}
```

Now the PIO program can read new data from the TX FIFO whenever it wants to:

```
.program squarewave
    set pindirs, 3   ; Set pin to output
    pull block

again:
  out pins,2
  out pins,2
  out pins,2
      pull block

  jmp again
```

In this case we send the first three pairs of bits to the output pins and then read the TX FIFO into the OSR to get new data. Notice that this program might well create timing problems if you reduce the clock divider. The reason is that the time to transfer data from the C program to the OSR is a few microseconds and if the OSR empties too fast the C program might not be able to keep up. Of course, usually you would use all of the data in the OSR before reloading it.

This standard task can be done automatically with the autopull which reloads the OSR whenever its contents fall below a threshold.

You set autopull using the last two parameters of:

```
sm_config_set_out_shift (pio_sm_config *c,  bool shift_right,
                    bool autopull, uint pull_threshold)
```

If you set autopull to true then the OSR will be reloaded from the TX FIFO when its contents fall below the pull_threshold.
Using this the PIO program becomes:

```
.program squarewave
again:
  out pins,2
  jmp again
```

On this occasion no attempt has been made to set the OUT group of pins to output. This will be done in the C program to illustrate how this works.

```c
#include "pico/stdlib.h"
#include "hardware/pio.h"
#include "sqwave.pio.h"

int main()
{
    uint offset = pio_add_program(pio0, &squarewave_program);
    uint sm = pio_claim_unused_sm(pio0, true);
    pio_sm_config c =
                squarewave_program_get_default_config(offset);
    sm_config_set_set_pins(&c, 2, 2);
    sm_config_set_out_pins(&c, 2, 2);
    pio_gpio_init(pio0, 2);
    pio_gpio_init(pio0, 3);
    pio_sm_set_consecutive_pindirs(pio0, sm, 2, 2, true);
    sm_config_set_clkdiv_int_frac(&c, 255, 0);
    sm_config_set_out_shift (&c, true, true, 6);
    pio_sm_init(pio0, sm, offset, &c);
    pio_sm_set_enabled(pio0, sm, true);
    while (true)
    {
        pio_sm_put_blocking(pio0, sm, 0xFEDCBA98);
    }
    return 0;
}
```

Notice that now:

```c
pio_sm_set_consecutive_pindirs(pio0, sm, 2, 2, true);
```

sets GPIO 2 and GPIO 3 to output before the state machine starts.

If you run this program you will find that it does the same job as the previous program, but in fewer instructions and fewer clock cycles.

There are some minor points of how autopull works we've not covered, but you now have the general principles.

Side Effects

Now we have encountered most of the ideas behind PIO output to the GPIO lines, but there is one more feature – set_side used as a side effect. As well as being able to explicitly set GPIO lines using set or out, we can also arrange for any instruction to set GPIO lines as part of its execution. In this sense, the setting of the GPIO lines is a "side effect" of the instruction. Side effects are usually thought of as something to avoid in a standard program – you want an instruction to do what it appears to do and nothing more. In the case of PIO programming, however, side effects are very useful because they allow you to set GPIO lines according to where the program is in its execution. That is, they can be used to signal to the outside world the state of the program. At a more utilitarian level, being able to set a GPIO line as a side effect of another instruction can save both time and instructions.

The only downside of side effects is that they are coded using the space in the PIO instruction that is normally used to specify a delay. There is a 5-bit field used to code the delay and the side effect and you can trade bits for each purpose. The default is that all five bits are used to specify a delay and this makes it possible to specify up to 31 clock cycles of delay.

You can allocate bits to be used as set sides using:

```
.side_set count opt pindirs
```

where `count` is the number of set-side bits to allocate, `opt` means that the set-side is optional on an instruction and `pindirs` is used to set the pin directions as a side effect. Setting `pindirs` as a side effect is useful if you need to change a line from `out` to `in` as the program progresses.

Alternatively you can use the SDK to set the same options when you configure the state machine:

```
sm_config_set_sideset (pio_sm_config *c, uint bit_count,
                                    bool optional, bool pindirs)
```

Both ways of setting the options apply to the entire program.

Obviously you should choose to use as few set-side bits as possible if you want to make use of a delay. The `side_set` directive has to come at the start of the program and it remains in effect for the entire program.

In addition to setting the number of `side_set` bits you also need to set the SIDESET GPIO group using:

```
sm_config_set_sideset_pins (pio_sm_config *c, uint sideset_base)
```

This sets the start of the SIDESET group and you can specify any number of contiguous GPIO lines that the number of set-side bits allows.

Finally to include a GPIO line to set as a side effect you can add:

```
side value
```

after any instruction and *value* will be used to set the SETSIDE pins (or their directions).

To show how all this works the simplest thing to do is write the square wave generator again, but this time using nothing but set-side options:

```
.program squarewave
.side_set 1 opt
again:
  nop side 1
  jmp  again side 0
```

The `side_set` directive specifies a single bit, which means that the SETSIDE group of GPIO lines is effectively a single line. `nop` has a side effect of setting the side effect lines to `1` and `jmp` sets it back to `0`.

The main program to make use of this is fairly standard, but we need to set the SETSIDE group to start at GPIO 2 if this is the line we want to toggle:

```
#include "pico/stdlib.h"
#include "hardware/pio.h"
#include "sqwave.pio.h"

int main()
{
    uint offset = pio_add_program(pio0, &squarewave_program);

    uint sm = pio_claim_unused_sm(pio0, true);
    pio_sm_config c =
                squarewave_program_get_default_config(offset);
    sm_config_set_sideset_pins(&c,2);
    pio_gpio_init(pio0, 2);
    pio_sm_set_consecutive_pindirs(pio0, sm, 2, 1, true);
    sm_config_set_clkdiv_int_frac(&c, 255, 0);
    pio_sm_init(pio0, sm, offset, &c);
    pio_sm_set_enabled(pio0, sm, true);
    while(true){};
    return 0;
}
```

If you run this program you will find that pin GPIO 2 is toggled in a 50% square wave at around 392kHz, without a single `out` or `set` instruction in sight. Notice that the rising edge occurs when the loop starts and the falling edge when the loop ends.

As an example of using more than one GPIO line as a side effect consider:

```
.program squarewave
.side_set 2 opt
again:
  nop side 2
  jmp  again side 1
```

Now we have set aside two bits to control set-side GPIO lines, which means we can control two of them. First we write two, `10` in binary, to the pair of lines and then one, or `01`, which switches the lines in anti-phase – when one of them is high the other is low.

The main program has to be changed to configure two GPIO lines:

```
pio_sm_set_consecutive_pindirs(pio0,sm,2,2,true);
pio_gpio_init(pio0, 2);
pio_gpio_init(pio0, 3);
```

Set-side lines can overlap with OUT and SET lines and if such instructions set the same GPIO line, the set-side instruction has precedent.

Input

Now that we have described most of the general ideas of PIO output to GPIO lines, it is time to consider input from GPIO lines. The good news is that this is easy to understand as long as you have followed the ideas involved in output. However, input is always harder than output and in the case of PIO programming you have to rethink how things work. As you don't have any edge-triggered events or timers, everything you do has to be conditioned on the state of the system and raw timings have to be based on how long instructions take to execute.

The basic mechanisms of input are the same as output. There is a 4-element, 32-bit RX FIFO buffer that you can read from your C program using:

```
static uint32_t pio_sm_get_blocking (PIO pio, uint sm)
```
and:

```
static uint32_t pio_sm_get (PIO pio, uint sm)
```

Whereas the first function blocks until there is some data to read, the second returns at once, either with data or with an undefined value.

You can find the current state of the RX FIFO using one of:

- ◆ `static bool pio_sm_is_rx_fifo_full (PIO pio, uint sm)`
- ◆ `static bool pio_sm_is_rx_fifo_empty (PIO pio, uint sm)`
- ◆ `static uint pio_sm_get_rx_fifo_level (PIO pio, uint sm)`

Again you need to remember that any interaction between the PIO and the C program is slower than for the Pico's PIO and hence timings will be different.

Data gets into the RX FIFO from the PIO via the Input Shift Register, ISR, which is the input equivalent of the OSR.

To transfer data from the GPIO lines you use the in instruction:

```
in pins,n
```

The in instruction moves n bits from the IN GPIO group into the ISR, shifting up any data that is already present. You can also use it to transfer n bits from the x or y registers and a few other sources. The IN group of GPIO lines is defined in the C program using:

```
sm_config_set_in_pins (pio_sm_config *c, uint in_base)
```

As in the case of the SETSIDE group, you only have to specify a base number as you can read from any GPIO line, even if it is an output. What this means is that an in instruction can read all of the 32 GPIO lines and only the numbering of the lines changes.

For example, after:

```
sm_config_set_in_pins (&c,10);
```

which sets the base to GP10, the instruction:

```
in pins,3
```

will transfer the state of GPIO 10, GPIO 11 and GPIO 12 to the ISR.

Once you have sufficient bits in the ISR, you can transfer the entire 32-bit value to the RX FIFO using the push instruction:

```
push block
```

This waits for a free space in the RX FIFO and clears the ISR ready for further use. You can also use autopush to transfer data to the RX FIFO automatically when a bit count threshold is reached. You can set the direction in which the ISR is shifted and the use of auto-push and threshold using:

```
static void sm_config_set_in_shift (pio_sm_config *c,
        bool shift_right,  bool autopush, uint push_threshold)
```

As the simplest example, let's read GPIO 2 and use its state to control GPIO 3. This isn't a useful program, but it is a good illustration of the basics. The PIO program is simply:

```
.program light
again:
 in pins,1
 push block
 jmp   again
```

You can see that this simply reads the state of the first INPUT pin and pushes it to the RX FIFO. Of course, after four reads and pushes, the RX FIFO will be full and the program will stall.

The C program simply has to set things up, read the data and set the on-board LED accordingly:

```
#include "pico/stdlib.h"
#include "hardware/pio.h"
#include "gpiod.h"
#include "light.pio.h"
int main()
{
    uint offset = pio_add_program(pio0, &light_program);
    uint sm = pio_claim_unused_sm(pio0, true);
    pio_sm_config c = light_program_get_default_config(offset);
    sm_config_set_in_pins(&c, 2);
    pio_gpio_init(pio0, 2);
    pio_sm_set_consecutive_pindirs(pio0, sm, 2, 1, false);
    sm_config_set_clkdiv_int_frac(&c, 255, 0);
    pio_sm_init(pio0, sm, offset, &c);
    pio_sm_set_enabled(pio0, sm, true);
```

```
    int res;
    while (true)
    {
        uint32_t flag = pio_sm_get_blocking(pio0, sm);
        if (flag == 0)
        {
            res = gpiod_ctxless_set_value("0", 3, 0,
                               1, "output test", NULL, NULL);
        }
        else
        {
            res = gpiod_ctxless_set_value("0", 3, 1,
                               1, "output test", NULL, NULL);
        }
    }
        return 0;
    }
```

Notice the use of `pio_sm_set_consecutive_pindirs` to set GPIO 2 to input. This is necessary for the program to work. If you connect GPIO 2 to high and low you will see GPIO 3 turn on and off. Notice that we are using gpiod to control the GPIO lines.

The problem with the program is that you have no idea when it reads the input line. All you can say is that the speed of reading is controlled by how fast the C program makes room for new data in the RX FIFO. Notice that currently you cannot use Gpio5 to control GPIO lines at the same time as using the PIO as they both define some of the same functions. To use Gpio5 with the PIO you would need to add _Gpio5 to the duplicate functions.

Edges

This is all there is to using input, but the big problem is when do you read the state of the GPIO lines? When you are implementing a data transfer protocol, it is usual that you output something and then wait a given time before reading. Alternatively, data is read in response to a clock state transition, often an edge, but we have no direct way of responding to an input edge.

The solution to the problem takes us a little way beyond the simple `in` instruction. The PIO supports a conditional wait and a conditional jump, based on the state of a GPIO line. The instruction:

`wait state pin n`

waits until the pin indexed by *n* in the INPUT group is in the specified state. Notice that n = 0 is the first pin in the group.

You can also select the pin by absolute GPIO number, so:

`wait state gpio n`

waits until GPIO *n* is in the specified state. You can also wait on an IRQ, but this is beyond the scope of this first look at the PIO system.

The conditional jump:

```
jmp pin target
```

jumps to the target if the pin specified by:

```
sm_config_set_jmp_pin (pio_sm_config *c, uint pin)
```

is a 1 and pin is a raw GPIO number and not specified by the INPUT group.

The wait instruction is about synchronizing the program to the outside world and the jmp is about determining what processing should occur according to the state of the outside world. For example, if you need to start a process based on the start of a rising edge you could use:

```
wait 0 pin 0
wait 1 pin 0
```

This works by waiting for the GPIO line to go to zero and hence, when the second wait ends, you know that a rising edge has just occurred. For this to be accurate, the clock rate should be high compared to the pulses being input. Notice that if you read the line after the second wait, the state will be one clock cycle after the rising edge. In general, whatever you do as a result of the edge will occur some number of clock cycles after the edge.

This need for a high clock rate to localize the edge can make other aspects of timing difficult. For example, we can generate a pulse that is close to the rising edge of an input pulse train. The PIO program is:

```
.program squarewave
again:
    wait 0 pin 0
    wait 1 pin 0
    set pins, 1
    set pins, 0
jmp   again
```

This waits on the first pin in the INPUT group to change from 0 to 1, i.e. a rising edge, and then toggles the first pin in the SET group.

The C program to make this work, using GPIO 2 as the input and GPIO 3 as the output, is:

```
#include "pico/stdlib.h"
#include "hardware/pio.h"
#include "squarewaveP337.pio.h"
int main()
{
    uint offset = pio_add_program(pio0, &squarewave_program);
    uint sm = pio_claim_unused_sm(pio0, true);
    pio_sm_config c =
                squarewave_program_get_default_config(offset);
    sm_config_set_set_pins(&c, 3, 1);
    sm_config_set_in_pins(&c, 2);
    pio_gpio_init(pio0, 2);
```

```
    pio_gpio_init(pio0, 3);
    pio_sm_set_consecutive_pindirs(pio0, sm, 2, 1, false);
    pio_sm_set_consecutive_pindirs(pio0, sm, 3, 1, true);
    sm_config_set_clkdiv_int_frac(&c, 255, 0);
    pio_sm_init(pio0, sm, offset, &c);
    pio_sm_set_enabled(pio0, sm, true);
    while(true){}
    return 0;
}
```

With the clock set to a low rate, you can see that the marker pulse isn't very close to the rising edge:

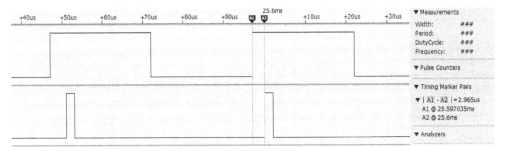

If you increase the clock rate to its maximum, the displacement becomes very small – 45n:

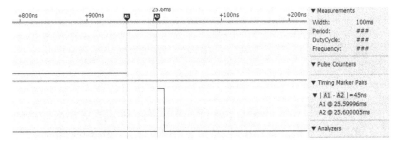

To see the problem, consider the task of moving the marker to the middle of the pulse where you might want to sample the line's state. At maximum clock rate this might be too many cycles to use a simple delay. A slower clock rate is easier, but less accurate in its alignment with the edge.

Advanced PIO

This first look at the PIO and its use has covered the main topics to make it possible for you to write PIO programs and use them from C. It isn't complete and there are many additional features that you still have to discover. Most of these features are about optimization. For example, nearly all PIO programs take the form of an infinite loop and this is a waste of one of the scarce 32 instruction locations and introduces a clock cycle delay.

As an alternative you can place:

```
.wrap_target
```

before the instruction that you want to restart the program at and:

```
.wrap
```

after the last instruction. For example, our previous program can be written:

```
.program squarewave
.wrap_target
    wait 0 pin 0
    wait 1 pin 0
    set pins, 1
    set pins, 0
.wrap
```

In this case there is no jmp instruction as the program counter is automatically set back to the target when it reaches the wrap. It is as if the program's address space was circular.

Other topics not discussed are the use of DMA, interrupts and the interaction between multiple PIOs. This is all very straightforward and logical once you have mastered the basics.

Now we move on to discover how the PIO can do useful work for us.

DHT22 Using the PIO – Counting

The DHT22 is not well suited to working with the PIO. The reason is that its protocol doesn't use fixed time slots for each bit or synchronization via a separate clock, two situations where it is usually possible to write compact PIO programs to send and receive data. The DHT22 relies on the length of the slot used to transmit a single bit to code zero or one and this means that the obvious way of decoding is a matter of measuring the time between edges. The PIO doesn't have access to a timer and implementing an instruction clock counter isn't straightforward, but it can be done.

The following PIO program does exactly this. However, it is a long program and it only just satisfies the constraints placed on it to make it work. After presenting the obvious algorithm with a slightly difficult implementation, a simpler and more direct, but less obvious, method is implemented.

Before going into details, it is worth explaining what the constraints are and what makes PIO access worth the effort. The bit-banging solution given earlier works and is perfectly good. However, it demands the full attention of the processor while the data is being read in. If an interrupt occurs during reading, the data will be corrupt. On the other hand, if you can implement a PIO program that reads in the data, the processor is free to do something else until it wants to use the data and interrupts have no effect. This all depends on the PIO being able to read the data from the device and keep it stored ready for when the processor wants to read it. If you consider this for a few moments, this means that you can hold data in the 4-word FIFO buffer and an additional word in the ISR, making a total of 160 bits of temporary storage, which seems to be more than enough for the 40 bits that the DHT22 produces.

For a timing-based protocol, however, things are more complicated. We can write a loop that counts instruction cycles when the input line is high and this count can be up to 32 bits in resolution. However, there is no easy way to convert the 32-bit count into single bits by applying a threshold, as in the bit-banging example. What this means is that we are forced to send the bit counts, rather than the decoded bits, back to the processor. A little arithmetic reveals that we can store the counts for all 40 bits as long as the count is represented as a 4-bit number. We can store the first 32-bits, the data in the four word FIFO buffer, with the counts for each byte, in a single element. The final byte can be stored in the ISR until the processor reads the FIFO register and frees up space. A count of 4 bits is enough to tell the difference between the times for a zero and a one and this makes the whole scheme possible, as long as we adjust the clock frequency correctly.

What all this means is that we can write a PIO program that can be set to read the data from the DHT22 and store the result in the FIFO and the ISR until the processor is ready to read it. The downside is that the processor has to convert the timing counts to bits and pack the results into bytes before processing the humidity, temperature and checksum – a small price to pay.

With all this worked out we can write the PIO program. The first problem is that we have to send a 1ms initialization pulse:

```
.program dht
        set pins, 1
        set pindirs, 1
again:
        pull block
        set pins, 0
        mov x, osr
loop1:
        jmp x--,loop1
        set pindirs, 0
```

This uses a data value written to the state machine by the C program to execute a delay loop that takes 1ms. It also serves to start the conversion. Also notice that the low pulse is terminated by setting the pin to input.

Next, we have to wait for two rising edges to pass before we get to the data pulses:

```
        wait 1 pin 0
        wait 0 pin 0
        wait 1 pin 0
        wait 0 pin 0
```

Finally, we can start reading in the four bytes of data:

```
        set y,31
bits:
        wait 1 pin 0
        set x, 0
loop2:
        jmp x--,continue
continue: jmp pin,loop2
        in x,4
        jmp y--,bits
```

The `bits` loop processes all 32 bits. The inner `loop2` processes each bit in turn. The x register is set to zero and then decremented using a forward jump to the end of the loop. The instruction:

```
jmp x--,continue
```

is used to implement an increment x instruction and always moves on to the next instruction. At the moment, decrementing a register that starts at zero increments it, but this is not part of the specification for the PIO so it could change. If you want to avoid this possibility then set x to its maximum value and decrement it to implement a count down.

The instruction:

```
continue: jmp pin,loop2
```

stops the loop when the "jump pin", set by the C program, goes low.

The whole loop effectively counts how long the GPIO line is high in terms of the number of clock cycles it runs for.

Once the loop has completed, the 4-bit count is transferred to the ISR and the next bit starts. Notice that it is assumed that auto-push is set so that the FIFO is automatically added to when the ISR is full.

We have to repeat the process for the checksum:

```
        set y,7
check:
        wait 1 pin 0
        set x, 0
loop3:
        jmp x--,continue2
continue2: jmp pin,loop3
        in x,4
        jmp y--,check
jmp again
```

Notice that if the C program hasn't read the FIFO then this blocks and waits for free space. Finally, we jump back to the start of the program to wait for the C program to write to the FIFO again and start the measurement over again.

The C program to make all this work is fairly straightforward, but it involves a lot of bit manipulation to convert the counts into bits:

```c
uint8_t getByte(PIO pio, uint sm)
{
    uint32_t count = pio_sm_get_blocking(pio0, sm);
    uint8_t byte = 0;
    for (int i = 0; i < 8; i++)
    {
        byte = byte << 1;
        if (((count >> i * 4) & 0x0F) > 8)
        {
            byte = byte | 1;
        }
    }
    return byte;
}
```

This reads a word from the PIO and converts it into a byte by comparing each 4-bit count with a threshold, i.e. 8.

Using this function we can obtain the five bytes needed to compute the humidity, temperature and checksum as per the previous program. All that is needed to complete the program is a function to get the data in a useful form and an initialization function.

The complete program is:

```c
#include <stdio.h>
#include "pico/stdlib.h"
#include "hardware/gpio.h"
#include "hardware/pio.h"
#include "DHT.pio.h"
uint dhtInitalize(PIO pio, int gpio)
{
    uint offset = pio_add_program(pio, &dht_program);

    uint sm = pio_claim_unused_sm(pio, true);
    pio_gpio_init(pio, gpio);
    pio_sm_config c = dht_program_get_default_config(offset);
    sm_config_set_clkdiv_int_frac(&c, 200, 0);
    sm_config_set_set_pins(&c, gpio, 1);
    sm_config_set_in_pins(&c, gpio);
    sm_config_set_jmp_pin(&c, gpio);
    sm_config_set_in_shift(&c, true, true, 32);
    pio_sm_init(pio0, sm, offset, &c);

    pio_sm_set_enabled(pio0, sm, true);
    return sm;
}
```

```
uint8_t getByte(PIO pio, uint sm)
{
    uint32_t count = pio_sm_get_blocking(pio0, sm);
    uint8_t byte = 0;
    for (int i = 0; i < 8; i++)
    {
        byte = byte << 1;
        if (((count >> i * 4) & 0x0F) > 8)
        {
            byte = byte | 1;
        }
    }
    return byte;
}

typedef struct
{
    float temperature;
    float humidity;
    bool error;
} dhtData;

void dhtread(PIO pio, uint sm, dhtData *reading)
{
    pio_sm_put_blocking(pio, sm, 1000);
    uint8_t byte1 = getByte(pio, sm);
    uint8_t byte2 = getByte(pio, sm);
    uint8_t byte3 = getByte(pio, sm);
    uint8_t byte4 = getByte(pio, sm);
    uint8_t checksum = getByte(pio, sm);
    reading->error = (checksum == (byte1 + byte2 + byte3 + byte4) &
                                                              0xFF);
    reading->humidity = (float)((byte1 << 8) | byte2) / 10.0;
    int neg = byte3 & 0x80;
    byte3 = byte3 & 0x7F;
    reading->temperature = (float)(byte3 << 8 | byte4) / 10.0;
    if (neg > 0) reading->temperature = -reading->temperature;
}
int main()
{
    stdio_init_all();
    uint sm = dhtInitalize(pio0, 2);
    dhtData reading;
    dhtread(pio0, sm, &reading);
    printf("Humidity= %f %\n", reading.humidity);
    printf("Temperature= %f C\n", reading.temperature);
    return 0;
}
```

The initialization program is the only function of additional interest as most of the rest of the program follows the previous example. The function dhtInitalize(PIO pio, int gpio) sets the clock frequency so that instructions take 1μs. This gives a count in the region of 4 to 13 and the threshold is set accordingly. At this clock speed, you also need to set the x register to 1000 to get the 1ms initialization pulse. It also sets the auto-push to 32 bits and a right-shift. Notice that as well as the SET and IN groups, you have to set the jump pin to the GPIO line being used or the counting loop doesn't work.

The PIO program is:

```
.program dht
    set pins, 1
    set pindirs, 1
again:
  pull block
  set pins, 0
mov x, osr
loop1:
    jmp x--,loop1
set pindirs, 0
wait 1 pin 0
wait 0 pin 0
wait 1 pin 0
wait 0 pin 0

    set y,31
bits:
    wait 1 pin 0
    set x, 0
loop2:
    jmp x--,continue
continue: jmp pin,loop2
    in x,4
    jmp y--,bits

    set y,7
check:
    wait 1 pin 0
    set x, 0
loop3:
    jmp x--,continue2
continue2: jmp pin,loop3
    in x,4
    jmp y--,check
jmp again
```

DHT22 Using the PIO – Sampling

A simpler alternative for decoding the data is to ignore the fact that it is the
width of each bit's frame that defines a zero, a short frame, or a one a long
frame, and notice that if you sample at a suitable fixed time from the rising
edge of a pulse then you will get a zero in a zero frame and a one in a one
frame:

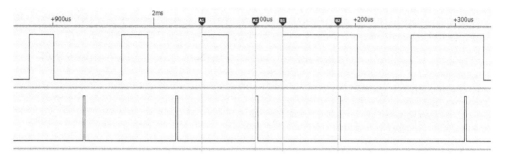

You can see the sampling times from the pulses on the lower trace of the
logic analyzer and the fact that you do indeed get a 0 in a zero frame and a 1
in a one frame. You can also see that the time to sample from the rising edge
is constant, even if the sampling period varies.

Surprisingly, the PIO program to implement this sampling isn't significantly
simpler than the previous program, but the entire four data bytes can now be
packed into a single FIFO entry and the checksum byte can occupy a second
entry.

The PIO program starts off in the same way:

```
.program dht
    set pins, 1
    set pindirs, 1
again:
  pull block
  set pins, 0
mov x, osr
loop1:
    jmp x--,loop1
set pindirs, 0
wait 1 pin 0
wait 0 pin 0
wait 1 pin 0
wait 0 pin 0
```

The wait instructions are placed at the start of the data and now we can wait for a rising edge and then delay until the sample time:

```
set y,31
bits:
   wait 1 pin 0 [25]
     in pins,1
     wait 0 pin 0
 jmp y--,bits
```

This too is very similar to the first program, only now we don't keep a count but simply add the single bit sampled from the input line to the ISR. When all 32 bits have been added, the autopush moves the data to the FIFO.

The eight checksum bits are just as easy to process and the complete PIO program is:

```
.program dht
 set pins, 1
 set pindirs, 1
again:
 pull block
 set pins, 0
mov x, osr
loop1:
 jmp x--,loop1
set pindirs, 0
wait 1 pin 0
wait 0 pin 0
wait 1 pin 0
wait 0 pin 0
set y,31
bits:
 wait 1 pin 0 [25]
 in pins,1
 wait 0 pin 0
 jmp y--,bits
 set y,7
check:
wait 1 pin 0 [25]
 in pins,1
 wait 0 pin 0
 jmp y--,check
push block
jmp again
```

Notice that we have to manually push the ISR because it doesn't fill up with just the final eight bits of the checksum.

The C program is also very like the previous program, but we have to change the clock frequency and the shift direction to make decoding the bytes from the 32-bit word easier:

```
 sm_config_set_clkdiv_int_frac(&c, 400, 0);
 sm_config_set_in_shift(&c, false, true, 32);
```

We need a slower clock speed to make the delay position the sample point about $50\mu s$ from the rising edge – recall that the delay is limited to 32 clock cycles.

The `dhtread` function can now read the FIFO and decode the data directly, which is a much simpler task:

```
void dhtread(PIO pio, uint sm, dhtData *reading)
{
    pio_sm_put_blocking(pio, sm, 500);
    uint32_t data = pio_sm_get_blocking(pio0, sm);
    uint8_t byte1 = (data >> 24 & 0xFF);
    uint8_t byte2 = (data >> 16 & 0xFF);
    uint8_t byte3 = (data >> 8 & 0xFF);
    uint8_t byte4 = (data & 0xFF);
    uint8_t checksum = pio_sm_get_blocking(pio0, sm) & 0xFF;
```

Notice the need to change the value sent to the input to account for the slower clock rate – 500 produces a 1ms initialization pulse. The rest of the program is unchanged as we now have the four data bytes and the checksum as before. This program is simpler to implement and can be extended to a protocol that needs to read in more than 40 bits at a time.

Complete Listing

```
#include <stdio.h>
#include "pico/stdlib.h"
#include "hardware/gpio.h"
#include "hardware/pio.h"
#include "DHT.pio.h"

uint dhtInitalize(PIO pio, int gpio)
{
    uint offset = pio_add_program(pio, &dht_program);
    uint sm = pio_claim_unused_sm(pio, true);
    pio_gpio_init(pio, gpio);
 pio_sm_config c = dht_program_get_default_config(offset);
 sm_config_set_clkdiv_int_frac(&c, 400, 0);
 sm_config_set_set_pins(&c, gpio, 1);
 sm_config_set_in_pins(&c, gpio);
 sm_config_set_in_shift(&c, false, true, 32);
 pio_sm_init(pio0, sm, offset, &c);
 pio_sm_set_enabled(pio0, sm, true);
 return sm;
}
typedef struct
{
 float temperature;
 float humidity;
 bool error;
} dhtData;
```

```c
void dhtread(PIO pio, uint sm, dhtData *reading)
{
 pio_sm_put_blocking(pio, sm, 500);

 uint32_t data = pio_sm_get_blocking(pio0, sm);
 uint8_t byte1 = (data >> 24 & 0xFF);
 uint8_t byte2 = (data >> 16 & 0xFF);
 uint8_t byte3 = (data >> 8 & 0xFF);
 uint8_t byte4 = (data & 0xFF);
 uint8_t checksum = pio_sm_get_blocking(pio0, sm) & 0xFF;

 reading->error = (checksum !=
 ((byte1 + byte2 + byte3 + byte4) & 0xFF));
 reading->humidity = (float)((byte1 << 8) | byte2) / 10.0;

 int neg = byte3 & 0x80;
 byte3 = byte3 & 0x7F;
 reading->temperature = (float)(byte3 << 8 | byte4) / 10.0;
 if (neg > 0)
 reading->temperature = -reading->temperature;
}

int main()
{
    stdio_init_all();
    uint sm = dhtInitalize(pio0, 2);
    dhtData reading;
    dhtread(pio0, sm, &reading);
    printf("Humidity= %f %\n", reading.humidity);
    printf("Temperature= %f C\n", reading.temperature);
    return 0;
}
```

The full PIO program is:

```
.program dht
    set pins, 1
    set pindirs, 1
again:
  pull block
  set pins, 0
mov x, osr
loop1:
    jmp x--,loop1
set pindirs, 0
wait 1 pin 0
wait 0 pin 0
wait 1 pin 0
wait 0 pin 0
```

```
set y,31
bits:
    wait 1 pin 0 [25]
      in pins,1
      wait 0 pin 0
  jmp y--,bits

  set y,7
check:
wait 1 pin 0 [25]
      in pins,1
      wait 0 pin 0
  jmp y--,check
push block
jmp again
```

A PIO DS18B20 Program

Implementing the 1-Wire protocol using a PIO is one of the most difficult tasks we tackle. It needs to both send and receive data and the master has to provide the start pulse for the slave to send data. The specification also makes it seem that we have to use a conditional to vary the timing of the data part of the pulse depending on sending a one or a zero. This is a lot of logic to fit into 32 instructions. In addition, a 1-Wire device can send far more data than the FIFO can hold. At first appraisal the idea of implementing the 1-Wire protocol in a PIO program seems hopeless, but a shift in emphasis makes it easier.

The main operations that you need to work with a 1-Wire device is to send a set of bytes and receive a set of bytes. In general, the timing requirements of the 1-Wire bus are at the bit level. That is, when you read data the device will generally store the data until you are ready for it. This means that if you can implement a byte read/write in the PIO then the main program can get on with something else while the 1-Wire device processes data. If the main program is interrupted then no harm is done as it can expect the PIO to continue to process the next byte ready for when it returns.

What all of this implies is that all we really have to do is implement a bit send and a bit receive facility. Using the way that 1-Wire protocol is usually described, this would be very difficult. In other words, trying to implement the simple-minded bit-banging protocol as a PIO program isn't going to work. A slightly different interpretation of the protocol, however, makes it very possible. If you think of each bit frame as starting with a short low pulse which signals the start of the frame, then a zero sends a low after the initial pulse and a one sends a high.

In other words, we can implement the write protocol as:

1) Send short "start bit" of about 6μs

2) Send the data bit, i.e. a 0 or a 1, for the rest of the frame – about 60μs

3) Set the line high for 10μs as a spacer between bit frames

The read protocol is much the same:

1) Send short "start bit" of about 6μs

2) After about 9μs sample the line and use this as the read bit

3) Do nothing for about 55μs as a spacer between bit frames

In this form the protocol doesn't need conditionals as the sending of a zero or a one and the receiving of a zero or a one follows the same steps – only the level changes between a 0 and a 1.

Using this version you could simplify the logic of the bit-banging example given earlier, but there is no real need to as there is plenty of space and computational power. Using a PIO is a very different matter and regularity in the implementation of a protocol is important.

There is also the problem of how to implement the PIO program so that the C program can make use of it. One possibility is to use one state machine for send and another to receive, but it is possible to create a single program to to do both jobs.

Start a new PIO project and create files called DS1820.c and DS1820.pio. The PIO program starts off with a presence pulse and, as this is long compared to the clock time, we use a loop set by the C program. As you generally don't need a presence pulse when reading data from a device, we can use a zero value to indicate that the operation is a read, not a write. That is, you use the program by pushing data onto the FIFO – the first byte starts the program off and if it is zero it starts a read operation and otherwise starts a write operation with its value setting the length of the initialization pulse:

```
.program DS1820
.wrap_target
again:
        pull block
        mov x, osr
        jmp !x, read

write:  set pindirs, 1
        set pins, 0
loop1:
        jmp x--,loop1
        set pindirs, 0 [31]
        wait 1 pin 0 [31]
```

Once the write part of the code gets started, the non-zero value passed in via the FIFO is used to create a long, 500μs, low pulse which the slave responds to with a 120μs low presence plus. The final instruction waits for the end of the pulse so that we can start to send some data.

358

The second byte pushed onto the FIFO gives the number of bytes to send and these are pushed onto the stack to follow. Notice that if there are more than four or five then the program might stall until the FIFO has space.

```
        pull block
        mov x, osr
bytes1:
        pull block
        set y, 7
        set pindirs, 1
bit1:
         set pins, 0 [1]
         out pins,1 [31]
         set pins, 1 [20]
        jmp y--,bit1
        jmp x--,bytes1
        set pindirs, 0 [31]
        jmp again
```

You can see that the inner loop starting at bit1 takes the data byte in the OSR and sends it out to the GPIO line, a bit at a time. The first instruction in the loop generates the short start pulse and the second instruction sets the line high or low for 32 clock cycles. The final instruction in the loop provides the space between the bit frames. The loop repeats until all eight bits have been sent when the outer loop gets another byte to send, if there is one. If not, the program restarts and waits for the next set of data.

The read part of the program is very similar to the write:

```
read:
        pull block
        mov x, osr
bytes2:
        set y, 7
        bit2:
        set pindirs, 1
        set pins, 0 [1]
        set pindirs, 0 [5]
        in pins,1 [10]
        jmp y--,bit2
 jmp x--,bytes2
.wrap
```

In this case the only data we need from the FIFO is the number of bytes to read. This is stored in the x register and controls the number of bytes processed. The inner loop, starting at bit2, reads each bit in turn. The first three instructions change the line to output, send the short start pulse and sets the line back to input. The in instruction samples the line after a short delay and gets the data which is auto-pushed onto the FIFO ready for the C program to read. Notice that if the C program fails to read the data then the

359

loop stalls, which is fine as long as the 1-Wire device can live with a pause and the DS18B20 can.

The entire program is 29 instructions, which leaves space for instructions to toggle another GPIO line for debugging purposes. It is very probable that it can be made even shorter.

Next we move on the C program. We first need an initialization function:

```
uint DS18Initalize(PIO pio, int gpio)
{
    uint offset = pio_add_program(pio, &DS1820_program);

    uint sm = pio_claim_unused_sm(pio, true);
    pio_gpio_init(pio, gpio);

    pio_sm_config c = DS1820_program_get_default_config(offset);
    sm_config_set_clkdiv_int_frac(&c, 400, 0);
    sm_config_set_set_pins(&c, gpio, 1);
    sm_config_set_out_pins(&c, gpio, 1);
    sm_config_set_in_pins(&c, gpio);
    sm_config_set_in_shift(&c, true, true, 8);
    pio_sm_init(pio0, sm, offset, &c);
    pio_sm_set_enabled(pio0, sm, true);
    return sm;
}
```

The frequency is selected to allow the pulse times to be implemented using delays from 1 to 31.

The PIO program is fairly general in that you could use it to talk to almost any 1-Wire device, but we are interested in the DS18B20 and it is easy enough to implement a function to read the temperature along the lines of the previous function:

```
float getTemperature(PIO pio, uint sm)
{
```

First we send an initialization pulse followed by a Skip ROM and a Convert command. The first item sets a write operation with an initialization pulse:

```
    pio_sm_put_blocking(pio, sm, 250);
    pio_sm_put_blocking(pio, sm, 1);
    pio_sm_put_blocking(pio, sm, 0xCC);
    pio_sm_put_blocking(pio, sm, 0x44);
```

Next we should wait until the conversion is complete, but for simplicity we wait for 1s – after which time the conversion is either complete or the device is broken.

Then we send another initialization pulse, a Skip ROM and a Read ScratchPad command:

```
sleep_ms(1000);
pio_sm_put_blocking(pio, sm, 250);
pio_sm_put_blocking(pio, sm, 1);
pio_sm_put_blocking(pio, sm, 0xCC);
pio_sm_put_blocking(pio, sm, 0xBE);
```

Finally we send a read command for nine bytes of data:

```
pio_sm_put_blocking(pio, sm, 0);
pio_sm_put_blocking(pio, sm, 8);
```

and read the nine bytes from the FIFO:

```
int i;
uint8_t data[9];
for (i = 0; i < 9; i++)
{
    data[i] = pio_sm_get_blocking(pio, sm) >> 24;
}
```

Now we have the same nine bytes of data as in the bit-banging example and the rest of the program is identical.

A better idea is to create two functions which read and write an array of bytes to the device:

```
void writeBytes(PIO pio, uint sm,uint8_t bytes[], int len){
    pio_sm_put_blocking(pio, sm, 250);
    pio_sm_put_blocking(pio, sm, len-1);
    for(int i=0;i<len;i++){
        pio_sm_put_blocking(pio, sm, bytes[i]);
    }
}
void readBytes(PIO pio, uint sm,uint8_t bytes[], int len){
    pio_sm_put_blocking(pio, sm, 0);
    pio_sm_put_blocking(pio, sm, len-1);
    for(int i=0;i<len;i++){
        bytes[i]=pio_sm_get_blocking(pio, sm) >> 24;
    }
}
```

Using these two functions the interaction with the 1-Wire device starts to look a lot like using the SPI or I2C bus.

This is about as complex a PIO program as you can implement. This raises the question of what to do if you need something more complex? You might think that using additional state machines might help, but you are still limited to 32 instructions in total. To reduce the need to store instructions you could use immediately executed instructions put directly into the state machine from the C program. This works for small tasks such as initialization, but it is too slow for data transfer.

The current program can only work with a single device on the 1-Wire bus. If you want to support more, you could implement the search algorithm outlined in Chapter 15 of *Raspberry Pi IOT in C, Third Edition*, although this is complex. A simpler solution is to use one state machine and one GPIO line per device.

Complete Listing

The C program using the read and write functions is:

```c
#include <stdio.h>
#include "pico/stdlib.h"
#include "hardware/gpio.h"
#include "DS1820.pio.h"

uint8_t crc8(uint8_t *data, uint8_t len)
{
    uint8_t i;
    uint8_t j;
    uint8_t temp;
    uint8_t databyte;
    uint8_t crc = 0;
    for (i = 0; i < len; i++)
    {
        databyte = data[i];
        for (j = 0; j < 8; j++)
        {
            temp = (crc ^ databyte) & 0x01;
            crc >>= 1;
            if (temp)
                crc ^= 0x8C;

            databyte >>= 1;
        }
    }
    return crc;
}
void writeBytes(PIO pio, uint sm, uint8_t bytes[], int len)
{
    pio_sm_put_blocking(pio, sm, 400);
    pio_sm_put_blocking(pio, sm, len - 1);
    for (int i = 0; i < len; i++)
    {
        pio_sm_put_blocking(pio, sm, bytes[i]);
    }
}
```

```c
void readBytes(PIO pio, uint sm, uint8_t bytes[], int len)
{
    pio_sm_put_blocking(pio, sm, 0);
    pio_sm_put_blocking(pio, sm, len - 1);
    for (int i = 0; i < len; i++)
    {
        bytes[i] = pio_sm_get_blocking(pio, sm) >> 24;
    }
}

float getTemperature(PIO pio, uint sm)
{
    writeBytes(pio, sm, (uint8_t[]){0xCC, 0x44}, 2);
    sleep_ms(1000);
    writeBytes(pio, sm, (uint8_t[]){0xCC, 0xBE}, 2);

    uint8_t data[9];
    readBytes(pio, sm, data, 9);

    uint8_t crc = crc8(data, 9);
    if (crc != 0)
        return -2000;
    int t1 = data[0];
    int t2 = data[1];
    int16_t temp1 = (t2 << 8 | t1);
    volatile float temp = (float)temp1 / 16;
    return temp;
}

uint DS18Initalize(PIO pio, int gpio)
{

    uint offset = pio_add_program(pio, &DS1820_program);

    uint sm = pio_claim_unused_sm(pio, true);
    pio_gpio_init(pio, gpio);

    pio_sm_config c = DS1820_program_get_default_config(offset);
    sm_config_set_clkdiv_int_frac(&c, 255, 0);
    sm_config_set_set_pins(&c, gpio, 1);
    sm_config_set_out_pins(&c, gpio, 1);
    sm_config_set_in_pins(&c, gpio);
    sm_config_set_in_shift(&c, true, true, 8);
    pio_sm_init(pio0, sm, offset, &c);
    pio_sm_set_enabled(pio0, sm, true);
    return sm;
}
```

```
int main()
{
    stdio_init_all();

    uint sm = DS18Initalize(pio0, 2);

    float t;
    for (;;)
    {
        do
        {
            t = getTemperature(pio0, sm);
        } while (t < -999);
        printf("temperature %f\r\n", t);
        sleep_ms(500);
    };

    return 0;
}
```

The PIO program is:

```
.program DS1820
.wrap_target
again:
 pull block
 mov x, osr
 jmp !x, read

write:  set pindirs, 1
 set pins, 0
loop1:
 jmp x--,loop1
set pindirs, 0 [31]
wait 1 pin 0 [31]

 pull block
 mov x, osr
bytes1:
 pull block
 set y, 7
 set pindirs, 1
bit1:
 set pins, 0 [1]
  out pins,1 [31]
    set pins, 1 [20]
   jmp y--,bit1
jmp x--,bytes1
set pindirs, 0 [31]
jmp again
```

```
read:
  pull block
  mov x, osr
bytes2:
  set y, 7
bit2:
  set pindirs, 1
  set pins, 0 [1]
  set pindirs, 0 [5]
  in pins,1 [10]
jmp y--,bit2
jmp x--,bytes2
.wrap
```

Summary

- The PIO and the state machine are special processors designed to interact with the outside world.

- You can use a PIO attempt to implement any otherwise unsupported protocol.

- The CM5 has one PIO with four state machines.

- The GPIO lines associated with the PIO are determined by a set of groups – OUT, SET, IN and SETSIDE. GPIO lines also have to be set to PIO mode before they will work in any of the groups.

- You can set the clock frequency that the PIO uses to execute instructions one per clock cycle.

- The clock should be set to a frequency that is suitable for the sort of pulses the PIO is working with.

- It is easy to toggle a GPIO line, but slightly harder to make it slow enough to flash an LED. To do this you need to implement a busy wait loop.

- The OSR and ISR are used to send data to and receive data from the GPIO lines.

- There are two FIFO stacks which can be used to send data to the OSR and ISR from the processor.

- Every instruction can change the state of GPIO lines in the SETSIDE group as a side effect of its execution.

- Working with edges isn't natural for the state machine, but it can be achieved using wait instructions.

- It is possible to implement the DHT22 protocol as defined in the data sheet using a PIO by using counting loops to time each pulse.

- A better use of the PIO is to notice that the protocol can be decoded by testing the state of the line a fixed time after the rising edge.

- With a shift in viewpoint, it is just possible to squeeze a 1-Wire bus protocol into a 32-instruction PIO program.

Chapter 17

Going Further With Drivers

Given the amount of space already devoted to using drivers, it may seem odd that this chapter is about drivers, However, it is worth going deeper so that you can customize your use of drivers. You can get a long way simply using overlays and what other people have worked out for you, but occasionally you have to go it alone. In such cases you need to know a little more about how things work. You need to know how drivers are manipulated and how to write your own overlays. This is a big topic and while this chapter provides a good introduction to the ideas you need, it can't cover everything - only provide you with the tools to solve new problems.

Loadable Kernel Modules

Drivers are a special case of Loadable Kernel Modules, LKMs. An LKM is a program that can be added to the Linux kernel after it has booted. It is a way to extend the kernel without having to "fork" it in its entirety before adding your own custom code to it. Most LKMs are drivers, i.e. they allow the kernel to work with hardware and provide a connection to user space programs so that they can also work with the hardware. Although much of what follows is described in terms of drivers, an LKM doesn't have to be just a driver - it can be a file system, a random number generator or even a "hello world" demo. However, in most cases the big advantage of running in kernel space is the access it provides to the hardware.

It isn't difficult to get started writing your own LKMs, but there is a lot to learn about programming in kernel space as most of the libraries that you have grown accustomed to using aren't available. Also, if you venture into writing your own drivers, this generally isn't a matter of starting from scratch. Each type of driver, IIO, hwmon and so on, has lots of code that you can make use of as a starting point, but there is also a lot to learn about that code. In most cases, writing a driver is a matter of finding an existing driver that is similar to what you want and modifying it. Depending on how you go about it, this task can leave a lot of uncertainty about how your final driver actually achieves its intended end product.

For most of us, using drivers that other programmers have created is the simplest option, even if it means restricting the hardware to supported devices.

Finding Modules

Modules are usually files with a `.ko` (for kernel object) extension. Standard modules are to be found in `/lib/modules` in a subdirectory that is specific to the kernel release that you are using. You can discover the kernel release that you are using automatically via the command `uname -r` the output of which can be quoted into other commands. So to discover the modules appropriate to your kernel you can use:

```
ls /lib/modules/`uname -r`
```

This will show a set of folders that group the modules into types. To see the total list of modules available, use the command `lsmod`, and to discover what modules are currently loaded use `modprobe -c` you might be surprised at how many there are. Some modules are built into the kernel and don't need to be loaded. To find out what these are you can use:

```
cat /lib/modules/$(uname -r)/modules.builtin
```

Loading Modules the Old Way

Before the device tree was introduced there were, and still are, commands that allow you to work with modules. It is worth knowing about this more fundamental way of doing things for times when it is the only way to make something work or to explore what it going on. In most cases, however, you should use the device tree and overlays to work with drivers.

There are two commands that let you insert a module into the kernel – `insmod` and `modprobe`. The `modprobe` command is far more versatile and it is the one to use in most cases. Simply, `modprobe modulename` installs the module and `modprobe -r modulename` removes it. The command automatically looks in the correct module directory for the version of Linux it is running on. It also uses configuration files to find what other modules the one being loaded depends on and makes sure that they are loaded first. You can see the configuration using the `-c` option and override it using the `-C` option.

Configurations are stored in the folder `/etc/modprobe.d` and any files ending in `.conf` are read and used to configure modules.

In addition to loading modules, you can also provide parameters in the form of key=value pairs following the module name. You can also pass parameters to modules loaded at boot time by adding:

```
modulename.parameter=value
```

to the boot loader's command line which you will find in `/boot/cmdline.txt`.

For example, you can load the 1-Wire driver using:

```
sudo modprobe w1-gpio gpiopin=4
```

Another complication is that modules can have aliases so that they can be loaded using a range of different names. Modules can also be blacklisted at boot time by creating .conf files in /etc/modprobe.d/ containing lines of the form:

```
blacklist modulename
```

You can manually load a blacklisted module at a later time and the module will be loaded anyway if it is used by a module that isn't blacklisted.

The device tree makes this approach mostly unnecessary but it is still used behind the scenes. For example:

```
dtoverlay=i2c-rtc,ds1307,addr=0x68
```

which causes i2c-rtc.dtb0 to be loaded into the device tree and is translated to:

```
modprobe i2c-bcm2835
modprobe rtc-ds1307
echo ds1307 0x68 > /sys/class/i2c-adapter/i2c-1/new_device
```

which is what you have to do to load the driver without the help of the device tree.

udev

Many of the things that blacklists and other ways of autoloading drivers were designed to take care of are now dealt with by udev. This is a dynamic device directory which takes account of hotplug devices. It is what takes care of finding and loading a driver when you plug in a USB device at any time after boot. When a device is created, udev automatically reads the corresponding sys directory to find out its attributes. These attributes are processed and stored as a database of currently active devices.

All important udev files are stored in /etc/udev/. Every received device event is matched against the set of rules read from files located in /lib/udev/rules.d and /run/udev/rules.d. You can add rules of your own to /etc/udev/rules.d and all rules files end in .rules. Files are processed in name order and earlier rules have precedence – this accounts for the common practice of using numbers at the start of the name of a rule file. There are also LABEL and GOTO commands that can be included in rule files to skip to a specific file, but they are best avoided.

Each rule is simple in theory, but can quickly become quite complex in practice. A rule consists of a set of key value pairs all on one line, use the continuation symbol / if you want to split lines. Keys come in two broad types – match keys and assignment keys. Match keys determine the event that the rule is activated for and assignment keys determine what the rule actually does when an event occurs. Assignment keys include RUN which allows you to run a script or a program when the event occurs so perhaps "assignment" isn't a good description of what they can do. The full list of keys is available in the documentation and they generally aren't difficult to understand.

The main use of udev is to deal with USB devices that are hot-plugged while the machine is running. Some common uses are to give a device a more human-oriented name. For example, you can write a rule that recognizes a particular USB stick and mounts it with a relevant name.

Another common use is to set the permissions on folders and files in the /sys folder so that they can be accessed without running as root. In principle, this is easy, but it is complicated by the fact that the folders and files in /sys are dynamically created. For example, you can create a rule that allows a folder to be used by a program running with a particular group's permission, but if the program writes something that configures the device in such a way that new folders or files are generated, the entire set of folders that represent the device are regenerated with the default permissions. It is difficult to catch all changes that need a udev rule to be triggered. For an example, see the PIO driver in Chapter 15.

Most IoT applications don't make use of hot plugging, the one big exception being the 1-Wire bus as described in the previous chapter. Another important exception is i-Buttons, which are intended to be hot plugged to provide identity based access. Although it isn't generally realized, the 1-Wire bus sends events to the kernel that udev can respond to. This is best explained by way of a simple example.

udev and the 1-Wire bus

When a device is added or removed from the 1-Wire bus it triggers a udev event that we can use to react to the change. We simply need to create a udev rule.

First we need a simple script that lets us know our rule has been used. Create a file /bin/device_added.sh and enter the lines:

```
#!/bin/bash
echo "USB device added at $(date)" >>/tmp/scripts.log
```

You also need to make the file executable:

```
sudo chmod +x /bin/device_added.sh
```

This script has nothing to do with udev – it is just a script to show that the rule has been activated by writing a message to a file.

To check that everything is working you can see what events udev is processing using:

```
su
udevadm monitor
```

If you try this out and disconnect and connect a 1-Wire device you will see something like:

```
pi@raspberrypi:/sys/bus/w1/devices/28-73fa511a64ff $ su
Password:
root@raspberrypi:/sys/bus/w1/devices/28-73fa511a64ff# udevadm monitor
monitor will print the received events for:
UDEV - the event which udev sends out after rule processing
KERNEL - the kernel uevent

KERNEL[635434.766262] remove    /devices/w1_bus_master1/28-73fa511a64ff/hwmon/hwmon3 (hwmon)
UDEV  [635434.794656] remove    /devices/w1_bus_master1/28-73fa511a64ff/hwmon/hwmon3 (hwmon)
KERNEL[635496.311780] add       /devices/w1_bus_master1/28-73fa511a64ff/hwmon/hwmon3 (hwmon)
KERNEL[635496.320597] add       /devices/w1_bus_master1/28-73fa511a64ff (w1)
UDEV  [635496.335529] add       /devices/w1_bus_master1/28-73fa511a64ff/hwmon/hwmon3 (hwmon)
UDEV  [635496.345868] add       /devices/w1_bus_master1/28-73fa511a64ff (w1)
```

This confirms that the devices are being added and removed with the help of udev.

You can find out more about the device using:
```
udevadm info —path=/sys/bus/w1/devices/w1_bus_master1
                                        —attribute-walk
```
which, for the device '/devices/w1_bus_master1', produces something like:

```
looking at device '/devices/w1_bus_master1':
 KERNEL=="w1_bus_master1"
 SUBSYSTEM=="w1"
 DRIVER=="w1_master_driver"
 ATTR{w1_master_timeout}=="10"
 ATTR{w1_master_slave_count}=="2"
 ATTR{w1_master_max_slave_count}=="64"
 ATTR{w1_master_timeout_us}=="0"
 ATTR{w1_master_remove}=="write device id xx-xxxxxxxxxxxx
                                        to remove slave"
 ATTR{w1_master_name}=="w1_bus_master1"
 ATTR{w1_master_attempts}=="67834"
 ATTR{w1_master_add}=="write device id xx-xxxxxxxxxxxx
                                        to add slave"
 ATTR{w1_master_pullup}=="1"
 ATTR{w1_master_pointer}=="0x58e38d87"
 ATTR{w1_master_search}=="-1"
 ATTR{therm_bulk_read}=="0"
```

Now that we know that the SUBSYSTEM is "w1" we can write a udev rule.

Create a text file /etc/udev/rules.d/100-w1.rules containing:

```
SUBSYSTEM=="w1",ACTION=="add",RUN+="/bin/device_added.sh"
```

The name of the file should ensure that it is the last loaded and so it is unlikely to be overridden. The match keys specify an add action in the w1 subsystem and when this event occurs our script is run. After you save the file you can restart `udev` using:

```
sudo udevadm control --reload-rules
```

This should restart the `udev` system, but sometimes a complete reboot is needed. Now when you add a new 1-Wire device you should see a message in the `/tmp/scripts.log` file.

If it doesn't seem to work you need to know that removing a 1-Wire device takes a few seconds because the driver doesn't immediately remove a device that is missing on one of its regular searches to allow for temporary loss of connectivity. You can check that events occur using `udevadm`.

Even for the 1-Wire bus, the actual usefulness of `udev` is limited. The time it takes to recognize a device being disconnected or connected can be too slow for many purposes and the range of things you can do usually don't fit in with controlling the device from code. Where `udev` does prove useful is if you have any USB devices that you want to set up the same way every time they are connected. Finally, notice that `udev` is the source of the file included in most device folders called `uevent`. It writes the latest relevant `udev` event into this folder.

Customizing the Device Tree

We have already met the Device Tree, DT, in Chapter 9, but only in the context of using supplied overlays to install device drivers. There often comes a time when a driver exists but the available overlays aren't quite what you need. There are also drivers which can support additional devices if you add an overlay that specifies what you want. Knowing how to create your own overlays is therefore useful and not that difficult. What is difficult is finding out what parameters are needed in your custom overlay – again the problem is lack of documentation.

A device tree, or an overlay to use with one, is written using a markup language usually referred to as Device Tree Source, DTS and stored in `.dts` files. The syntax of DTS is C-like and you should recognize its general form. Before a device tree or overlay is used it has to be compiled to a binary format known as a Flattened Device Tree, FDT, or a Device Tree Blob, DTB, stored in `.dtb` files. The tools you need to compile a device tree are installed as standard. DTS files that are to be included in other DTS files, using a C-like include instruction, by convention have file names ending `.dtsi`.

You can look up the syntax of the full DTS which you need to create a complete overlay, but for most of us the smaller task of creating overlays means we have to master a subset of the language and use it in a slightly different way. Few of us have to create a device tree for a completely new device, but being able to modify or add devices by way of overlays is more common.

The first thing to say is that not all drivers are compatible with device trees in the sense that they might well be loaded from a device tree node, but they don't necessarily understand everything that might be included in that node. For example, which device driver should be loaded is specified using `compatible = name` where, at its simplest, *name* is the actual filename of the driver. A device tree-aware driver will also recognize names that are not the file name of the driver and indicate a wider range of use. You can generally find the name of the compatible driver in the bindings documentation at `/linux/Documentation/devicetree/bindings/` in the GitHub repo, but this is not always everything you need to know.

The best way of getting started is to look at a typical overlay.

Custom LEDs

The driver for the existing LEDs, `gpio-leds`, introduced in Chapter 3, has the ability to support new LED devices on any GPIO line. To find out how this works you need to look up the documentation in: `linux/Documentation/devicetree/bindings/leds/leds-gpio.txt`

It says:

> *Each LED is represented as a sub-node of the gpio-leds device.*
> *Each node's name represents the name of the corresponding LED.*

What this means is that we can use an overlay to introduce a new sub-node to the `gpio-led` node. Following this, a lot of sub-node properties are listed, but as we are considering adding a simple LED on a GPIO line the one that is relevant is `gpios`, which should specify the LED's GPIO, see "gpios property" in `Documentation/devicetree/bindings/gpio/gpio.txt`.

Active low LEDs should be indicated using flags in the GPIO specifier.

Clearly we can use this to add an LED on a specific GPIO, but we need to know how to specify a GPIO line. The documentation says that you specify a GPIO line using something like `<controller,line offset, options>`. It then says that the options are controller-dependent, which means you now have to look elsewhere for details. However, the general documentation says:

> *The exact meaning of each specifier cell is controller specific, and must be documented in the device tree binding for the device, but it is strongly recommended to use the two-cell approach.*

Before this the "two-cell approach" is specified as using a single option for active state - a `0` for active high and `1` for active low.

Putting all this together and we can write a simple overlay:

```
/dts-v1/;
/plugin/;
/ {
    compatible = "brcm,bcm2708";
    fragment@0 {
        target = <&leds>;
        __overlay__ {
            my_led: myled {
                gpios = <&gpio 4 0>;
            };
        };
    };
};
```

The first two lines are standard comments. The `compatible` line is also standard and is defined to be an overlay that works on all Pis and `compatible =` is used to specify the driver to be used by the node.

The `fragment@0` starts the actual details of the overlay. You can write a number of fragments in the file, but they have to be numbered sequentially. The `target =` determines the node that the overlay will modify. In this case it is identified by a label `&leds`, which is set within the main device tree to reference the `gpio-leds` node. You can only discover this by reading the device tree or seeing it used in an example as it doesn't seem to be documented anywhere. After this the `__overlay__` block defines what is added to the node and in this case we add a single LED on GPIO 4:

```
  my_led: myled {
            gpios = <&gpio 4 0>;
          };
```

Again, you have to know that `gpio` is a label for GPIO controller 0 and you can only find this out by reading the device tree or seeing it used in another example. Notice that we have also created a label for our new node. We can use `my_led` as an alternative name for the node within the overlay.

Start a new text file and enter all of the above to produce a file called `MyLed.dts`:

```
/dts-v1/;
/plugin/;
/ {
    compatible = "brcm,bcm2708";
    fragment@0 {
        target = <&leds>;
        __overlay__ {
            my_led: myled {
                gpios = <&gpio 4 0>;
            };
        };
    };
};
```

Once you have saved the file you need to compile it using:

```
dtc -@ -I dts -O dtb -o MyLed.dtbo MyLed.dts
```

You can look up the details of the options for the dtc compiler, but this is typical for compiling an overlay. After this you need to copy the compiled file into the overlay directory:

```
sudo cp MyLed.dtbo /boot/firmware/overlays/
```

In the case of other drivers you would now load the overlay dynamically, but the gpio-leds driver doesn't support this. As a result you need to add dtoverlay=MyLed to /boot/firmware/config.txt and reboot. Note: make sure that there are no spaces around =.

With this change, you will find that there is a new LED device that you can control in the usual way:

```
#include <stdio.h>
#include <errno.h>
#include <unistd.h>
#include <fcntl.h>
int main(int argc, char **argv)
{

    int fd = open("/sys/class/leds/myled/brightness", O_WRONLY);
    while (1)
    {
        write(fd, "0",1);
        sleep(2);
        write(fd, "1",1);
        sleep(2);
    }
}
```

For this program to work it has to be run with root permissions.

You can see that the custom LED is installed with the standard set of files in the appropriate folder:

If this doesn't work then add:

dtdebug=1

to the start of the /boot/firmware/config.txt file and after rebooting use:

sudo vclog --msg

to see the error messages.

You might find it interesting to see what the compiler has generated using the command:

```
fdtdump /boot/overlays/MyLed.dtbo
****fdtdump is a low-level debugging tool,not meant for general
use.
**** If you want to decompile a dtb, you probably want
**** dtc -I dtb -O dts <filename>
/dts-v1/;
// magic:            0xd00dfeed
// totalsize:        0x1b1 (433)
// off_dt_struct:    0x38
// off_dt_strings:   0x180
// off_mem_rsvmap:   0x28
// version:          17
// last_comp_version:      16
// boot_cpuid_phys: 0x0
// size_dt_strings: 0x31
// size_dt_struct:  0x148
/ {
    compatible = "brcm,bcm2708";
    fragment@0 {
        target = <0xffffffff>;
        __overlay__ {
            myled {
                gpios = <0xffffffff 0x00000004 0x00000000>;
                phandle = <0x00000001>;
            };
        };
    };
    __symbols__ {
        my_led = "/fragment@0/__overlay__/myled";
    };
    __fixups__ {
        leds = "/fragment@0:target:0";
        gpio = "/fragment@0/__overlay__/myled:gpios:0";
    };
};
```

The __fixups__ section lists the symbols that don't have values yet as they haven't been merged with the full device tree where they do have values.

You can, as the previous listing suggests, use the decompiler option to get slightly less information:

```
dtc -I dtb -O dts /boot/overlays/MyLed.dtbo
```

You can also use the decompiler to get a complete listing of the current state of the device tree:

```
$ dtc -I fs -O dts /proc/device-tree
```

If you do this you can find the node that the LED overlay adds to:

```
leds {
        compatible = "gpio-leds";
        phandle = < 0x7a >;

        act {
                gpios = < 0x0a 0x2f 0x01 >;
                label = "led0";
                phandle = < 0x2d >;
                default-state = "keep";
                linux,default-trigger = "actpwr";
        };

        myled {
                gpios = < 0x0a 0x04 0x00 >;
                phandle = < 0x7d >;
        };
};
```

You can see that it hasn't added quite as much information as for the standard act LED.

Once you have a basic overlay you can start to improve on it. For example the documentation says:

linux,default-trigger   *This parameter, if present, is a string*
                             defining the trigger assigned to the
LED. Current triggers are:
    "backlight"   *LED will act as a back-light, controlled*
                             by the framebuffer system
    "default-on"   *LED will turn on (but for leds-gpio*
                             see "default-state" property in
                             Documentation/devicetree/
                             bindings/leds/leds-gpio.txt)
    "heartbeat"   *LED flashes at a load average rate*
    "disk-activity"   *LED indicates disk activity*
    "ide-disk"   *IDE disk activity (deprecated),*
                             in new implementations use
                             "disk-activity"
    "timer"   *LED flashes at a fixed, configurable*
                             rate
    "pattern"   *LED alters the brightness for the*
                             specified duration with one software
                             timer (requires "led-pattern" property)

Of course, the Pi supports more than this, see Chapter 3. Another useful section is the aliases node, which lists many of the labels used in overlays.

With this information, setting a default trigger for the new LED is easy:

```
ts-v1/;
/plugin/;
/ {
    compatible = "brcm,bcm2708";
    fragment@0 {
        target =<&leds>;
        __overlay__ {
            my_led: myled {
                gpios = <&gpio 4 0>;
                linux,default-trigger = "heartbeat";
            };
        };
    };
};
```

After a reboot you will see the standard double-flash heartbeat on GPIO4.

Parameters

We can make overlays more useful by way of parameters. In fact, we have been making use of parameters to customize overlays since our first encounter with them. In the case of the custom LED overlay, for example, it would be better to allow the user to define the default trigger and the GPIO pin to use via parameters. You can define any parameters that you might want to set in an __overrides__ node.

Parameters are defined using a standard syntax:

```
name = <&label>,"property";
```

where *name* is the name of the parameter, i.e. it is what you use in the dtparam or dtoverlay line to set the property, and *label* is the node that the property you want the parameter to set is in.

There are different ways to specify the property according to how you want the value that is assigned to the parameter to change it. The simplest is a string property, which simply takes whatever is assigned to the parameter and sets the property equal to it. For example:

```
trigger =  <&my_led>,"linux,default-trigger";
```

sets the linux,default-trigger property within the node labeled my_led to whatever the user specifies for the trigger parameter as part of a dtparam or dtoverlay.

A complete example is:

```
/dts-v1/;
/plugin/;
/ {
    compatible = "brcm,bcm2708";
    fragment@0 {
        target =<&leds>;
        __overlay__ {
            my_led: myled {
                gpios = <&gpio 4 0>;
                linux,default-trigger = "heartbeat";
            };
        };
    };
    __overrides__{
    trigger =  <&my_led>,"linux,default-trigger";

    };
};
```

If you now change `config.txt` to read:

```
dtoverlay = MyLed
dtparam = trigger = none
```

the trigger will be set to none and the LED won't flash at all. You can set the trigger to be anything that is supported. You can set multiple properties using the same parameter – just write a comma-separated list of labels and properties.

Setting a simple string via a parameter is easy, but what about selecting the GPIO pin number? The problem here is that the number is embedded in a list of values:

```
gpios = <&gpio 4 0>;
```

How can you change a single value in a list of values? The answer is to make use of the offset specification. If you want to define an integer parameter then there a number of possible forms depending on the size of the integer:

- `name = <&label>,"property.offset"; // 8-bit`
- `name = <&label>,"property;offset"; // 16-bit`
- `name = <&label>,"property:offset"; // 32-bit`
- `name = <&label>,"property#offset"; // 64-bit`

This looks straightforward, but the key is the offset specification. A numeric property is treated as a set of bytes and the offset, in bytes, determines where the parameter's value will be inserted into the set.

For example:

```
gpios = <&gpio 4 0>;
```

is a set of 32-bit integers where the first four are the GPIO controller number, the next four are the GPIO pin number and the final four are the active high/low selector. To store a value in the GPIO pin number we need to store a 32-bit integer offset by four bytes. That is:

```
gpio_pin = <&my_led>,"gpios:4"
```

This creates a `gpio_pin` parameter and sets bytes 4, 5, 6 and 7 of the `gpios` property to its value as a 32-bit integer.

If you now change `config.txt` to read:

```
dtoverlay=MyLed
dtparam=trigger=none
dtparam=gpio_pin=4
```

you will discover that you can customize the new LED device to use any trigger and any GPIO pin.

The complete overlay is:

```
/dts-v1/;
/plugin/;
/ {
    compatible = "brcm,bcm2708";
    fragment@0 {
        target =<&leds>;
        __overlay__ {
                    my_led: myled {
                    gpios = <&gpio 4 0>;
                    linux,default-trigger = "heartbeat";
                    };
            };
        };
    __overrides__{
        trigger =  <&my_led>,"linux,default-trigger";
        gpio_pin = <&my_led>,"gpios:4";
        };
};
```

Device Tree – Where Next?

The device tree is a relatively young idea and is still being developed. This brief introduction is enough to get you started writing overlays, but there are many topics that have been omitted. In particular, we haven't touched on the topic of specifying hardware in terms of addresses and interrupts, and we haven't looked at loading and configuring device drivers that aren't officially supported. The reason for these omissions is that they are not common requirements when creating custom overlays for existing devices. This said, we have encountered many of the basic ideas and techniques. If you want to take this further than the best advice is to read existing overlays and bindings and see how they work.

Summary

- Loadable Kernel Modules, LKMs, are a way of extending the Linux kernel after it has booted.

- LKMs are most often used for drivers, but they are completely general and can be used to implement any desired behavior.

- Writing an LKM isn't difficult, but there is a great deal to learn as you no longer have access to user space libraries, and drivers in particular tend to have their own frameworks.

- Module are usually stored in /lib/modules and you can load and generally work with a module using modprobe, although the device tree is the preferred way of doing most things relating to drivers.

- udev is the Linux subsystem that deals with devices, mostly USB devices, that can be hot-plugged.

- When a device changes its state a udev event is triggered and you can define actions to be taken in a .rules file.

- IoT devices are generally not hot-plugged, but 1-Wire bus devices can be handled using udev rules.

- You can write custom overlays to add to or modify the device tree. For example, you can add additional LEDs for the LED driver to control.

- Custom overlays can be made more general with the use of parameters.

Chapter 18

Almost Real-Time Linux

This chapter is about advanced scheduling and not every C programmer needs to know about this. Overall you can use the ideas to achieve a smaller latency and some aspects of real-time service, but you cannot eliminate the possibility of your program being interrupted.

You can write real-time programs using standard Linux as long as you know how to control scheduling. In fact, this turns out to be relatively easy and it enables the CM5 to do things you might not think it capable of. Scheduling in single-core systems is relatively simple, but the CM5 has four cores which means four threads can be running at the same time and this makes scheduling more complicated.

If you are writing a real-time system there are two things that should concern you - how fast the system can act and how poor this response can be in the worst case. We usually divide this response into throughput and latency. Throughput is how many events you can deal with per second and it is what we have been concerned with so far. Latency is how quickly the system responds to a one-off event. Throughput is mostly a hardware matter, but latency is very much affected by the software and the need to multitask and keep the system running. The machine may have the hardware speed to respond to an event, but it might not be able to because it is doing something else.

After learning how to generate accurate and fast pulses, we now have the ability to work with I/O down in the microsecond region, but we still have the problem that our program can be interrupted at any time by the operating system. This means that our outputs and inputs can go drastically wrong. For example, if you generate a fast pulse train in the 1ms range using a standard GPIO line and set a logic analyzer to trigger on a long pulse, you will eventually find one or more very long pulses, typically in the millisecond range. This problem becomes worse the more the CPU is loaded as the operating system switches between tasks to make sure that everything has an opportunity to progress. There are many situations where this is not just inconvenient, but completely unacceptable. Pi OS is not a real-time operating system and we cannot turn it into one, but there is a great deal we can do to lessen the problem.

The Scheduling Problem

If you are familiar with microcontrollers such as the PIC, AMTEL, etc, then the idea that there could be something getting between you and the hardware will be new. The majority of simple microcontrollers do nothing but run the program you download. Any talk of an "operating system" generally refers to code that does the downloading or minimal system preparation. When you write a control loop then you can safely assume that the loop will run as you wrote it and without interruption, unless of course you have coded an interrupt handler.

The point is that in many situations your program is the only program running and you are in complete charge of the processor. In the case of running a program on the Pi's ARM processor, the situation is very different. Your program is just one of a number of programs running at any given time. The CM5 has four cores and this means that four programs can be running at any given time. The operating system is responsible for starting and stopping programs so that each and every program has a turn to run. This is called "scheduling" and it is a problem if you are trying to write a real-time system.

The problem is that you might write a program that toggles a GPIO line between high and low with a given timing, but whether this timing is honored depends not just on your program but on the operating system as well. You can't even be sure how the operating system will treat your program because it depends, in a fairly complex way, on what else is running on the system and exactly what the other programs are doing.

Sometimes this is expressed as program execution being non-deterministic, whereas in a simple microcontroller unit (mcu) it is deterministic. This means that if you run the same program twice you probably don't get exactly the same result, whereas on an mcu this is a reasonable expectation.

The whole subject of multitasking operating systems, and scheduling in particular, is a large one. It is usually taught as part of a computer science degree, but generally not as it applies to real-time programming. What this means is that there is often a lot of guesswork involved in getting programs with real-time demands to work properly under general operating systems such as Linux. In fact, it is often stated that you can't do real-time processing under Linux because you cannot even place a bound, an upper limit, on how long your program might be suspended by the OS. This isn't true and real-time processing on standard Linux is possible, as long as you are able to live within the constraints.

As an alternative you could opt to run a specially designed real-time OS that does provide guarantees on how quickly a request will be serviced. There are such real-time versions of Linux that you can install, but, since version 3.14, the Linux Kernel has had sufficient real-time facilities for many applications, so you don't need to move to anything different to the standard Pi OS.

It is important to realize that there is no way that a real-time operating system can increase the speed of operation of the processor; the maximum speed of operation cannot be improved upon. What a real-time OS does provide is higher consistency of that response time. It isn't perfect, however, and despite all of the features of real-time Linux there will still be small periods of time when your program isn't operating and there is little to be done about this.

The Scheduler and Preemption

Unfortunately the Linux Scheduler has evolved faster than the documentation and there are many misconceptions about how it all works based on how it used to work. The first version of the Linux Scheduler was very simple and it survived for a surprisingly long time. After 2007 most versions of Linux made use of a default scheduler called the Completely Fair Scheduler (CFS) which, despite its name, was not really completely fair. The current Linux kernel makes use of a modified CFS scheduler - the EEVDS Earliest Eligible Virtual Deadline Scheduler. At the time of writing, the EEVDS is implemented in the same source code files as the CFS used to be and it lacks documentation about how to tune it or modify it in any way.

Another confusion is the historical role of the Jiffy, the unit of time associated with the scheduler. How often the scheduler was called depended on a kernel constant USER_HZ which is set when the kernel is compiled. In other words, it is not an easy value to change unless you are happy about compiling the kernel. You can find the current setting using the command line:

```
getconf CLK_TCK
```

If you try this out on a CM5 you will find that the tick rate is 100 per second or 10ms between interrupts, i.e. a Jiffy is 10ms. The Jiffy is still used for timing and backward compatibility, but it is no longer used to invoke the scheduler.

Most accounts of the scheduler concentrate on how it allocates time to threads. For the typical IoT application this is not the main concern. As threads are run on multiple cores, every now and again a thread will initiate an action, typically an I/O task, that causes it to have to wait. This causes the scheduler to be called to work out what task should replace the waiting task. In many cases there are enough I/O-bound tasks to ensure that the scheduler is called often enough to ensure that every task gets its share of the processor's cores. Consider, however, what happens if the cores are all running tasks that perform no I/O – they are CPU-bound. In this case none of the tasks will need to enter a wait state and the scheduler will never be called. This is where preemption comes into the story. The scheduler is also called at a regular interval as part of a timer interrupt. When the scheduler is called it examines the running processes and if there are tasks that are waiting and deserve to be run then the scheduler will forcibly place the thread into a suspended state and run another more deserving thread. This is preemption and it is how CPU-bound threads are interrupted by the scheduler to allow other threads to run.

As IoT programs are mostly CPU-bound - even if they have to wait for external events they tend to do so by polling - preemption is our biggest concern. What matters is how long a thread gets to run before it is suspended and how often it is going to be suspended that is of most importance. What thread gets to replace it is often irrelevant and the fairness of the scheduler is of less concern.

For the EEVDS the only parameter you can change is `sched_base_slice` which sets the time a thread can run for without being preempted. Of course if there are no more deserving threads to run it may not be preempted. Notice that under the CFS `sched_base_slice` was called `sched_min_granularity` and this causes confusion in the documentation.

At the time of writing you cannot change `sched_base_slice` without recompiling the kernel, which doesn't seem to be a very sensible choice.

Based on observation, for the CM5, and Pi5 in general, `sched_base_slice` is 4 ms.

Group Scheduling

There is yet another twist to the story. It is possible to group processes together so that they are scheduled as if they were a single entity. For example, if you have two groups, one consisting of a single process and of the other containing three processes, then the two groups each get 50% of the processor time, which means one process gets 50% and the three in the other group get 50%/3 each. Group scheduling would be a footnote and not something we needed to get into, but for the adoption of auto-grouping.

This approach automatically forms groups according to the console process that starts each process. So if you run a process from a console, or an implied console, it forms a group. Run another process from the same source and it is added to the group and the time allotted to the group is shared between them. The idea is that, for a desktop system, the time should be shared between the different consoles to seem more responsive to the user. If a user starts a video editor, that is one group. Then they start compiling a program using multiple threads and all of those threads form another group. If this were not the case, each thread would get an equal share of time and the video editor would slow to a crawl.

Auto-grouping is said to be the single biggest improvement in desktop Linux in terms of interactivity, but it can cause problems for IoT programs if you don't know about it.

Exploring Scheduling

To explore exactly how scheduling affects your programs you need to run other programs with well-defined properties concurrently. The most commonly used is the stress utility:

```
sudo apt-get install stress
```

You can start n CPU-hogging programs using:

```
stress --cpu n
```

These carry on running until you interrupt the command using Ctrl-C. If you need to stop all of the stress programs running then use:

```
sudo killall stress
```

and to see how they are being scheduled use:

```
top
```

in another console.

For example:

```
stress --cpu 4
```

with another CPU-bound task already running results in:

PID	USER	PR	NI	VIRT	RES	SHR	S	%CPU	%MEM	TIME+	COMMAND
6545	root	20	0	67696	512	512	R	100.0	0.0	1:03.58	test
6582	root	20	0	2944	0	0	R	78.7	0.0	0:43.45	stress
6584	root	20	0	2944	0	0	R	77.4	0.0	0:41.89	stress
6585	root	20	0	2944	0	0	R	71.8	0.0	0:41.16	stress
6583	root	20	0	2944	0	0	R	70.8	0.0	0:42.73	stress

The four stress programs get 50% of the total cores and the test program gets the other 50%, ignoring all the other programs running. This is because the four stress programs were started from the same console and so count as a single program as far as the scheduler is concerned. This means that the test program should get 200% of the four cores. However, as it can only use one core, it is allocated 100% and the remaining 300% is divided equally between the four stress programs, i.e. they get 75% each of the remaining three cores.

Compare this to what happens if all five programs are started from the same console session:

```
sudo stress --cpu 4 & sudo /root/document/test
```

PID	USER	PR	NI	VIRT	RES	SHR	S	%CPU	%MEM	TIME+	COMMAND
7679	root	20	0	2944	0	0	R	86.4	0.0	95:35.50	stress
7677	root	20	0	2944	0	0	R	81.7	0.0	95:38.11	stress
7680	root	20	0	2944	0	0	R	79.1	0.0	95:39.54	stress
7676	root	20	0	2944	0	0	R	77.7	0.0	95:34.62	stress
7678	root	20	0	67696	512	512	R	75.1	0.0	98:42.71	test

Now all five programs share the same allocation so each gets 400%/5 = 80%

Clearly with auto-grouping on it matters how a program is started.

Now let's look at the way this affects the test program, which is simply a loop that toggles a GPIO line as fast as possible. If you examine the output you will see that the program is suspended every 4ms or so:

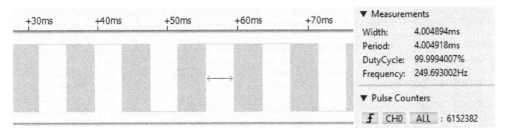

Some of the time, due to the way the schedule is implemented, the program will have the benefit of a core for more than a single time slice.

You might think that if the test program manages to secure 100% of a core simply because there are no other CPU-hogging programs running then the signal generation would be glitch free – this is not the case. If you sample the output and filter out all pulses that are as short as the typical signal then you will see something like:

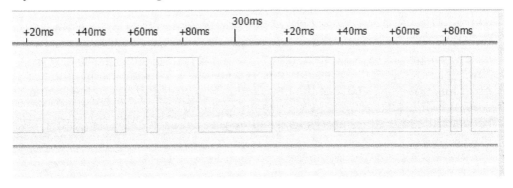

388

Each of the edges in this trace correspond to pulses larger than the signal and are due to the program being interrupted. For example, the two pulses at the far right are about 4ms and correspond to the program being preempted. The unfiltered signal near the leading edge of the first of the two pulses is:

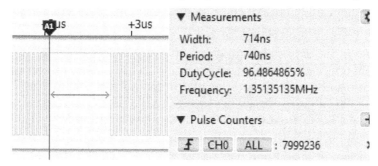

You can see that the program is only interrupted for just over 700ns. However there are larger interruptions, typically no more than $100\mu s$.

The point is that scheduling is complicated and depends on what else is running at the same time, but even if the load is such that the program can have 100% of a core allocated to it there are still interruptions.

Real-Time Scheduling

Every Linux thread is assigned a scheduling policy and a static priority. The normal scheduling algorithm that Linux uses, SCHED_OTHER, applies to all threads with static priority zero. If you are not using real-time scheduling then all the threads run at priority zero. In place of a static priority, each thread is assigned a dynamic priority which increases each time it is passed over for execution by the scheduler. The scheduler gives the thread with the highest dynamic priority an opportunity to run for one time slice. A thread can be suspended before its time slice is up because it has to wait for I/O or because it is blocked in some other way. Any time a thread makes a system call it is also a candidate to be suspended in favor of another thread.
You have only a little control over the computation of the dynamic priority.

The normal scheduling algorithm doesn't provide much control over what runs. It is "fair" in the sense that all threads get a turn at running, but it isn't possible to set a thread to have a high priority so that it runs in preference to all others. To do this we need to look at the real-time scheduling options. The ones that are important for us are SCHED_FIFO, SCHED_DEADLINE and, in some cases SCHED_RR. These apply to real-time threads with static priorities from 1 (low) to 99 (high).

The first thing to note is that a thread with priority greater than zero will always run in preference to a thread with zero priority and so all real-time threads will run before a thread using the normal EEVDS scheduling algorithm.

Deadline scheduling is tricky and it is discussed in detail later.

First In First Out (FIFO) scheduling.

What happens in FIFO scheduling is that the system maintains queues of threads that are ready to run at each priority. It then looks for the list with the highest priority with threads ready to run and it starts the thread at the head of the list. When a thread is started it is added to the back of its priority queue. Once a FIFO thread gets to run it can be preempted by a thread with a higher static priority that is ready to run.

If a FIFO thread is suspended because of a higher priority thread, it goes back to the head of the queue. This makes it the next thread to resume. This is the sense in which the schedule is First In First Out. If a thread is suspended by another thread of higher priority that becomes runnable then it is restarted as soon as the thread that replaced it is suspended or stops running. Finally, if a thread explicitly yields, by calling yield, it goes to the end of the priority queue.

Round Robin (RR) scheduling is a very simple modification to FIFO scheduling. The only difference is that a thread that has been running for its allotted time period or longer is placed at the end of the queue. This results in threads running in an A, B, C, A, B, C order. You can see that this allows each thread to run for around one timeslice in turn.

You may be wondering how Linux can manage to operate with threads that have different scheduling policies? The answer is that Linux has a modular scheduler which can be expanded by the addition of new classes. At the moment there are four scheduler classes, idle, cfs, rt and dl in order of priority. Any Deadline tasks are scheduled first, then FIFO, then RR and finally Normal. What this means is that if there are any runnable Deadline threads, these take precedence over any other type of thread. However, to keep the system running, Linux only allows Deadline tasks to add up to 95% of the available compute time. This leaves no less than 5% for the other schedulers.

Setting Scheduling Priority

This sounds like a recipe for chaos with multiple scheduling systems working at the same time and a range of different priorities, but if you think about it for a moment and start simply, you will see that it provides most of what you are looking for. You are in full control of the CM5 and so you can determine exactly how many non-zero priority threads there are. By default, all of the standard threads are priority zero and scheduled by the normal scheduler and your real-time threads are priority 1 and above.

Now consider what happens if you start a FIFO scheduled thread with priority 1. It starts and is added to the end of the priority 1 queue. Of course, it is the only priority 1 process and so it starts immediately on one of the available cores. If the process never makes a call that causes it to wait for I/O or become blocked in some other way then it will execute without being interrupted by any other process. In principle, this should ensure that your process never delivers anything but its fastest response time.

This is almost, but not quite, true. There are more complex situations you can invent with threads at different priorities according to how important they are, but this gets complicated very quickly.

In most cases for real-time programming the SCHED_FIFO scheduler is what you need and in its simplest form. Its complete set of scheduling commands supported by #include <sched.h> are:

sched_setscheduler	Set the scheduling policy and parameters of a thread
sched_getscheduler	Return the scheduling policy of a thread
sched_setparam	Set the scheduling parameters of a thread
sched_getparam	Fetch the scheduling parameters of a thread
sched_get_priority_max	Return the maximum priority available in a scheduling policy
sched_get_priority_min	Return the minimum priority available in a scheduling policy
sched_rr_get_interval	Fetch the quantum used for threads that are scheduled under the round-robin scheduling policy
sched_yield	Cause the caller to relinquish the CPU, so that some other thread be executed
sched_setaffinity	Set the CPU affinity of a thread
sched_getaffinity	Get the CPU affinity of a thread
sched_setattr	Set the scheduling policy and parameters of a thread
sched_getattr	Fetch the scheduling policy and parameters of a thread

The scheduling types supported are:

SCHED_OTHER   The standard time-sharing policy
SCHED_BATCH   For "batch" style execution of processes
SCHED_IDLE   For running very low priority background jobs
SCHED_FIFO   A first-in first-out policy
SCHED_RR   A round-robin policy

where only the final two are real-time schedulers. Also notice that all the scheduling functions return an error code which you should check to make sure things have worked.

For example, to set the current thread to FIFO scheduling with a `priority` Struct you need to use:

```
sched_setscheduler(pid, sched, &priority);
```

where *pid* is the thread id and if it is 0 then the calling thread is used.

For example:

```
#include <sched.h>
…

const struct sched_param priority = {1};
sched_setscheduler(0, SCHED_FIFO, &priority);
```

If this is the only thread with a priority as high as 1 then it will not be interrupted by other threads and only the kernel will cause short interruptions in its running – typically a few tens of nanoseconds every now and again. Even if there are other threads with the same or higher priorities, as long as there are sufficient cores to run them, the thread will still not be interrupted.

Real Time FIFO Scheduling

Now we can try the same stress test given earlier, but with FIFO real-time scheduling selected. To set FIFO scheduling we need to use the function:

```
sched_setscheduler(pid SCHED_FIFO &priority);
```

where *pid* is the thread id and if it is 0 then the calling thread is used.

The second parameter sets the type of scheduling used, FIFO in this case, and the final parameter is a pointer to a struct that specifies the priority.

Notice you need to include <sched.h> to make use of the scheduling functions.

The modified program is:

```c
#include <stdio.h>
#include <stdlib.h>
#include "Gpio5.h"
#include <sched.h>

int main(int argc, char **argv)
{

    const struct sched_param priority = {1};
    sched_setscheduler(0, SCHED_FIFO, &priority);
    rp1_Init();
    gpio_init(2);
    gpio_set_dir(2, true);
    while (true)
    {
        gpio_put(2, 1);
        gpio_put(2, 0);
    }
    return (EXIT_SUCCESS);
}
```

If you run a logic analyzer then there is a surprise. The program runs for one second and then it is interrupted for around 50ms. Clearly something with a higher priority is now interrupting your program and probably keeping the console and other essentials running. If you now run a CPU-hogging task you will discover that there is no change in the behavior of your program. It runs for a second and then is interrupted for 50ms.

In short, running your IoT program in FIFO or RR mode makes it look as if it is the only task, but it doesn't get rid of the timer ticks or other system interrupts.

Deadline Scheduling

FIFO scheduling can be used to lock a single process into a core so that it gets the maximum time possible, but there are more subtle ways of managing things using Earliest Deadline Scheduling (EDS) instead of the default scheduling policy.

A SCHED_DEADLINE thread is associated with three parameters – *runtime*, *period* and *deadline*. The thread will receive *runtime* nanoseconds of execution every *period* nanoseconds and *deadline* specifies in nanoseconds the time by which the action has to be completed. Notice that if the thread is interrupted then it could take longer than its estimated runtime. The scheduler attempts to schedule the thread so that it is completed in the specified deadline.

393

In terms of what you are trying to do, the runtime you specify is used by the scheduler to work out if it is possible to satisfy all of the requirements. The deadline is more important to you because it represents the maximum elapsed time that the task should take.

The period is just the rate that you want the task to be repeated. For example, suppose you are monitoring a batch of chemicals in a tank and you need to take a set of measurements of temperature at different depths in the tank every second then the period is obviously one second.

The deadline is more difficult to determine – how long can you wait for the reading? Clearly this has to be less than one second or you will have missed a reading. You might say that everything is going to be fine if the reading is available after 250ms from the start of the period – then this is your deadline.

Finally you need to estimate how long it will actually take to get the readings – suppose each sensor takes 1ms to read and you have five sensors to read then the runtime can be estimated to be 5ms. With these estimates the scheduler will attempt to run your thread every second and it will ensure that within that time it gets 5ms of runtime, possibly spread over the first 250ms due to other threads preempting it. As long as the system isn't overloaded, the scheduling algorithm will meet the specifications of period and deadline. If a thread takes longer than its runtime period the operating system suspends it and restarts it at its next activation period.

It is also useful to know that in this case `sched_yield` suspends the thread until its next time period starts. This means you can give time back to the system if you have overestimated how long a task should take.

To set deadline scheduling you have to use the Linux-specific calls and these are not available as easy-to-call functions in the GNU libraries. Fortunately it is very easy to use a direct Linux `syscall`:

```
int sched_setattr(pid, struct sched_attr *attr, flags);
```

where *pid* is the Linux process id and not the thread id returned by `Pthreads`. If this is 0 then the current thread is used. The second parameter is a pointer to a new struct which sets the properties of the scheduling policy and the third, `flags`, is an integer which is currently unused and should be set to 0.

To make use of this function we need a definition of the new struct. While there is a definition in one of the Linux-specific headers, it is simpler to explicitly add it to your program:

```
struct sched_attr {
    uint32_t size;
    uint32_t sched_policy;
    uint64_t sched_flags;
    int32_t  sched_nice;
    uint32_t sched_priority;
    uint64_t sched_runtime;
    uint64_t sched_deadline;
    uint64_t sched_period;
};
```

with size as the size of struct and policy specifying the policy, using the same constants as used earlier plus the new SCHED_DEADLINE. The flags field is to control what happens if you fork the thread and what to do if the time constraints aren't met and can mostly be set to zero and ignored. The next two fields control what happens under SCHED_OTHER/BATCH and SCHED_FIFO/RR respectively. The final three fields control SCHED_DEADLINE. To use these constants you need to add:

```
#include <linux/sched.h>
```

The function call has to be implemented as a Linux syscall so you also need to add:

```
#include <sys/syscall.h>
int sched_setattr(pid_t pid, const struct sched_attr *attr,
                                     unsigned int flags) {
    return syscall(__NR_sched_setattr, pid, attr, flags);
}
```

There is also a related getattr call:

```
int sched_getattr(pid_t pid struct sched_attr *attr,
                    unsigned int size, unsigned int flags){
    return syscall(__NR_sched_getattr, pid, attr, size, flags);
}
```

You can be sure that the deadlines you specify will be met because the scheduler computes the feasibility of the requested schedule and setattr will return with an EBUSY error when you add a thread that makes it impossible to meet all of the deadlines you have defined.

To see how this works, let's implement a simple task that prints "sensor" every two seconds. The first problem is specifying the times to allocate. Currently these have to satisfy:

sched_runtime ≤ sched_deadline ≤ sched_period

and all times have to be greater than 1024ns and smaller than 2^{63}ns. Particular systems also set limits on the size of sched_period. For the CM5 the smallest sched_period is 100μs which means you can't use deadline scheduling for tasks that take less than 100us.

If we select two seconds for sched_period and assume the runtime to print the message is likely to be less than 10ms, the deadline can be 11ms. Thus the struct can be initialized as:

```
struct sched_attr attr = {
    .size = sizeof (attr)
    .sched_policy = SCHED_DEADLINE
    .sched_runtime = 10 * 1000 * 1000
    .sched_period = 2 * 1000 * 1000 * 1000
    .sched_deadline = 11 * 1000 * 1000
};
```

The task will be repeated every two seconds, but it can take up to 11ms to complete.

The thread function is simply:

```
sched_setattr(0, &attr, 0);
for (;;) {
    printf("sensor\n");
    fflush(0);
    sched_yield();
};
```

Notice that, after we set the scheduling policy, the thread simply loops printing the message. The key point is that in this case the yield causes the thread to be suspended until the start of its next time period.

Putting all of this together gives:

```
#include <stdio.h>
#include <stdlib.h>
#include <sys/syscall.h>
#include <unistd.h>
#include <linux/sched.h>
#include <pthread.h>
#include <stdint.h>
```

```
struct sched_attr {
    uint32_t size;
    uint32_t sched_policy;
    uint64_t sched_flags;
    int32_t sched_nice;
    uint32_t sched_priority;
    uint64_t sched_runtime;
    uint64_t sched_deadline;
    uint64_t sched_period;
};

int sched_setattr(pid_t pid, const struct sched_attr *attr,
        unsigned int flags) {
    return syscall(__NR_sched_setattr, pid, attr, flags);
}

void * threadA(void *p) {
    struct sched_attr attr = {
        .size = sizeof (attr),
        .sched_policy = SCHED_DEADLINE,
        .sched_runtime = 10 * 1000 * 1000,
        .sched_deadline = 11 * 1000 * 1000,
        .sched_period = 2 * 1000 * 1000 * 1000,
    };
    sched_setattr(0, &attr, 0);
    for (;;) {
        printf("sensor\n");
        fflush(0);
        sched_yield();
    };
}

int main(int argc, char** argv) {
    pthread_t pthreadA;
    pthread_create(&pthreadA, NULL, threadA, NULL);
    pthread_exit(0);
    return (EXIT_SUCCESS);
}
```

In this case the main program simply stops its thread leaving the Deadline thread to run every two seconds. Notice that when the scheduler makes the thread active it continues to run after the sched_yield – its state is stored when it is suspended and restored when it is activated.

In a real instance, the main program could continue to run using any of the other scheduling policies.

To make the program work it has to be run as root or similar, see Chapter 3 if you need to know how to do this.

As an example more in keeping with the previous goal of generating a fast signal without dropout, we can arrange to use deadline scheduling to toggle a GPIO line at 100μs intervals. Change the thread function to read:

```
void *threadA(void *p)
{
    struct sched_attr attr = {
        .size = sizeof(attr),
        .sched_policy = SCHED_DEADLINE,
        .sched_runtime = 10 * 1000,
        .sched_deadline = 25 * 1000,
        .sched_period = 100* 1000,
    };
    int result =sched_setattr(0, &attr, 0);
    for (;;)
    {
        gpio_xor_mask(0x4);
        sched_yield();
    };
}
```

This sets up the schedule for a repeat rate of 100us with a deadline of 24μs and a runtime of 10us. These figures are reasonable, but are far from the only choice. Making them more precise would allow the scheduler to succeed in meeting the requirements in a more loaded system.

The main program has to set up the GPIO line:

```
int main(int argc, char **argv)
{
    rp1_Init();
    gpio_init(2);
    gpio_set_dir(2, true);
    pthread_t pthreadA;
    pthread_create(&pthreadA, NULL, threadA, NULL);
    pthread_exit(0);
    return (EXIT_SUCCESS);
}
```

If you try this out you will find that it generates a fairly accurate 200μs 50% square wave with no detectable large anomalies and a jitter around 0.5us. The jitter increases with the loading, but not more than 1μs for even 32 core-hogging threads.

If you configure things carefully, deadline scheduling means you really don't need to use a full real-time version of Linux or a real-time operating system. It is good enough for most situations where you have a set of short, duration-repetitive tasks. You can also be sure that the task will get its allocated time without interruption and meet its specified deadline.

Managing Cores

The CM5 has four cores, core 0 to 3, and these can be used to minimize the problems of multitasking. It is important to notice that, as each core runs code out of its own isolated L1 cache, you can think of them as isolated machines. Even when they appear to be operating on the same variable, they are in fact working with their own copy of the variable. This would mean that each core had its own view of the state of the machine if it wasn't for cache coherency mechanisms. When a core updates its level 1 (L1) cache then that change is propagated to all of the L1 caches by special cache coherency hardware. This means that, even though updates to a variable by each cache occur in an isolated fashion, the change is propagated and all threads see the same updated value. What is not guaranteed by cache coherency is the order of update of different variables, which can be changed by the hardware for efficiency reasons.

You can often simply ignore the structure of the processor and allow the operating system to manage allocation of threads to cores. Threads are generally created with a natural CPU affinity. This means that the operating system will assign a thread to a core and from then on attempt to run the thread on the same core. So, in most cases, you can let the operating system manage a machine's cores, but sometimes you will want to intervene.

The reasons why you would want to manually allocate threads to cores are usually specific to the application. For example, you might have a computation-bound thread and an I/O-bound thread. Clearly, scheduling these on the same single core would allow the computational thread to make use of the core when the I/O thread was waiting for the external world. Other reasons include placing a high priority thread into a core that no other thread was allowed to use so that it wasn't interrupted, placing a thread into a core that has preferential access to particular hardware, and so on.

Another consideration is warm versus cold cache. When a thread starts running on a core then none of the data it needs will be in the cache and so it will run slowly. As it transfers the data and instructions it uses, its working set, into the cache, the cache slowly "warms up". If the thread is switched out of the core and another thread takes it over, then restoring the original thread to the original core means that it is still possible that the cache has the data that it requires, that the cache is still warm.

Affinity

The operating system tries to keep threads associated with particular cores, but sometimes you need to enforce this. If you can ensure that the machine is lightly loaded and there is spare computing power, then the operating system will do the right thing. If this isn't the case you may need to specify the core your program is going to use.

There is no standard POSIX way of determining which core a thread will use, but there is a Linux extension of the Pthreads library that does the job. The `setaffinity` function:

```
int pthread_setaffinity_np(pthread_t thread, size_t cpusetsize,
                            const cpu_set_t *cpuset);
```

sets the specified thread to run on one of a set of possible CPUs as specified by the `cpuset`, the affinity mask.

The `getaffinity` function will return the affinity mask of the specified thread:

```
int pthread_getaffinity_np(pthread_t thread, size_t cpusetsize,
                            cpu_set_t *cpuset);
```

Notice the thread is specified as a `pthread` id not a `pid` or a `tid`. You can also use a Linux process id if you use the alternative `get` and `set` functions defined in `sched.h`:

```
int sched_setaffinity(pid_t pid, size_t cpusetsize,
                            const cpu_set_t *mask);
int sched_getaffinity(pid_t pid, size_t cpusetsize,
                            cpu_set_t *mask);
```

Notice that these work with the Linux process id rather than the thread id and this can sometimes be useful. In practice, Pthreads functions call the functions defined in `sched.h`.

The other thing we need to know is how to set the affinity mask. This uses a single bit to control access to each of the physical and logical cores. You can't simply set or reset these bits. You have to use the set of macros designed for the job. There are a large number of these, but the ones that you use most often are:

```
CPU_ZERO(&cpuset);          Sets all bits to 0
CPU_SET(n &cpuset);         Sets the bit corresponding to core n
CPU_CLR(n &cpuset);         Resets the bit corresponding to core n
```

How do you find out which core corresponds to which bit in the mask?

As long as your system is set up correctly you should be able to get details by reading the `/proc/cpuinfo` file, or you could use the `lstopo` tool.

For example, suppose you want to run two threads on separate cores. First we need two functions to run:

```
volatile int j;
volatile int i;

void * threadA(void *p) {
    for (i = 0;; i++) {
    };
}

void * threadB(void *p) {
    for (j = 0;; j++) {
    };
}
```

These simply run a for loop with a global counter to let us know how many times the loop has been executed. The global counters have to be marked as volatile to stop the compiler optimizing the empty loops away.

To set the thread affinity we need to use the macros:

```
cpu_set_t cpuset;
CPU_ZERO(&cpuset);
CPU_SET(1, &cpuset);
```

This sets the mask to core 1. Next we start the first thread and set its affinity:

```
pthread_t pthreadA;
pthread_create(&pthreadA, NULL, threadA, NULL);
pthread_setaffinity_np(pthreadA, sizeof (cpu_set_t), &cpuset);
```

The second thread is to run on core 2 so we need to change the mask and then start the thread:

```
CPU_ZERO(&cpuset);
CPU_SET(2, &cpuset);
pthread_t pthreadB;
pthread_create(&pthreadB, NULL, threadB, NULL);
pthread_setaffinity_np(pthreadB, sizeof (cpu_set_t), &cpuset);
```

Now we can let the main thread sleep for a few seconds and print the value of the counters to give an indication of how many loops each thread has performed.

The complete program is:

```
#define _GNU_SOURCE
#include <stdio.h>
#include <stdlib.h>

#include <pthread.h>
#include <sched.h>
#include <unistd.h>

volatile int j;
volatile int i;

void * threadA(void *p) {
    for (i = 0;; i++) {
    };
}

void * threadB(void *p) {
    for (j = 0;; j++) {
    };
}

int main(int argc, char** argv) {
    cpu_set_t cpuset;
    CPU_ZERO(&cpuset);
    CPU_SET(1, &cpuset);

    pthread_t pthreadA;
    pthread_create(&pthreadA, NULL, threadA, NULL);
    pthread_setaffinity_np(pthreadA, sizeof (cpu_set_t), &cpuset);

    CPU_ZERO(&cpuset);
    CPU_SET(2, &cpuset);
    pthread_t pthreadB;
    pthread_create(&pthreadB, NULL, threadB, NULL);
    pthread_setaffinity_np(pthreadB, sizeof (cpu_set_t), &cpuset);

    sleep(5);

    printf("%d %d", i, j);
    return (EXIT_SUCCESS);
}
```

If you run the program you will find that each thread executes roughly the same number of loops.

Now if you set the second thread to run on the same core by changing:

```
CPU_SET(2, &cpuset);
```

to:

```
CPU_SET(1, &cpuset);
```

and run it again, you will discover that each thread now loops for about half the previous total. This is what you would expect as each of the two threads now only gets to run on the core for half of the total time.

If you run the same program without setting affinities you will discover that, for a lightly loaded machine, they will automatically be allocated to different cores and as the load goes up they will eventually share a core.

There are Linux tools that will allow you to discover what core a process is running on and change its affinity. There is also the cpuset facility, which can be used to dynamically change what cores are used. However, if your goal is to allocate a single core to a single important thread, then the best and simplest way of doing this, is to first prohibit Linux from using the core by adding:

```
isolcpus = core_number
```

to the boot loader. You can use a comma separated list of cores not to use.

For the CM5 the Linux configuration is stored in /boot/firmware/cmdline.txt. Simply add:

```
isolcpus=3
```

to the end of the list and reboot. Make sure that you don't add spaces or line breaks to the command. When the machine starts up, core 3 will not be used by the system. You can, however, still use thread affinity to run a user thread on core 3. There are other ways, such as cpuset, to disable a core dynamically, but these suffer from problems such as not removing any thread that is already running. You can check that this worked and find out what cores are isolated using:

```
cat /sys/devices/system/cpu/isolated
```

The system will still occasionally interrupt a thread running on an isolated core, but the interference is much less than encountered in normal scheduling.

You can discover which cores are being used for interrupt handlers using the command:

```
cat /proc/interrupts
```

This gives you a list of interrupt numbers and the cores that have handled them. Some interrupts have names rather than numbers and these are the ones that you can't tamper with. Isolated cores only handle interrupts that are essential – rescheduling interrupts for example.

It is sometimes possible to control which cores are used for particular interrupts – as long as they have an interrupt number and as long as they support IO-APIC, and many don't. There are none on the CM5, for example. To discover which cores a particular interrupt is assigned to use:

```
cat /proc/irq/n/smp_affinity
```

where n is the interrupt number. This returns a bitmask with the low-order bit corresponding to core 0. You can set the bitmask to determine which processors will handle the interrupt using:

```
echo m > /proc/irq/n/smp_affinity
```

where n is the interrupt number and m is the new mask.

For example, to have all timer interrupts, irq 17, handled by core 0 you would use:

```
echo "1" > /proc/irq/17/smp_affinity
```

Note that if the interrupt is not IO-APIC compatible you will get a read/write error. You also have to give the entire command as root, e.g. use sudo -i.

We can now run the pulse-generating program in core 3 after isolating it so that nothing else uses it:

```
#define _GNU_SOURCE
#include <stdio.h>
#include <stdlib.h>
#include <sched.h>
#include "Gpio5.h"
int main(int argc, char **argv)
{
    cpu_set_t cpuset;
    CPU_ZERO(&cpuset);
    CPU_SET(3, &cpuset);
    int res = sched_setaffinity(getpid(), sizeof(cpu_set_t),
                                &cpuset);
    rp1_Init();
    gpio_init(2);
    gpio_set_dir(2, true);
    while (1)
    {
        gpio_xor_mask(0x4);
    }
    return 0;
}
```

Notice the use of the sched_setaffinity to allocate the core to the current process. The result is that we still see rescheduling interrupts every so often, but these only last a maximum of $7\mu s$. This isn't very different to what happens under EEVDS default scheduling.

Where it does make a big difference is when auto-grouping is off or the pulse program is run with other CPU-hogging programs from the same console. In this case, if you don't lock the program to a core, it gets a decreasingly small amount of CPU time as the load increases. If you do lock it to core 3 then it gets close to 100% of the core's time, no matter what the scheduler tries to do.

Summary

- Working with Linux isn't like working with a microcontroller. The difference is that the operating system schedules programs to run and services interrupts and this means you cannot be sure that your program is running at any given time.

- The Linux scheduler has been developed over many years and it's current default configuration is better suited to running desktop applications than anything else.

- The default scheduler has recently been updated. It is now the EEVDS, Earliest Eligible Virtual Deadline Scheduler, which works well, but makes much of the documentation for the previous CFS Scheduler obsolete and misleading.

- The CM5 has four cores and a lot depends on which one your program runs and which one the scheduler interrupt uses.

- A recent feature of Linux scheduling, designed to make desktop apps more responsive, is group scheduling. Put simply, all processes that are started from the same console share the same time allocation.

- There are some real-time scheduling methods - SCHED_FIFO, SCHED_RR and the more recent SCHED_DEADLINE which attempt to meet a set of timing constraints.

- SCHED_DEADLINE is easy to use and, if you can work with its $100\mu s$ minimum period, solves many scheduling tasks that usually need real-time Linux.

- You can control which core your program runs on using thread affinity and you can isolate a core and tell Linux not to use it.

Gpio5 is the library devised for the purposes of this book and its companion volume Raspberry Pi 5 IoT in C: Drivers and Gpio5, ISBN: 978187196294.It is open source under the MIT License and can be downloaded or forked from it its GitHub repo, https://github.com/IOPress/Gpio5.

Gpio5.h

Main branch 1st March 2025

```
#ifndef GPIO5_H
#define GPIO5_H

#undef _POSIX_C_SOURCE
#define _POSIX_C_SOURCE 199309L

#include <stdio.h>
#include <stdint.h>
#include <stdbool.h>
#include <sys/mman.h>
#include <errno.h>
#include <fcntl.h>
#include <string.h>
#include <unistd.h>
#include <time.h>

#define GPIO_OUT 1
#define GPIO_IN 0

#define rp1_GPIO_FSEL_INPT 1
#define rp1_GPIO_FSEL_OUTP 2

enum gpio_function_rp1
{
    GPIO_FUNC_I2C = 3,
    GPIO_FUNC_PWM1 = 0,
    GPIO_FUNC_SPI = 0,
    GPIO_FUNC_PWM2 = 3,
    GPIO_FUNC_RIO = 5,
    GPIO_FUNC_NULL = 0x1f
};
```

```c
enum gpio_slew_rate
{
    GPIO_SLEW_RATE_SLOW = 0, ///< Slew rate limiting enabled
    GPIO_SLEW_RATE_FAST = 1  ///< Slew rate limiting disabled
};
enum gpio_drive_strength
{
    GPIO_DRIVE_STRENGTH_2MA = 0, ///< 2 mA nominal drive strength
    GPIO_DRIVE_STRENGTH_4MA = 1, ///< 4 mA nominal drive strength
    GPIO_DRIVE_STRENGTH_8MA = 2, ///< 8 mA nominal drive strength
    GPIO_DRIVE_STRENGTH_12MA = 3 ///< 12 mA nominal drive strength
};

typedef struct
{
    uint32_t status;
    uint32_t ctrl;
} GPIOregs;
#define GPIO ((GPIOregs *)GPIOBase)

typedef struct
{
    uint32_t Out;
    uint32_t OE;
    uint32_t In;
    uint32_t InSync;
} rioregs;

#define rio ((rioregs *)RIOBase)
#define rioXOR ((rioregs *)(RIOBase + 0x1000 / 4))
#define rioSET ((rioregs *)(RIOBase + 0x2000 / 4))
#define rioCLR ((rioregs *)(RIOBase + 0x3000 / 4))

// CLOCKS
typedef struct
{
    uint32_t PWM0_CTRL;
    uint32_t PWM0_DIV_INT;
    uint32_t PWM0_DIV_FRAC;
    uint32_t PWM0_SEL;
} pwmclockregs;
#define PWMCLK ((pwmclockregs *)(ClockBase + 0x74 / 4))

// PWM
typedef struct
{
    uint32_t Ctrl;
    uint32_t Range;
    uint32_t Phase;
    uint32_t Duty;
} PWMregs;
#define PWM ((PWMregs *)(PWMBase + 0x14 / 4))
```

```c
enum pwm_mode_rp1
{
    Zero = 0x0,
    TrailingEdge = 0x1,
    PhaseCorrect = 0x2,
    PDE = 0x3,
    MSBSerial = 0x4,
    PPM = 0x5,
    LeadingEdge = 0x6,
    LSBSerial = 0x7
};

#define PWMClock 50000000

// SPI
extern uint32_t *PERIBase;

volatile typedef struct
{
    int32_t CTRLR0; // frame format, clock polarity, phase
    int32_t CTRLR1;
    int32_t SSIENR; // enable/disable
    int32_t MWCR;
    int32_t SER;    // slave CS enable
    int32_t BAUDR; // baud rate - clock divisor
    int32_t TXFTLR;
    int32_t RXFTLR;
    int32_t TXFLR;
    int32_t RXFLR;
    int32_t SR;   // status register
    int32_t IMR; // interrupt mask register
    int32_t ISR;
    int32_t RISR;
    int32_t TXOICR;
    int32_t RXOICR;
    int32_t RXUICR;
    int32_t MSTICR;
    int32_t ICR;
    int32_t DMACR;
    int32_t DMATDLR;
    int32_t DMARDLR;
    int32_t IDR;
    int32_t SSI_VERSION_ID;
    int32_t DR; // data register
    int32_t DRx[35];
    int32_t RX_SAMPLE_DLY;
    int32_t SPI_CTRLR0;
    int32_t TXD_DRIVE_EDGE;
} SPIregs;

typedef SPIregs *SPI;
```

409

```
#define RP1_SPI0_BASE 0x050000
#define RP1_SPI1_BASE 0x054000
#define RP1_SPI2_BASE 0x058000
#define RP1_SPI3_BASE 0x05c000
#define RP1_SPI4_BASE 0x060000
#define RP1_SPI5_BASE 0x064000

#define SPI0 ((SPI)(PERIBase + RP1_SPI0_BASE / 4))
#define SPI1 ((SPI)(PERIBase + RP1_SPI1_BASE / 4))
#define SPI2 ((SPI)(PERIBase + RP1_SPI2_BASE / 4))
#define SPI3 ((SPI)(PERIBase + RP1_SPI3_BASE / 4))
#define SPI4 ((SPI)(PERIBase + RP1_SPI4_BASE / 4))
#define SPI5 ((SPI)(PERIBase + RP1_SPI5_BASE / 4))

#define SPIClock 200000000

typedef enum
{
    SPI_OK = 0,
    SPI_ERROR = 1,
    SPI_BUSY = 2,
    SPI_TIMEOUT = 3,
    SPI_INVALID = 4
} spi_status_t;
typedef enum
{
    SPI_CPHA_0 = 0,
    SPI_CPHA_1 = 1
} spi_cpha_t;

typedef enum
{
    SPI_CPOL_0 = 0,
    SPI_CPOL_1 = 1
} spi_cpol_t;

typedef enum
{
    SPI_LSB_FIRST = 0,
    SPI_MSB_FIRST = 1
} spi_order_t;

// I2C

volatile typedef struct
{
    int32_t con;
    int32_t tar;
    int32_t sar;
    uint32_t _pad0;
    int32_t data_cmd;
```

410

```c
        int32_t ss_scl_hcnt;
        int32_t ss_scl_lcnt;
        int32_t fs_scl_hcnt;
        int32_t fs_scl_lcnt;
        uint32_t _pad1[2];
        uint32_t intr_stat;
        int32_t intr_mask;
        int32_t raw_intr_stat;
        int32_t rx_tl;
        int32_t tx_tl;
        int32_t clr_intr;
        int32_t clr_rx_under;
        int32_t clr_rx_over;
        int32_t clr_tx_over;
        int32_t clr_rd_req;
        int32_t clr_tx_abrt;
        int32_t clr_rx_done;
        int32_t clr_activity;
        int32_t clr_stop_det;
        int32_t clr_start_det;
        int32_t clr_gen_call;
        int32_t enable;
        int32_t status;
        int32_t txflr;
        int32_t rxflr;
        int32_t sda_hold;
        int32_t tx_abrt_source;
        int32_t slv_data_nack_only;
        int32_t dma_cr;
        int32_t dma_tdlr;
        int32_t dma_rdlr;
        int32_t sda_setup;
        int32_t ack_general_call;
        int32_t enable_status;
        int32_t fs_spklen;
        uint32_t _pad2;
        int32_t clr_restart_det;
        int32_t SCL_STUCK_AT_LOW_TIMEOUT;
        int32_t IC_SDA_STUCK_AT_LOW_TIMEOUT;
        uint32_t _pad3[16];
        uint32_t comp_param_1;
        uint32_t comp_version;
        uint32_t comp_type;
} i2cregs;

typedef i2cregs *I2C;
#define RP1_I2C0_BASE 0x070000
#define RP1_I2C1_BASE 0x074000
#define RP1_I2C2_BASE 0x078000
#define RP1_I2C3_BASE 0x07c000
#define RP1_I2C4_BASE 0x080000
#define RP1_I2C5_BASE 0x084000
```

```
#define RP1_I2C6_BASE 0x088000

#define I2C0 ((I2C)(PERIBase + RP1_I2C0_BASE / 4))
#define I2C1 ((I2C)(PERIBase + RP1_I2C1_BASE / 4))
#define I2C2 ((I2C)(PERIBase + RP1_I2C2_BASE / 4))
#define I2C3 ((I2C)(PERIBase + RP1_I2C3_BASE / 4))
#define I2C4 ((I2C)(PERIBase + RP1_I2C4_BASE / 4))
#define I2C5 ((I2C)(PERIBase + RP1_I2C5_BASE / 4))

#define I2CClock 200000000
#define I2C_TX_BUFFER_DEPTH 32;

// Function declarations
int rp1_Init();

int sleep_ms(int ms);
void sleep_us(int us);
uint32_t time_us_32();
void gpio_set_dir(uint32_t gpio, bool out);
void gpio_set_dir_in_masked(uint32_t mask);
void gpio_set_dir_out_masked(uint32_t mask);
void gpio_set_dir_masked(uint32_t mask, uint32_t value);

void gpio_set_mask(uint32_t mask);
void gpio_clr_mask(uint32_t mask);
void gpio_xor_mask(uint32_t mask);

void gpio_put(uint32_t gpio, bool value);
void gpio_put_masked(uint32_t mask, uint32_t value);
bool gpio_get(uint32_t gpio);
uint32_t gpio_get_all(void);
void gpio_set_function(uint32_t gpio, enum gpio_function_rp1 fn);
void gpio_init(uint32_t gpio);
void gpio_init_mask(uint32_t gpio_mask);
// PAD
// Pull
void gpio_set_pulls(uint32_t gpio, bool up, bool down);
void gpio_pull_down(uint32_t gpio);
void gpio_pull_up(uint32_t gpio);
void gpio_disable_pulls(uint32_t gpio);
bool gpio_is_pulled_up(uint32_t gpio);
bool gpio_is_pulled_down(uint32_t gpio);
// Other
void gpio_set_input_hysteresis_enabled(uint32_t gpio,
                                       bool enabled);
bool gpio_is_input_hysteresis_enabled(uint32_t gpio);
void gpio_set_slew_rate(uint32_t gpio, enum gpio_slew_rate slew);
enum gpio_slew_rate gpio_get_slew_rate(uint32_t gpio);
void gpio_set_drive_strength(uint32_t gpio,
                             enum gpio_drive_strength drive);
enum gpio_drive_strength gpio_get_drive_strength(uint32_t gpio);
```

```
// PWM
int pwm_setup(uint32_t gpio, enum pwm_mode_rp1 mode);
int pwm_enable(uint32_t gpio);
int pwm_disable(uint32_t gpio);
void pwm_set_clock(uint32_t div, uint32_t frac);
int pwm_set_invert(int32_t gpio);
int pwm_clr_invert(int32_t gpio);
int pwm_set_range_duty_phase(int32_t gpio, uint32_t range,
                                    uint32_t duty, uint32_t phase);
int pwm_set_frequency_duty(int32_t gpio, int32_t freq,
                                            int dutyPercent);
// SPI
void spi_init(SPI spi, int32_t baudrate);
void spi_set_format(SPI spi, uint32_t data_bits, spi_cpol_t cpol,
                            spi_cpha_t cpha, spi_order_t order);
void spi_set_baudrate(SPI spi, int32_t baudrate);
int32_t spi_get_baudrate(SPI spi);
void spi_set_slave(SPI spi, int slave);
void spi_set_CS_toggle(SPI spi, bool enable);

int spi_write_read_blocking(SPI spi, const uint8_t *src,
                                    uint8_t *dst, size_t len);
int spi_write_blocking(SPI spi, const uint8_t *src, size_t len);
int spi_read_blocking(SPI spi, uint8_t repeated_tx_data,
                                    uint8_t *dst, size_t len);
int spi_write16_read16_blocking(SPI spi, const uint16_t *src,
                                    uint16_t *dst, size_t len);
int spi_write16_blocking(SPI spi, const uint16_t *src, size_t len);
int spi_read16_blocking(SPI spi, uint16_t repeated_tx_data,
                                    uint16_t *dst, size_t len);

int spi_write32_read32_blocking(SPI spi, const uint32_t *src,
                                    uint32_t *dst, size_t len);
int spi_write32_blocking(SPI spi, const uint32_t *src, size_t len);
int spi_read32_blocking(SPI spi, uint32_t repeated_tx_data,
                                    uint32_t *dst, size_t len);
uint32_t i2c_init(I2C i2c, uint32_t baudrate);
int32_t i2c_set_baudrate(I2C i2c, int32_t baudrate);
void i2c_reset(I2C i2c);
int i2c_read_blocking(I2C i2c, uint8_t addr, uint8_t *dst,
                                        size_t len, bool nostop);
int i2c_write_blocking(I2C i2c, uint8_t addr, const uint8_t *src,
                                        size_t len, bool nostop);
int i2c_write_timeout_per_char_us(I2C i2c, uint8_t addr, const
        uint8_t *src, size_t len, bool nostop,
                            uint32_t timeout_per_char_us);
int i2c_read_timeout_per_char_us(I2C i2c, uint8_t addr,
            uint8_t *dst, size_t len, bool nostop, uint32_t
                                        timeout_per_char_us);

#endif
```

Gpio5.c

```c
#include "Gpio5.h"
uint32_t *PERIBase;
uint32_t *GPIOBase;
uint32_t *RIOBase;
uint32_t *PADBase;
uint32_t *pad;

uint32_t *ClockBase;
uint32_t *PWMBase;

int sleep_ms(int ms)
{
    struct timespec delay = {0, ms * 1000 * 1000};
    return nanosleep(&delay, NULL);
}

void sleep_us(int us){
    if (us < 100)
    {
        volatile int i;
        for (i = 0; i < 403*us-5;)          {
            i++;
        }
  }
    else
    {
        struct timespec delay = {0, us * 1000};
        nanosleep(&delay, NULL);
    }
    return;
}


uint32_t time_us_32()
{
    struct timespec t;
    clock_gettime(CLOCK_REALTIME, &t);
    return t.tv_sec * 1000 * 1000 + t.tv_nsec / 1000;
}
```

```c
int rp1_Init()
{
    int memfd = open("/dev/mem", O_RDWR | O_SYNC);
    uint32_t *map = (uint32_t *)mmap(
        NULL,
        64 * 1024 * 1024,
        (PROT_READ | PROT_WRITE),
        MAP_SHARED,
        memfd,
        0x1f00000000);
    close(memfd);
    PERIBase = map;
    if (map == MAP_FAILED)
    {
        int memfd = open("/dev/gpiomem0", O_RDWR | O_SYNC);
        uint32_t *map = (uint32_t *)mmap(
            NULL,
            576 * 1024,
            (PROT_READ | PROT_WRITE),
            MAP_SHARED,
            memfd,
            0x0);
        if (map == MAP_FAILED)
        {
            printf("mmap failed: %s\n", strerror(errno));
            return (-1);
        };
        close(memfd);
        PERIBase = map - 0xD0000 / 4;
    };

    GPIOBase = PERIBase + 0xD0000 / 4;
    RIOBase = PERIBase + 0xe0000 / 4;
    PADBase = PERIBase + 0xf0000 / 4;
    pad = PADBase + 1;
    ClockBase = PERIBase + 0x18000 / 4;
    PWMBase = PERIBase + 0x98000 / 4;
    return 0;
}

// Initialize GPIO lines
void gpio_init(uint32_t gpio)
{
    gpio_set_dir(gpio, GPIO_IN);
    gpio_put(gpio, 0);
    gpio_set_function(gpio, GPIO_FUNC_RIO);
}

void gpio_deinit(uint32_t gpio)
{
    gpio_set_function(gpio, GPIO_FUNC_NULL);
}
```

```c
void gpio_init_mask(uint32_t gpio_mask)
{
    for (int i = 0; i < 29; i++)
    {
        if (gpio_mask & 1)
        {
            gpio_init(i);
        }
        gpio_mask >>= 1;
    }
}
void gpio_set_function(uint32_t gpio, enum gpio_function_rp1 fn)
{
    pad[gpio] = 0x50;
    GPIO[gpio].ctrl = fn;
}

// Set Direction
void gpio_set_dir(uint32_t gpio, bool out)
{
    uint32_t mask = 1ul << gpio;
    if (out)
        gpio_set_dir_out_masked(mask);
    else
        gpio_set_dir_in_masked(mask);
}
void gpio_set_dir_in_masked(uint32_t mask)
{
    rioCLR->OE = mask;
}
void gpio_set_dir_out_masked(uint32_t mask)
{
    rioSET->OE = mask;
}
void gpio_set_dir_masked(uint32_t mask, uint32_t value)
{
    rioXOR->OE = (rio->OE ^ value) & mask;
}

// SETGET GPIO
inline void gpio_set_mask(uint32_t mask)
{
    rioSET->Out = mask;
}

inline void gpio_clr_mask(uint32_t mask)
{
    rioCLR->Out = mask;
}
```

```
inline void gpio_xor_mask(uint32_t mask)
{

    rioXOR->Out = mask;
}

inline void gpio_put(uint32_t gpio, bool value)
{
    uint32_t mask = 1ul << gpio;
    if (value)
        gpio_set_mask(mask);
    else
        gpio_clr_mask(mask);
}

inline void gpio_put_masked(uint32_t mask, uint32_t value)
{
    rioXOR->Out = (rio->Out ^ value) & mask;
}

inline bool gpio_get(uint32_t gpio)
{
    return rio->In & (1u << gpio);
}

inline uint32_t gpio_get_all(void)
{
    return rio->In;
}

// PAD Configure
void gpio_set_pulls(uint32_t gpio, bool up, bool down)
{
    pad[gpio] = pad[gpio] & ~0xC;
    if (up)
    {
        pad[gpio] = pad[gpio] | 0x8;
    };
    if (down)
    {
        pad[gpio] = pad[gpio] | 0x4;
    }
}
void gpio_pull_down(uint32_t gpio)
{
    gpio_set_pulls(gpio, false, true);
}
void gpio_pull_up(uint32_t gpio)
{
    gpio_set_pulls(gpio, true, false);
}
```

```
void gpio_disable_pulls(uint32_t gpio)
{
    gpio_set_pulls(gpio, false, false);
}
bool gpio_is_pulled_up(uint32_t gpio)
{
    return (pad[gpio] & 0x8) != 0;
}
bool gpio_is_pulled_down(uint32_t gpio)
{
    return (pad[gpio] & 0x4) != 0;
}
void gpio_set_input_hysteresis_enabled(uint32_t gpio, bool enabled)
{
    if (enabled)
        pad[gpio] = pad[gpio] | 0x2;
    else
        pad[gpio] = pad[gpio] & !0x2;
}
bool gpio_is_input_hysteresis_enabled(uint32_t gpio)
{
    return (pad[gpio] & 0x2) != 0;
}
void gpio_set_slew_rate(uint32_t gpio, enum gpio_slew_rate slew)
{
    if (slew == GPIO_SLEW_RATE_FAST)
    {
        pad[gpio] = pad[gpio] | 1;
    }
    else
    {
        pad[gpio] = pad[gpio] & ~1;
    }
}
enum gpio_slew_rate gpio_get_slew_rate(uint32_t gpio)
{
    return (enum gpio_slew_rate)(pad[gpio] & 1);
}

void gpio_set_drive_strength(uint32_t gpio,
                             enum gpio_drive_strength drive)
{
    pad[gpio] = (pad[gpio] & ~0x30) |
                        (0x30 & (uint32_t)drive << 4);
}
enum gpio_drive_strength gpio_get_drive_strength(uint32_t gpio)
{
    return (enum gpio_drive_strength)((pad[gpio] & 0x30) >> 4);
}
```

```
// PWM

int getPWM(uint32_t gpio)
{
    switch (gpio)
    {
    case 12:
        return 0;
    case 13:
        return 1;
    case 14:
        return 2;
    case 15:
        return 3;
    case 18:
        return 2;
    case 19:
        return 3;
    }
    return -1;
}

int pwm_enable(uint32_t gpio)
{
    int pwm = getPWM(gpio);
    if (pwm < 0)
        return -1;
    uint32_t temp = 1 << pwm;
    *PWMBase = *PWMBase | temp | 0x80000000;
}
int pwm_disable(uint32_t gpio)
{
    int pwm = getPWM(gpio);
    if (pwm < 0)
        return -1;
    uint32_t temp = 1 << pwm;
    temp = ~temp & 0xf;
    *PWMBase = (*PWMBase & temp) | 0x80000000;
}

void pwm_init_clock(void)
{
    PWMCLK->PWM0_CTRL = 0x11000840;
    PWMCLK->PWM0_SEL = 1;
}
void pwm_set_clock(uint32_t div, uint32_t frac)
{
    PWMCLK->PWM0_DIV_INT = div;
    PWMCLK->PWM0_DIV_FRAC = frac;
}
```

```c
int pwm_setup(uint32_t gpio, enum pwm_mode_rp1 mode)
{
    int pwm = getPWM(gpio);
    if (pwm < 0)
        return -1;
    pwm_init_clock();
    if (gpio == 18 | gpio == 19)
    {
        gpio_set_function(gpio, GPIO_FUNC_PWM2);
    }
    else
    {
        gpio_set_function(gpio, GPIO_FUNC_PWM1);
    }
    PWM[pwm].Ctrl = mode;
    pwm_disable(gpio);
}

int pwm_set_invert(int32_t gpio)
{
    int pwm = getPWM(gpio);
    if (pwm < 0)
        return -1;
    PWM[pwm].Ctrl = PWM[pwm].Ctrl | 0x8;
    *PWMBase = *PWMBase | 0x80000000;
}
int pwm_clr_invert(int32_t gpio)
{
    int pwm = getPWM(gpio);
    if (pwm < 0)
        return -1;
    PWM[pwm].Ctrl = PWM[pwm].Ctrl & ~0x8ul;
    *PWMBase = *PWMBase | 0x80000000;
}

int pwm_set_range_duty_phase(int32_t gpio, uint32_t range,
                             uint32_t duty, uint32_t phase)
{
    int pwm = getPWM(gpio);
    if (pwm < 0)
        return -1;
    PWM[pwm].Range = range;
    PWM[pwm].Duty = duty;
    PWM[pwm].Phase = phase;
    *PWMBase = *PWMBase | 0x80000000;
}
```

```c
int pwm_set_frequency_duty(int32_t gpio, int32_t freq,
                                              int dutyPercent)
{
    int32_t div = PWMCLK->PWM0_DIV_INT;
    int32_t frac = PWMCLK->PWM0_DIV_FRAC;
    int32_t pwmf = PWMClock / div;
    int32_t range = pwmf / freq-1;
    int32_t duty = range * dutyPercent / 1000+1;
    pwm_set_range_duty_phase(gpio, range, duty, 0);
}

// SPI
void dump_all_spi_regs(SPI spi, const char *msg)
{

    printf("\nSPI register dump:%s\n", msg);
    uint32_t *i;
    int j = 1;
    for (i = (uint32_t *)spi; i <= (uint32_t *)&
                                  (spi->SSI_VERSION_ID); i++)
    {
        printf("spi reg %x @  %x %p: %x\n", j++,
                           (char *)i - (char *)spi, i, *i);
    }
}
void spi_enable(SPI spi, bool enable)
{
    if (enable)
    {
        spi->SSIENR = 0x1;
    }
    else
    {
        spi->SSIENR = 0x0;
    }
}
void spi_init(SPI spi, int32_t baudrate)
{
    //  dump_all_spi_regs(spi, "Just after spi created");
    spi_set_baudrate(spi, baudrate);
    spi->BAUDR = SPIClock / baudrate;
    spi_enable(spi, false); // set CPOL and CHPA
    spi_set_format(spi, 8, SPI_CPOL_0, SPI_CPHA_0, SPI_MSB_FIRST);
    spi_enable(spi, false);
    // set CE to stay active (bit 24 set low)
    spi->CTRLR0 = (spi->CTRLR0) & 0xFFFFFFFFFEFFFFFF;
    // set CE0 as default
    spi->SER = 1;   //  clear interrupts
    uint32_t reg_icr = spi->ICR;
    spi_enable(spi, true);
}
```

```c
void spi_set_format(SPI spi, uint32_t data_bits, spi_cpol_t cpol,
                            spi_cpha_t cpha, spi_order_t order)
{
    spi_enable(spi, false);
    // Bit 16 to 20 databits
    //   6 CPHA
    //   7 CPOL
    uint32_t mask = 0x1F00C0;
    data_bits = (data_bits - 1) & 0x1F;
    uint32_t value = data_bits << 16 | cpol << 7 | cpha << 6;
    int32_t data = spi->CTRLR0;
    spi->CTRLR0 = (data & ~mask) | (value & mask);
    spi_enable(spi, true);
}

bool spi_is_writable(SPI spi)
{
    return (spi->SR) & 0x2;
}

bool spi_is_readable(SPI spi)
{
    return spi->SR & 0x8;
}

bool spi_is_busy(SPI spi)
{
    return spi->SR & 0x1;
}
bool spi_rx_full(SPI spi)
{
    return spi->SR & 0x10;
}

int spi_rx_num(SPI spi)
{
    return spi->RXFLR;
}
int spi_tx_num(SPI spi)
{
    return spi->TXFLR;
}

void spi_set_baudrate(SPI spi, int32_t baudrate)
{
    int32_t div = SPIClock / baudrate;
    if (div % 2 != 0)
        div = div - 1;
    spi_enable(spi, false);
    spi->BAUDR = div;
    spi_enable(spi, true);
}
```

```
int32_t spi_get_baudrate(SPI spi)
{
    return SPIClock / (spi->BAUDR);
}
int spi_write_read_blocking(SPI spi, const uint8_t *src,
                                        uint8_t *dst, size_t len)
{
    const size_t fifo_depth = 64;
    size_t rx_remaining = len, tx_remaining = len;
    for (int i = 0; i < (fifo_depth < len ?
                                        fifo_depth : len) - 1; i++)
    {
        spi->DR = (uint32_t)*src++;
        --tx_remaining;
    }
    while (rx_remaining || tx_remaining)
    {
        if (tx_remaining && spi_is_writable(spi) &&
                                spi_rx_num(spi) < fifo_depth)
        {
            spi->DR = (uint32_t)*src++;
            --tx_remaining;
        }
        if (rx_remaining && spi_is_readable(spi))
        {
            *dst++ = (uint8_t)spi->DR;
            --rx_remaining;
        }
    }
    return (int)len;
}
int spi_write16_read16_blocking(SPI spi, const uint16_t *src,
                                        uint16_t *dst, size_t len)
{
    const size_t fifo_depth = 64;
    size_t rx_remaining = len, tx_remaining = len;
    for (int i = 0; i < (fifo_depth < len ?
                                        fifo_depth : len) - 1; i++)
    {
        spi->DR = (uint32_t)*src++;
        --tx_remaining;
    }
    while (rx_remaining || tx_remaining)
    {
        if (tx_remaining && spi_is_writable(spi) &&
                                spi_rx_num(spi) < fifo_depth)
        {
            spi->DR = (uint32_t)*src++;
            --tx_remaining;
        }
```

```
   if (rx_remaining && spi_is_readable(spi))
        {
            *dst++ = (uint16_t)spi->DR;
            --rx_remaining;
        }
    }
    return (int)len;
}
int spi_write32_read32_blocking(SPI spi,
            const uint32_t *src, uint32_t *dst, size_t len)
{
    const size_t fifo_depth = 64;
    size_t rx_remaining = len, tx_remaining = len;
    for (int i = 0; i < (fifo_depth < len ?
                         fifo_depth : len) - 1; i++)
    {
        spi->DR = (uint32_t)*src++;
        --tx_remaining;
    }
    while (rx_remaining || tx_remaining)
    {
        if (tx_remaining && spi_is_writable(spi) &&
                              spi_rx_num(spi) < fifo_depth)
        {
            spi->DR = (uint32_t)*src++;
            --tx_remaining;
        }
        if (rx_remaining && spi_is_readable(spi))
        {
            *dst++ = (uint32_t)spi->DR;
            --rx_remaining;
        }
    }
    return (int)len;
}

int spi_write_blocking(SPI spi, const uint8_t *src, size_t len)
{
    uint8_t dst[len];
    return spi_write_read_blocking(spi, src, dst, len);
}

int spi_read_blocking(SPI spi, uint8_t repeated_tx_data,
                                    uint8_t *dst, size_t len)
{
    uint8_t src[len];
    for (int i = 0; i < len; i++)
    {
        src[i] = repeated_tx_data;
    }
    return spi_write_read_blocking(spi, src, dst, len);
}
```

```c
int spi_write16_blocking(SPI spi, const uint16_t *src, size_t len)
{
    uint16_t dst[len];
    return spi_write16_read16_blocking(spi, src, dst, len);
}

int spi_read16_blocking(SPI spi, uint16_t repeated_tx_data,
                                    uint16_t *dst, size_t len)
{
    uint16_t src[len];
    for (int i = 0; i < len; i++)
    {
        src[i] = repeated_tx_data;
    }
    return spi_write16_read16_blocking(spi, src, dst, len);
}
int spi_write32_blocking(SPI spi, const uint32_t *src, size_t len)
{
    uint32_t dst[len];
    return spi_write32_read32_blocking(spi, src, dst, len);
}

int spi_read32_blocking(SPI spi, uint32_t repeated_tx_data,
                                    uint32_t *dst, size_t len)
{
    uint32_t src[len];
    for (int i = 0; i < len; i++)
    {
        src[i] = repeated_tx_data;
    }
    return spi_write32_read32_blocking(spi, src, dst, len);
}

void spi_set_slave(SPI spi, int slave)
{
    spi_enable(spi, false);
    spi->SER = 1ul << slave;
    spi_enable(spi, true);
}
void spi_set_CS_toggle(SPI spi, bool enable)
{
    spi_enable(spi, false);
    if (enable)
    {
        spi->CTRLR0 = (spi->CTRLR0) | 0x1000000;
    }
    else
    {
        spi->CTRLR0 = (spi->CTRLR0) & 0xFFFFFFFFFEFFFFFF;
    }
    spi_enable(spi, true);
}
```

```c
// I2C
void dump_all_i2c_regs(I2C i2c, const char *msg)
{
    printf("\nI2C register dump:%s\n", msg);
    uint32_t *i;
    int j = 1;
    for (i = (uint32_t *)i2c; i <= (uint32_t *)&
                                      (i2c->comp_type); i++)
    {
        printf("i2c reg %x @  %x %p: %x\n", j++,
                             (char *)i - (char *)i2c, i, *i);
    }
}

void i2c_enable(I2C i2c, bool enable)
{
    i2c->enable = enable ? 1 : 0;
}

uint32_t i2c_init(I2C i2c, uint32_t baudrate)
{
    // dump_all_i2c_regs(i2c, "Before init");
    i2c_enable(i2c, false);
    // Configure as a fast-mode master with
    // RepStart support, 7-bit addresses
    i2c->con = (0x2ul << 1) | 0x01 | 0x040 | 0x20 | 0x100;
    // Set FIFO watermarks to 1
    i2c->tx_tl = 0;
    i2c->rx_tl = 0;
    return i2c_set_baudrate(i2c, baudrate);
}
int32_t i2c_set_baudrate(I2C i2c, int32_t baudrate)
{
    i2c_enable(i2c, false);
    // use "fast" mode
    i2c->con = (i2c->con & ~0x06ul) | (0x02 << 1 & 0x06ul);
    // set frequency and duty
    uint32_t period = (I2CClock + baudrate / 2) / baudrate;
    i2c->fs_scl_lcnt = period * 3 / 5; // 40% duty cycle
    i2c->fs_scl_hcnt = period - i2c->fs_scl_lcnt;

    // set spike suppression
    i2c->fs_spklen = i2c->fs_scl_lcnt < 16 ?
                                      1 : i2c->fs_scl_lcnt / 16;

    // set hold time
    uint32_t sda_tx_hold_count = (baudrate < 1000000) ?
       ((I2CClock * 3) / 10000000) + 1 :
                ((I2CClock * 3) / 25000000) + 1;
    i2c->sda_hold = (i2c->sda_hold & ~0x0000ffff) |
                                (sda_tx_hold_count & 0x0000ffff);
```

```
    i2c_enable(i2c, true);
    // dump_all_i2c_regs(i2c, "after init");
    return I2CClock / period;
}

void i2c_reset(I2C spi)
{
    uint32_t *resetreg = PERIBase + 14000 / 4;
    uint32_t *resetdonereg = PERIBase + 14004 / 4;
    volatile int32_t temp = *resetreg;
    *resetreg = *resetreg | 0x00020000;
    temp = *resetreg;
}
bool restart_on_next = false;

uint64_t micros()
{
    struct timespec ts;
    clock_gettime(CLOCK_MONOTONIC_RAW, &ts);
    uint64_t us = ts.tv_sec * 1000000 + ts.tv_nsec / 1000;
    return us;
}

int32_t i2c_handleAbort(I2C i2c, bool timeout, int32_t abortreason)
{
    if (timeout)
        return 1 << 31 | 1 << 30; // bit 30 set for timout
    return abortreason | 1 << 31;
}

int i2c_write_blocking_internal(I2C i2c, uint8_t addr,
                const uint8_t *src, size_t len, bool nostop,
                                        uint32_t timeout_per_char_us)
{
    i2c_enable(i2c, false);
    i2c->tar = addr;
    i2c_enable(i2c, true);

    bool abort = false;
    bool timeout = false;
    uint32_t abort_reason = 0;

    int byte_ctr;

    int ilen = (int)len;
    for (byte_ctr = 0; byte_ctr < ilen; ++byte_ctr)
    {
        bool first = byte_ctr == 0;
        bool last = byte_ctr == ilen - 1;

        uint32_t startbitnext = ((uint32_t)!!
                            (first && restart_on_next)) << 10;
```

```
            uint32_t stopbit = ((uint32_t)!!(last && !nostop)) << 9;
            uint64_t tm = micros() + timeout_per_char_us;
            i2c->data_cmd = startbitnext | stopbit | *src++;
            do
            {
                if (micros() > tm)
                    timeout = true;
            } while (!timeout && !(i2c->raw_intr_stat & 0x10));

            if (timeout)
                break;

            // check for non-timeout abort
            abort_reason = i2c->tx_abrt_source;
            if (abort_reason)
            {
                int32_t temp = i2c->clr_tx_abrt;
                abort = true;
            }
        }
    restart_on_next = nostop;
    if (abort || timeout)
        return i2c_handleAbort(i2c, timeout, abort_reason);
    return byte_ctr;
}

size_t i2c_get_write_available(I2C i2c)
{
    return I2C_TX_BUFFER_DEPTH - (i2c->txflr);
}
size_t i2c_get_read_available(I2C i2c)
{
    return i2c->rxflr;
}

int i2c_read_blocking_internal(I2C i2c, uint8_t addr, uint8_t *dst,
            size_t len, bool nostop, uint32_t timeout_per_char_us)
{

    i2c_enable(i2c, false);
    i2c->tar = addr;
    i2c_enable(i2c, true);

    bool abort = false;
    bool timeout = false;
    uint32_t abort_reason;

    int byte_ctr;
    int ilen = (int)len;

    for (byte_ctr = 0; byte_ctr < ilen; ++byte_ctr)
    {
```

```
            bool first = byte_ctr == 0;
            bool last = byte_ctr == ilen - 1;

            while (!i2c_get_write_available(i2c))
            {
            };

            uint32_t startbitnext = (uint32_t)!!
                               (first && restart_on_next) << 10;
            uint32_t stopbit = (uint32_t)!!(last && !nostop) << 9;
            uint64_t tm = micros() + timeout_per_char_us;
            i2c->data_cmd = startbitnext | stopbit | 0x100;

            do
            {
                if (micros() > tm)
                {
                    timeout = true;
                    abort = true;
                }
                abort_reason = i2c->tx_abrt_source;
                // check tx abort bits
                if (i2c->raw_intr_stat & 0x40)
                {
                    abort = true;
                    i2c->clr_tx_abrt;
                }

            } while (!abort && !i2c_get_read_available(i2c));

            if (abort)
                break;

            *dst++ = (uint8_t)i2c->data_cmd;
        }
        restart_on_next = nostop;
        if (abort)
            return i2c_handleAbort(i2c, timeout, abort_reason);
        return byte_ctr;
}
int i2c_read_blocking(I2C i2c, uint8_t addr, uint8_t *dst,
                                        size_t len, bool nostop)
{
        return i2c_read_blocking_internal(i2c, addr, dst,
                                        len, nostop, 0xFFFFFFFF);
}
int i2c_write_blocking(I2C i2c, uint8_t addr, const uint8_t *src,
                                        size_t len, bool nostop)
{
        return i2c_write_blocking_internal(i2c, addr, src,
                                        len, nostop, 0xFFFFFFFF);
}
```

```
int i2c_write_timeout_per_char_us(I2C i2c, uint8_t addr,
     const uint8_t *src, size_t len, bool nostop,
                                 uint32_t timeout_per_char_us)
{
    return i2c_write_blocking_internal(i2c, addr, src, len,
                                 nostop, timeout_per_char_us);
}

int i2c_read_timeout_per_char_us(I2C i2c, uint8_t addr,
        uint8_t *dst, size_t len, bool nostop,
                                 uint32_t timeout_per_char_us)
{

    return i2c_read_blocking_internal(i2c, addr, dst, len,
                                 nostop, timeout_per_char_us);
}
```

Index

435

438

Raspberry Pi IoT in C, Third Edition
ISBN: 978-1871962840 (Paperback)
ISBN: 978-1871962154 (Hardback)

In this book you will find a practical approach to understanding electronic circuits and datasheets and translating this to code, specifically using the C programming language. The main reason for choosing C is speed, a crucial factor when you are writing programs to communicate with the outside world. If you are familiar with another programming language, C shouldn't be hard to pick up. This third edition has been brought up-to-date and includes the Pi Zero 2W and the latest OS. An entire chapter is devoted to the Pi 5 and it is covered elsewhere in the book wherever possible.

Raspberry Pi IoT in Python With Linux Drivers, 2nd Edition
ISBN: 9781871962864 (Paperback)
ISBN: 9781871962178 (Hardback)

This is the Python version of this book and covers much of the same ground. It explains how to use Python to connect to and control external devices with the full current range of Raspberry Pis, including the Pi 5 and the Raspberry Pi Zero 2W using the standard Linux drivers.

Raspberry Pi IoT in C With Linux Drivers, 2nd Edition
ISBN: 978-1871962857(Paperback)
ISBN: 9781871962161 (Hardback)

This second edition has been updated and expanded to cover the Raspberry Pi 5 and the Raspberry Pi Zero W/2W. There are Linux drivers for many off-the-shelf IoT devices and they provide a very easy-to-use, high-level way of working. The big problem is that there is very little documentation to help you get started. This book explains the principles so that you can tackle new devices.

Programming The Raspberry Pi Pico/W In C, 2nd Edition

ISBN: 978-1871962796

This book explains the many reasons for wanting to use C with the Pico, not least of which is the fact that it is much faster. This makes it ideal for serious experimentation and delving into parts of the hardware that are otherwise inaccessible. Using C is the way to get the maximum from the Pico and to really understand how it works.

Master the Raspberry Pi Pico
ISBN: 978-1871962819

There is far too much to the Pico to cover in a single book and this follow-on volume takes your Pico C programming to the next level. Chapters are devoted to more advanced PIO programming, using the second core and many of the more advanced hardware features such as DMA, watchdog timer and saving power. For the Pico W it covers TLS/HTTPS connections, access point mode, other protocols and using FreeRTOS.

Programming the Raspberry Pi Pico/W in MicroPython, 2nd Edition
ISBN: 978-1871962802

MicroPython is a good choice of language to program the Pico. It isn't the fastest way, but in most cases it is fast enough to interface with the Pico's hardware and its big advantage is that it is easy to use.

The purpose of the book is to reveal what you can do with the Pico's GPIO lines together with widely used sensors, servos and motors and ADCs. One of the key advantages of the Pico is its PIO (Programmable I/O) and while this is an advanced feature, it is introduced in this book. After finding out how the PIO works, we apply it to writing a PIO program for the DHT22 and the 1-Wire bus.

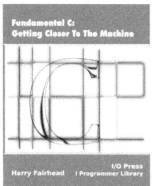

Fundamental C: Getting Closer To The Machine
ISBN: 978-1871962604

For beginners, the book covers installing an IDE and GCC before writing a Hello World program and then presents the fundamental building blocks of any program - variables, assignment and expressions, flow of control using conditionals and loops.

When programming in C you need to think about the way data is represented, and this book emphasizes the idea of modifying how a bit pattern is treated using type punning and unions and tackles the topic of undefined behavior, which is ignored in many books on C.

Applying C For The IoT With Linux
ISBN: 978-1871962611

If you are using C to write low-level code using small Single Board Computers (SBCs) that run Linux, or if you do any coding in C that interacts with the hardware, this book brings together low-level, hardware-oriented and often hardware-specific information.

It starts by looking at how programs work with user-mode Linux. When working with hardware, arithmetic cannot be ignored, so separate chapters are devoted to integer, fixed-point and floating-point arithmetic. It goes on to the pseudo file system, memory-mapped files and sockets as a general-purpose way of communicating over networks and similar infrastructure. It continues by looking at multitasking, locking, using mutex and condition variables, and scheduling. It rounds out with a short look at how to mix assembler with C.

Deep C Dives: Adventures in C
ISBN: 978-1871962888

This book provides in-depth exploration of the essence of C, identifying the strengths of its distinctive traits. This reveals that C has a very special place among the programming languages of today as a powerful and versatile option for low-level programming, something that is often overlooked in books written by programmers who would really rather be using a higher-level language. To emphasize the way in which chapters of this book focus on specific topics, they are referred to as "dives", something that also implies a deep examination of the subject.

Programming The ESP32 In C Using The Espressif IDF
ISBN: 978-1871962918

C is the ideal choice of language to program the ESP32, ensuring that your programs are fast and efficient, and here it is used with the Espressif IoT Development Framework, ESP-IDF and VS Code, a combination which makes it simple to get started and provides a wealth of functions not found elsewhere.

The purpose of this book is to reveal what you can do with the ESP32's GPIO lines together with widely used sensors, servos and motors and ADCs. After covering the GPIO, outputs and inputs, events and interrupts, it gives you hands-on experience of PWM (Pulse Width Modulation), PWM for Motor control, the SPI bus, the I2C bus and the 1-Wire bus, the UARTs and of course WiFi. To round out, it covers direct access to the hardware, adding an SD Card reader, sleep states to save power, the RTC, RMT and touch sensors. It also devotes a chapter to FreeRTOS which takes us into the realm of asynchronous processing.

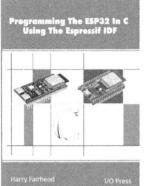

Programming the ESP32 in MicroPython
ISBN: 978-1871962826

Although MicroPython is slower than C, most of the time this doesn't matter and it is much easier to use. It is based on Python 3 and is fully object-oriented.

Another good thing about MicroPython on the ESP32 is that it is very easy to get started. After a simple installation procedure you have a working MicroPython machine which you can program almost at once using the Thonny IDE or PyCharm which has more extensive syntax checking and input prompting.

The purpose of the book is to reveal what you can do with the ESP's GPIO lines together with widely used sensors, servos and motors and ADCs. After covering the GPIO, outputs and inputs, events and interrupts, it gives you hands-on experience of PWM (Pulse Width Modulation), the SPI bus, the I2C bus and the 1-Wire bus. We also cover direct access to the hardware, adding an SD Card reader, sleep states to save power, the RTC, RMT and touch sensors, not to mention how to use WiFi.

www.ingramcontent.com/pod-product-compliance
Lightning Source LLC
LaVergne TN
LVHW062301060326
832902LV00013B/1989